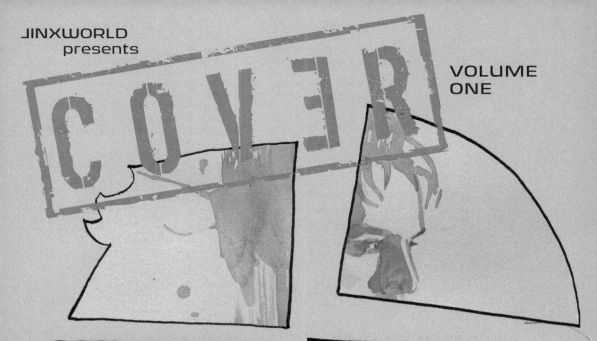

JINXWORLD
presents

COVER

VOLUME ONE

CREATED BY
BRIAN MICHAEL BENDIS
AND
DAVID MACK

DIGITAL COLORING
ZU ORZU

LETTERS
CARLOS M. MANGUAL

DESIGN
CURTIS KING JR.

EDITING
MICHAEL McCALISTER

MODEL FOR JULIA
SUSAN HEYWARD

PUBLISHER
ALISA BENDIS

NINJA SWORD
ODYSSEY SCRIPT
AND LETTERING BY
DAVID MACK

ESSAD SINNS ART
IN CHAPTER 3 BY
BILL SIENKIEWICZ

OWEN ART
IN CHAPTERS 4–5 BY
MICHAEL AVON OEMING

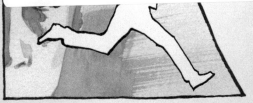

MACK

COVER VOLUME ONE

Published by DC Comics. Compilation and all new material
Copyright © 2019 Jinxworld, Inc. All Rights Reserved.

Originally published in single magazine form in COVER 1-6. Copyright © 2018, 2019 Jinxworld, Inc.
All Rights Reserved. Cover, its logo design, the Jinxworld logo, all characters, their distinctive
likenesses and related elements featured in this publication are trademarks of Jinxworld, Inc.
The stories, characters and incidents featured in this publication are entirely fictional.
DC Comics does not read or accept unsolicited submissions of ideas, stories or artwork.

DC Comics, 2900 West Alameda Ave., Burbank, CA 91505

Printed by LSC Communications, Owensville, MO, USA. 4/19/19.
First Printing. ISBN: 978-1-4012-9104-4

Library of Congress Cataloging-in-Publication Data is available.

INTRODUCTION

Brian Michael Bendis and I have been friends and have worked together since 1993. We met in Chicago signing our creator-owned books at a comics convention. At the time, Brian was writing and drawing his indie books and looking for work as an artist. I was writing *Kabuki* and looking for an artist to draw it. We decided that Brian was going to be the artist on *Kabuki*, and on the first day we met he got me a job as his inker on some other projects. I was barely 20 years old, and we were both fascinated with the possibilities of storytelling in this visual field and enthusiastic to create personal works and to learn from each other as much as possible.

Brian opened my eyes to a world of cinematography and directors and writers, and our early conversations during those formative years shaped me deeply as a storyteller. We shared with each other pages from the projects we were working on and traded feedback and encouragement as we created our early stories.

I ended up doing the art for *Kabuki* myself, and it was published while I was in college as my senior thesis in Literature. My writing on *Kabuki* got me the offer to write *Daredevil* for Marvel Comics.

While I was working on *Daredevil*, I sent Brian's crime comics (which he had both written and drawn) to Joe Quesada, who was the artist on my *Daredevil* story and who had just become Marvel's editor-in-chief. Joe liked Brian's writing and offered us the chance to work together on *Daredevil* after Joe's run ended. This was 1999, and Brian and I felt like we were finally working on a project worthy of our friendship.

I tell you all of this because, while we worked on *Jessica Jones* together and co-wrote *Daredevil: End of Days* together, we always talked about the creator-owned project that we wanted to collaborate on—our own special story that we could invent and make together.

Fast-forward 18 years later to the end of 2017, when Brian had a near-death experience. He nearly died. And in a moment that still moves me when I think about it, he told me that as he was lying in his hospital bed, blind and possibly dying, one thing that made him sad was that we had not created our own special project together.

Let that sink in.

Brian survived and recovered fully, becoming stronger than ever, and once he was better we decided that we were going to make our book together *right now*.

COVER

During the last few years I have been traveling overseas for the State Department as a cultural ambassador. I was in North Africa, Asia, and the former Soviet areas. I was in refugee camps; I taught at schools for the deaf in Tunisia, Singapore and the country of Georgia; I taught at universities, prisons and a variety of schools, with students from a multitude of cultural and ethnic backgrounds who spoke an array of languages; and I worked with different embassies and parts of the State Department.

My work in Tunisia was under the CVE (Countering Violent Extremism) program, and its agenda was to interact with at-risk youth and make them less susceptible to recruitment by extremist groups. There were extremist groups from Libya attempting to recruit young people on the borders of Tunisia, and I was driven around in a bullet-resistant embassy vehicle from town to town, where I taught storytelling workshops with very talented and bright young people in a variety of schools and encouraged them to follow their dreams.

I was telling Brian about an episode in Libya that I was involved with, in which I was a speaker at an event that was shut down by a militia who took many of the organizers prisoner, and how I spent the next two months doing everything I could behind the scenes to aid in their release, as well as trying to secure legal advocacy and medication for them (two were diabetic).

It was an intense time for me, and Brian had just been through an intense experience as well, and we decided during our conversation that our new project would be inspired by these personal events and my experiences overseas. And that is the origin of the book you now hold in your hands.

I told Brian that someday, when I would be able to do so, I wanted to tell a directly non-fictional story of my State Department work—but for now, we decided to tell this collaborative story inspired by real events, which would also be a love letter to our formative years when we were figuring out how to create comics, building a friendship while telling personal truths and integrating it all into our art.

I want to take this opportunity to give a sincere thank-you to Brian for being my friend for all of these years, and for his inspiration as a person and a creator—both when we were kids just starting out and now.

A big thank-you also goes out to Brian's wife, Alisa, for making these Jinxworld books happen as a publisher; and to our tireless DC editor, Michael McCalister; and to Zu, who colored my inks in this story and who was a part of some of my State Department trips in North Africa and Asia.

I also send a heartfelt shout-out to Tom King, who was originally going to write this introduction but had a scheduling conflict. I first heard of Tom King a few years ago when I was in the country of Georgia and my Georgian and Russian translator Giorgi told me about him—something I told Tom about when we first met. Tom, you can write the introduction to the next volume!

Finally, a word of gratitude to my State Department liaisons, foreign affairs officers and cultural attachés: Damian Wampler and Tamar (Tako) Rtveliashvili of the U.S. embassy in Georgia (Sakarvelo); Giorgi Sabanashvili, my translator; Sara Ferchichi, Hazel Cipolle and Najla Abbes of the U.S. embassy in Tunisia; Allyson Coyne of the U.S. embassy in Singapore; Allison Lee of the U.S. embassy in Libya; Jennifer Phillips in Washington, D.C.; Julia and all those who are unnamed and who work tirelessly to make a difference even though you never hear about it. Gratitude.

This book is dedicated to you.

—**David Mack**
March 7, 2019
Venice, Los Angeles

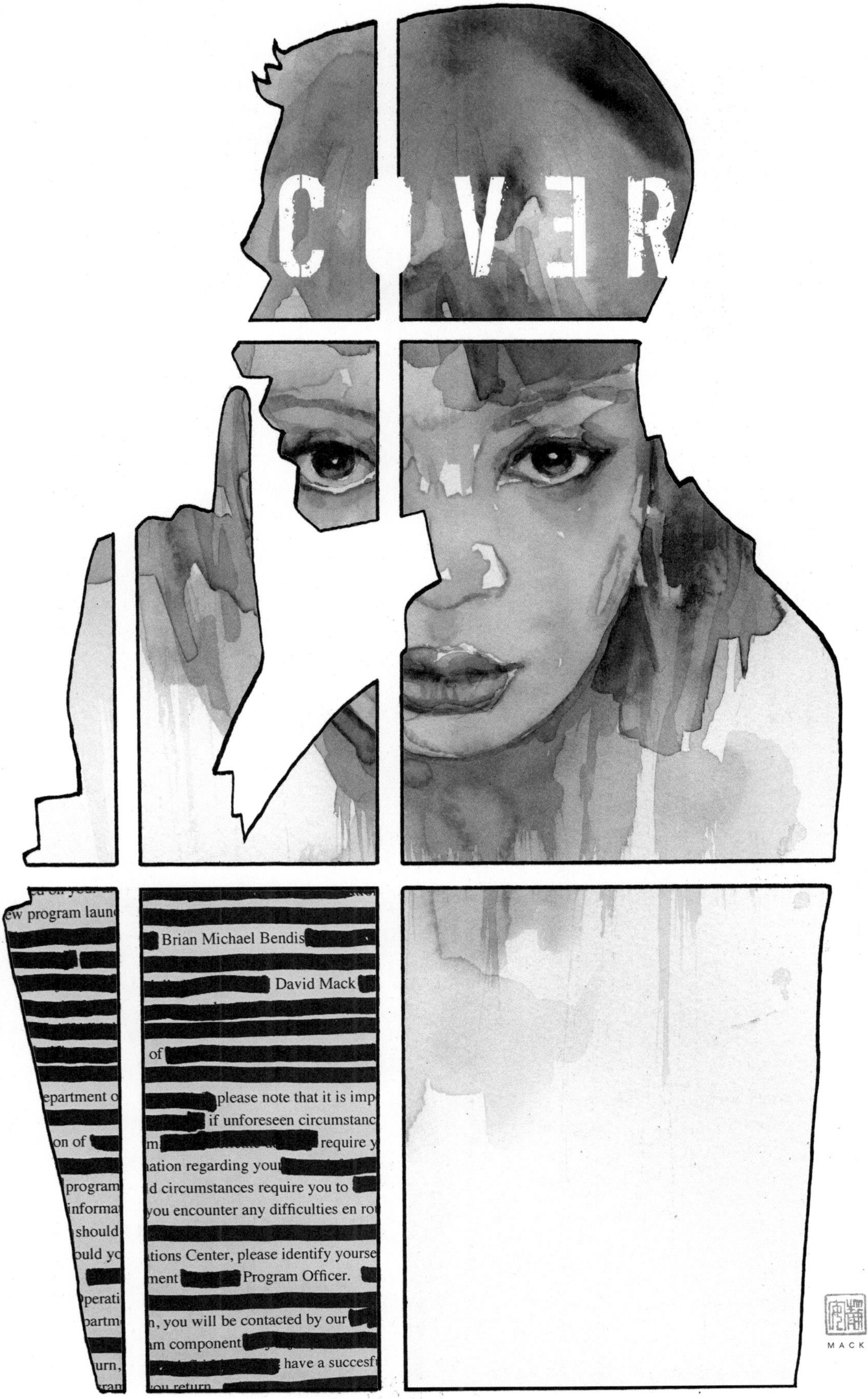
COVER
ew program launc
[redacted] Brian Michael Bendis [redacted]
[redacted] David Mack [redacted]
of [redacted]
epartment o [redacted] please note that it is impo
[redacted] if unforeseen circumstanc
on of [redacted] require y
[redacted] nation regarding you [redacted]
program ld circumstances require you to [redacted]
informa you encounter any difficulties en ro
should
ould yo ations Center, please identify yourse
[redacted] ment [redacted] Program Officer. [redacted]
Operati
partm n, you will be contacted by our [redacted]
am component [redacted]
urn, [redacted] have a succesf
MACK

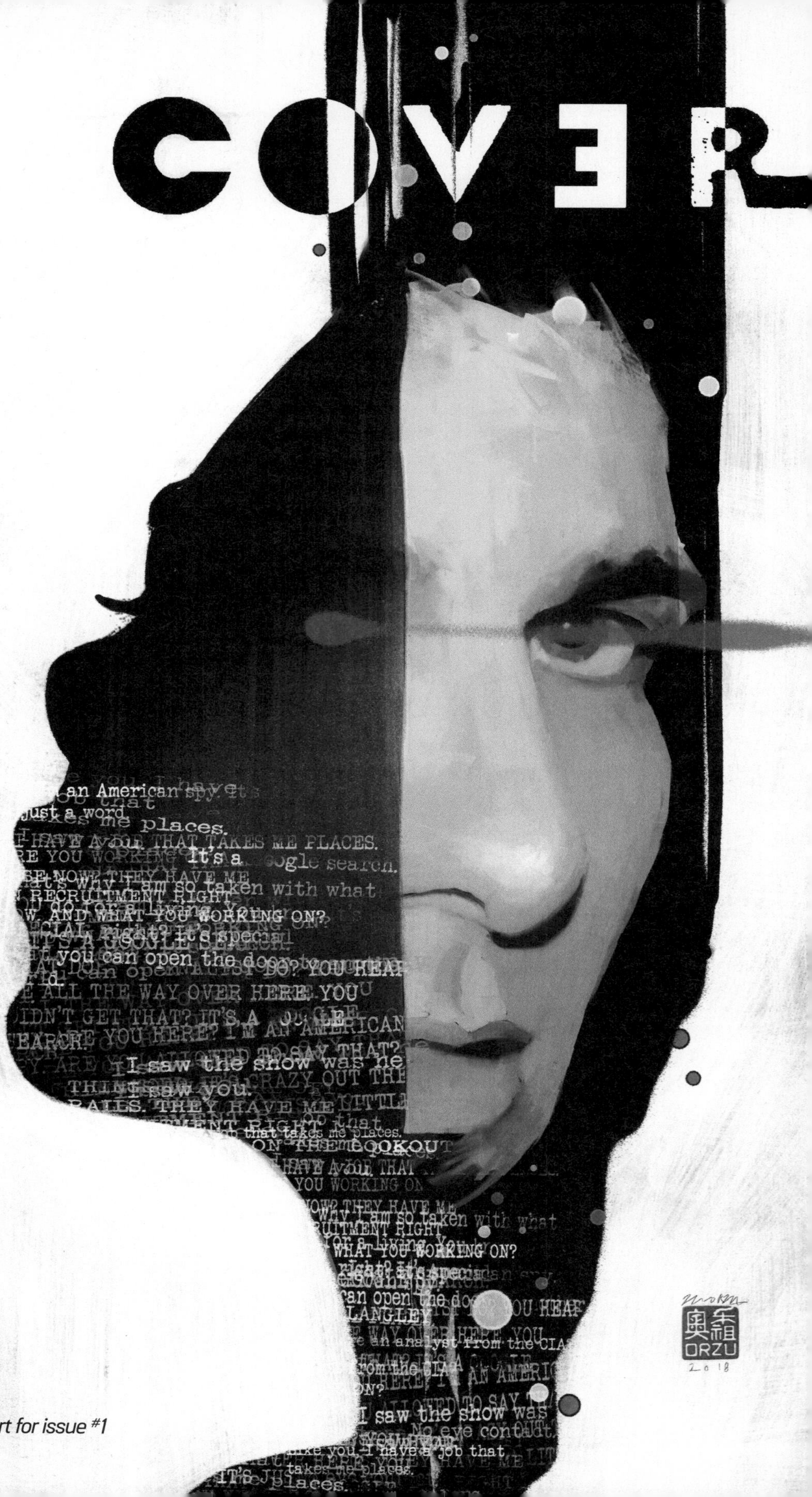
COVER
ORZU
2018

Variant cover art for issue #1
by ***Zu Orzu***

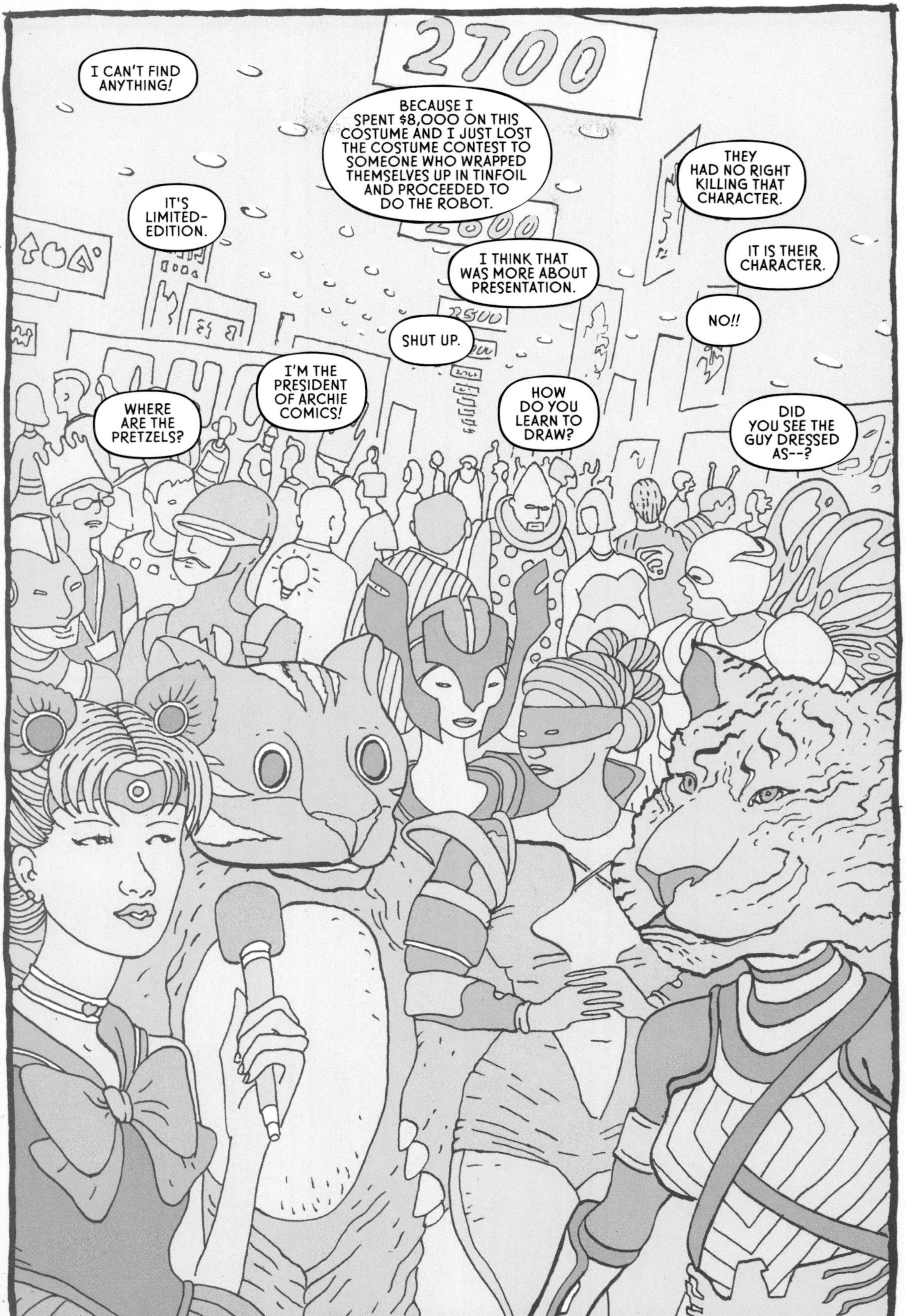
2700
I CAN'T FIND ANYTHING!
BECAUSE I SPENT $8,000 ON THIS COSTUME AND I JUST LOST THE COSTUME CONTEST TO SOMEONE WHO WRAPPED THEMSELVES UP IN TINFOIL AND PROCEEDED TO DO THE ROBOT.
IT'S LIMITED-EDITION.
I THINK THAT WAS MORE ABOUT PRESENTATION.
THEY HAD NO RIGHT KILLING THAT CHARACTER.
IT IS THEIR CHARACTER.
NO!!
SHUT UP.
I'M THE PRESIDENT OF ARCHIE COMICS!
WHERE ARE THE PRETZELS?
HOW DO YOU LEARN TO DRAW?
DID YOU SEE THE GUY DRESSED AS--?

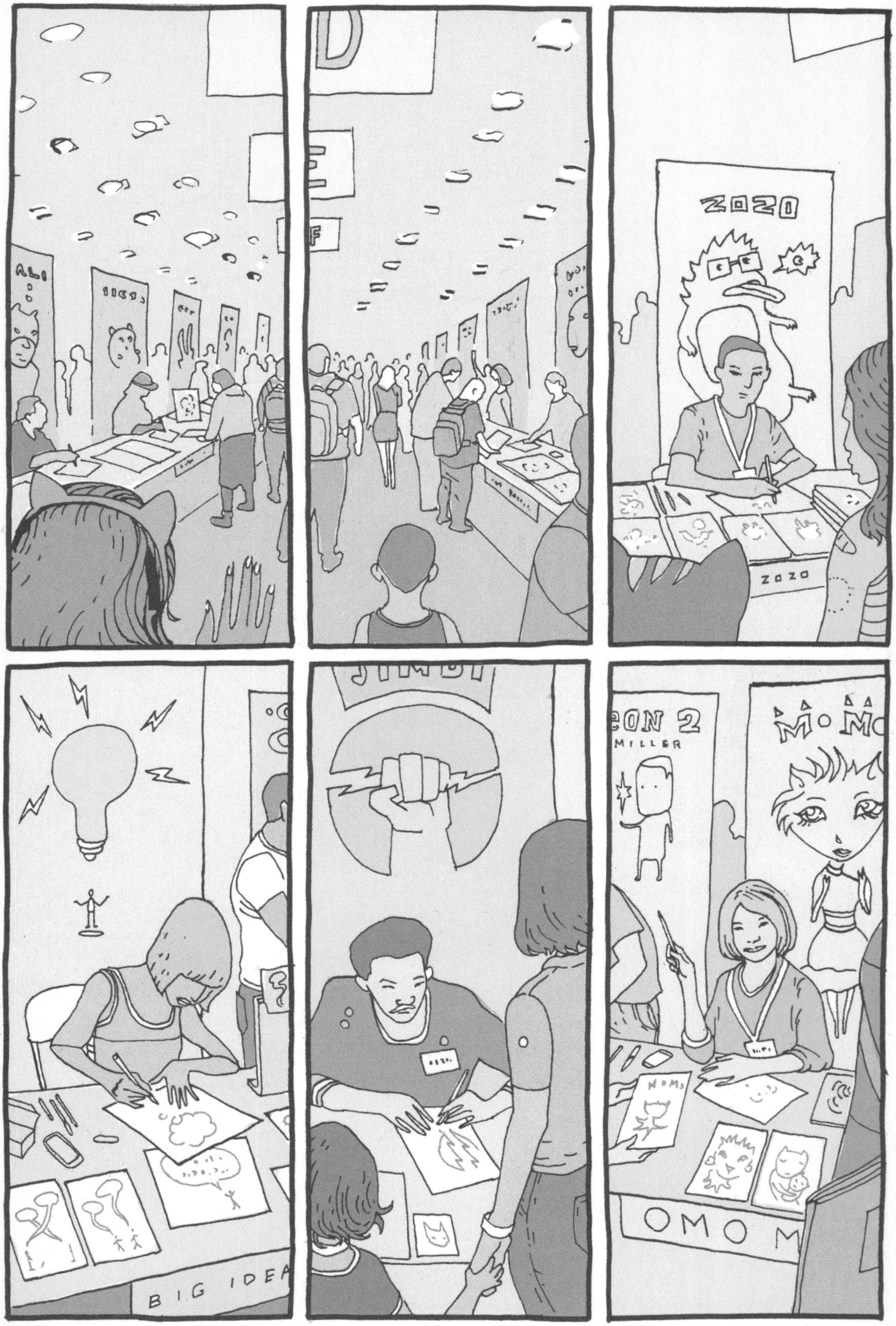
MILLER
BIG IDEA
OMO M

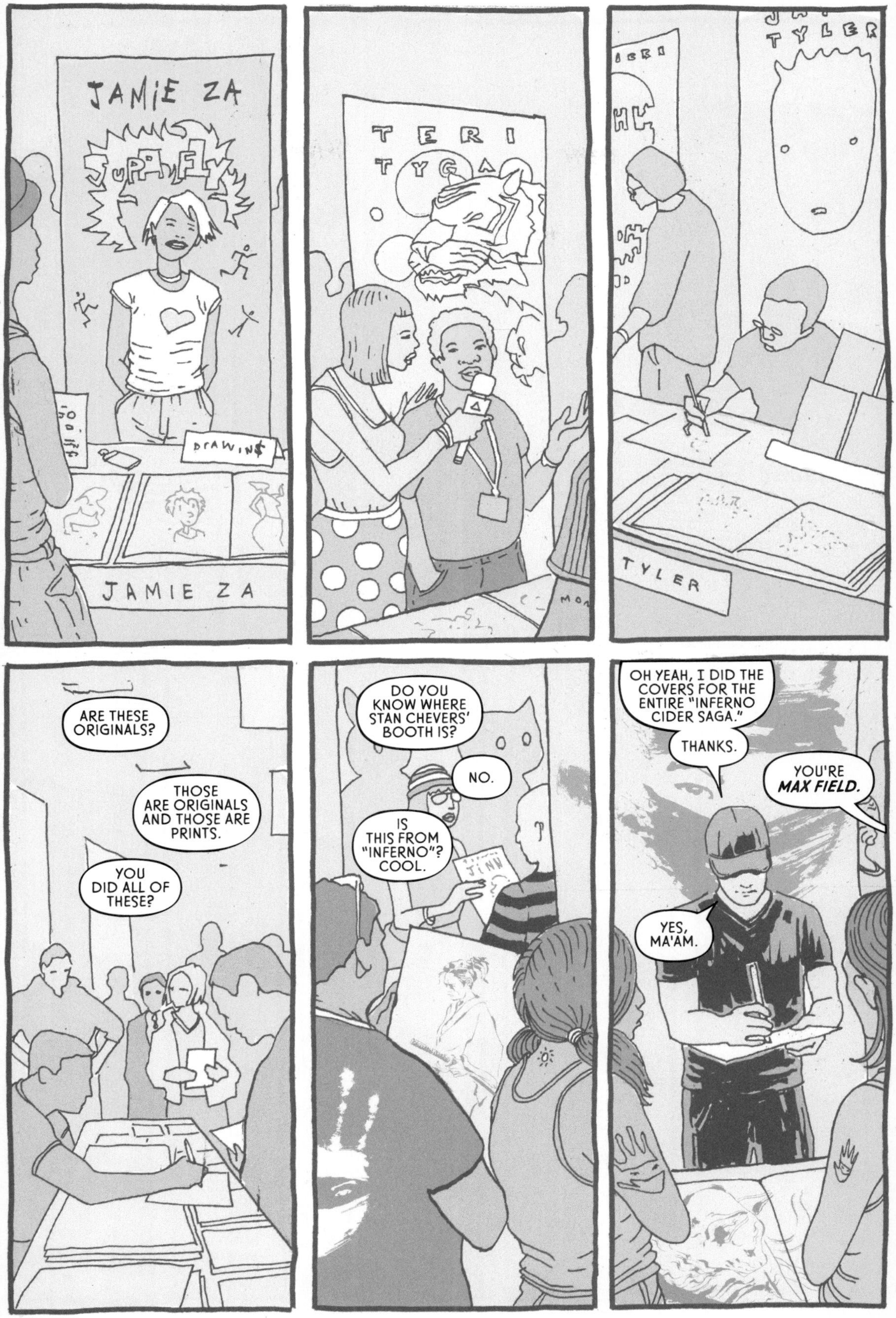
JAMIE ZA
DRAWIN$
JAMIE ZA
TERI TYGA
TYLER
TYLER
ARE THESE ORIGINALS?
THOSE ARE ORIGINALS AND THOSE ARE PRINTS.
YOU DID ALL OF THESE?
DO YOU KNOW WHERE STAN CHEVERS' BOOTH IS?
NO.
IS THIS FROM "INFERNO"? COOL.
OH YEAH, I DID THE COVERS FOR THE ENTIRE "INFERNO CIDER SAGA."
THANKS.
YOU'RE **MAX FIELD.**
YES, MA'AM.

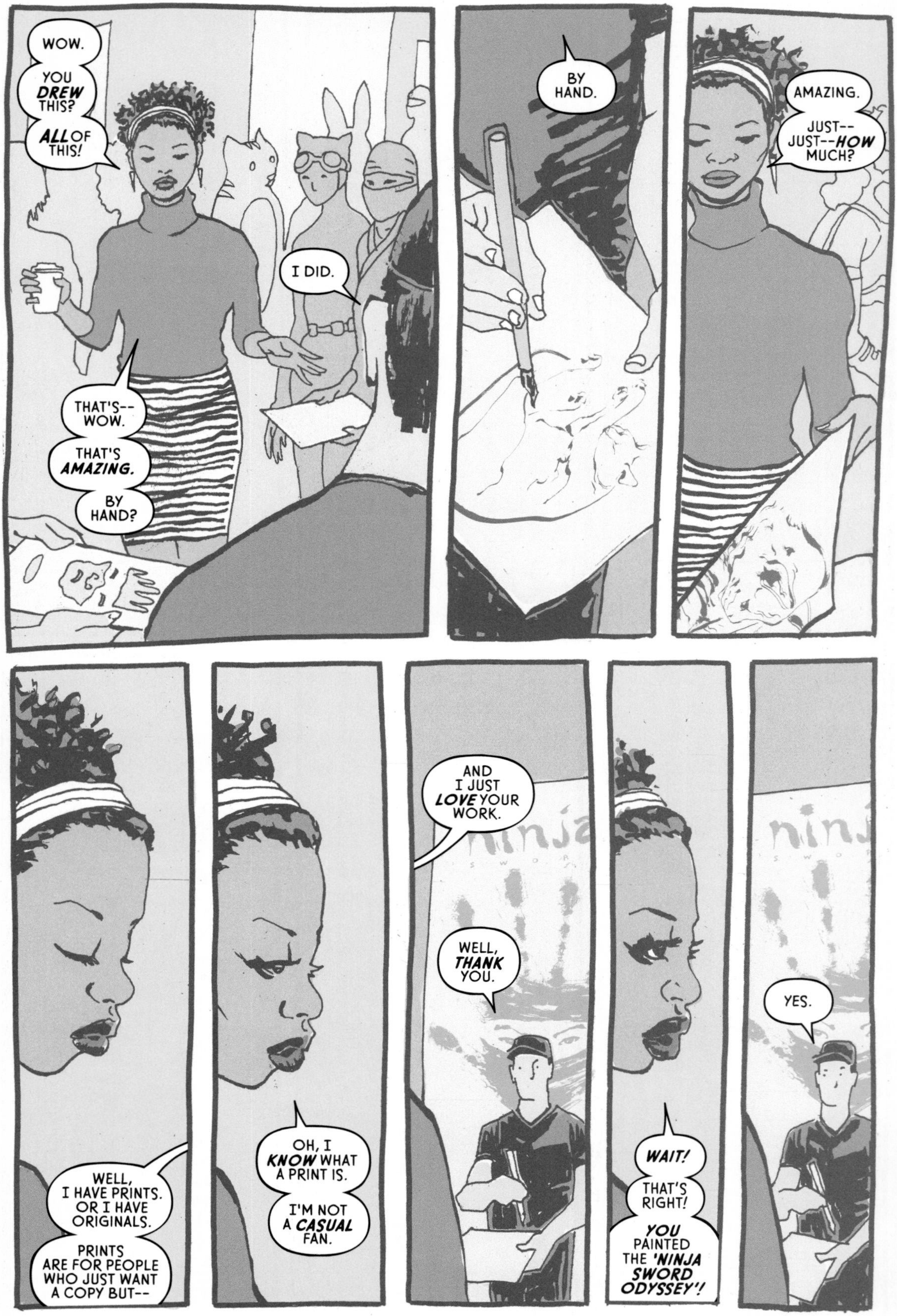
WOW.
YOU DREW THIS?
ALL OF THIS!
I DID.
THAT'S-- WOW.
THAT'S AMAZING.
BY HAND?
BY HAND.
AMAZING.
JUST-- JUST--HOW MUCH?
WELL, I HAVE PRINTS. OR I HAVE ORIGINALS.
PRINTS ARE FOR PEOPLE WHO JUST WANT A COPY BUT--
OH, I KNOW WHAT A PRINT IS.
I'M NOT A CASUAL FAN.
AND I JUST LOVE YOUR WORK.
WELL, THANK YOU.
WAIT!
THAT'S RIGHT!
YOU PAINTED THE 'NINJA SWORD ODYSSEY'!
YES.

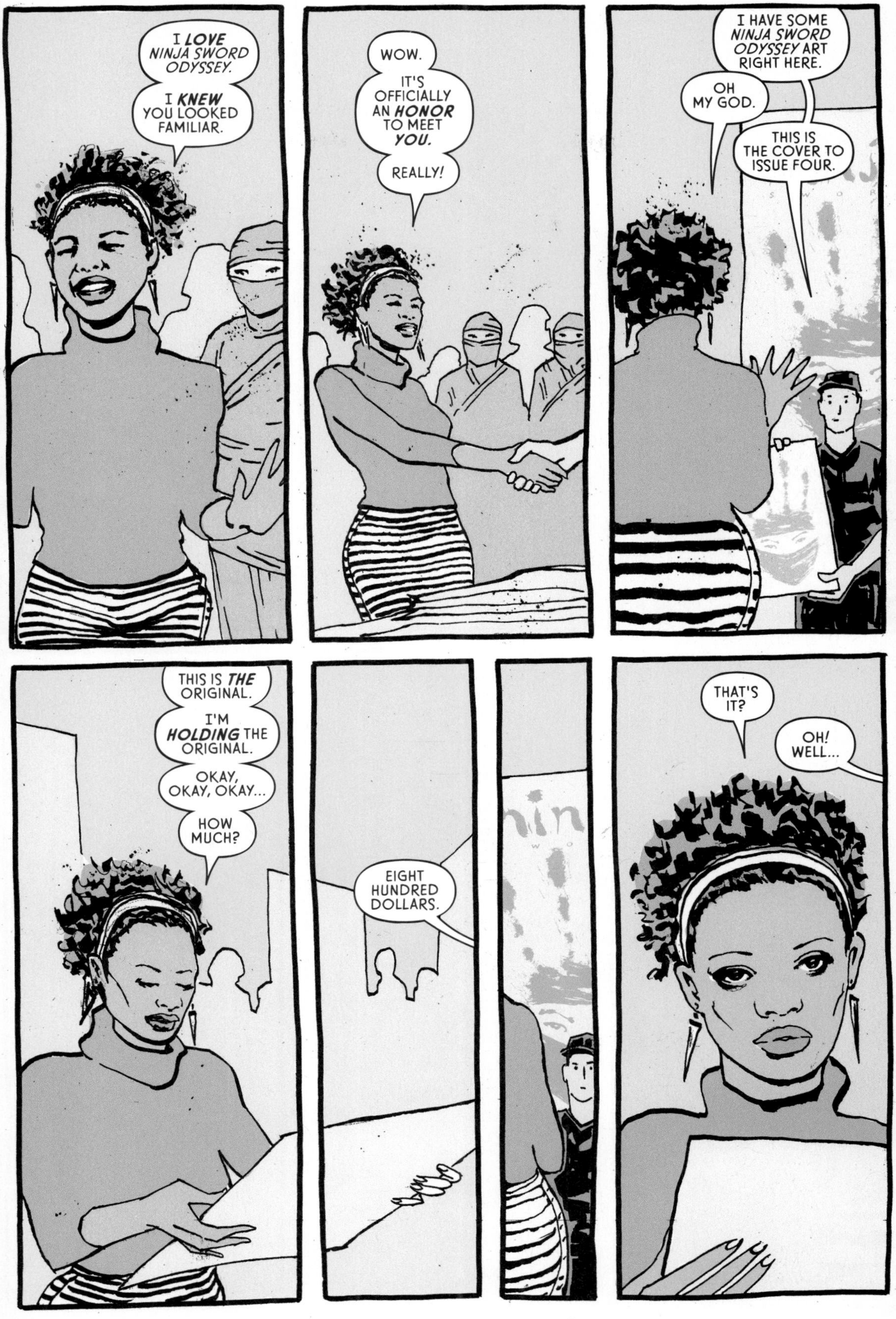
I LOVE NINJA SWORD ODYSSEY.
I KNEW YOU LOOKED FAMILIAR.
WOW.
IT'S OFFICIALLY AN HONOR TO MEET YOU.
REALLY!
I HAVE SOME NINJA SWORD ODYSSEY ART RIGHT HERE.
OH MY GOD.
THIS IS THE COVER TO ISSUE FOUR.
THIS IS THE ORIGINAL.
I'M HOLDING THE ORIGINAL.
OKAY, OKAY, OKAY...
HOW MUCH?
EIGHT HUNDRED DOLLARS.
THAT'S IT?
OH! WELL...

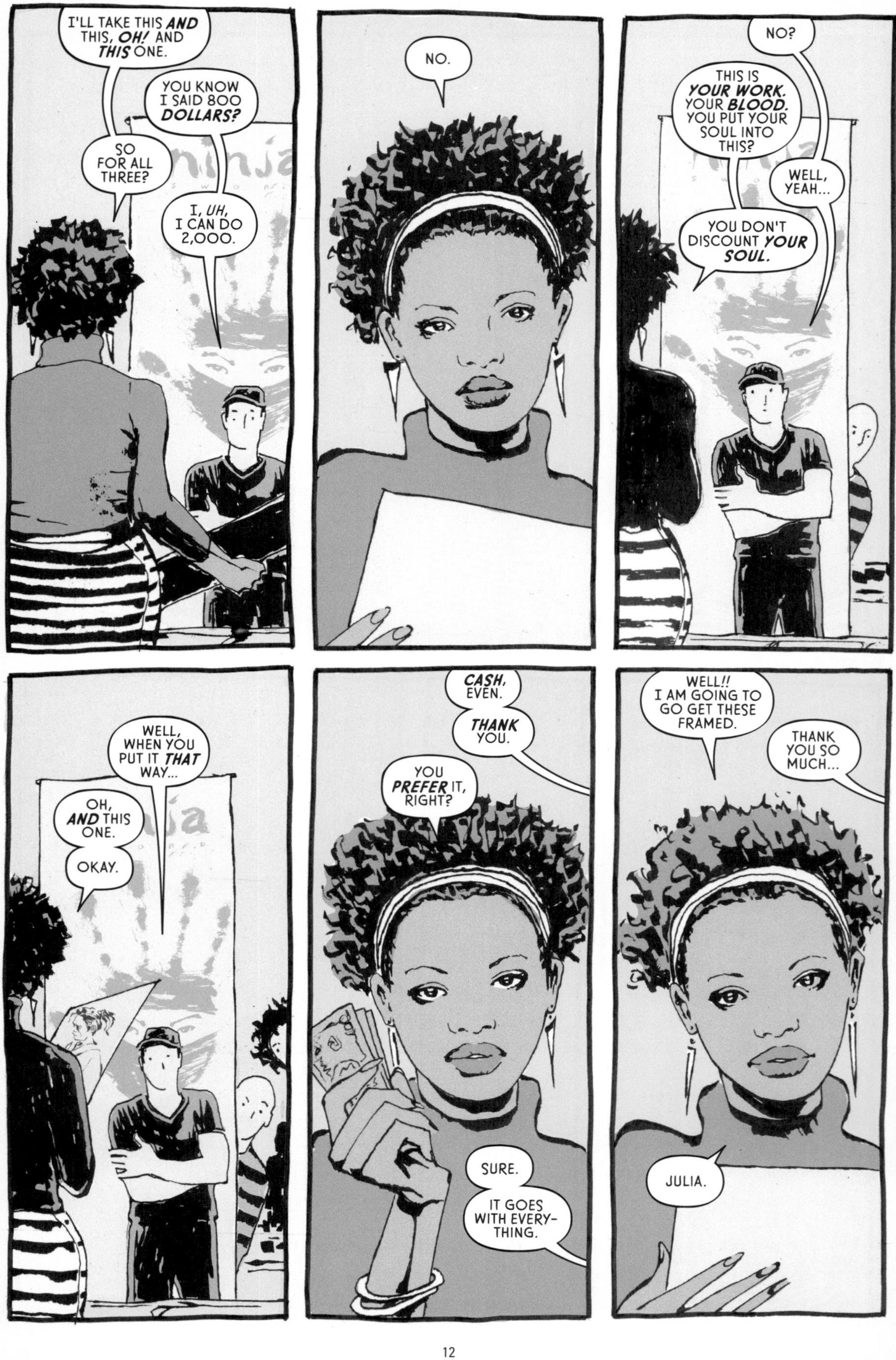
I'LL TAKE THIS AND THIS, OH! AND THIS ONE.
YOU KNOW I SAID 800 DOLLARS?
SO FOR ALL THREE?
I, UH, I CAN DO 2,000.
NO.
NO?
THIS IS YOUR WORK. YOUR BLOOD. YOU PUT YOUR SOUL INTO THIS?
WELL, YEAH...
YOU DON'T DISCOUNT YOUR SOUL.
WELL, WHEN YOU PUT IT THAT WAY...
OH, AND THIS ONE.
OKAY.
CASH, EVEN.
THANK YOU.
YOU PREFER IT, RIGHT?
SURE.
IT GOES WITH EVERY-THING.
WELL!! I AM GOING TO GO GET THESE FRAMED.
THANK YOU SO MUCH...
JULIA.

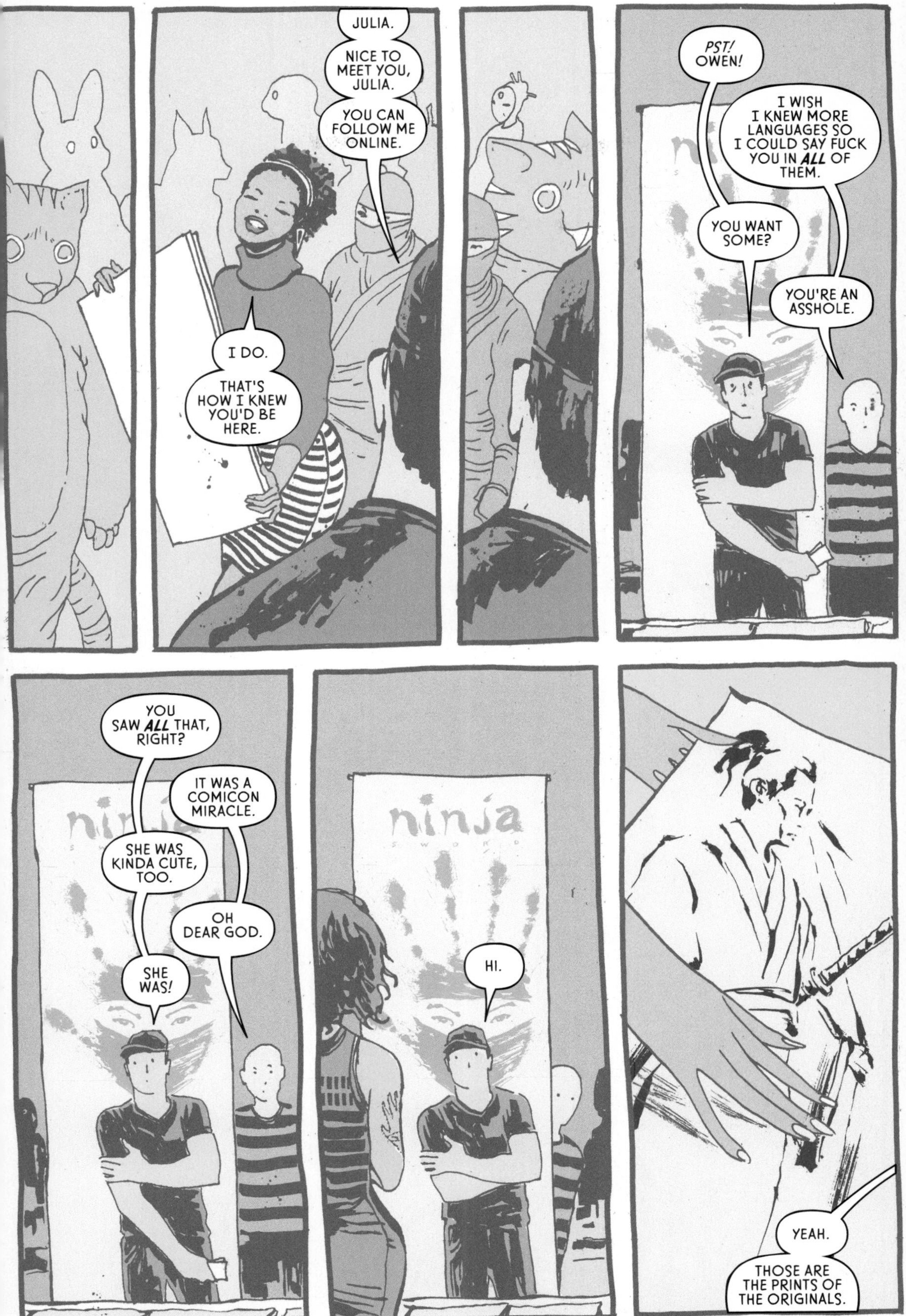

JULIA.
NICE TO MEET YOU, JULIA.
YOU CAN FOLLOW ME ONLINE.
I DO.
THAT'S HOW I KNEW YOU'D BE HERE.
PST! OWEN!
I WISH I KNEW MORE LANGUAGES SO I COULD SAY FUCK YOU IN ALL OF THEM.
YOU WANT SOME?
YOU'RE AN ASSHOLE.
YOU SAW ALL THAT, RIGHT?
IT WAS A COMICON MIRACLE.
SHE WAS KINDA CUTE, TOO.
OH DEAR GOD.
SHE WAS!
HI.
YEAH.
THOSE ARE THE PRINTS OF THE ORIGINALS.

Father came home.
After many battles.
The rules had changed
and he no longer had
his old job.

He now had jobs
without rules.

And he trained me
for this work too.

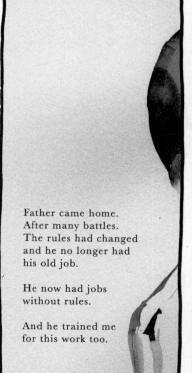

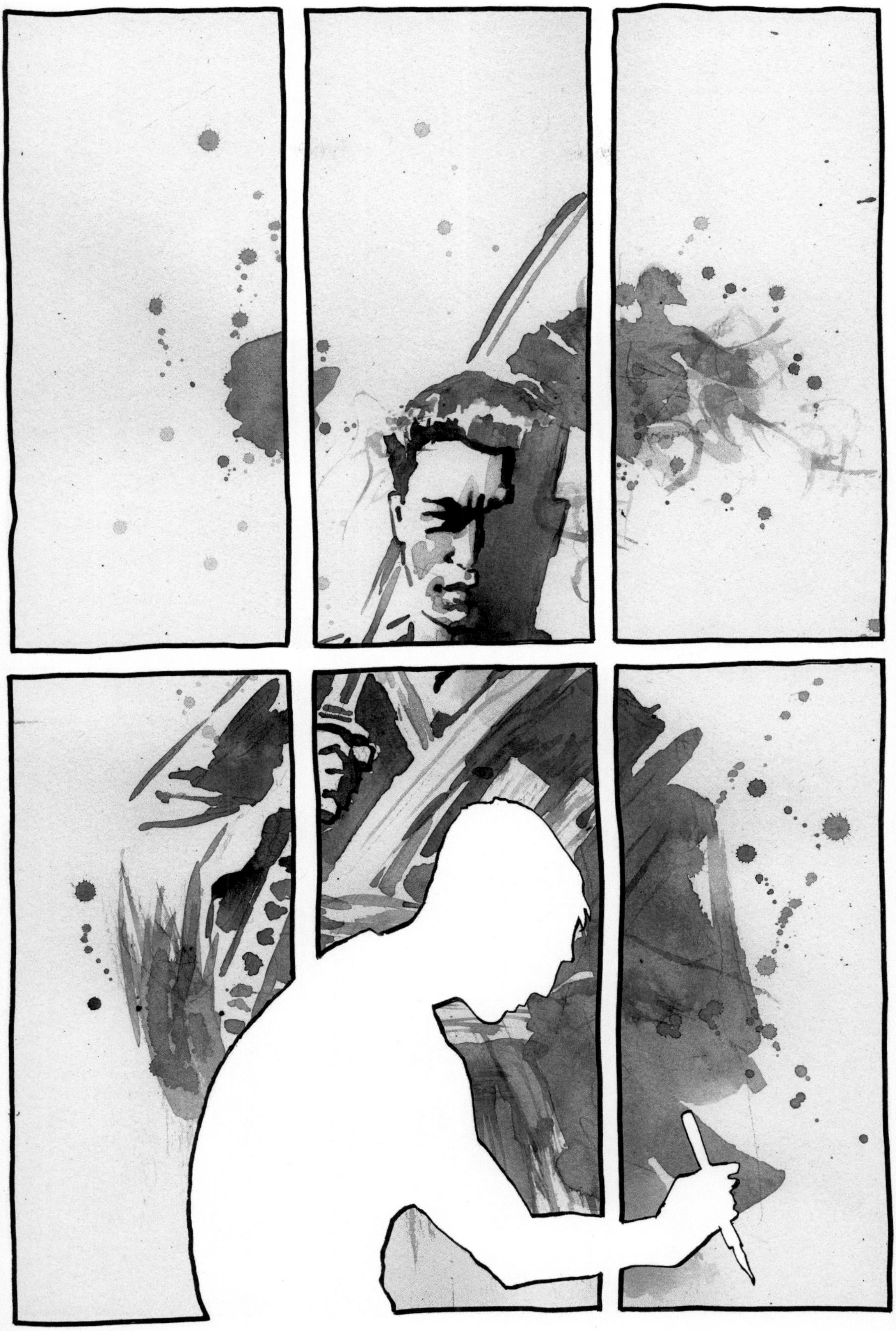

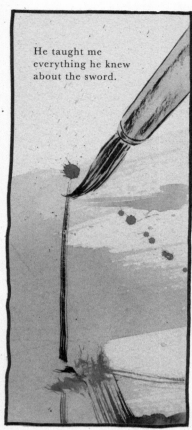

He taught me
everything he knew
about the sword.

About rules.
And no rules.

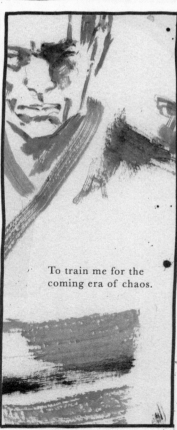

To train me for the
coming era of chaos.

He said there would be a time
when he was gone.
And that I would have to
change my name.

I would have to
blend in.
I would have to live
in the night and
hide in the day
in plain sight.

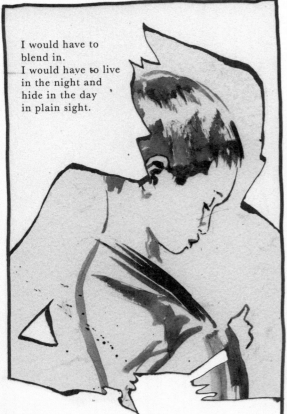

His teaching
was brutal.

I learned
it well.

FATHER, WHY
did you...

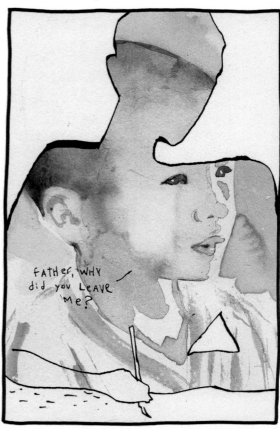

FATHER, WHY
did you LEAVE
me?

DING
DONG

I HEAR
YA IN THERE,
MAXXY.

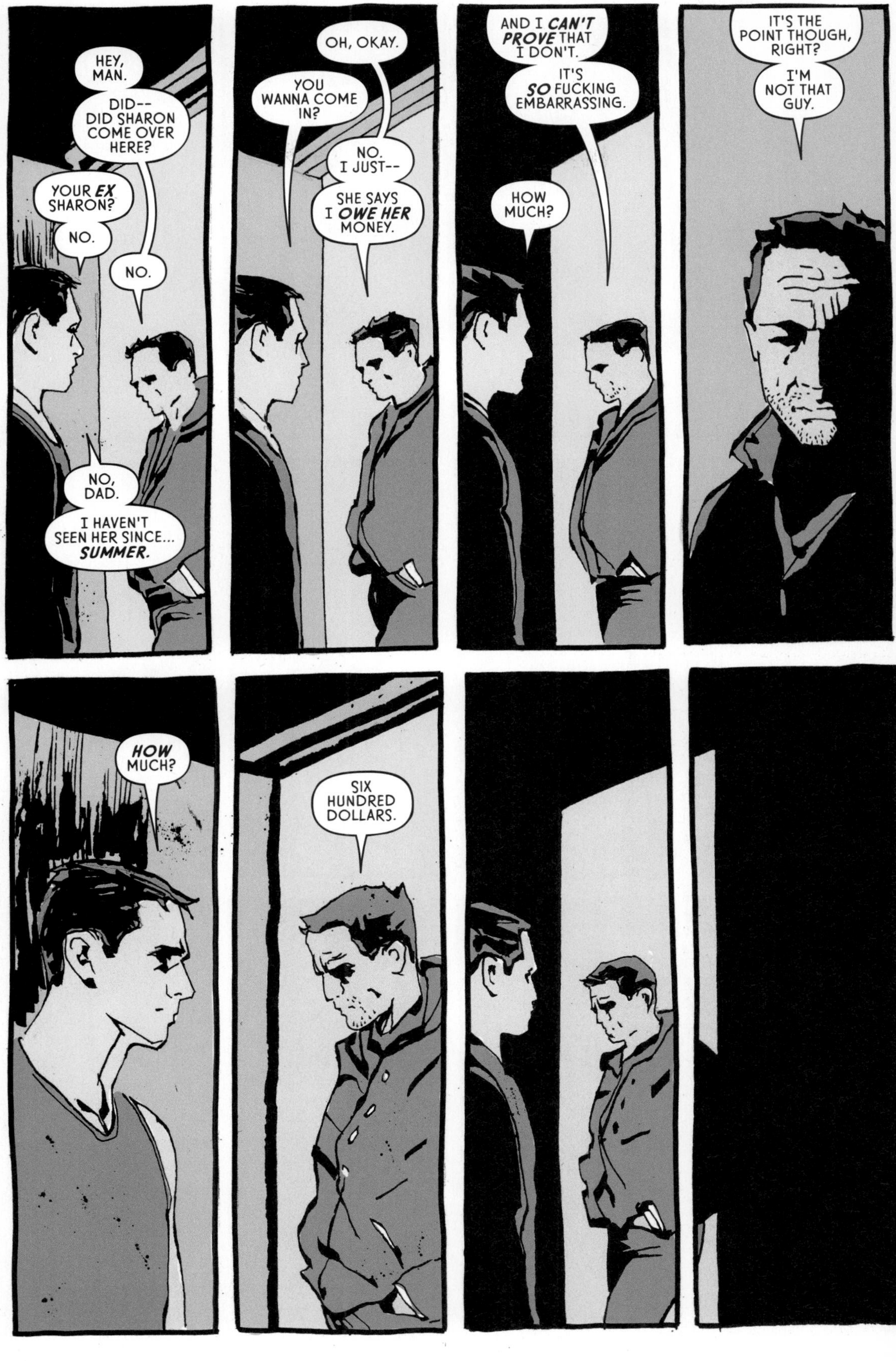
HEY, MAN.
DID-- DID SHARON COME OVER HERE?
YOUR EX SHARON?
NO.
NO.
NO, DAD.
I HAVEN'T SEEN HER SINCE... SUMMER.
OH, OKAY.
YOU WANNA COME IN?
NO. I JUST--
SHE SAYS I OWE HER MONEY.
AND I CAN'T PROVE THAT I DON'T.
IT'S SO FUCKING EMBARRASSING.
HOW MUCH?
IT'S THE POINT THOUGH, RIGHT?
I'M NOT THAT GUY.
HOW MUCH?
SIX HUNDRED DOLLARS.

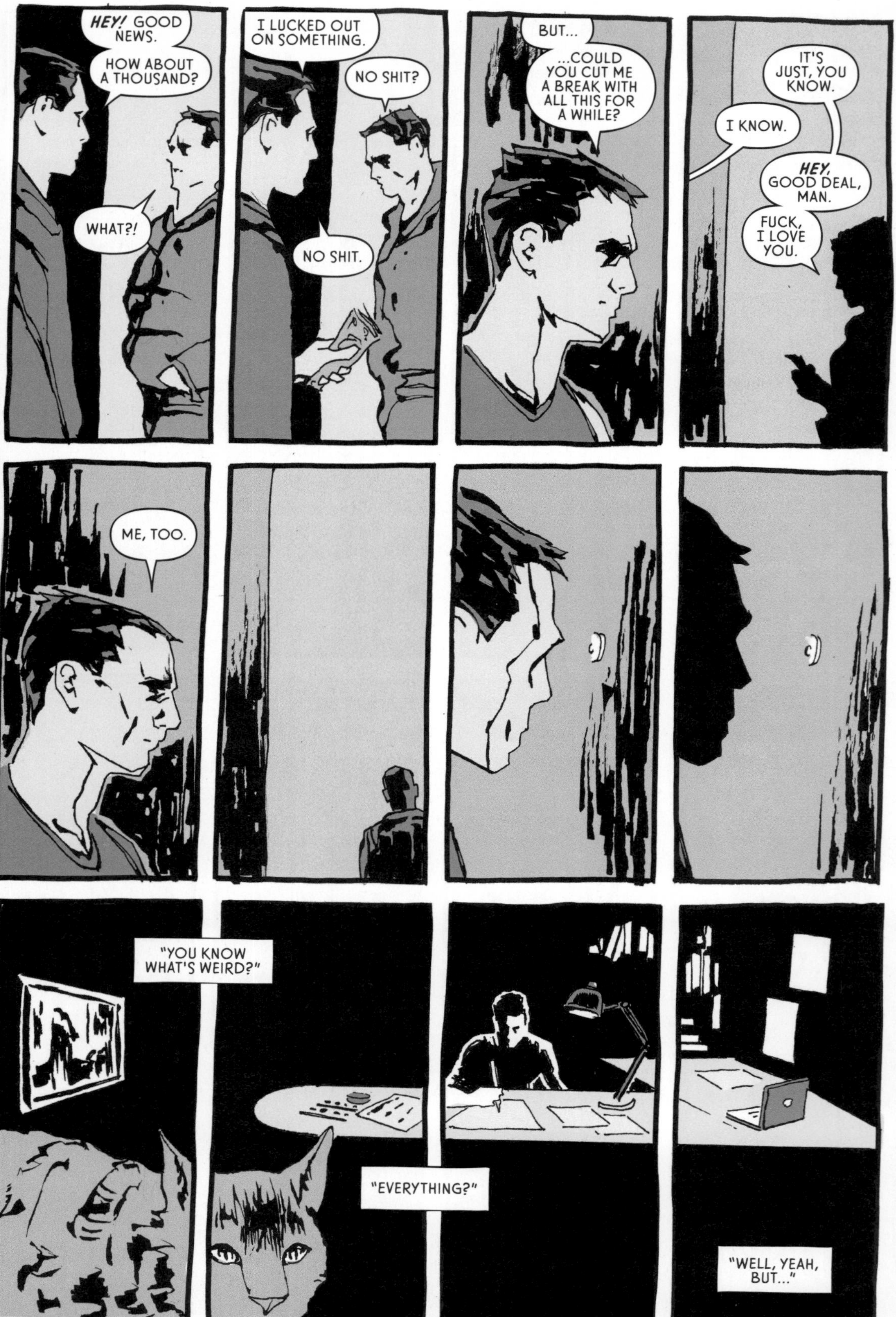

HEY! GOOD NEWS.
HOW ABOUT A THOUSAND?
WHAT?!
I LUCKED OUT ON SOMETHING.
NO SHIT?
NO SHIT.
BUT...
...COULD YOU CUT ME A BREAK WITH ALL THIS FOR A WHILE?
IT'S JUST, YOU KNOW.
I KNOW.
HEY, GOOD DEAL, MAN.
FUCK, I LOVE YOU.
ME, TOO.
"YOU KNOW WHAT'S WEIRD?"
"EVERYTHING?"
"WELL, YEAH, BUT..."

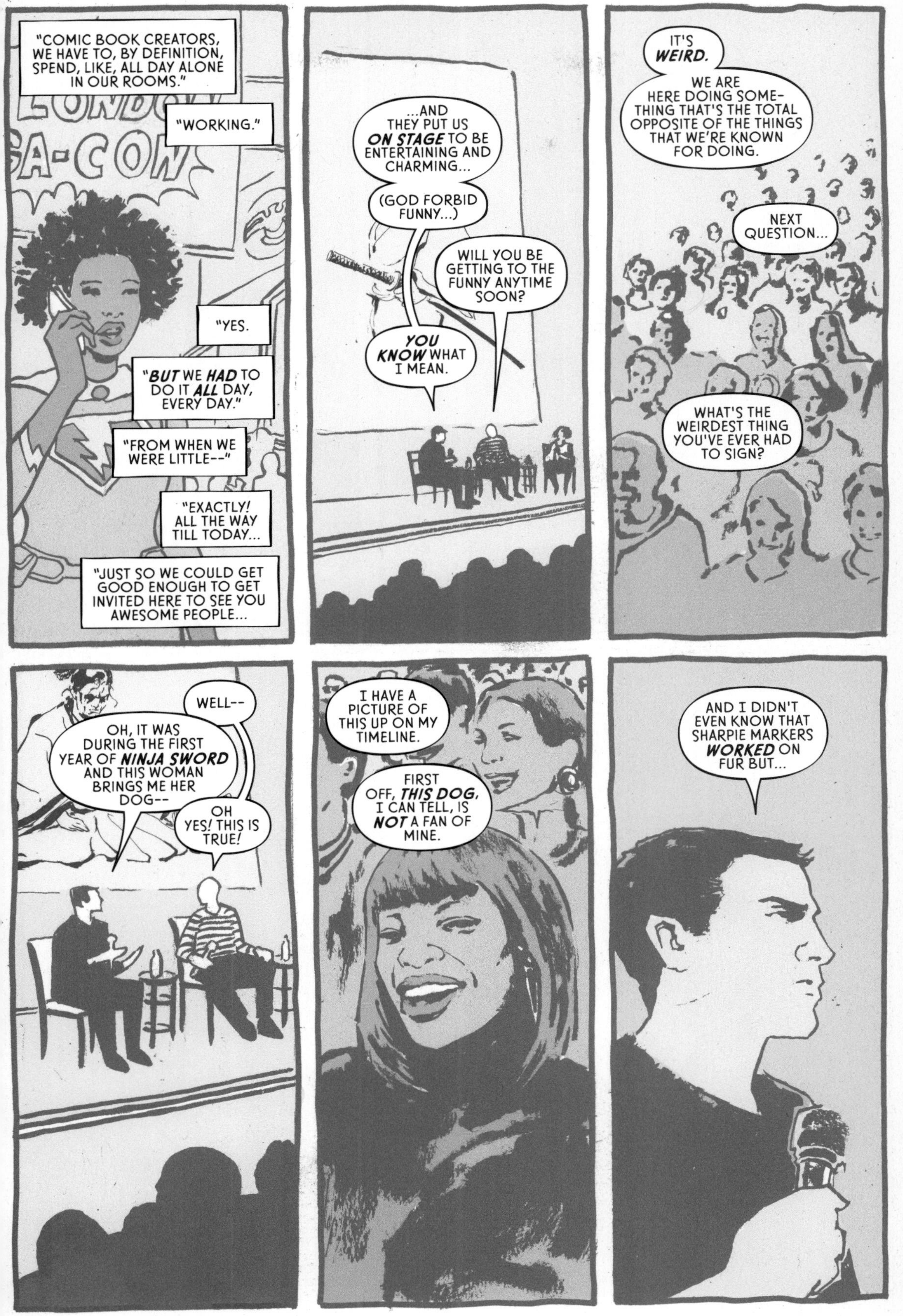
"COMIC BOOK CREATORS, WE HAVE TO, BY DEFINITION, SPEND, LIKE, ALL DAY ALONE IN OUR ROOMS."
"WORKING."
"YES.
"BUT WE HAD TO DO IT ALL DAY, EVERY DAY."
"FROM WHEN WE WERE LITTLE--"
"EXACTLY! ALL THE WAY TILL TODAY...
"JUST SO WE COULD GET GOOD ENOUGH TO GET INVITED HERE TO SEE YOU AWESOME PEOPLE...
...AND THEY PUT US ON STAGE TO BE ENTERTAINING AND CHARMING...
(GOD FORBID FUNNY...)
WILL YOU BE GETTING TO THE FUNNY ANYTIME SOON?
YOU KNOW WHAT I MEAN.
IT'S WEIRD.
WE ARE HERE DOING SOME-THING THAT'S THE TOTAL OPPOSITE OF THE THINGS THAT WE'RE KNOWN FOR DOING.
NEXT QUESTION...
WHAT'S THE WEIRDEST THING YOU'VE EVER HAD TO SIGN?
WELL--
OH, IT WAS DURING THE FIRST YEAR OF NINJA SWORD AND THIS WOMAN BRINGS ME HER DOG--
OH YES! THIS IS TRUE!
I HAVE A PICTURE OF THIS UP ON MY TIMELINE.
FIRST OFF, THIS DOG, I CAN TELL, IS NOT A FAN OF MINE.
AND I DIDN'T EVEN KNOW THAT SHARPIE MARKERS WORKED ON FUR BUT...

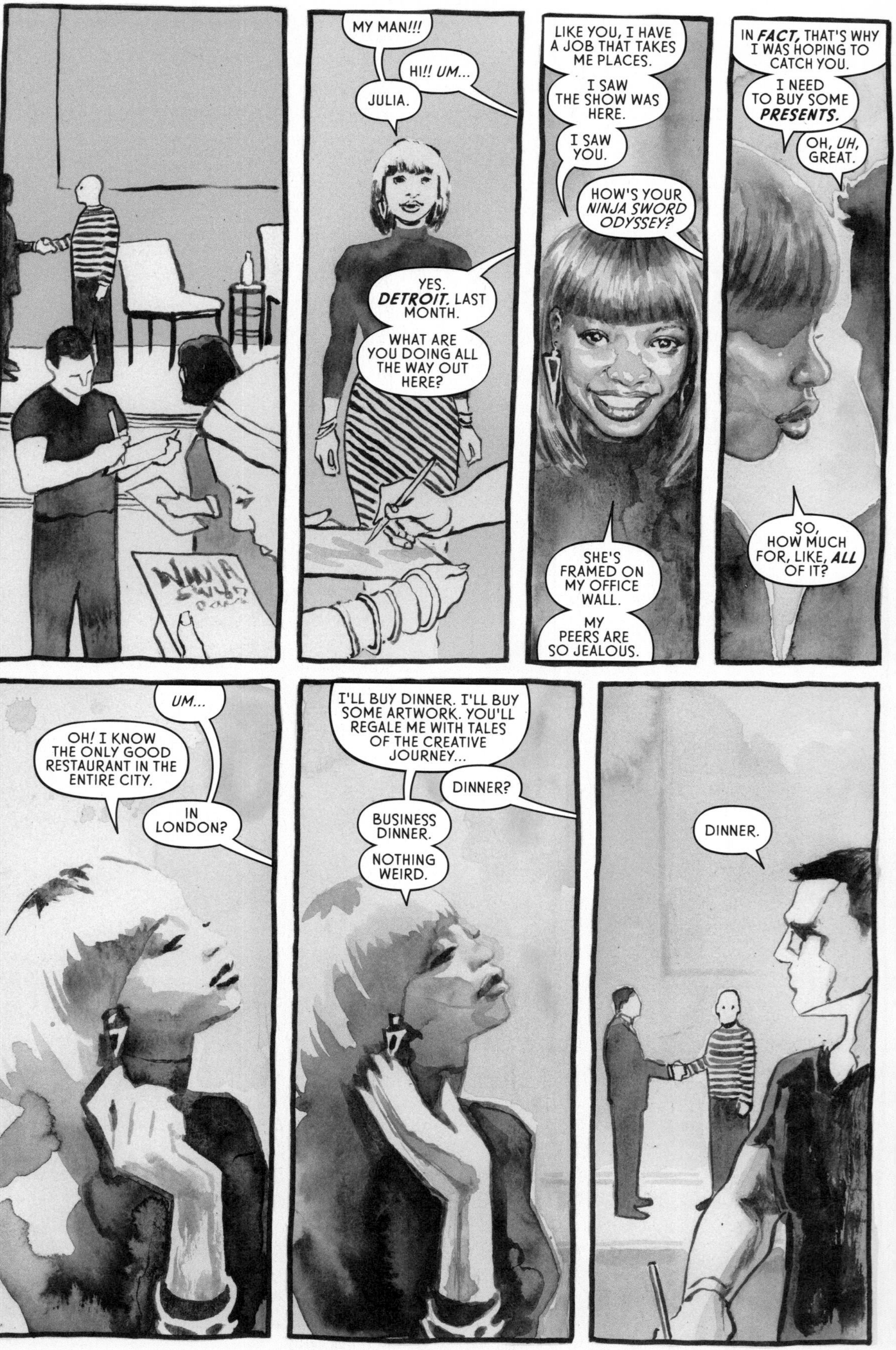
MY MAN!!!
HI!! *UM...*
JULIA.
YES. ***DETROIT.*** LAST MONTH.
WHAT ARE YOU DOING ALL THE WAY OUT HERE?
LIKE YOU, I HAVE A JOB THAT TAKES ME PLACES.
I SAW THE SHOW WAS HERE.
I SAW YOU.
HOW'S YOUR *NINJA SWORD ODYSSEY?*
SHE'S FRAMED ON MY OFFICE WALL.
MY PEERS ARE SO JEALOUS.
IN ***FACT,*** THAT'S WHY I WAS HOPING TO CATCH YOU.
I NEED TO BUY SOME ***PRESENTS.***
OH, *UH,* GREAT.
SO, HOW MUCH FOR, LIKE, ***ALL*** OF IT?
UM...
OH! I KNOW THE ONLY GOOD RESTAURANT IN THE ENTIRE CITY.
IN LONDON?
I'LL BUY DINNER. I'LL BUY SOME ARTWORK. YOU'LL REGALE ME WITH TALES OF THE CREATIVE JOURNEY...
DINNER?
BUSINESS DINNER.
NOTHING WEIRD.
DINNER.

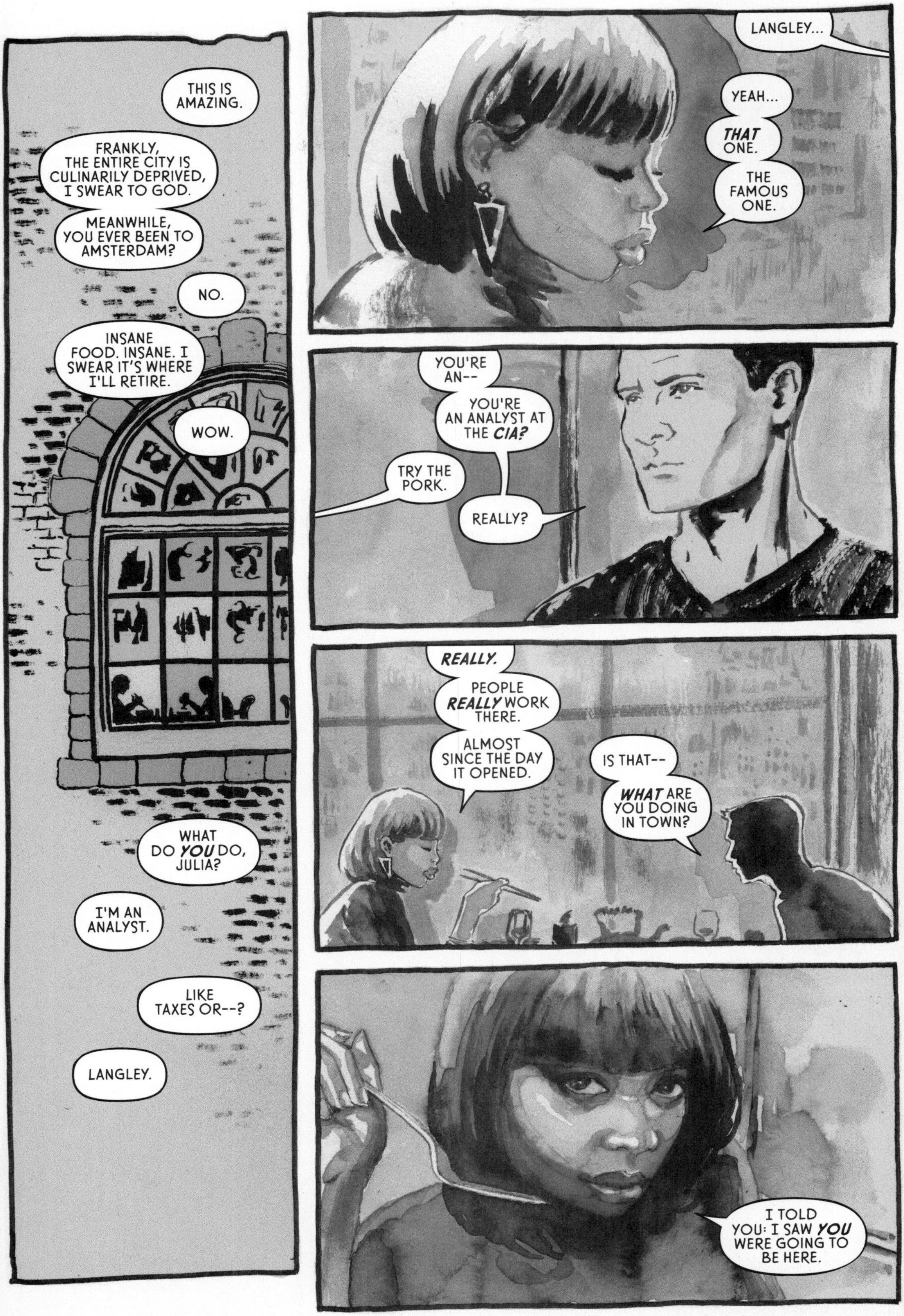
THIS IS AMAZING.
FRANKLY, THE ENTIRE CITY IS CULINARILY DEPRIVED, I SWEAR TO GOD.
MEANWHILE, YOU EVER BEEN TO AMSTERDAM?
NO.
INSANE FOOD. INSANE. I SWEAR IT'S WHERE I'LL RETIRE.
WOW.
WHAT DO *YOU* DO, JULIA?
I'M AN ANALYST.
LIKE TAXES OR--?
LANGLEY.
LANGLEY...
YEAH...
THAT ONE.
THE FAMOUS ONE.
YOU'RE AN--
YOU'RE AN ANALYST AT THE *CIA?*
TRY THE PORK.
REALLY?
REALLY.
PEOPLE *REALLY* WORK THERE.
ALMOST SINCE THE DAY IT OPENED.
IS THAT--
WHAT ARE YOU DOING IN TOWN?
I TOLD YOU: I SAW *YOU* WERE GOING TO BE HERE.

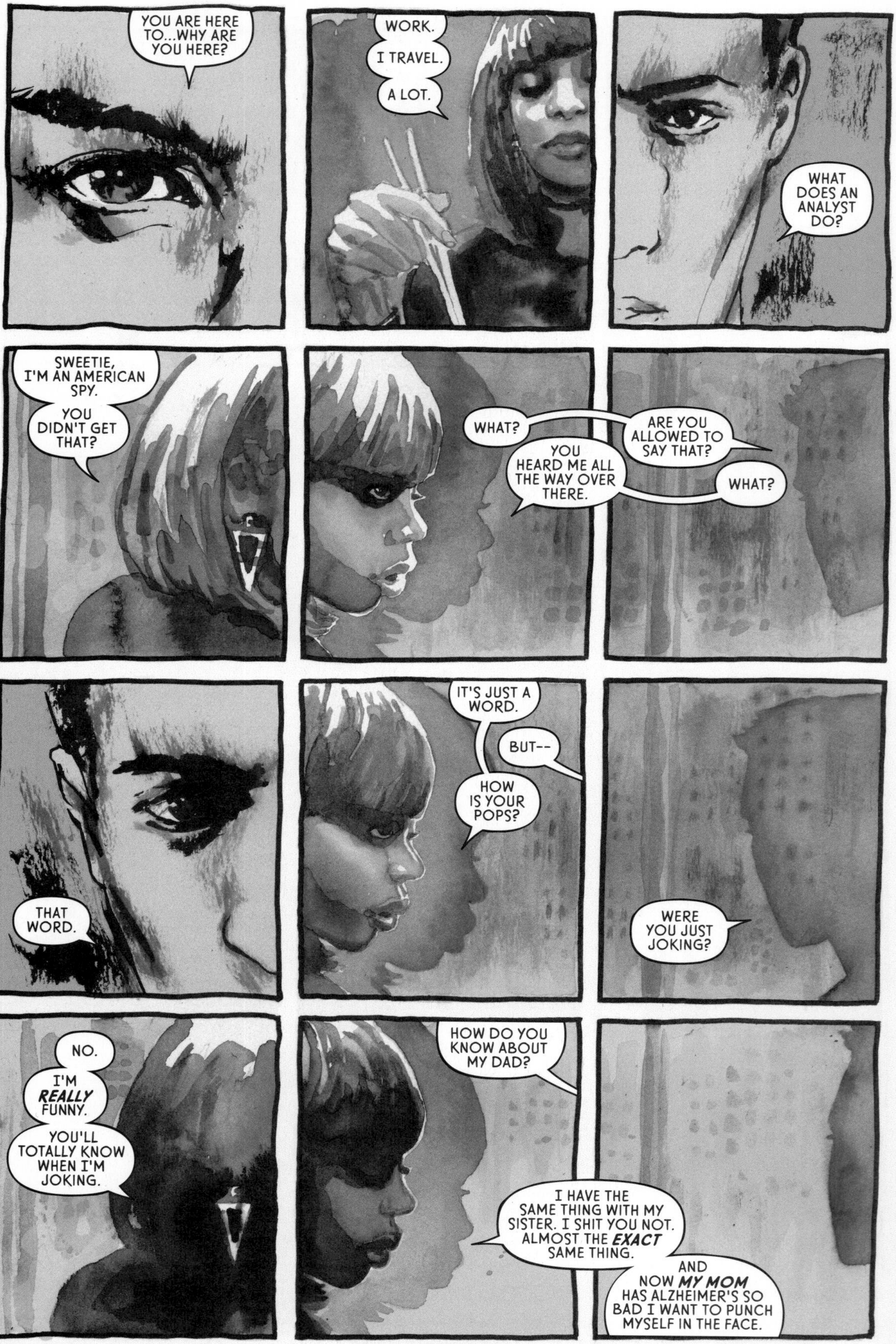
YOU ARE HERE TO...WHY ARE YOU HERE?
WORK.
I TRAVEL.
A LOT.
WHAT DOES AN ANALYST DO?
SWEETIE, I'M AN AMERICAN SPY.
YOU DIDN'T GET THAT?
WHAT?
ARE YOU ALLOWED TO SAY THAT?
YOU HEARD ME ALL THE WAY OVER THERE.
WHAT?
THAT WORD.
IT'S JUST A WORD.
BUT--
HOW IS YOUR POPS?
WERE YOU JUST JOKING?
NO.
I'M ***REALLY*** FUNNY.
YOU'LL TOTALLY KNOW WHEN I'M JOKING.
HOW DO YOU KNOW ABOUT MY DAD?
I HAVE THE SAME THING WITH MY SISTER. I SHIT YOU NOT. ALMOST THE ***EXACT*** SAME THING.
AND NOW ***MY MOM*** HAS ALZHEIMER'S SO BAD I WANT TO PUNCH MYSELF IN THE FACE.

YOU LOOKED INTO ME?

IT'S A GOOGLE SEARCH, MAX.

ALSO, YOU TALKED A LITTLE ABOUT IT ON THAT WORD BALLOON PODCAST.

DID MY FATHER DO SOMETHING WRONG?

HE SHOULDN'T HAVE PUT ANY PART OF HIMSELF IN THAT ASSHOLE NAMED SHARON.

WOW.

SORRY. THAT WAS A LITTLE JUDGY--

NO. THAT WAS-- THAT WAS RIGHT.

YOU'RE NOT IN TROUBLE.

NO ONE IS IN TROUBLE.

I AM *A FAN.* YOUR WORK REALLY GETS TO ME.

WHAT DO YOU DO AS THE THING YOU SAID YOU ARE?

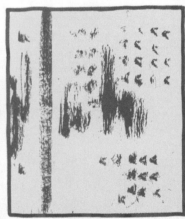

I HANDLE CASEWORK. CASES.

OKAY. WHAT KIND OF CASES?

25

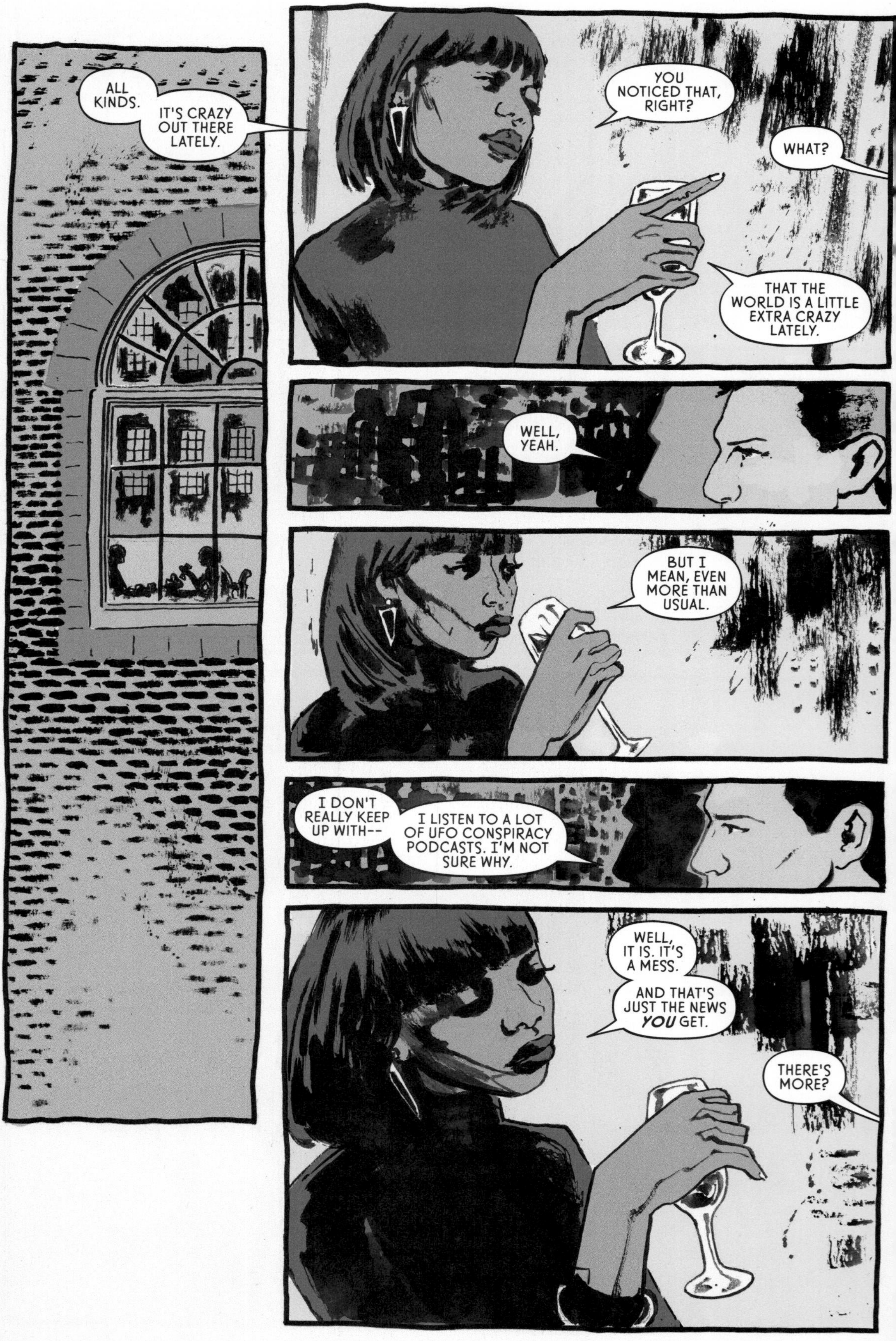
ALL KINDS.
IT'S CRAZY OUT THERE LATELY.
YOU NOTICED THAT, RIGHT?
WHAT?
THAT THE WORLD IS A LITTLE EXTRA CRAZY LATELY.
WELL, YEAH.
BUT I MEAN, EVEN MORE THAN USUAL.
I DON'T REALLY KEEP UP WITH--
I LISTEN TO A LOT OF UFO CONSPIRACY PODCASTS. I'M NOT SURE WHY.
WELL, IT IS. IT'S A MESS.
AND THAT'S JUST THE NEWS *YOU* GET.
THERE'S MORE?

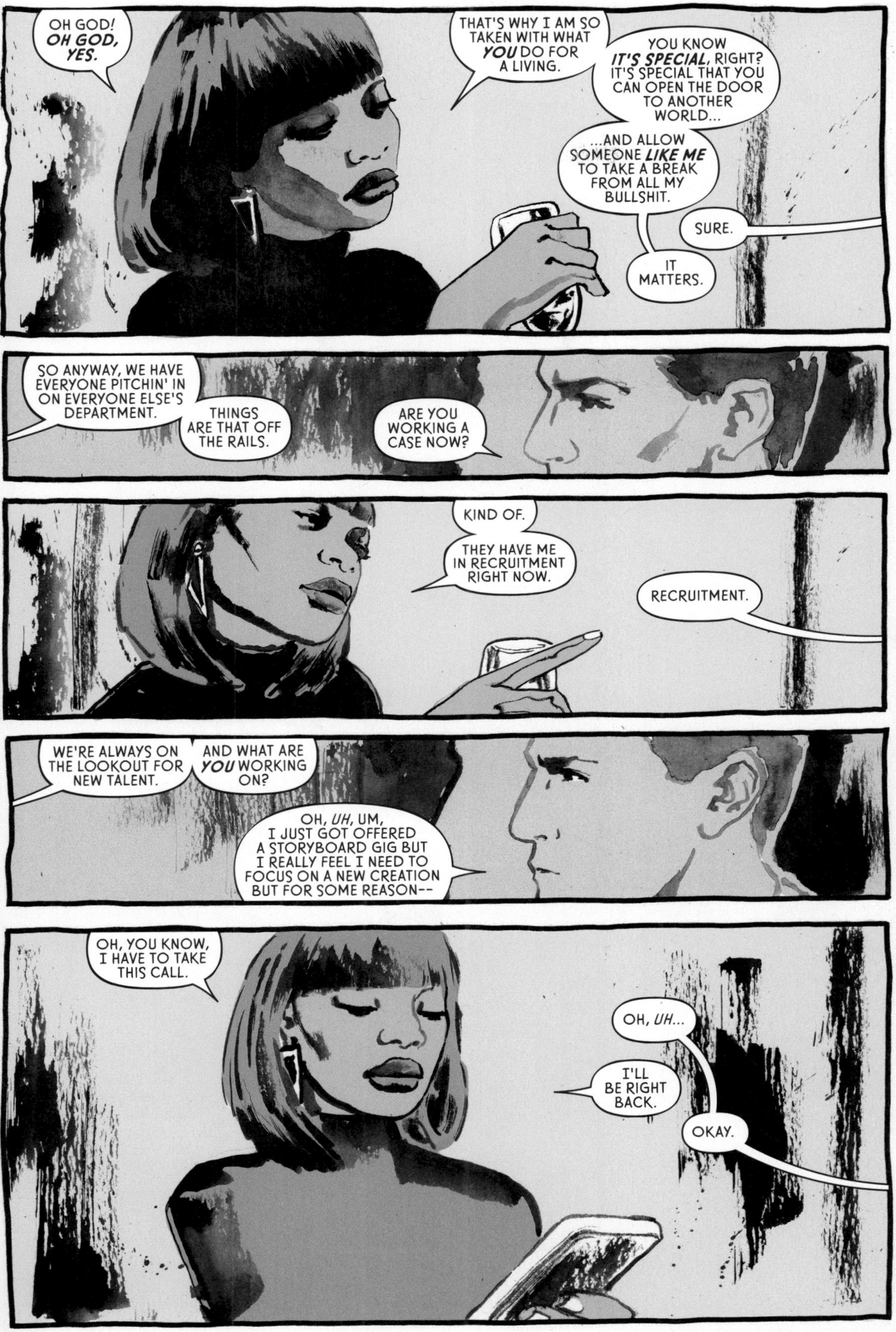
OH GOD! ***OH GOD, YES.***
THAT'S WHY I AM SO TAKEN WITH WHAT ***YOU*** DO FOR A LIVING.
YOU KNOW ***IT'S SPECIAL***, RIGHT? IT'S SPECIAL THAT YOU CAN OPEN THE DOOR TO ANOTHER WORLD...
...AND ALLOW SOMEONE ***LIKE ME*** TO TAKE A BREAK FROM ALL MY BULLSHIT.
SURE.
IT MATTERS.
SO ANYWAY, WE HAVE EVERYONE PITCHIN' IN ON EVERYONE ELSE'S DEPARTMENT.
THINGS ARE THAT OFF THE RAILS.
ARE YOU WORKING A CASE NOW?
KIND OF.
THEY HAVE ME IN RECRUITMENT RIGHT NOW.
RECRUITMENT.
WE'RE ALWAYS ON THE LOOKOUT FOR NEW TALENT.
AND WHAT ARE ***YOU*** WORKING ON?
OH, *UH*, UM, I JUST GOT OFFERED A STORYBOARD GIG BUT I REALLY FEEL I NEED TO FOCUS ON A NEW CREATION BUT FOR SOME REASON--
OH, YOU KNOW, I HAVE TO TAKE THIS CALL.
OH, *UH*...
I'LL BE RIGHT BACK.
OKAY.

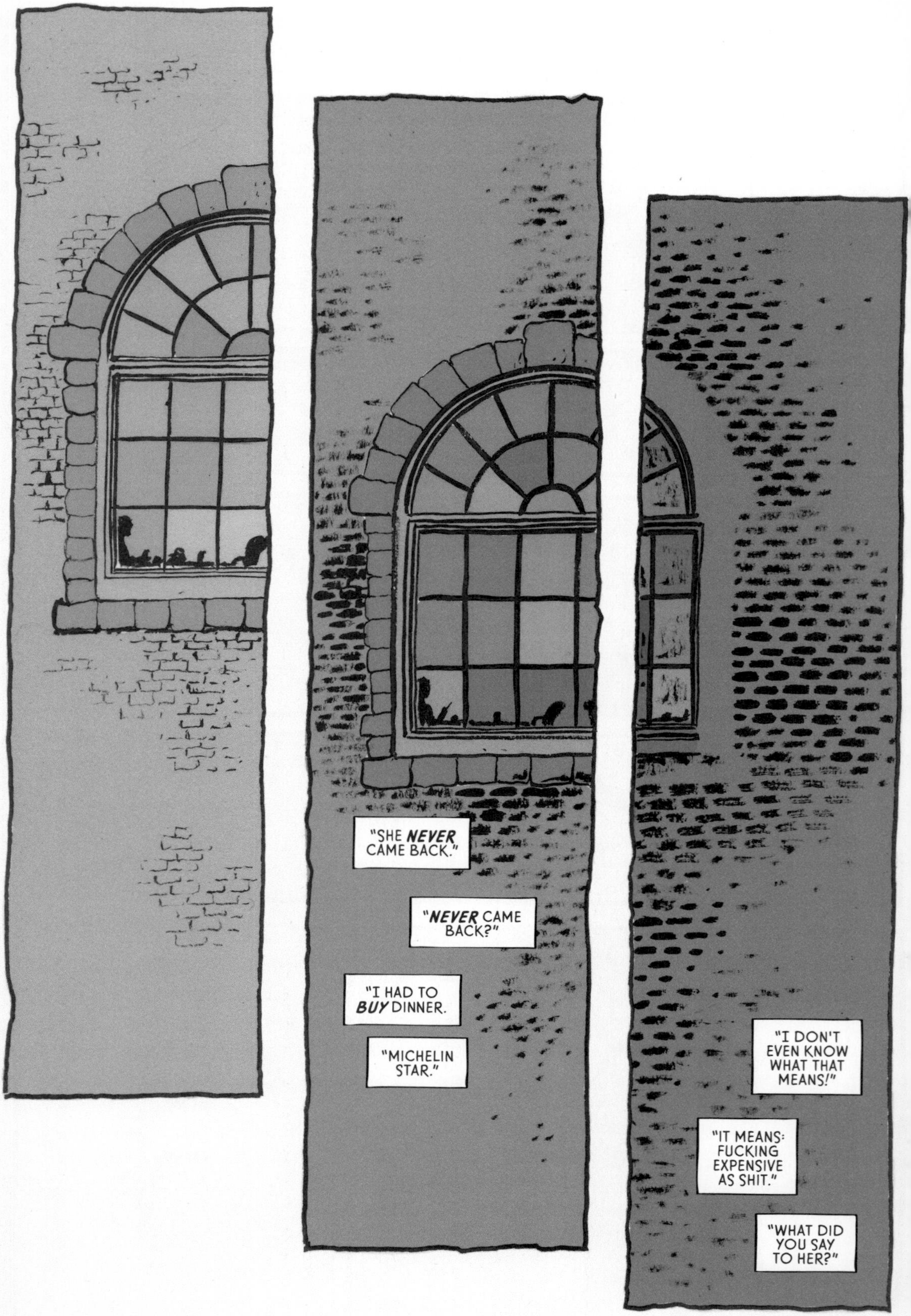
"SHE NEVER CAME BACK."
"NEVER CAME BACK?"
"I HAD TO BUY DINNER.
"MICHELIN STAR."
"I DON'T EVEN KNOW WHAT THAT MEANS!"
"IT MEANS: FUCKING EXPENSIVE AS SHIT."
"WHAT DID YOU SAY TO HER?"

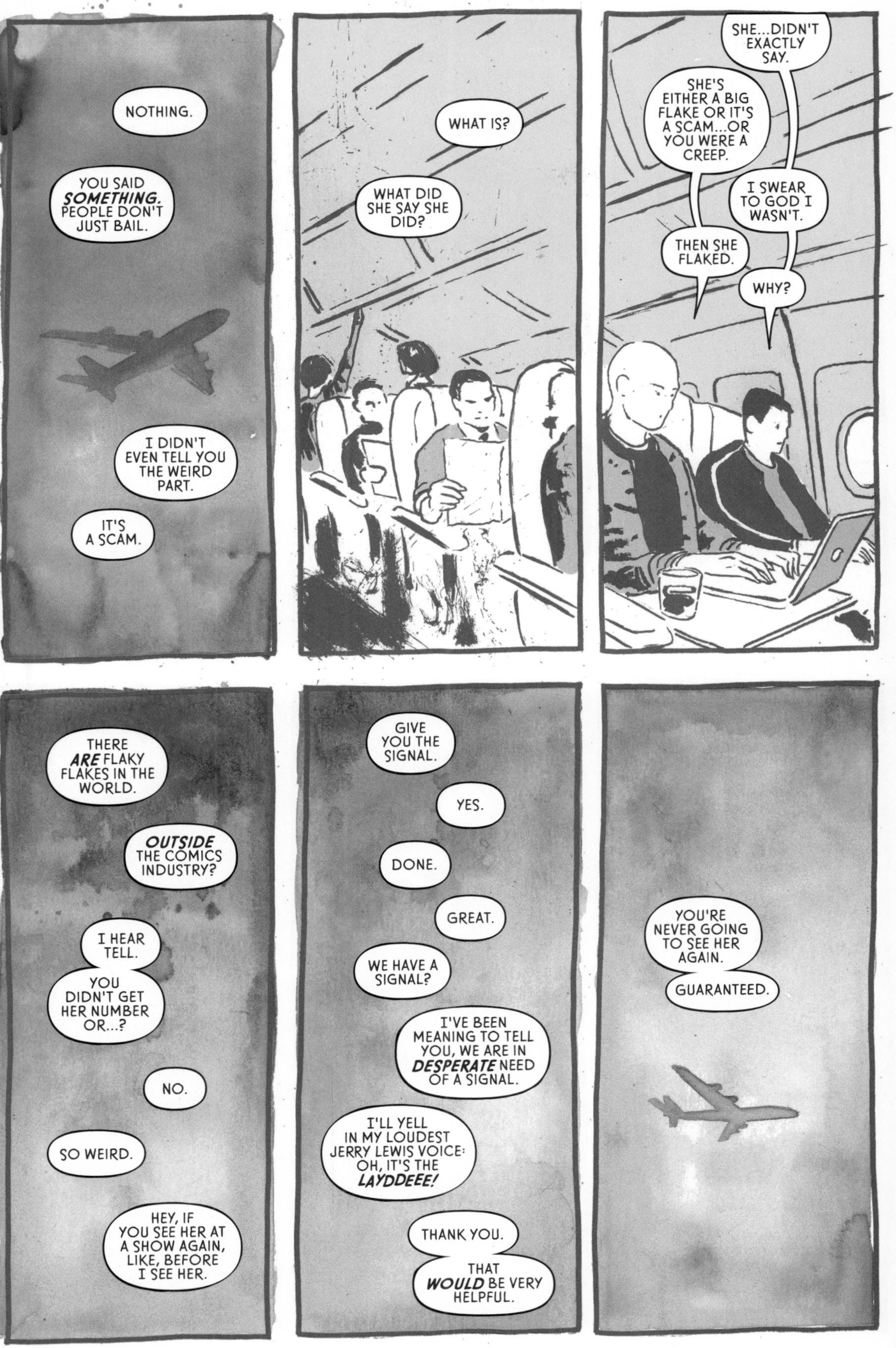
NOTHING.
YOU SAID SOMETHING. PEOPLE DON'T JUST BAIL.
I DIDN'T EVEN TELL YOU THE WEIRD PART.
IT'S A SCAM.
WHAT IS?
WHAT DID SHE SAY SHE DID?
SHE...DIDN'T EXACTLY SAY.
SHE'S EITHER A BIG FLAKE OR IT'S A SCAM...OR YOU WERE A CREEP.
I SWEAR TO GOD I WASN'T.
THEN SHE FLAKED.
WHY?
THERE ARE FLAKY FLAKES IN THE WORLD.
OUTSIDE THE COMICS INDUSTRY?
I HEAR TELL.
YOU DIDN'T GET HER NUMBER OR...?
NO.
SO WEIRD.
HEY, IF YOU SEE HER AT A SHOW AGAIN, LIKE, BEFORE I SEE HER.
GIVE YOU THE SIGNAL.
YES.
DONE.
GREAT.
WE HAVE A SIGNAL?
I'VE BEEN MEANING TO TELL YOU, WE ARE IN DESPERATE NEED OF A SIGNAL.
I'LL YELL IN MY LOUDEST JERRY LEWIS VOICE: OH, IT'S THE LAYDDEEE!
THANK YOU.
THAT WOULD BE VERY HELPFUL.
YOU'RE NEVER GOING TO SEE HER AGAIN.
GUARANTEED.

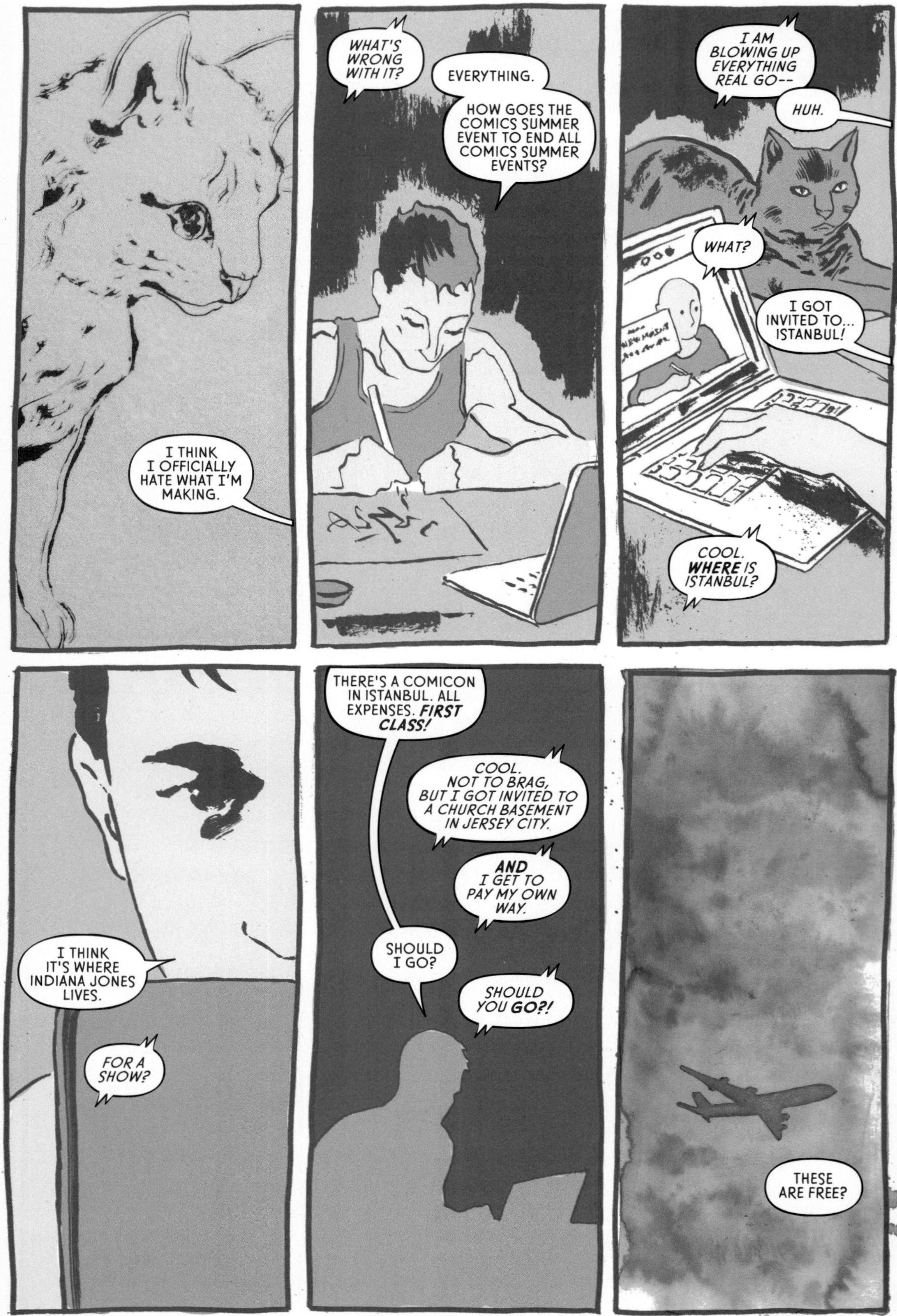
I THINK I OFFICIALLY HATE WHAT I'M MAKING.
WHAT'S WRONG WITH IT?
EVERYTHING.
HOW GOES THE COMICS SUMMER EVENT TO END ALL COMICS SUMMER EVENTS?
I AM BLOWING UP EVERYTHING REAL GO--
HUH.
WHAT?
I GOT INVITED TO... ISTANBUL!
COOL. WHERE IS ISTANBUL?
I THINK IT'S WHERE INDIANA JONES LIVES.
FOR A SHOW?
THERE'S A COMICON IN ISTANBUL. ALL EXPENSES. FIRST CLASS!
COOL. NOT TO BRAG, BUT I GOT INVITED TO A CHURCH BASEMENT IN JERSEY CITY.
AND I GET TO PAY MY OWN WAY.
SHOULD I GO?
SHOULD YOU GO?!
THESE ARE FREE?

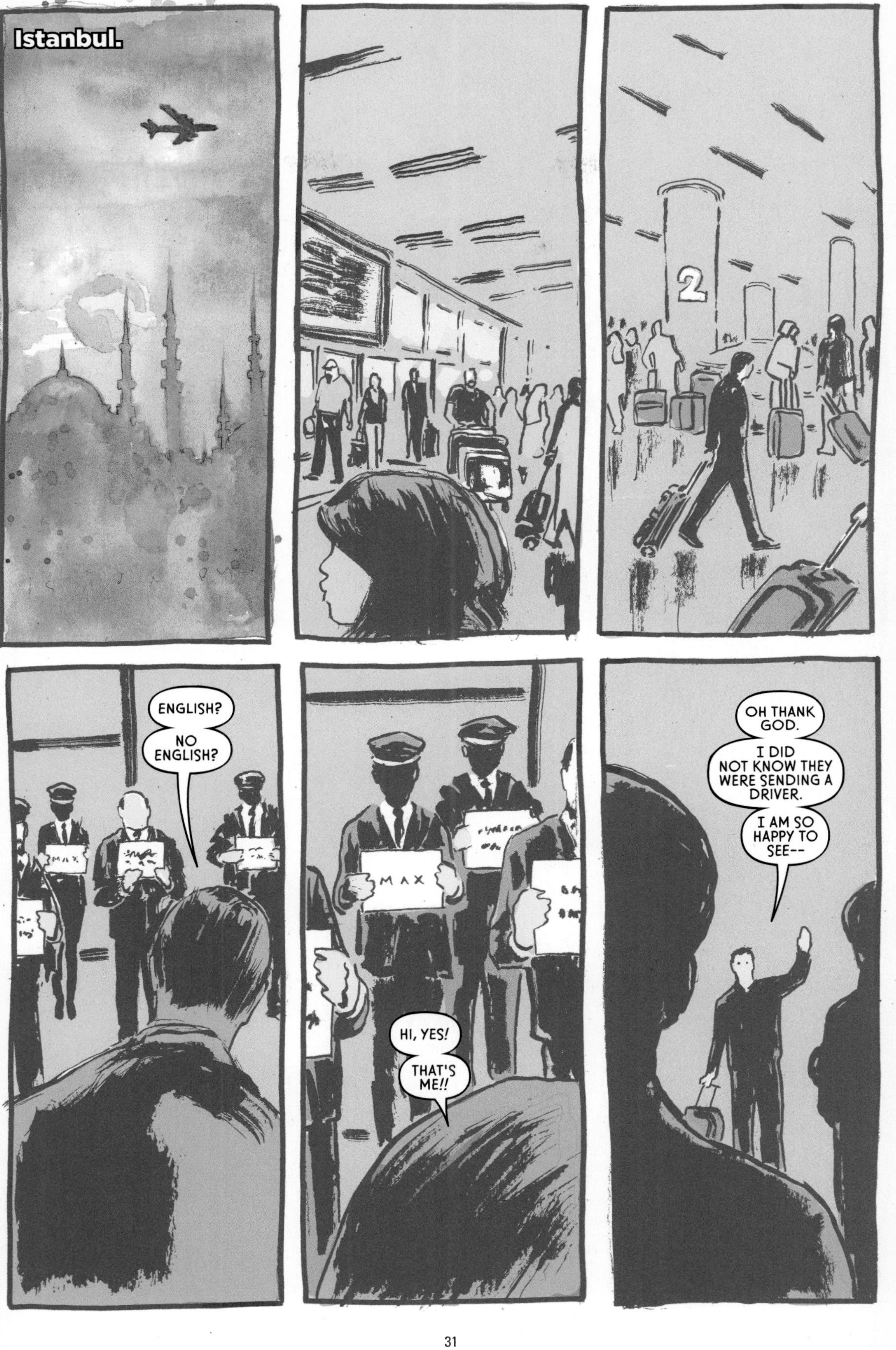
Istanbul.
2
ENGLISH?
NO ENGLISH?
MAX
HI, YES!
THAT'S ME!!
OH THANK GOD.
I DID NOT KNOW THEY WERE SENDING A DRIVER.
I AM SO HAPPY TO SEE--

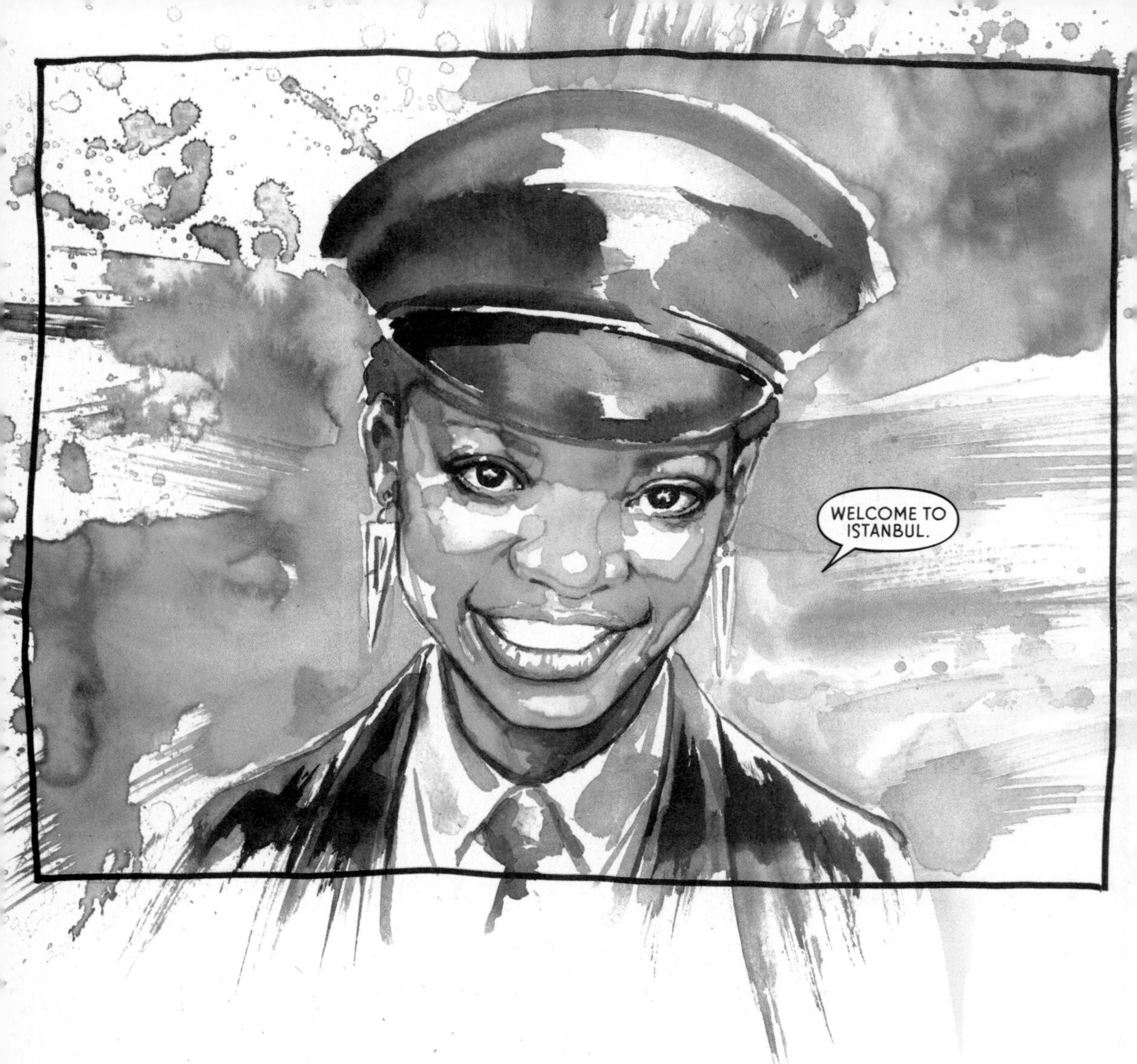
WELCOME TO ISTANBUL.

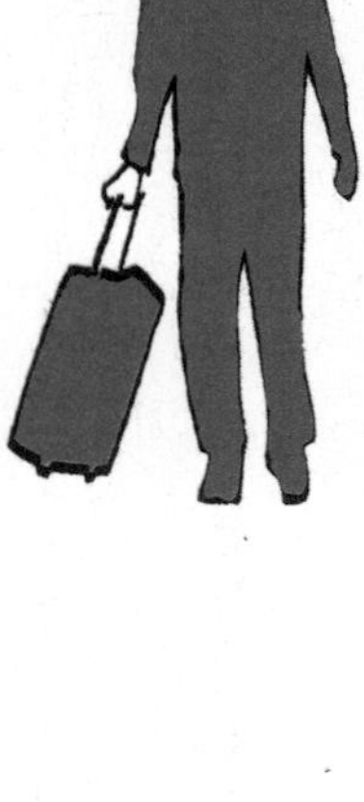

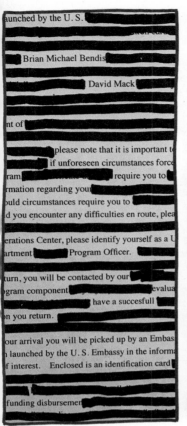

aunched by the U. S. [redacted]
[redacted] Brian Michael Bendis [redacted]
[redacted] David Mack [redacted]
nt of [redacted]
[redacted] please note that it is important t
[redacted] if unforeseen circumstances force
ram [redacted] require you to [redacted]
rmation regarding your [redacted]
ould circumstances require you to [redacted]
d you encounter any difficulties en route, plea
erations Center, please identify yourself as a U
artment [redacted] Program Officer. [redacted]
turn, you will be contacted by our [redacted]
gram component [redacted] evalua
[redacted] have a succesfull [redacted]
n you return. [redacted]
our arrival you will be picked up by an Embass
launched by the U. S. Embassy in the informa
f interest. Enclosed is an identification card [redacted]
funding disbursemen [redacted]
COVER
MACK

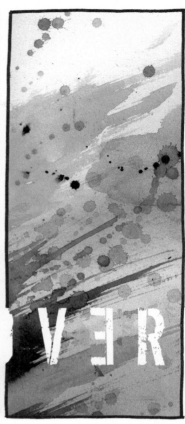

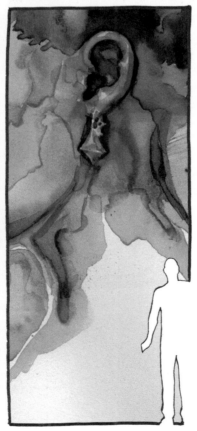

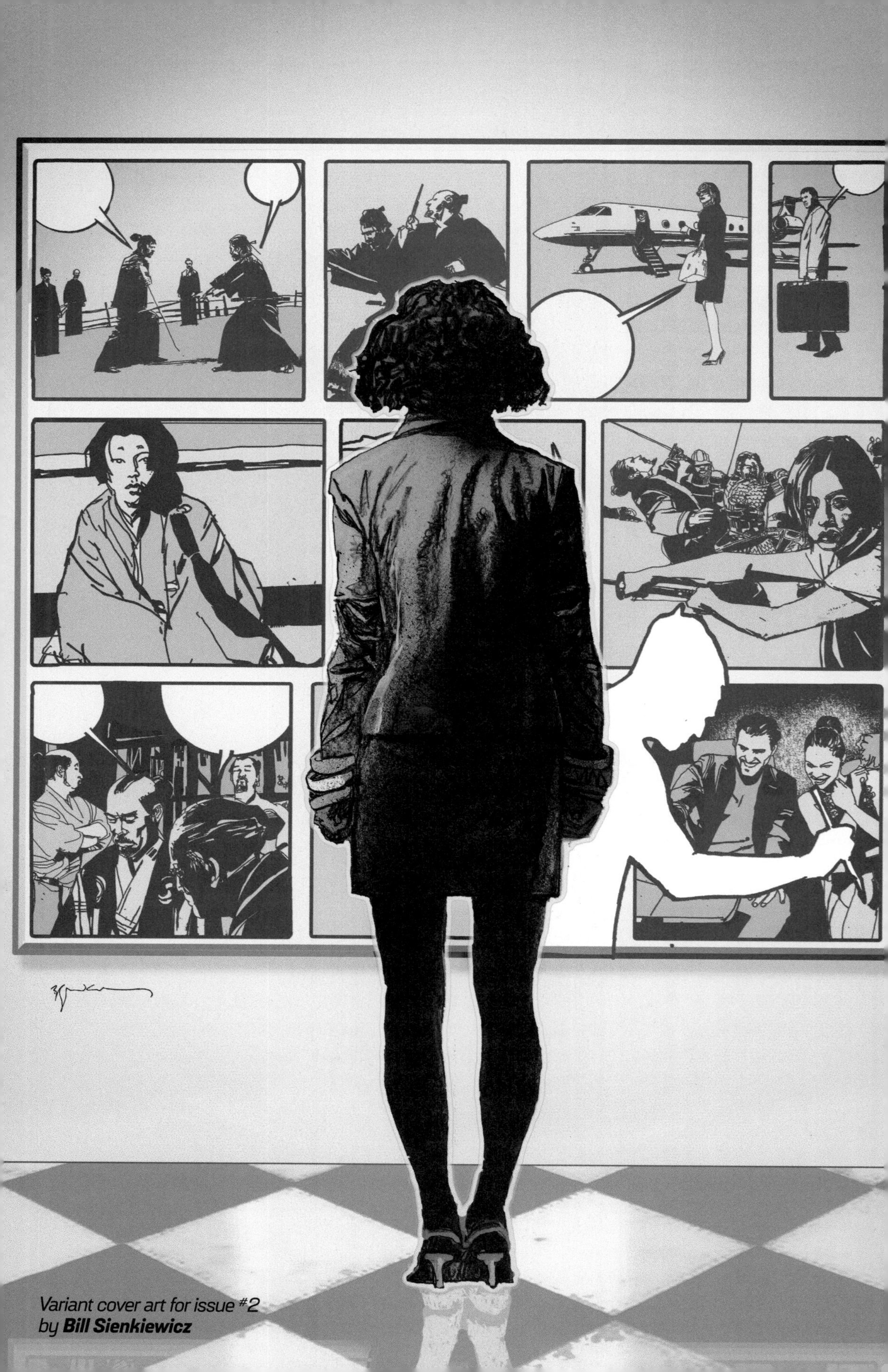

Variant cover art for issue #2
by ***Bill Sienkiewicz***

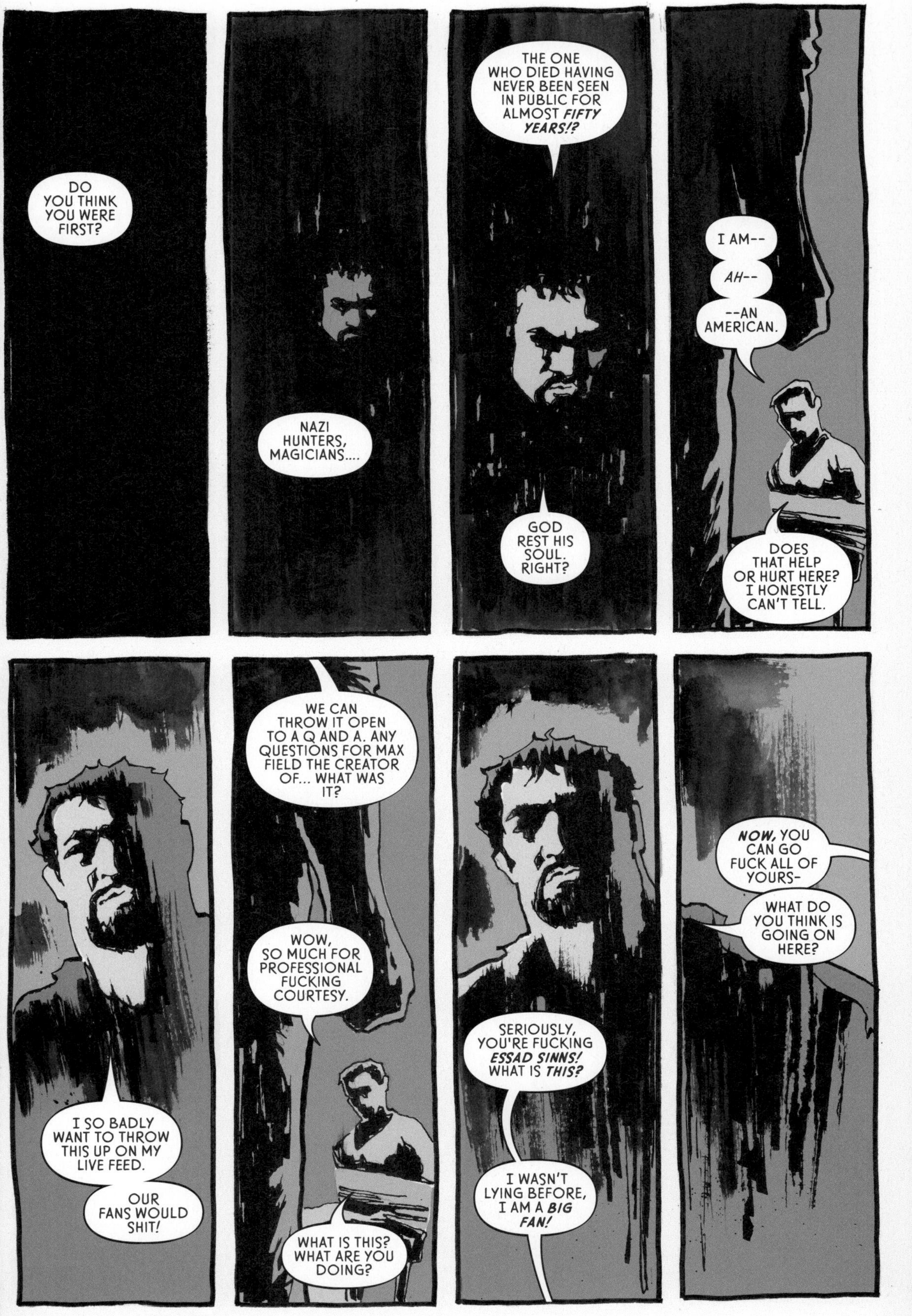
DO YOU THINK YOU WERE FIRST?
NAZI HUNTERS, MAGICIANS....
THE ONE WHO DIED HAVING NEVER BEEN SEEN IN PUBLIC FOR ALMOST *FIFTY YEARS!?*
GOD REST HIS SOUL. RIGHT?
I AM--
AH--
--AN AMERICAN.
DOES THAT HELP OR HURT HERE? I HONESTLY CAN'T TELL.
I SO BADLY WANT TO THROW THIS UP ON MY LIVE FEED.
OUR FANS WOULD SHIT!
WE CAN THROW IT OPEN TO A Q AND A. ANY QUESTIONS FOR MAX FIELD THE CREATOR OF... WHAT WAS IT?
WOW, SO MUCH FOR PROFESSIONAL FUCKING COURTESY.
WHAT IS THIS? WHAT ARE YOU DOING?
SERIOUSLY, YOU'RE FUCKING *ESSAD SINNS!* WHAT IS *THIS?*
I WASN'T LYING BEFORE, I AM A *BIG FAN!*
NOW, YOU CAN GO FUCK ALL OF YOURS-
WHAT DO YOU THINK IS GOING ON HERE?

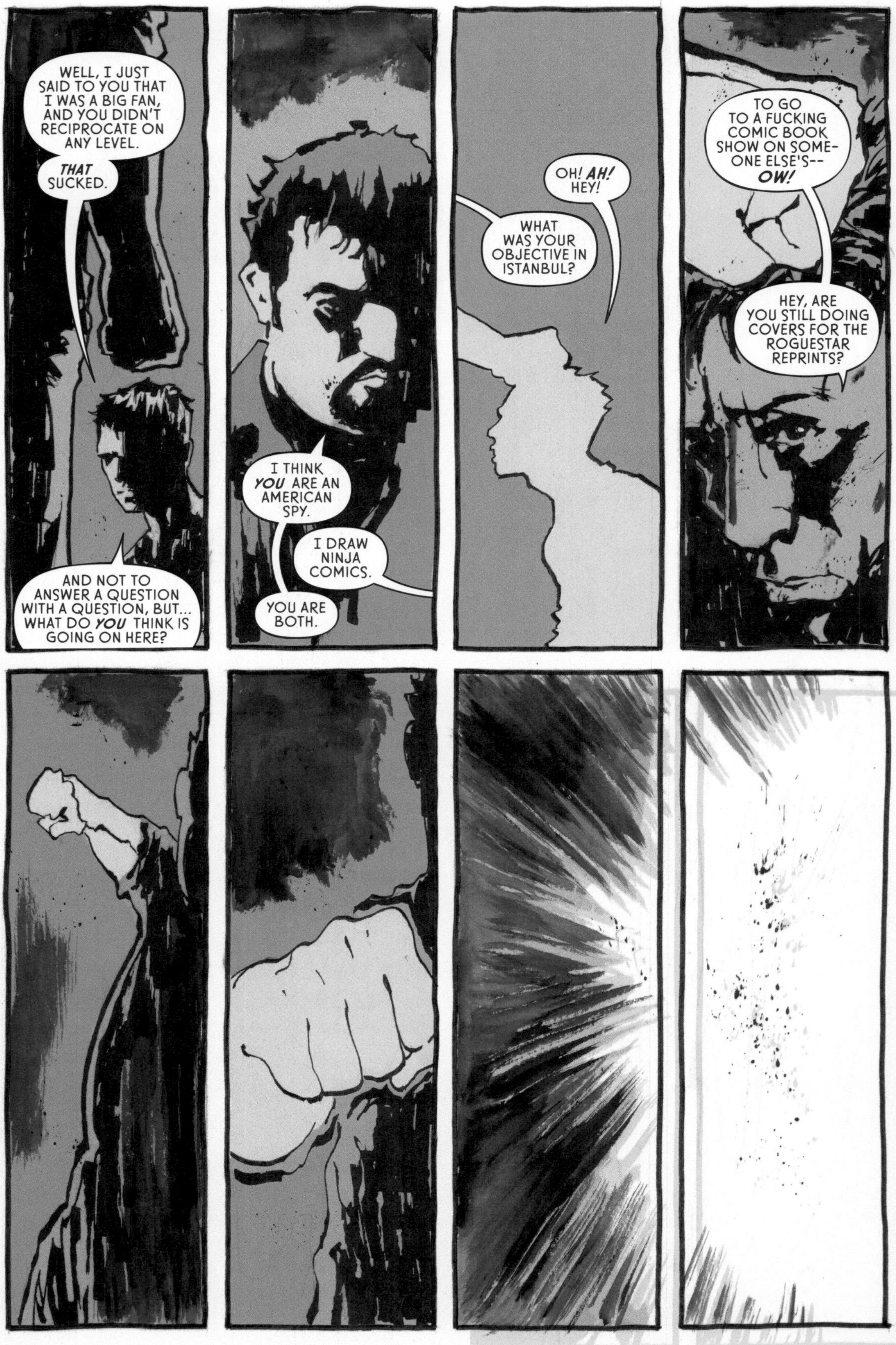
WELL, I JUST SAID TO YOU THAT I WAS A BIG FAN, AND YOU DIDN'T RECIPROCATE ON ANY LEVEL.
THAT SUCKED.
AND NOT TO ANSWER A QUESTION WITH A QUESTION, BUT... WHAT DO YOU THINK IS GOING ON HERE?
I THINK YOU ARE AN AMERICAN SPY.
I DRAW NINJA COMICS.
YOU ARE BOTH.
WHAT WAS YOUR OBJECTIVE IN ISTANBUL?
OH! AH! HEY!
TO GO TO A FUCKING COMIC BOOK SHOW ON SOME-ONE ELSE'S-- OW!
HEY, ARE YOU STILL DOING COVERS FOR THE ROGUESTAR REPRINTS?

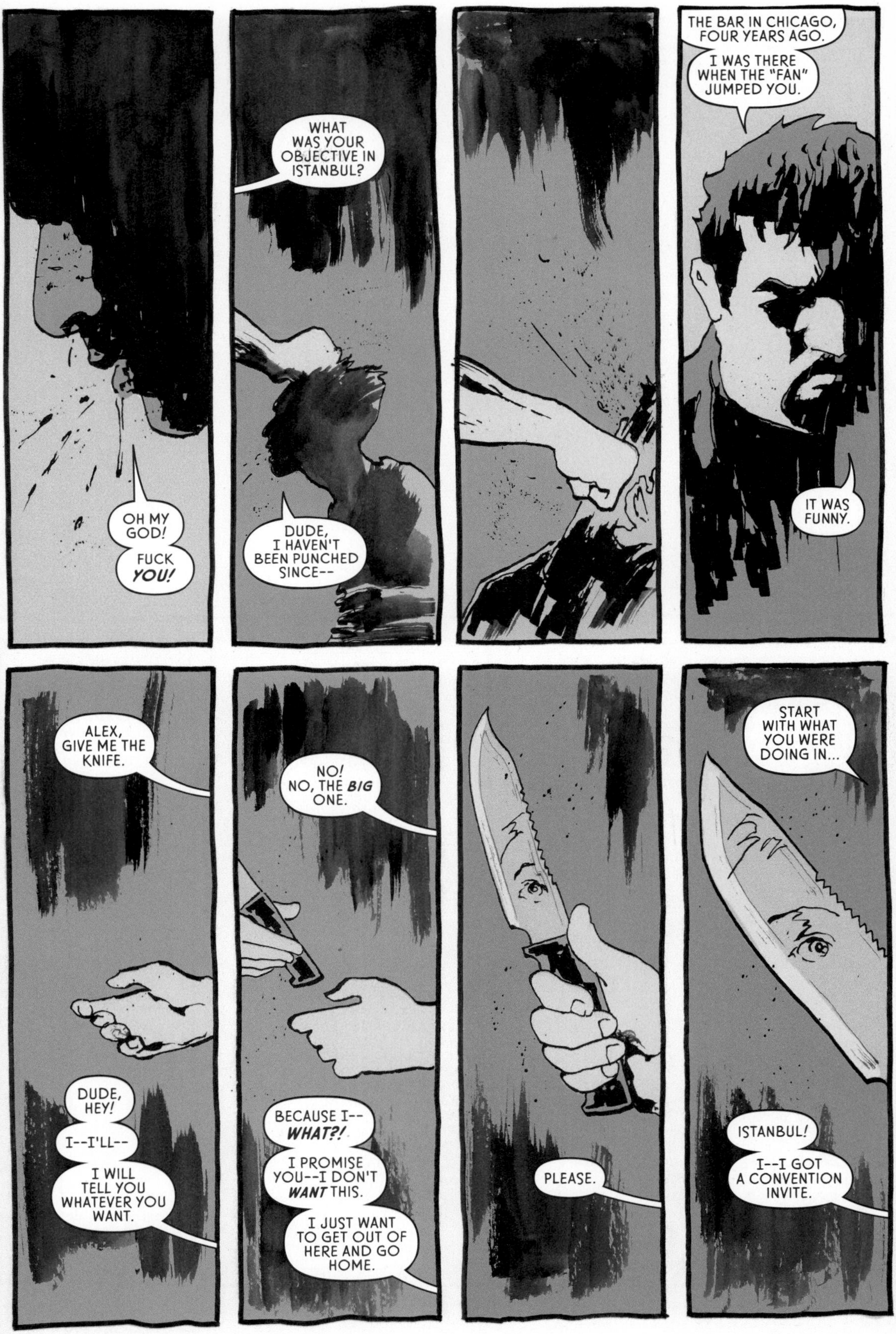
OH MY GOD!
FUCK YOU!
WHAT WAS YOUR OBJECTIVE IN ISTANBUL?
DUDE, I HAVEN'T BEEN PUNCHED SINCE--
THE BAR IN CHICAGO, FOUR YEARS AGO.
I WAS THERE WHEN THE "FAN" JUMPED YOU.
IT WAS FUNNY.
ALEX, GIVE ME THE KNIFE.
DUDE, HEY!
I--I'LL--
I WILL TELL YOU WHATEVER YOU WANT.
NO! NO, THE BIG ONE.
BECAUSE I-- WHAT?!
I PROMISE YOU--I DON'T WANT THIS.
I JUST WANT TO GET OUT OF HERE AND GO HOME.
PLEASE.
START WITH WHAT YOU WERE DOING IN...
ISTANBUL!
I--I GOT A CONVENTION INVITE.

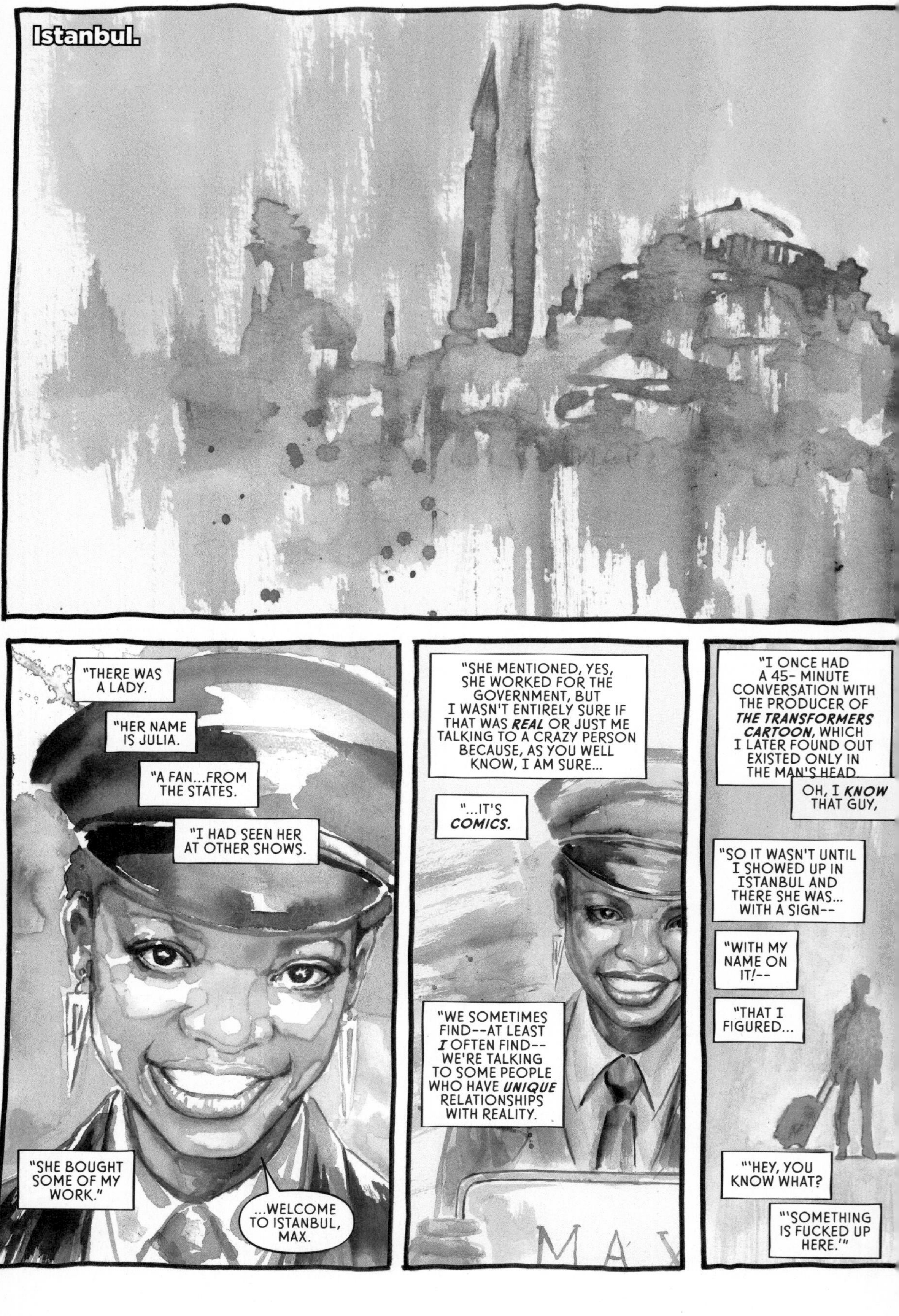
Istanbul.
"THERE WAS A LADY.
"HER NAME IS JULIA.
"A FAN...FROM THE STATES.
"I HAD SEEN HER AT OTHER SHOWS.
"SHE BOUGHT SOME OF MY WORK."
...WELCOME TO ISTANBUL, MAX.
"SHE MENTIONED, YES, SHE WORKED FOR THE GOVERNMENT, BUT I WASN'T ENTIRELY SURE IF THAT WAS *REAL* OR JUST ME TALKING TO A CRAZY PERSON BECAUSE, AS YOU WELL KNOW, I AM SURE...
"...IT'S *COMICS.*
"WE SOMETIMES FIND--AT LEAST *I* OFTEN FIND--WE'RE TALKING TO SOME PEOPLE WHO HAVE *UNIQUE* RELATIONSHIPS WITH REALITY.
"I ONCE HAD A 45- MINUTE CONVERSATION WITH THE PRODUCER OF *THE TRANSFORMERS CARTOON*, WHICH I LATER FOUND OUT EXISTED ONLY IN THE MAN'S HEAD.
OH, I *KNOW* THAT GUY,
"SO IT WASN'T UNTIL I SHOWED UP IN ISTANBUL AND THERE SHE WAS... WITH A SIGN--
"WITH MY NAME ON IT!--
"THAT I FIGURED...
"'HEY, YOU KNOW WHAT?
"'SOMETHING IS FUCKED UP HERE.'"

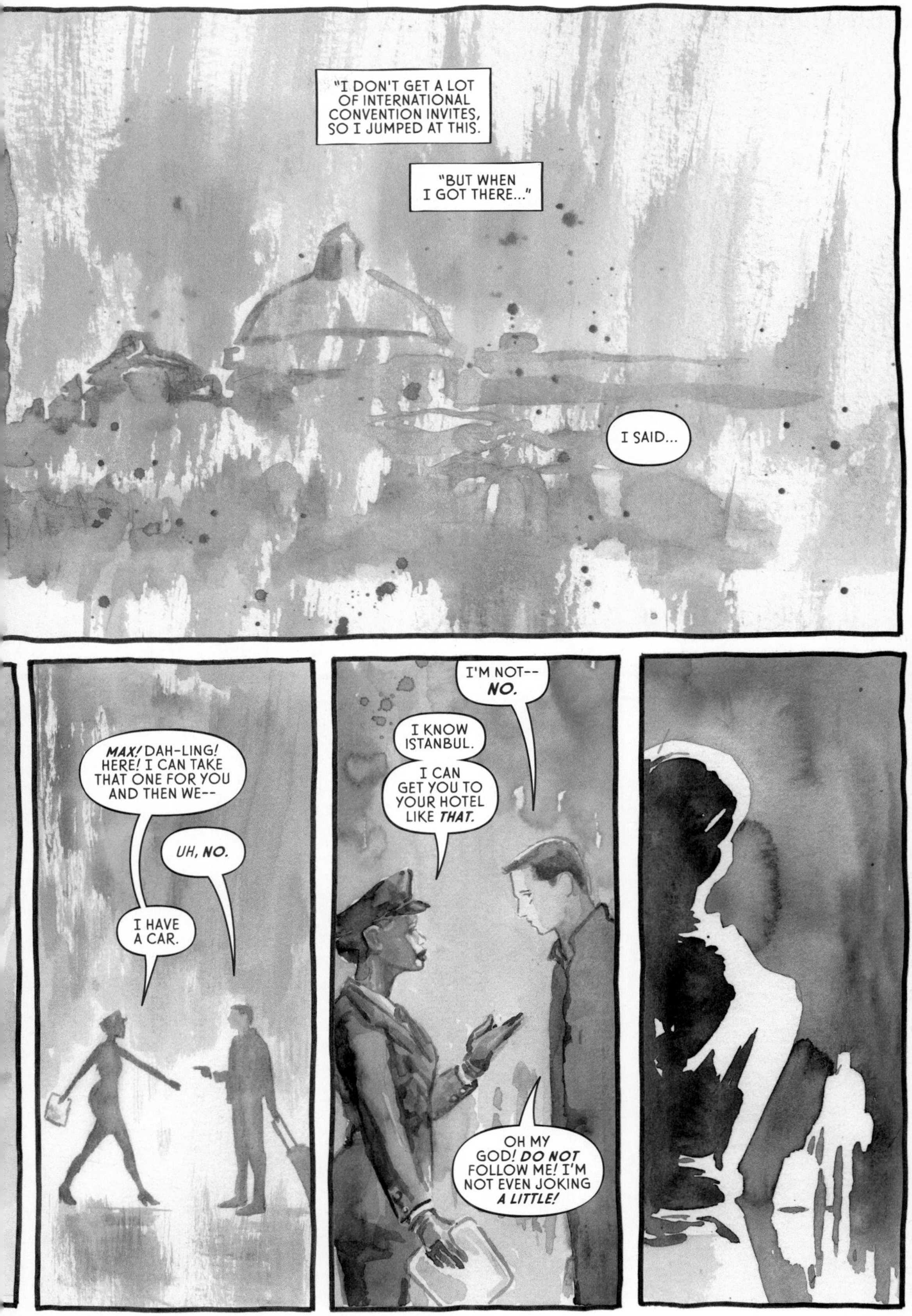
"I DON'T GET A LOT OF INTERNATIONAL CONVENTION INVITES, SO I JUMPED AT THIS.
"BUT WHEN I GOT THERE..."
I SAID...
MAX! DAH-LING! HERE! I CAN TAKE THAT ONE FOR YOU AND THEN WE--
UH, **NO.**
I HAVE A CAR.
I'M NOT-- ***NO.***
I KNOW ISTANBUL.
I CAN GET YOU TO YOUR HOTEL LIKE ***THAT.***
OH MY GOD! ***DO NOT*** FOLLOW ME! I'M NOT EVEN JOKING ***A LITTLE!***

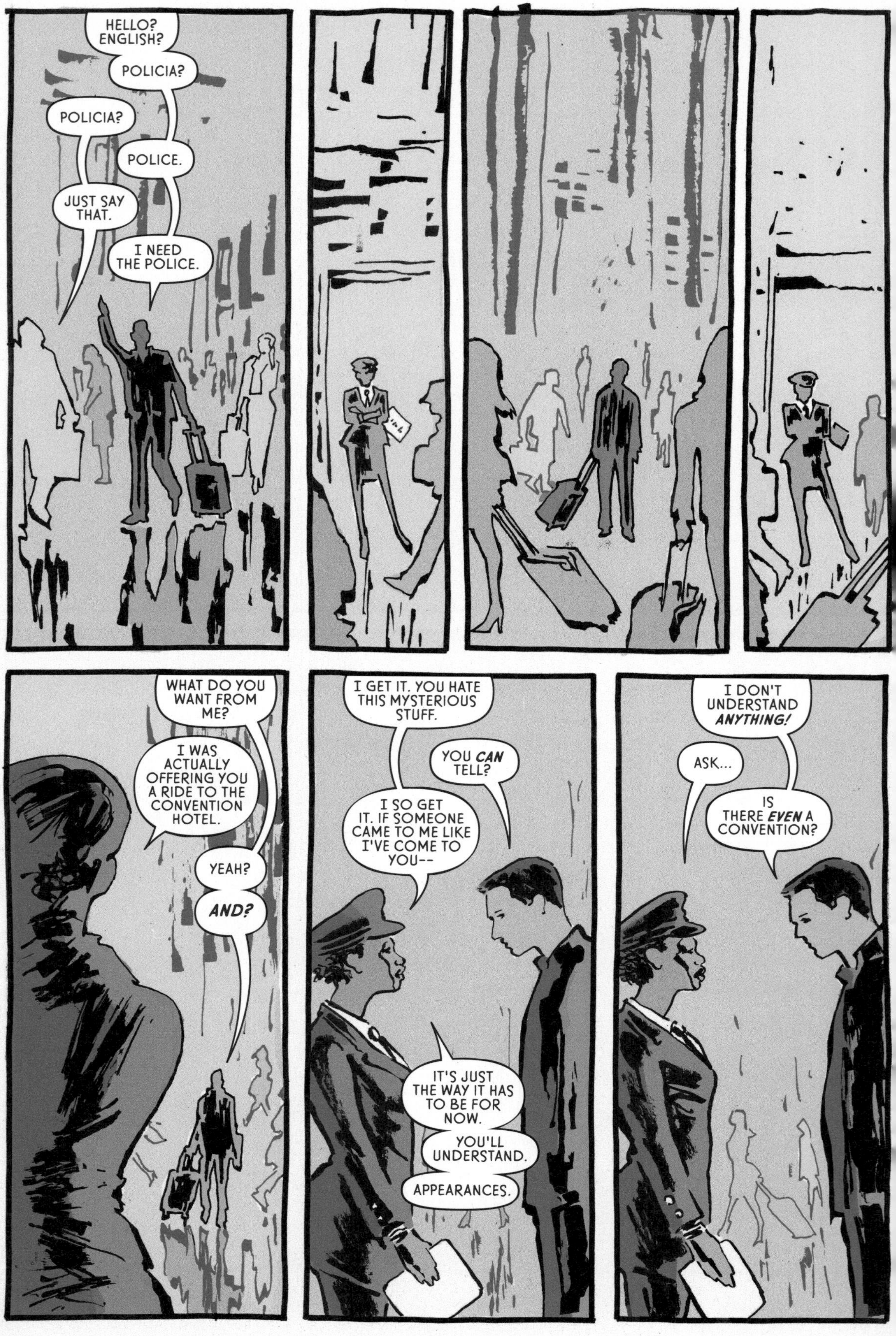
HELLO? ENGLISH?
POLICIA?
POLICIA?
POLICE.
JUST SAY THAT.
I NEED THE POLICE.
WHAT DO YOU WANT FROM ME?
I WAS ACTUALLY OFFERING YOU A RIDE TO THE CONVENTION HOTEL.
YEAH?
AND?
I GET IT. YOU HATE THIS MYSTERIOUS STUFF.
YOU CAN TELL?
I SO GET IT. IF SOMEONE CAME TO ME LIKE I'VE COME TO YOU--
IT'S JUST THE WAY IT HAS TO BE FOR NOW.
YOU'LL UNDERSTAND.
APPEARANCES.
I DON'T UNDERSTAND ANYTHING!
ASK...
IS THERE EVEN A CONVENTION?

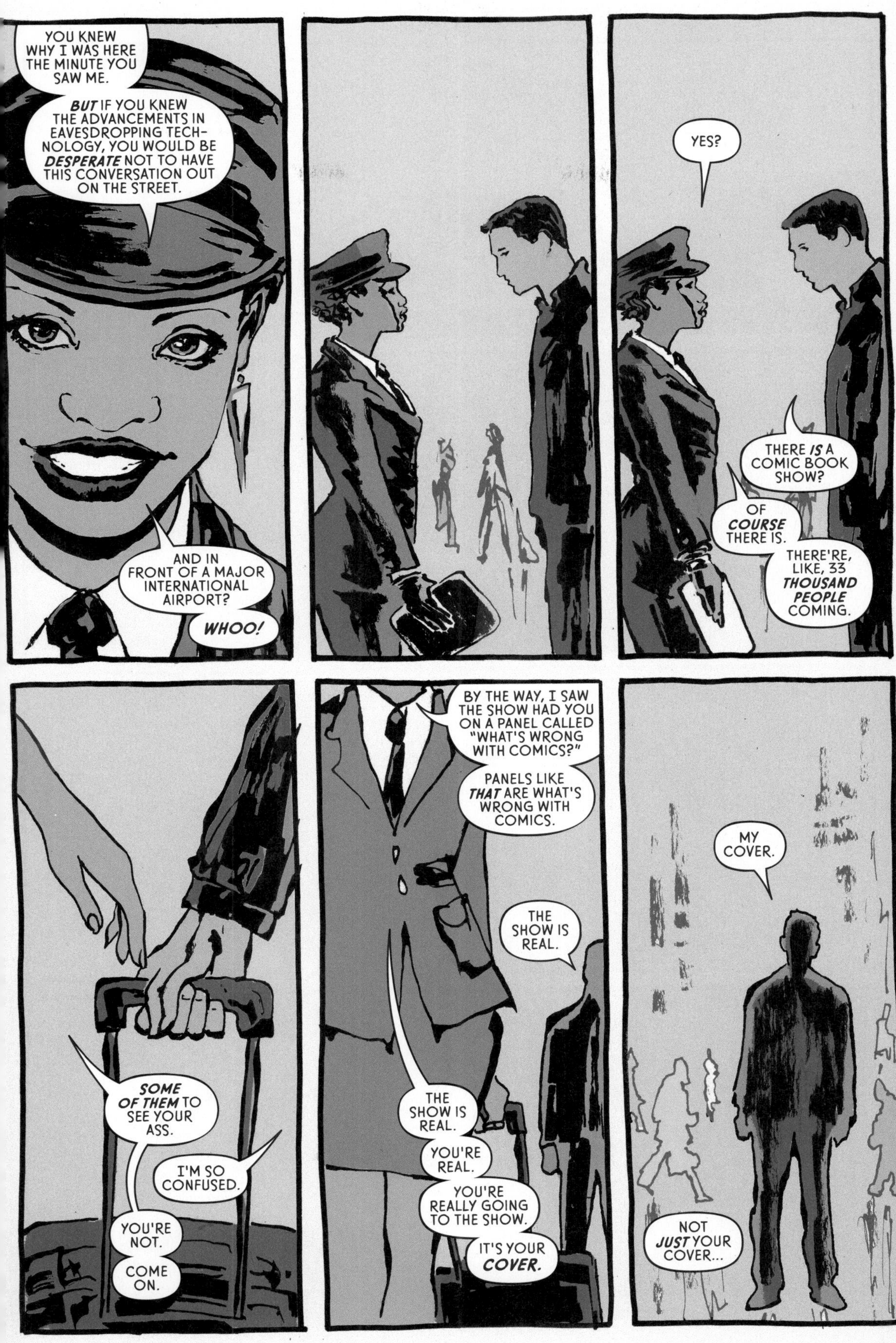
YOU KNEW WHY I WAS HERE THE MINUTE YOU SAW ME.
BUT IF YOU KNEW THE ADVANCEMENTS IN EAVESDROPPING TECH-NOLOGY, YOU WOULD BE *DESPERATE* NOT TO HAVE THIS CONVERSATION OUT ON THE STREET.
AND IN FRONT OF A MAJOR INTERNATIONAL AIRPORT?
WHOO!
YES?
THERE *IS* A COMIC BOOK SHOW?
OF *COURSE* THERE IS.
THERE'RE, LIKE, 33 *THOUSAND PEOPLE* COMING.
SOME OF THEM TO SEE YOUR ASS.
I'M SO CONFUSED.
YOU'RE NOT.
COME ON.
BY THE WAY, I SAW THE SHOW HAD YOU ON A PANEL CALLED "WHAT'S WRONG WITH COMICS?"
PANELS LIKE *THAT* ARE WHAT'S WRONG WITH COMICS.
THE SHOW IS REAL.
THE SHOW IS REAL.
YOU'RE REAL.
YOU'RE REALLY GOING TO THE SHOW.
IT'S YOUR *COVER.*
MY COVER.
NOT *JUST* YOUR COVER...

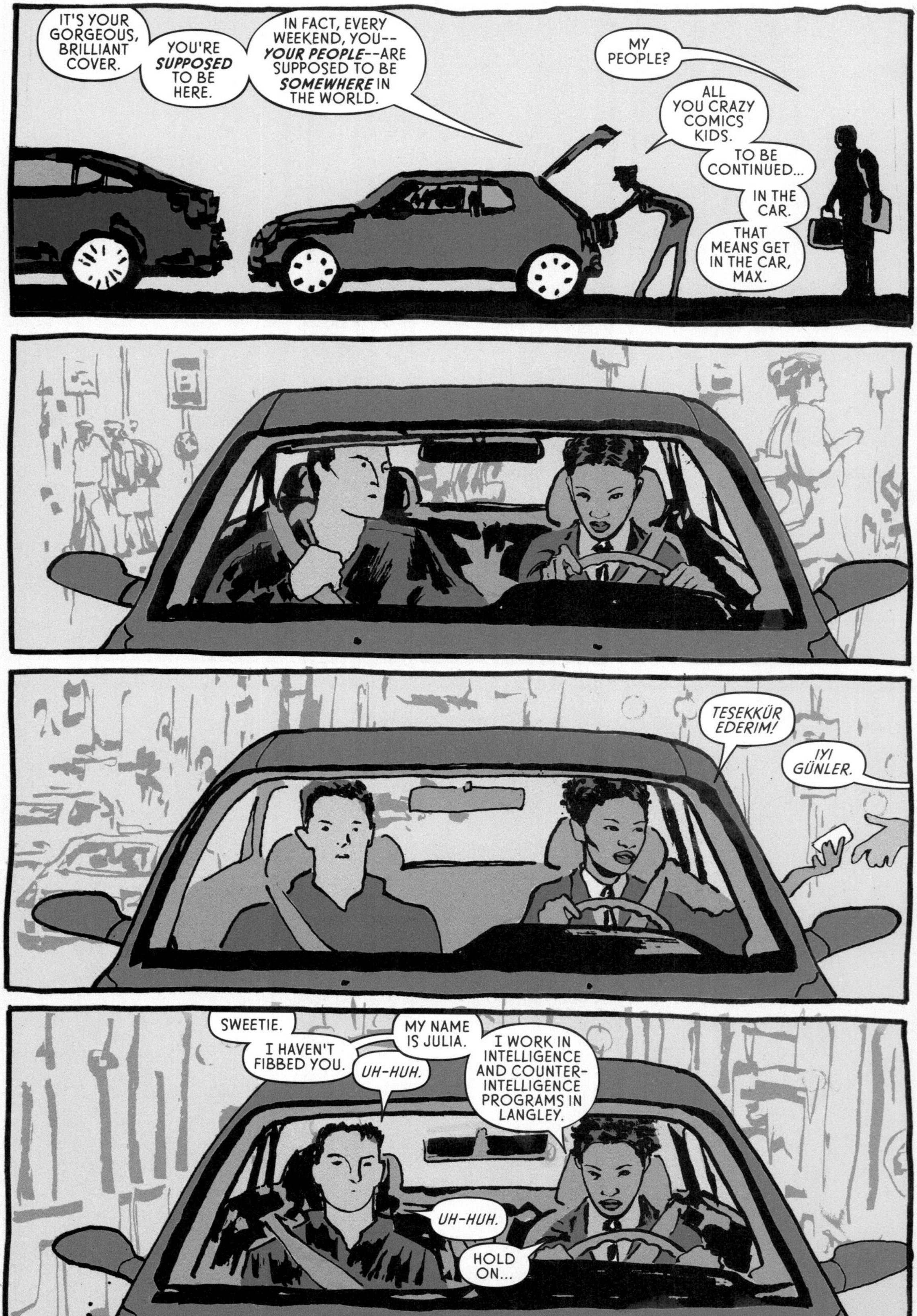
IT'S YOUR GORGEOUS, BRILLIANT COVER.
YOU'RE *SUPPOSED* TO BE HERE.
IN FACT, EVERY WEEKEND, YOU-- ***YOUR PEOPLE***--ARE SUPPOSED TO BE ***SOMEWHERE*** IN THE WORLD.
MY PEOPLE?
ALL YOU CRAZY COMICS KIDS.
TO BE CONTINUED...
IN THE CAR.
THAT MEANS GET IN THE CAR, MAX.
TEŞEKKÜR EDERIM!
IYI GÜNLER.
SWEETIE.
I HAVEN'T FIBBED YOU.
MY NAME IS JULIA.
UH-HUH.
I WORK IN INTELLIGENCE AND COUNTER-INTELLIGENCE PROGRAMS IN LANGLEY.
UH-HUH.
HOLD ON...

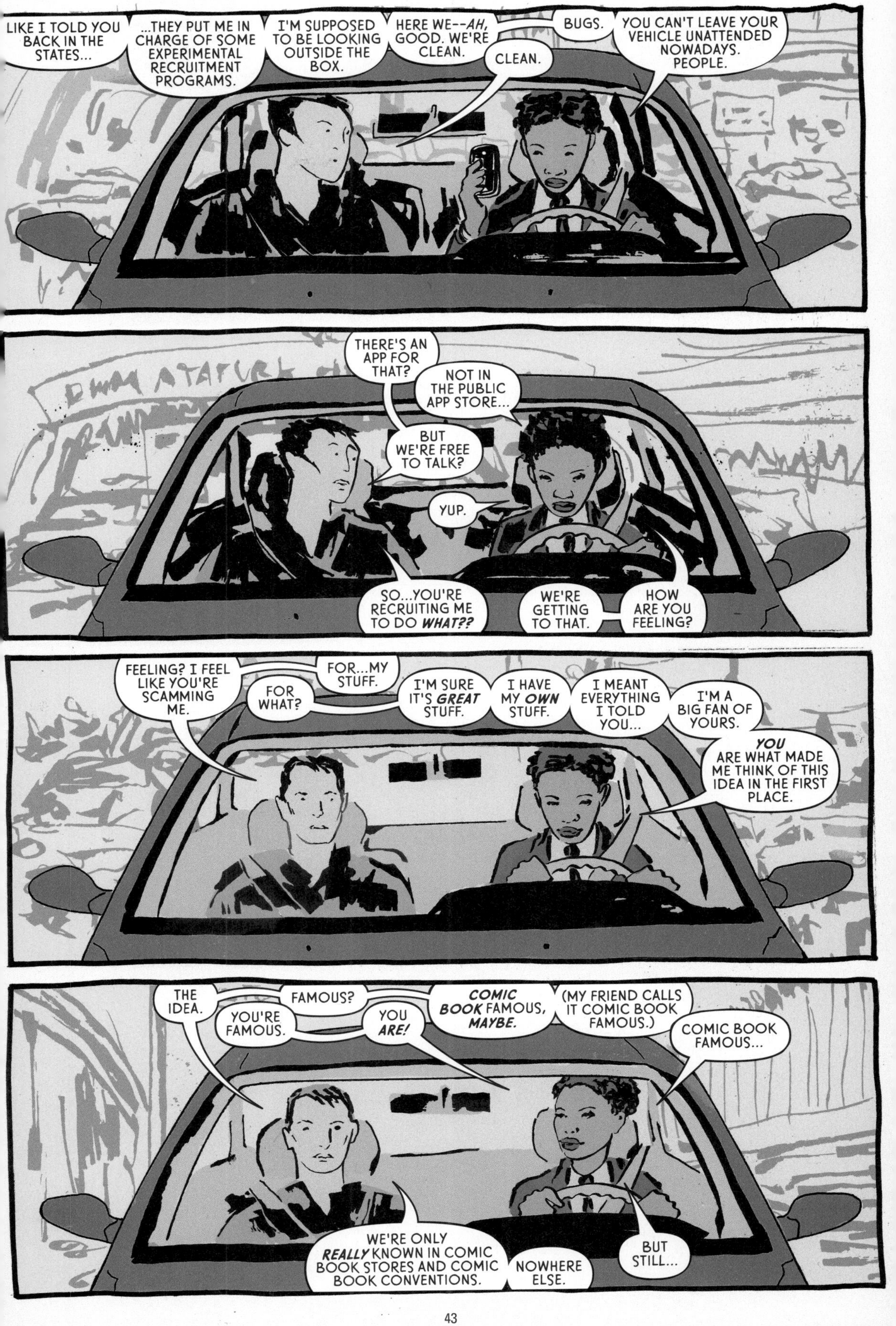
LIKE I TOLD YOU BACK IN THE STATES...
...THEY PUT ME IN CHARGE OF SOME EXPERIMENTAL RECRUITMENT PROGRAMS.
I'M SUPPOSED TO BE LOOKING OUTSIDE THE BOX.
HERE WE--*AH,* GOOD. WE'RE CLEAN.
BUGS.
CLEAN.
YOU CAN'T LEAVE YOUR VEHICLE UNATTENDED NOWADAYS. PEOPLE.
THERE'S AN APP FOR THAT?
NOT IN THE PUBLIC APP STORE...
BUT WE'RE FREE TO TALK?
YUP.
SO...YOU'RE RECRUITING ME TO DO *WHAT??*
WE'RE GETTING TO THAT.
HOW ARE YOU FEELING?
FEELING? I FEEL LIKE YOU'RE SCAMMING ME.
FOR WHAT?
FOR...MY STUFF.
I'M SURE IT'S *GREAT* STUFF.
I HAVE MY *OWN* STUFF.
I MEANT EVERYTHING I TOLD YOU...
I'M A BIG FAN OF YOURS.
YOU ARE WHAT MADE ME THINK OF THIS IDEA IN THE FIRST PLACE.
THE IDEA.
YOU'RE FAMOUS.
FAMOUS?
YOU *ARE!*
COMIC BOOK FAMOUS, *MAYBE.*
(MY FRIEND CALLS IT COMIC BOOK FAMOUS.)
COMIC BOOK FAMOUS...
WE'RE ONLY *REALLY* KNOWN IN COMIC BOOK STORES AND COMIC BOOK CONVENTIONS.
NOWHERE ELSE.
BUT STILL...

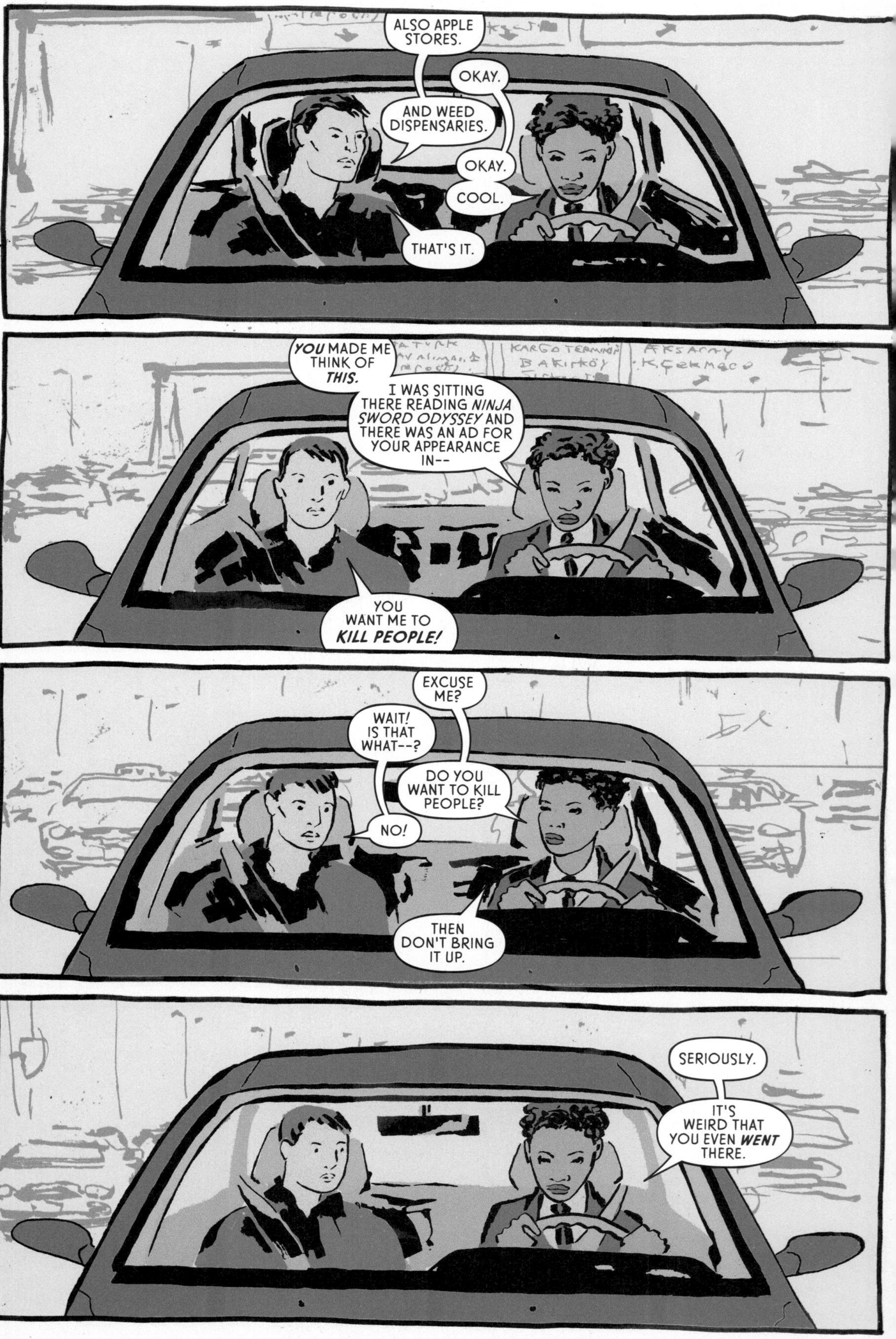
ALSO APPLE STORES.
OKAY.
AND WEED DISPENSARIES.
OKAY.
COOL.
THAT'S IT.
YOU MADE ME THINK OF *THIS.*
I WAS SITTING THERE READING *NINJA SWORD ODYSSEY* AND THERE WAS AN AD FOR YOUR APPEARANCE IN--
YOU WANT ME TO *KILL PEOPLE!*
EXCUSE ME?
WAIT! IS THAT WHAT--?
DO YOU WANT TO KILL PEOPLE?
NO!
THEN DON'T BRING IT UP.
SERIOUSLY.
IT'S WEIRD THAT YOU EVEN *WENT* THERE.

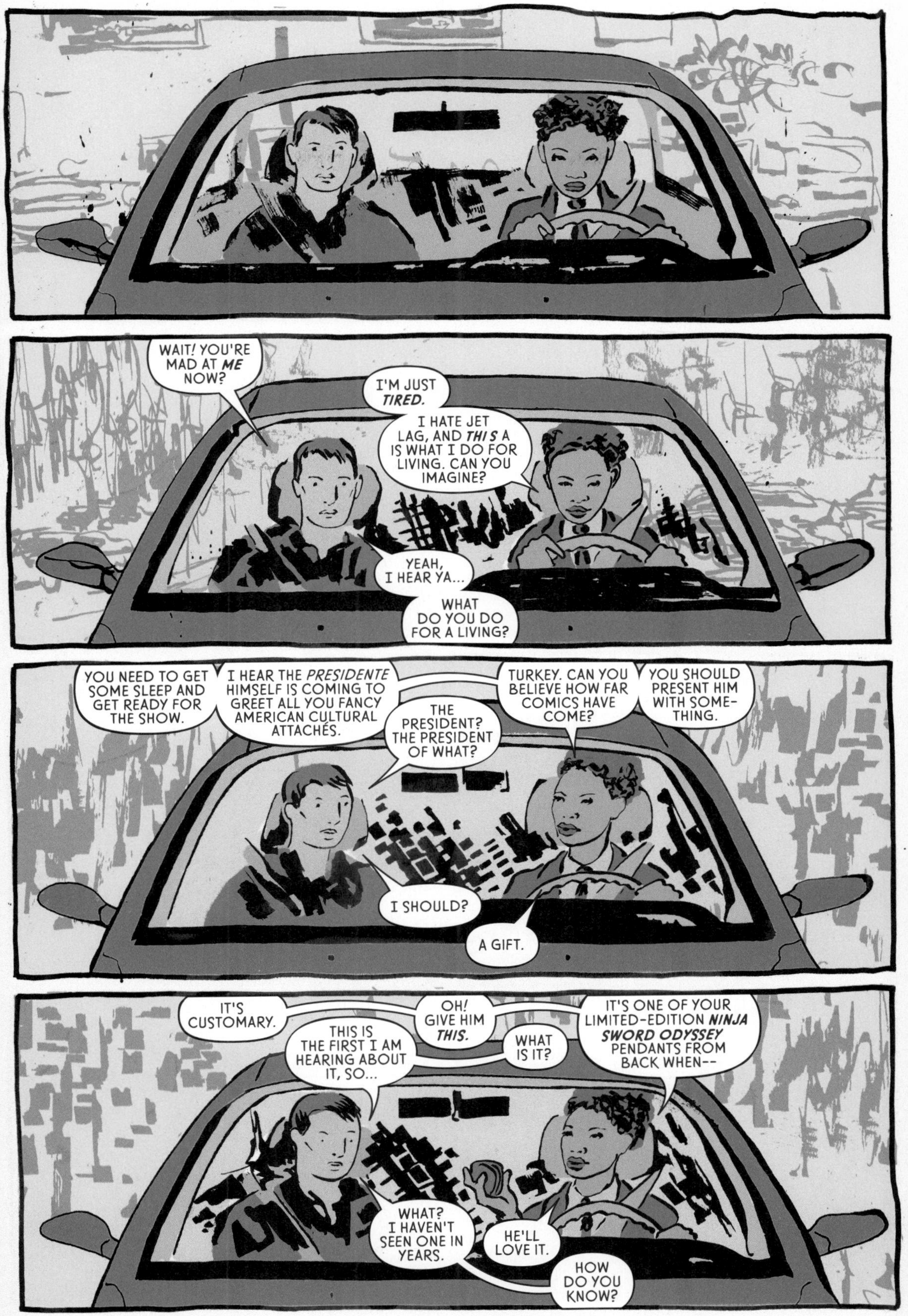
WAIT! YOU'RE MAD AT *ME* NOW?
I'M JUST *TIRED.*
I HATE JET LAG, AND *THIS* IS WHAT I DO FOR A LIVING. CAN YOU IMAGINE?
YEAH, I HEAR YA...
WHAT DO YOU DO FOR A LIVING?
YOU NEED TO GET SOME SLEEP AND GET READY FOR THE SHOW.
I HEAR THE *PRESIDENTE* HIMSELF IS COMING TO GREET ALL YOU FANCY AMERICAN CULTURAL ATTACHÉS.
THE PRESIDENT? THE PRESIDENT OF WHAT?
TURKEY. CAN YOU BELIEVE HOW FAR COMICS HAVE COME?
YOU SHOULD PRESENT HIM WITH SOME-THING.
I SHOULD?
A GIFT.
IT'S CUSTOMARY.
THIS IS THE FIRST I AM HEARING ABOUT IT, SO...
OH! GIVE HIM *THIS.*
WHAT IS IT?
IT'S ONE OF YOUR LIMITED-EDITION ***NINJA SWORD ODYSSEY*** PENDANTS FROM BACK WHEN--
WHAT? I HAVEN'T SEEN ONE IN YEARS.
HE'LL LOVE IT.
HOW DO YOU KNOW?

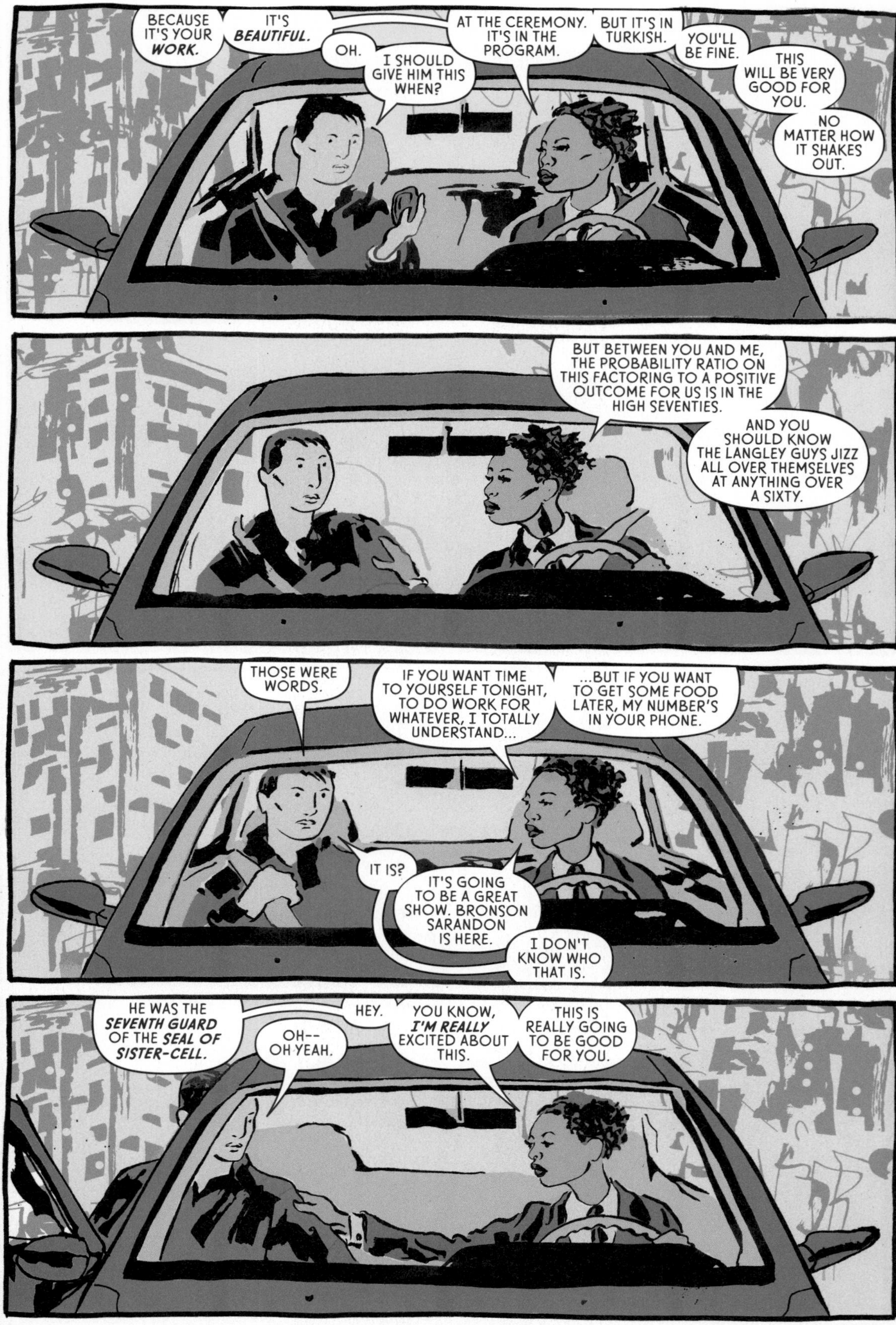

BECAUSE IT'S YOUR **WORK.**
IT'S **BEAUTIFUL.**
OH.
I SHOULD GIVE HIM THIS WHEN?
AT THE CEREMONY. IT'S IN THE PROGRAM.
BUT IT'S IN TURKISH.
YOU'LL BE FINE.
THIS WILL BE VERY GOOD FOR YOU.
NO MATTER HOW IT SHAKES OUT.
BUT BETWEEN YOU AND ME, THE PROBABILITY RATIO ON THIS FACTORING TO A POSITIVE OUTCOME FOR US IS IN THE HIGH SEVENTIES.
AND YOU SHOULD KNOW THE LANGLEY GUYS JIZZ ALL OVER THEMSELVES AT ANYTHING OVER A SIXTY.
THOSE WERE WORDS.
IF YOU WANT TIME TO YOURSELF TONIGHT, TO DO WORK FOR WHATEVER, I TOTALLY UNDERSTAND...
...BUT IF YOU WANT TO GET SOME FOOD LATER, MY NUMBER'S IN YOUR PHONE.
IT IS?
IT'S GOING TO BE A GREAT SHOW. BRONSON SARANDON IS HERE.
I DON'T KNOW WHO THAT IS.
HE WAS THE **SEVENTH GUARD** OF THE **SEAL OF SISTER-CELL.**
OH-- OH YEAH.
HEY.
YOU KNOW, ***I'M REALLY*** EXCITED ABOUT THIS.
THIS IS REALLY GOING TO BE GOOD FOR YOU.

When Father came back from the wars he was different. Hollow. Missing something.

He gave me a tsuba without a sword. He said it belonged to a teacher. A sword maker who taught him how to survive.

Father said he was having a new sword built for me. The only one I would ever need. The sword would fit inside his old teacher's tsuba.

His teacher and his teacher's sword were gone. All that remained is his teacher's tsuba, the empty place where a sword used to be.

I don't know if any of this is true. But it is what he said.

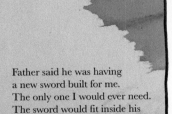

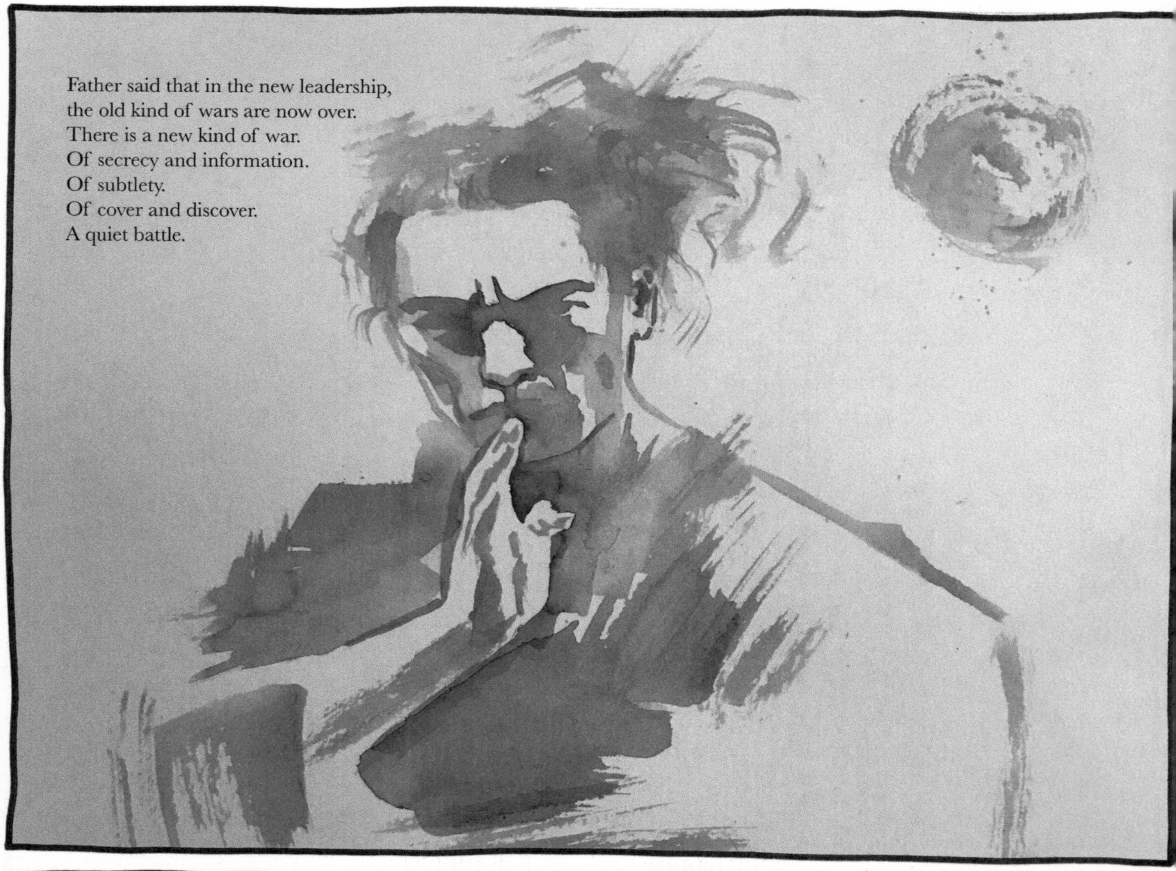
Father said that in the new leadership,
the old kind of wars are now over.
There is a new kind of war.
Of secrecy and information.
Of subtlety.
Of cover and discover.
A quiet battle.

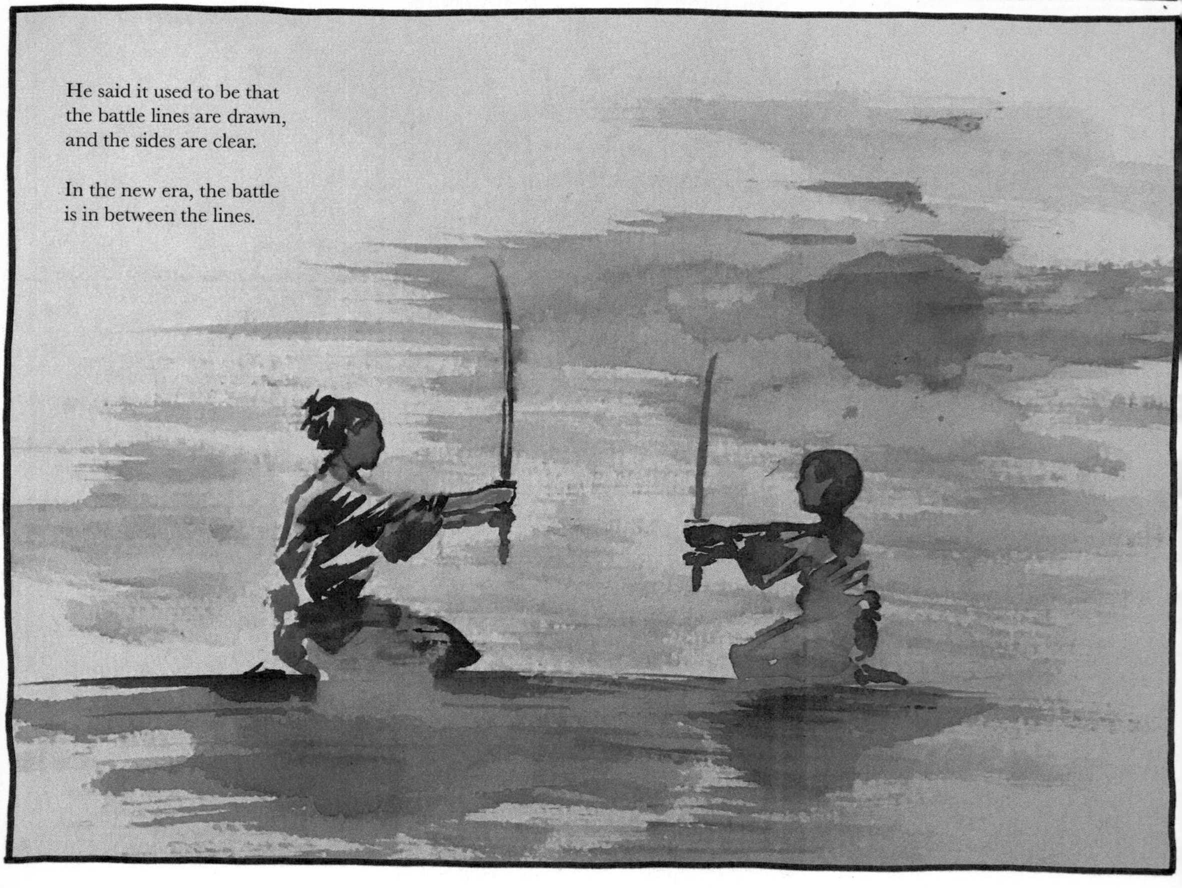
He said it used to be that
the battle lines are drawn,
and the sides are clear.

In the new era, the battle
is in between the lines.

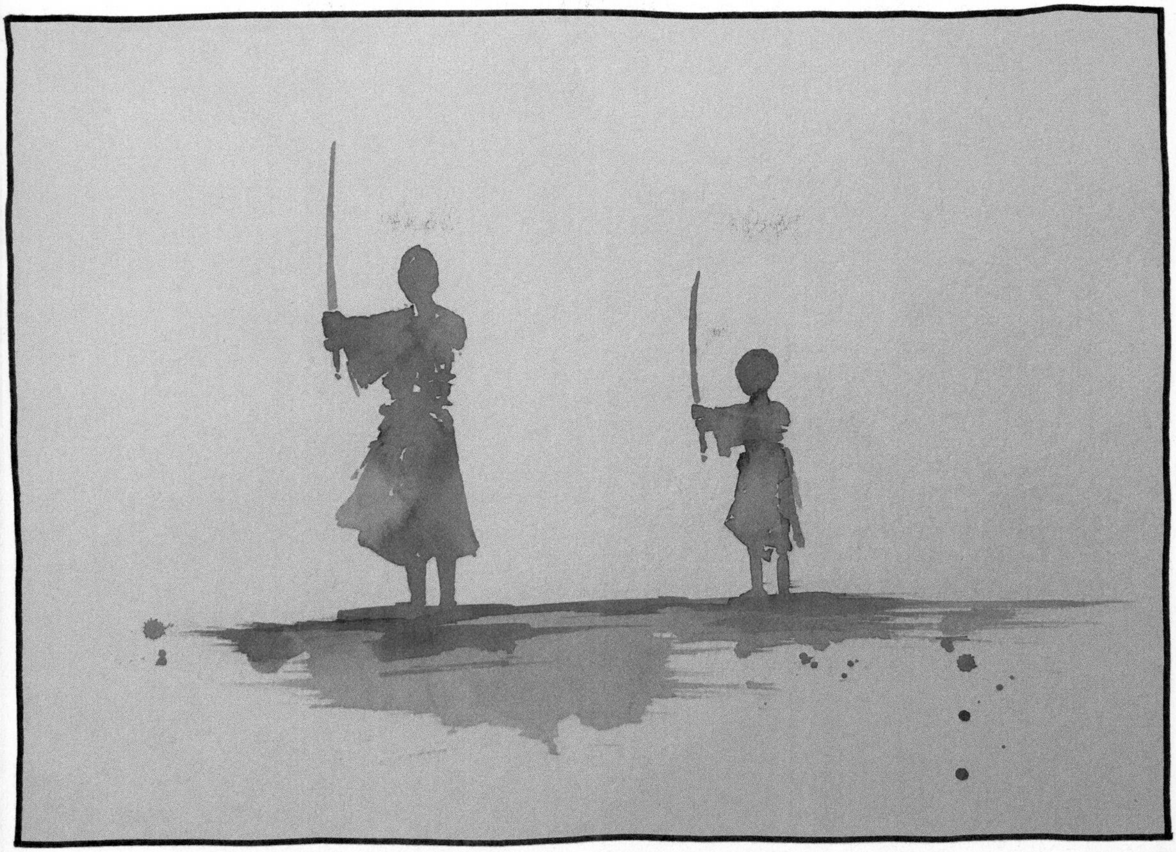

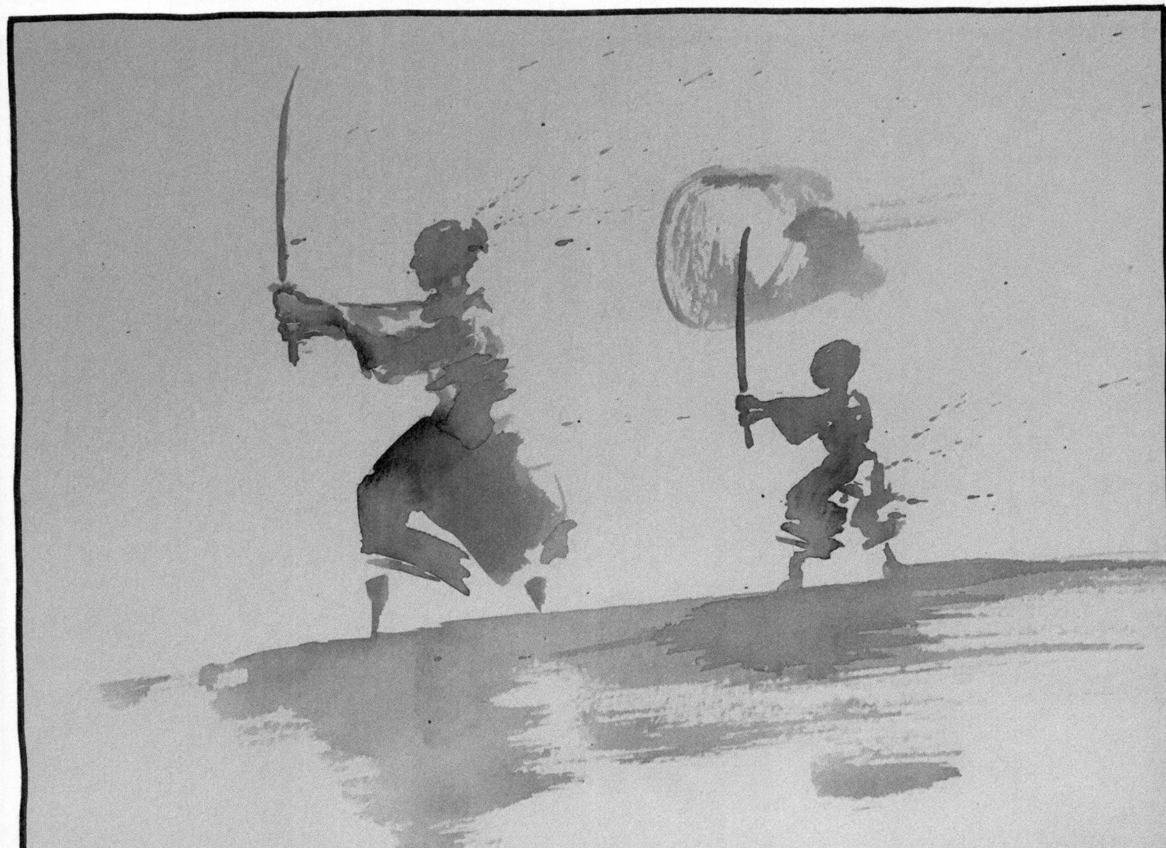

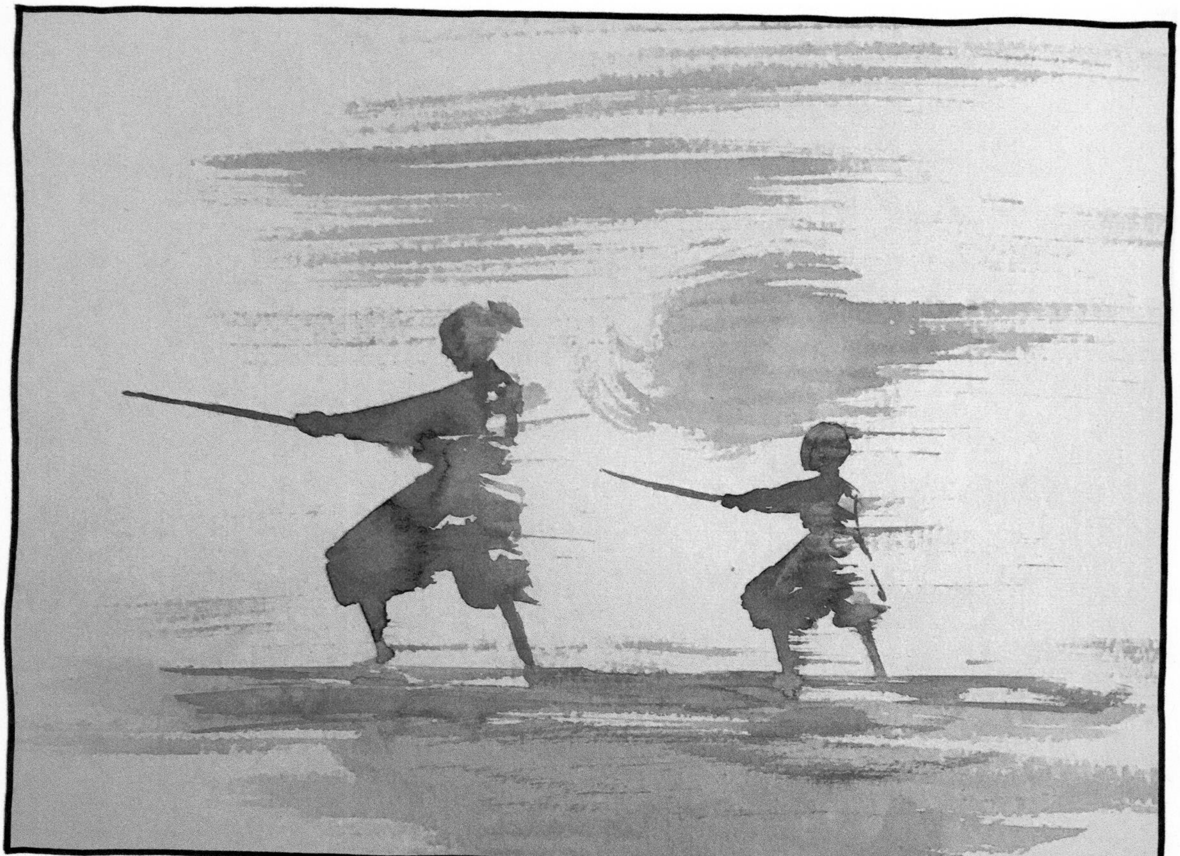

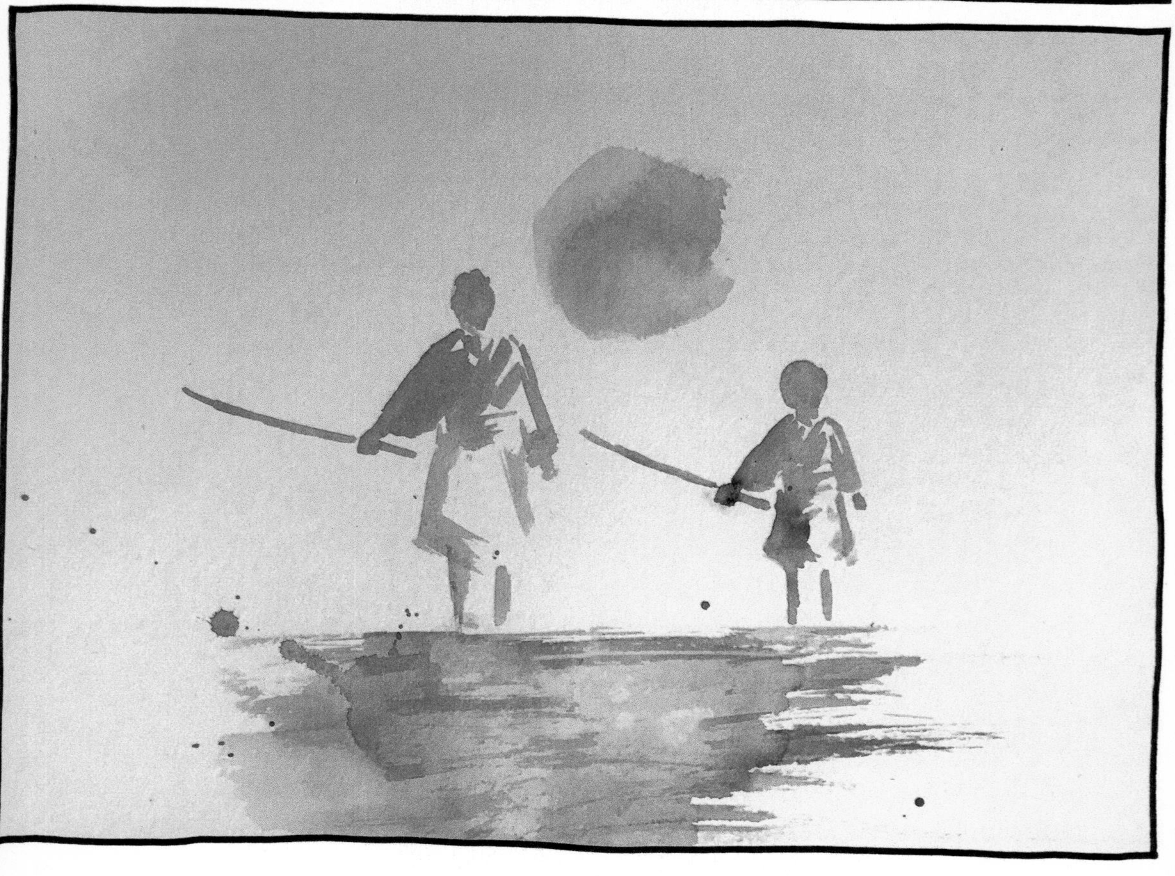

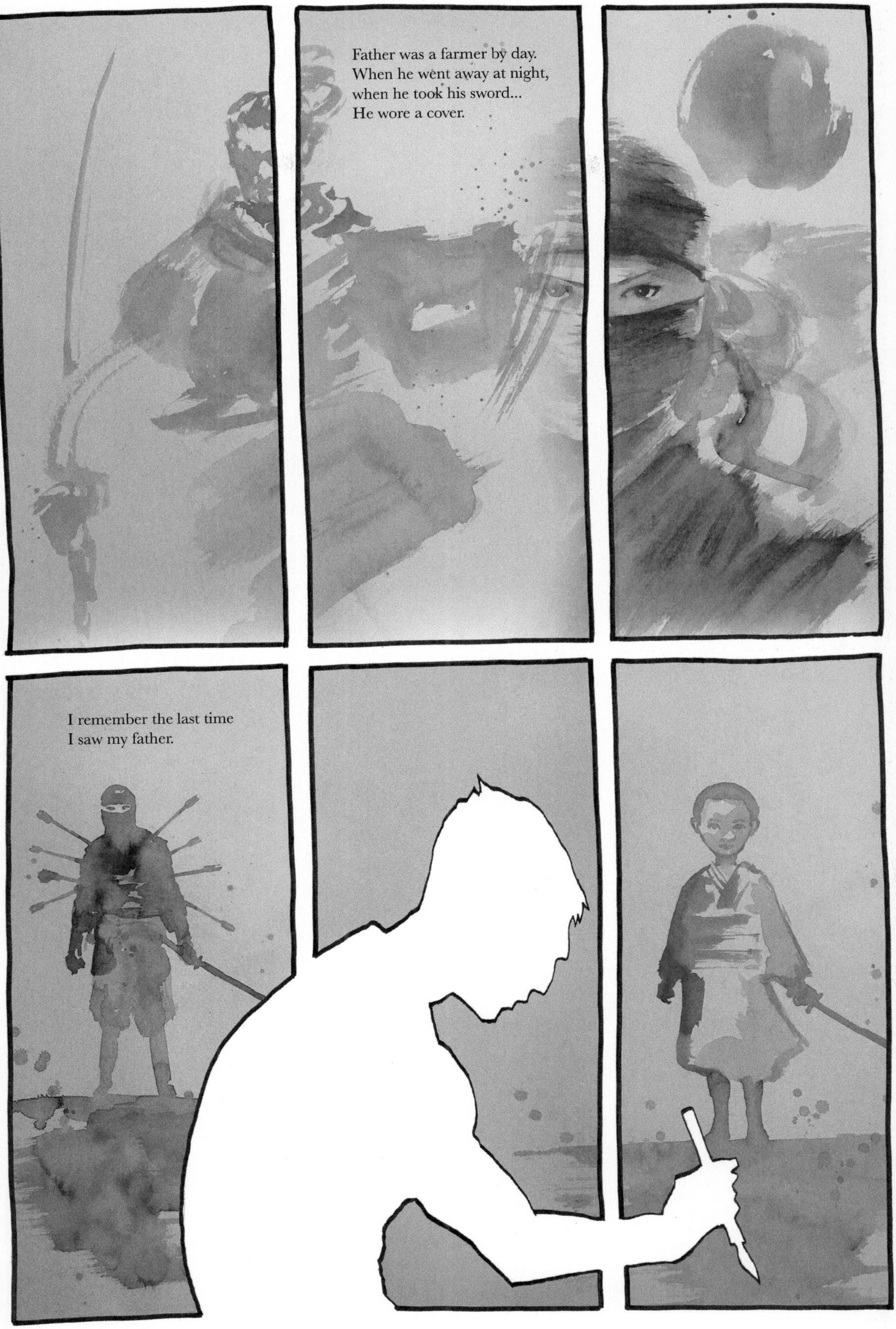

Father was a farmer by day.
When he went away at night,
when he took his sword...
He wore a cover.
I remember the last time
I saw my father.

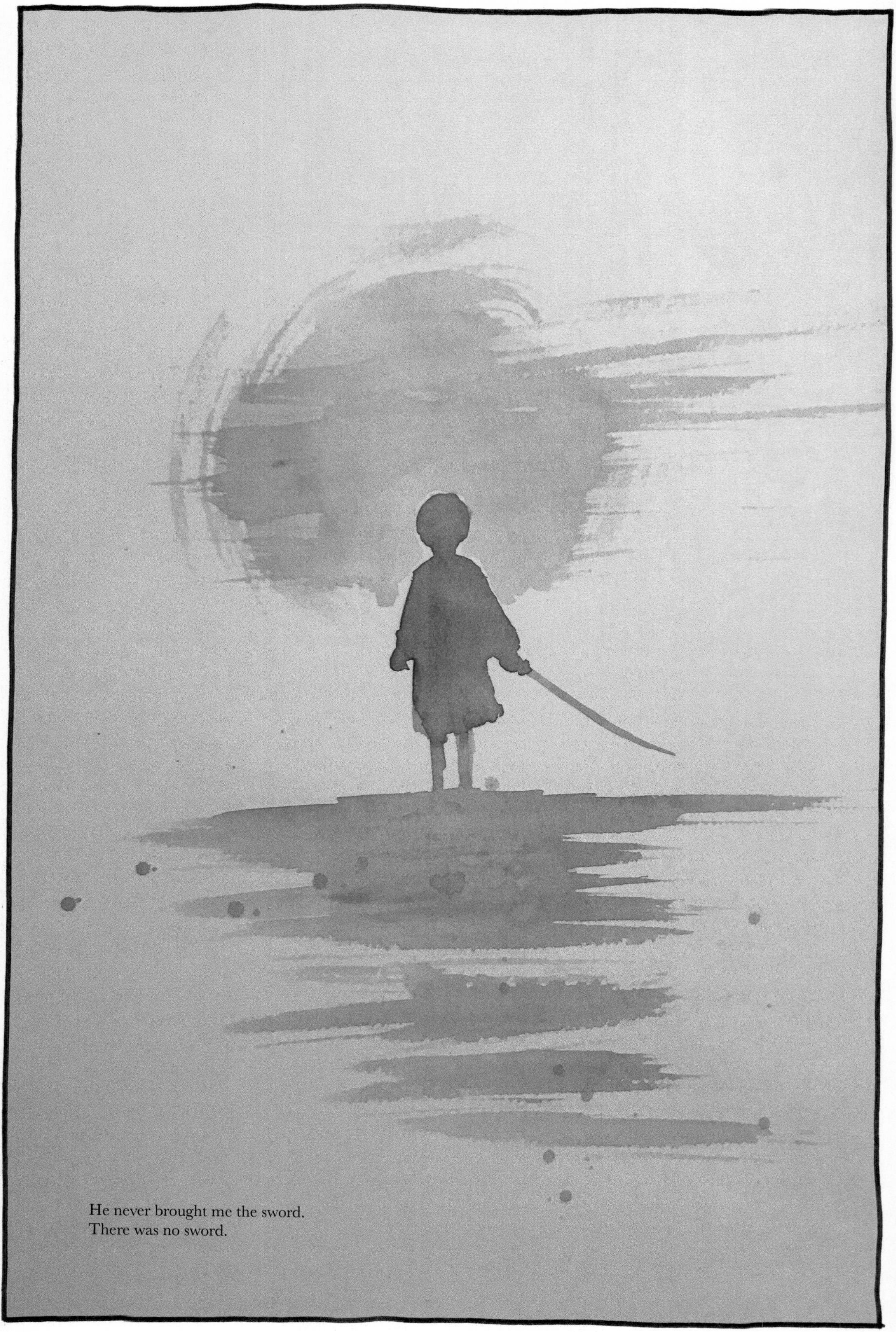
He never brought me the sword.
There was no sword.

I went searching for the sword maker whose crest was on the tsuba.

The man that the tsuba belonged to. Who Father said would give me a sword for it.

I was told there never was a sword for the empty tsuba.
A sword made with pressure and fire and foldings and beatings.

I was told, "The sword being made... was you."

"You are the sword."

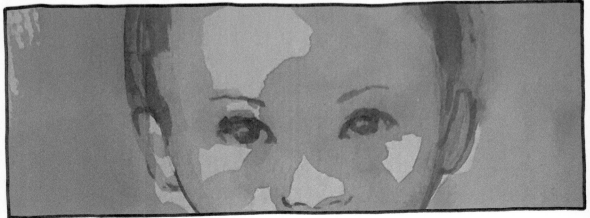

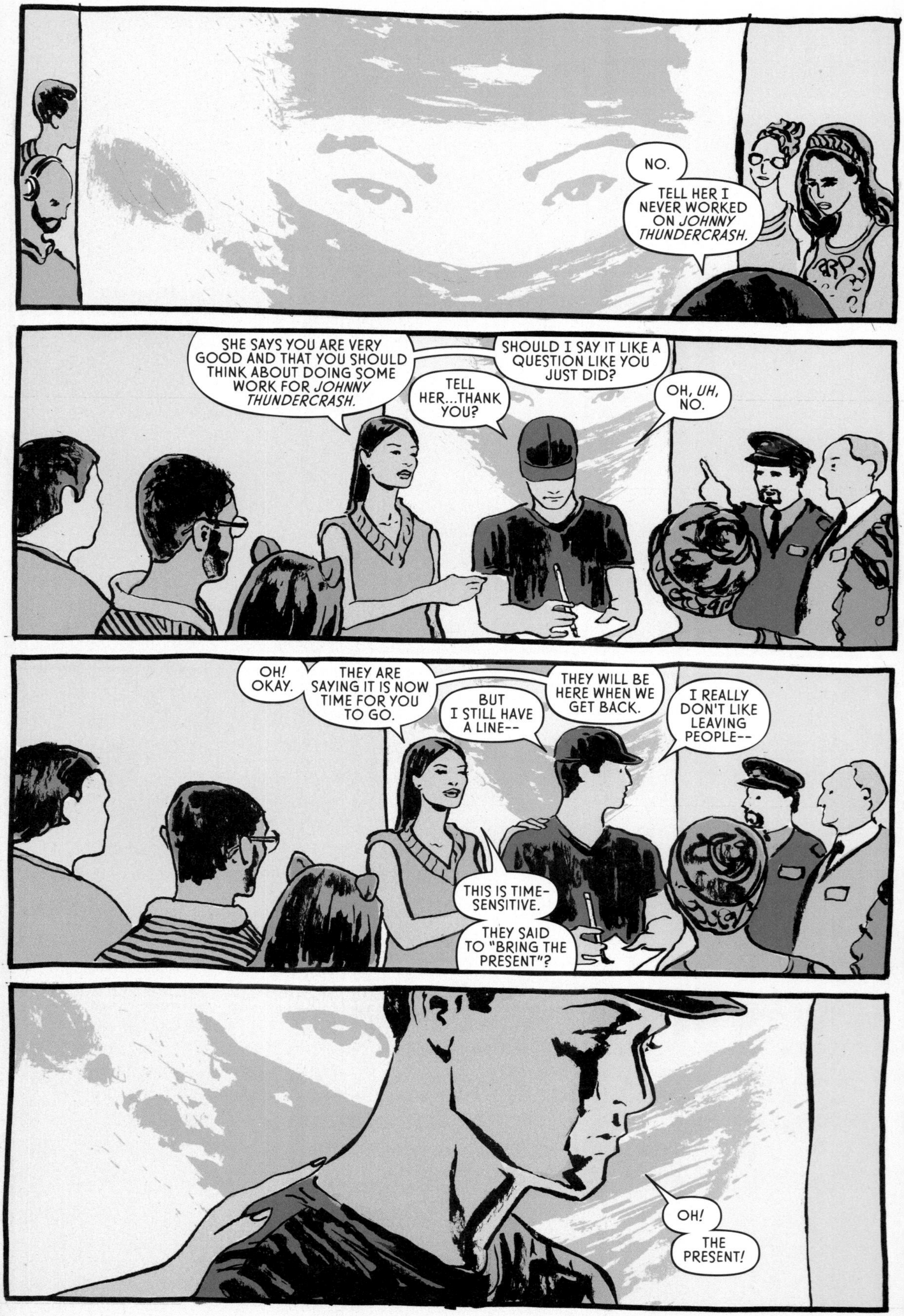
NO.
TELL HER I NEVER WORKED ON *JOHNNY THUNDERCRASH.*
SHE SAYS YOU ARE VERY GOOD AND THAT YOU SHOULD THINK ABOUT DOING SOME WORK FOR *JOHNNY THUNDERCRASH.*
TELL HER...THANK YOU?
SHOULD I SAY IT LIKE A QUESTION LIKE YOU JUST DID?
OH, *UH,* NO.
OH! OKAY.
THEY ARE SAYING IT IS NOW TIME FOR YOU TO GO.
BUT I STILL HAVE A LINE--
THEY WILL BE HERE WHEN WE GET BACK.
I REALLY DON'T LIKE LEAVING PEOPLE--
THIS IS TIME-SENSITIVE.
THEY SAID TO "BRING THE PRESENT"?
OH!
THE PRESENT!

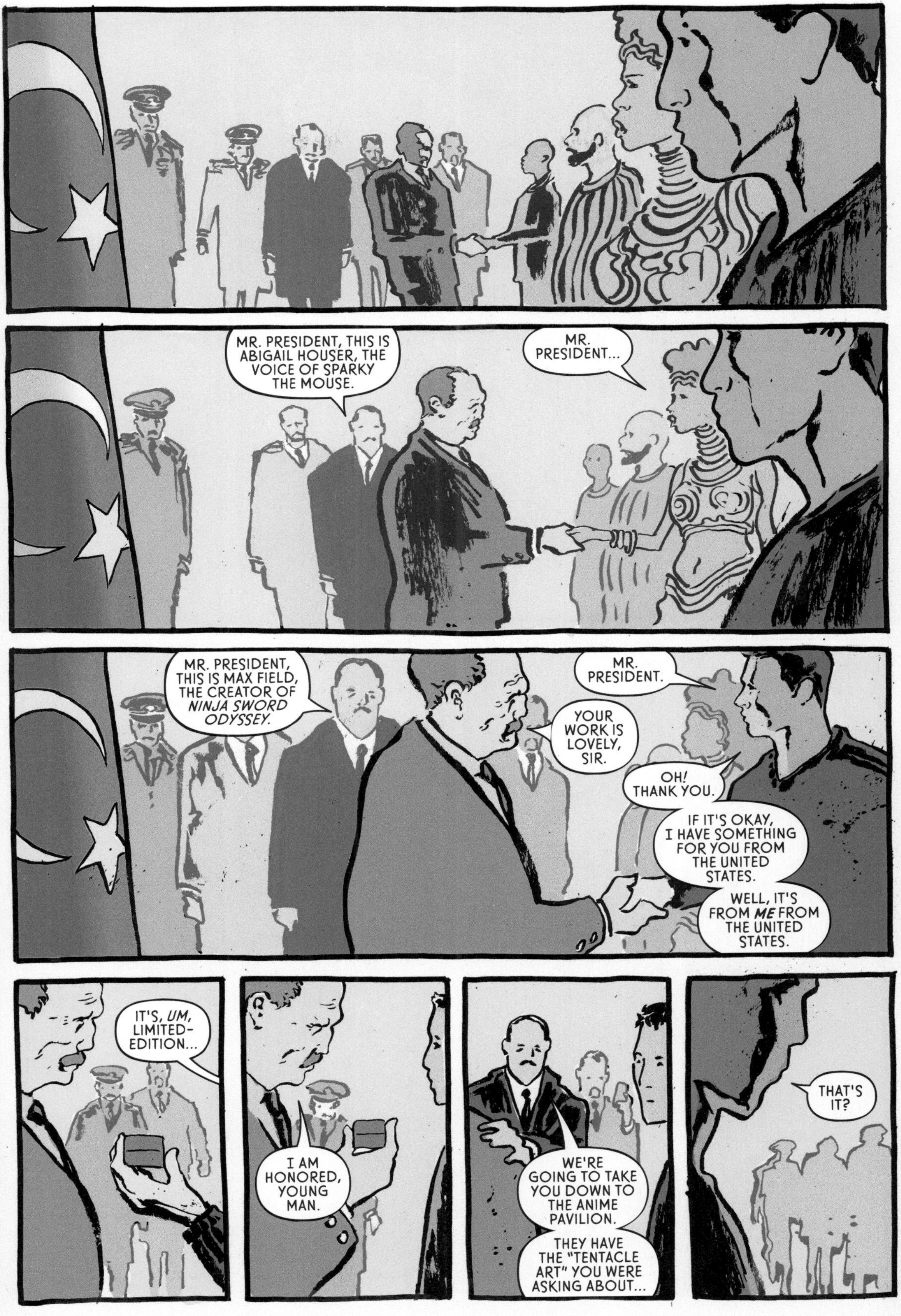

MR. PRESIDENT, THIS IS ABIGAIL HOUSER, THE VOICE OF SPARKY THE MOUSE.
MR. PRESIDENT...
MR. PRESIDENT, THIS IS MAX FIELD, THE CREATOR OF *NINJA SWORD ODYSSEY.*
MR. PRESIDENT.
YOUR WORK IS LOVELY, SIR.
OH! THANK YOU.
IF IT'S OKAY, I HAVE SOMETHING FOR YOU FROM THE UNITED STATES.
WELL, IT'S FROM ***ME*** FROM THE UNITED STATES.
IT'S, *UM,* LIMITED-EDITION...
I AM HONORED, YOUNG MAN.
WE'RE GOING TO TAKE YOU DOWN TO THE ANIME PAVILION.
THEY HAVE THE "TENTACLE ART" YOU WERE ASKING ABOUT...
THAT'S IT?

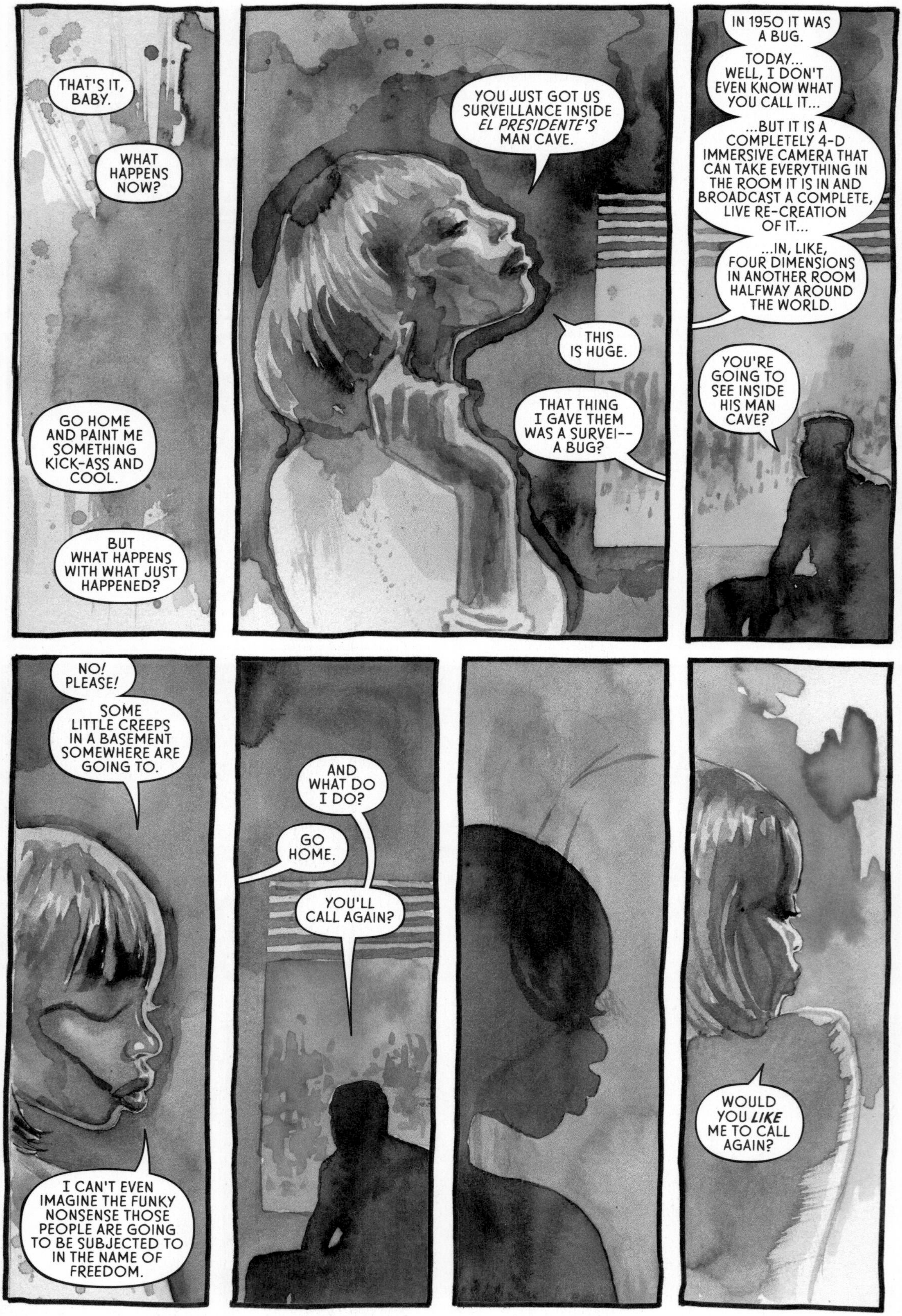
THAT'S IT, BABY.
WHAT HAPPENS NOW?
GO HOME AND PAINT ME SOMETHING KICK-ASS AND COOL.
BUT WHAT HAPPENS WITH WHAT JUST HAPPENED?
YOU JUST GOT US SURVEILLANCE INSIDE *EL PRESIDENTE'S* MAN CAVE.
THIS IS HUGE.
THAT THING I GAVE THEM WAS A SURVEI-- A BUG?
IN 1950 IT WAS A BUG.
TODAY... WELL, I DON'T EVEN KNOW WHAT YOU CALL IT...
...BUT IT IS A COMPLETELY 4-D IMMERSIVE CAMERA THAT CAN TAKE EVERYTHING IN THE ROOM IT IS IN AND BROADCAST A COMPLETE, LIVE RE-CREATION OF IT...
...IN, LIKE, FOUR DIMENSIONS IN ANOTHER ROOM HALFWAY AROUND THE WORLD.
YOU'RE GOING TO SEE INSIDE HIS MAN CAVE?
NO! PLEASE!
SOME LITTLE CREEPS IN A BASEMENT SOMEWHERE ARE GOING TO.
I CAN'T EVEN IMAGINE THE FUNKY NONSENSE THOSE PEOPLE ARE GOING TO BE SUBJECTED TO IN THE NAME OF FREEDOM.
AND WHAT DO I DO?
GO HOME.
YOU'LL CALL AGAIN?
WOULD YOU ***LIKE*** ME TO CALL AGAIN?

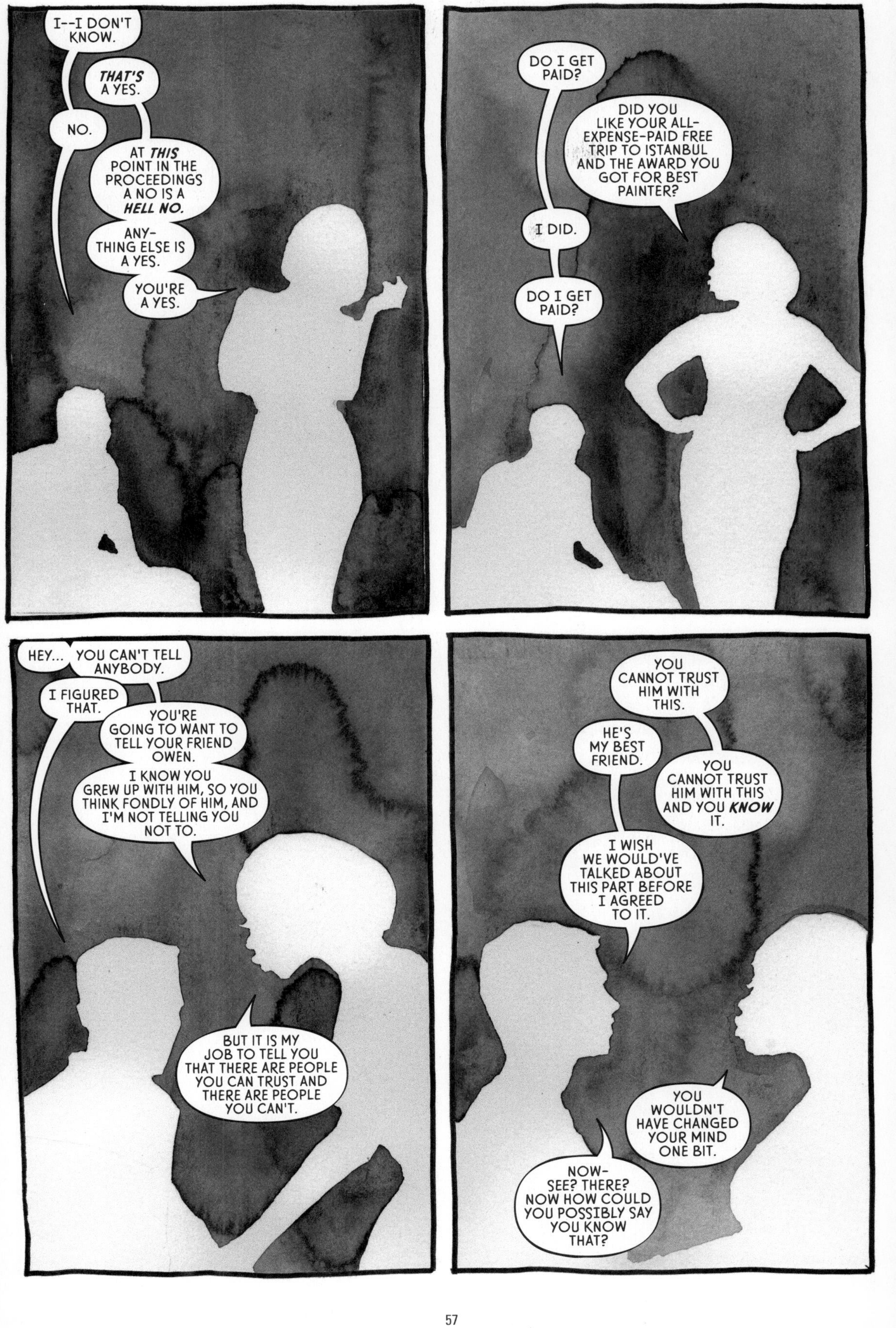
I--I DON'T KNOW.
THAT'S A YES.
NO.
AT *THIS* POINT IN THE PROCEEDINGS A NO IS A *HELL NO.*
ANY-THING ELSE IS A YES.
YOU'RE A YES.
DO I GET PAID?
DID YOU LIKE YOUR ALL-EXPENSE-PAID FREE TRIP TO ISTANBUL AND THE AWARD YOU GOT FOR BEST PAINTER?
I DID.
DO I GET PAID?
HEY...
YOU CAN'T TELL ANYBODY.
I FIGURED THAT.
YOU'RE GOING TO WANT TO TELL YOUR FRIEND OWEN.
I KNOW YOU GREW UP WITH HIM, SO YOU THINK FONDLY OF HIM, AND I'M NOT TELLING YOU NOT TO.
BUT IT IS MY JOB TO TELL YOU THAT THERE ARE PEOPLE YOU CAN TRUST AND THERE ARE PEOPLE YOU CAN'T.
YOU CANNOT TRUST HIM WITH THIS.
HE'S MY BEST FRIEND.
YOU CANNOT TRUST HIM WITH THIS AND YOU *KNOW* IT.
I WISH WE WOULD'VE TALKED ABOUT THIS PART BEFORE I AGREED TO IT.
YOU WOULDN'T HAVE CHANGED YOUR MIND ONE BIT.
NOW-SEE? THERE? NOW HOW COULD YOU POSSIBLY SAY YOU KNOW THAT?

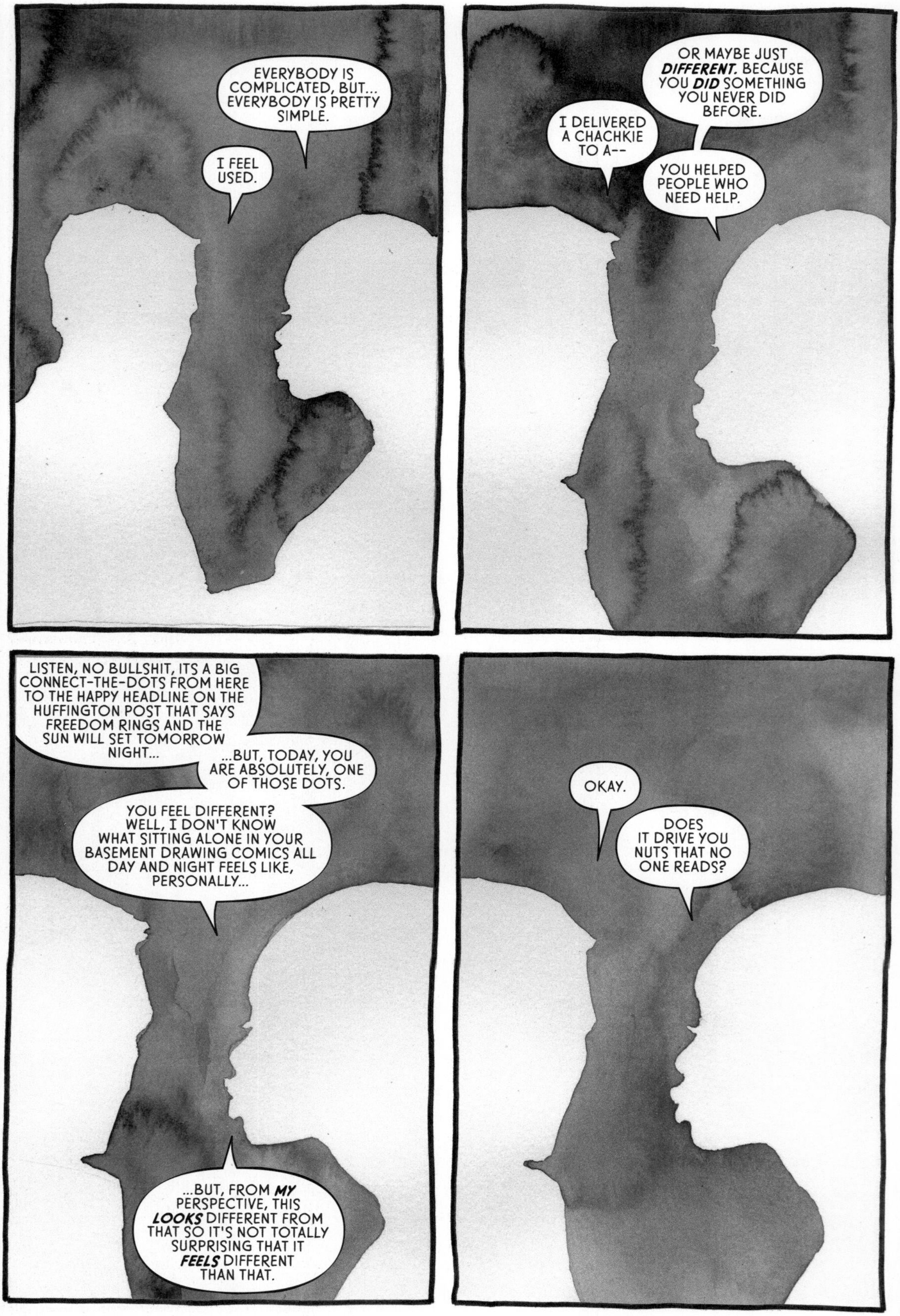
EVERYBODY IS COMPLICATED, BUT... EVERYBODY IS PRETTY SIMPLE.
I FEEL USED.
OR MAYBE JUST DIFFERENT. BECAUSE YOU DID SOMETHING YOU NEVER DID BEFORE.
I DELIVERED A CHACHKIE TO A--
YOU HELPED PEOPLE WHO NEED HELP.
LISTEN, NO BULLSHIT, ITS A BIG CONNECT-THE-DOTS FROM HERE TO THE HAPPY HEADLINE ON THE HUFFINGTON POST THAT SAYS FREEDOM RINGS AND THE SUN WILL SET TOMORROW NIGHT...
...BUT, TODAY, YOU ARE ABSOLUTELY, ONE OF THOSE DOTS.
YOU FEEL DIFFERENT? WELL, I DON'T KNOW WHAT SITTING ALONE IN YOUR BASEMENT DRAWING COMICS ALL DAY AND NIGHT FEELS LIKE, PERSONALLY...
...BUT, FROM MY PERSPECTIVE, THIS LOOKS DIFFERENT FROM THAT SO IT'S NOT TOTALLY SURPRISING THAT IT FEELS DIFFERENT THAN THAT.
OKAY.
DOES IT DRIVE YOU NUTS THAT NO ONE READS?

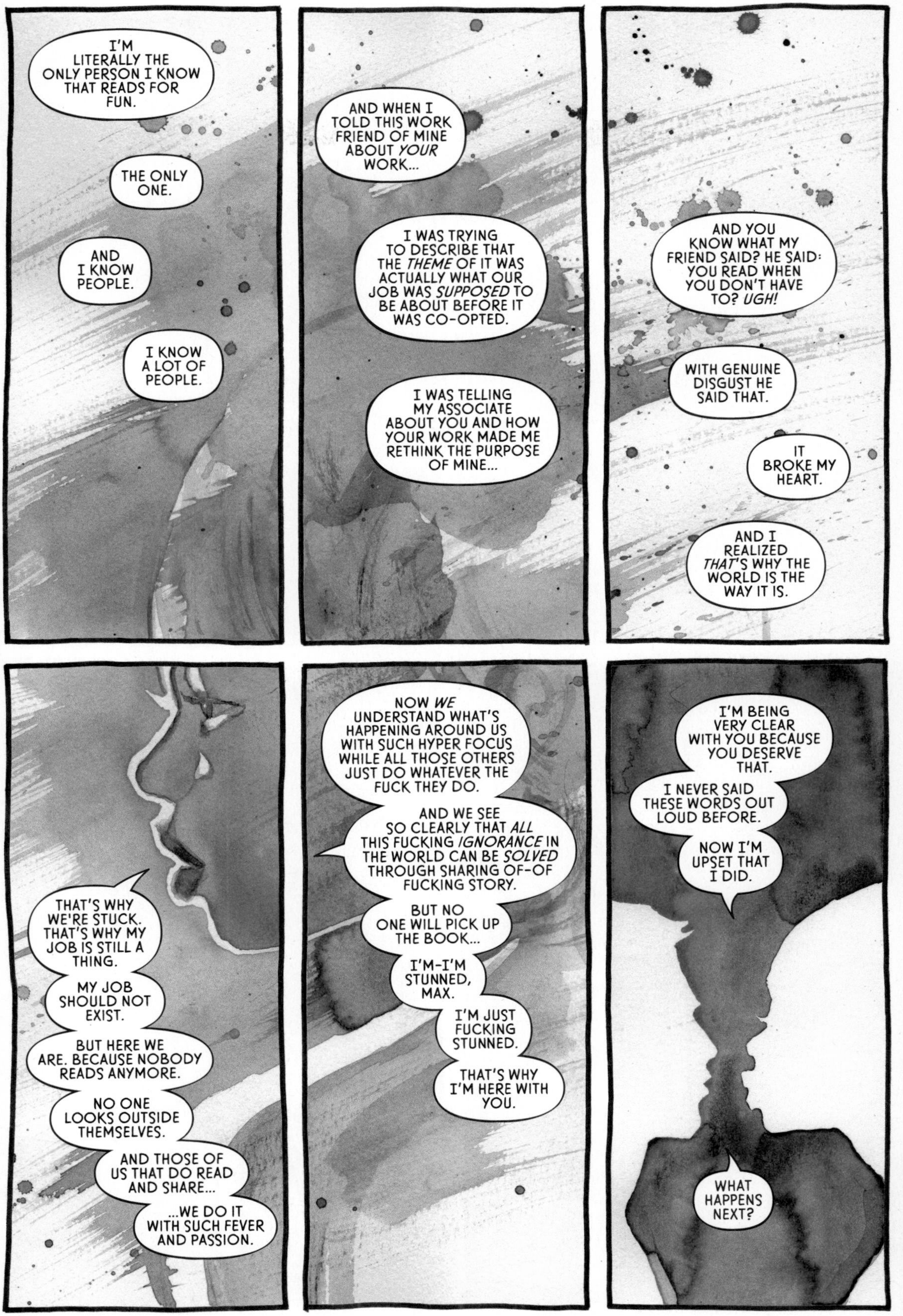
I'M LITERALLY THE ONLY PERSON I KNOW THAT READS FOR FUN.
THE ONLY ONE.
AND I KNOW PEOPLE.
I KNOW A LOT OF PEOPLE.
AND WHEN I TOLD THIS WORK FRIEND OF MINE ABOUT *YOUR* WORK...
I WAS TRYING TO DESCRIBE THAT THE *THEME* OF IT WAS ACTUALLY WHAT OUR JOB WAS *SUPPOSED* TO BE ABOUT BEFORE IT WAS CO-OPTED.
I WAS TELLING MY ASSOCIATE ABOUT YOU AND HOW YOUR WORK MADE ME RETHINK THE PURPOSE OF MINE...
AND YOU KNOW WHAT MY FRIEND SAID? HE SAID: YOU READ WHEN YOU DON'T HAVE TO? *UGH!*
WITH GENUINE DISGUST HE SAID THAT.
IT BROKE MY HEART.
AND I REALIZED *THAT*'S WHY THE WORLD IS THE WAY IT IS.
THAT'S WHY WE'RE STUCK. THAT'S WHY MY JOB IS STILL A THING.
MY JOB SHOULD NOT EXIST.
BUT HERE WE ARE. BECAUSE NOBODY READS ANYMORE.
NO ONE LOOKS OUTSIDE THEMSELVES.
AND THOSE OF US THAT DO READ AND SHARE...
...WE DO IT WITH SUCH FEVER AND PASSION.
NOW *WE* UNDERSTAND WHAT'S HAPPENING AROUND US WITH SUCH HYPER FOCUS WHILE ALL THOSE OTHERS JUST DO WHATEVER THE FUCK THEY DO.
AND WE SEE SO CLEARLY THAT *ALL* THIS FUCKING *IGNORANCE* IN THE WORLD CAN BE *SOLVED* THROUGH SHARING OF-OF FUCKING STORY.
BUT NO ONE WILL PICK UP THE BOOK...
I'M-I'M STUNNED, MAX.
I'M JUST FUCKING STUNNED.
THAT'S WHY I'M HERE WITH YOU.
I'M BEING VERY CLEAR WITH YOU BECAUSE YOU DESERVE THAT.
I NEVER SAID THESE WORDS OUT LOUD BEFORE.
NOW I'M UPSET THAT I DID.
WHAT HAPPENS NEXT?

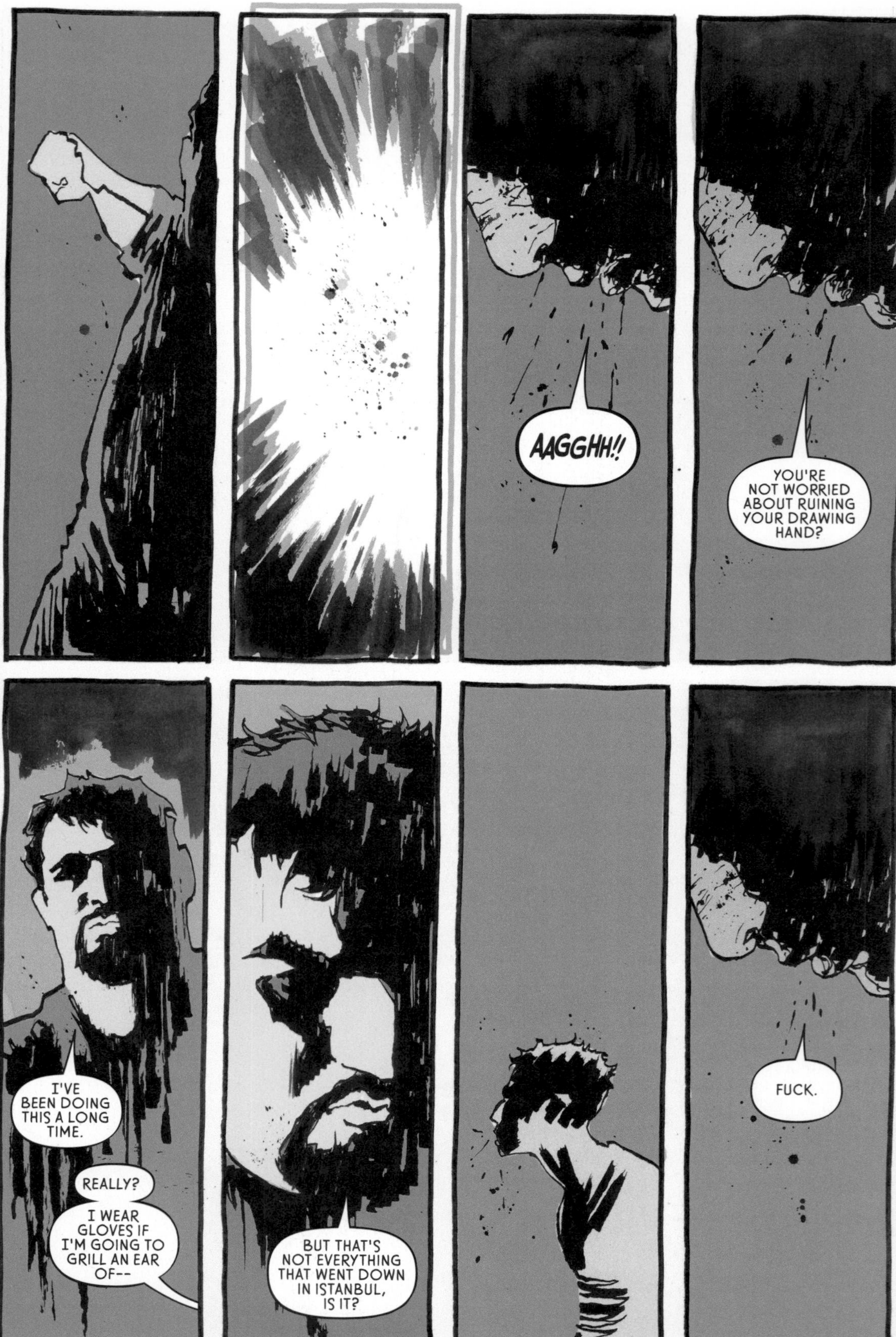
AAGGHH!!
YOU'RE NOT WORRIED ABOUT RUINING YOUR DRAWING HAND?
I'VE BEEN DOING THIS A LONG TIME.
REALLY?
I WEAR GLOVES IF I'M GOING TO GRILL AN EAR OF--
BUT THAT'S NOT EVERYTHING THAT WENT DOWN IN ISTANBUL, IS IT?
FUCK.

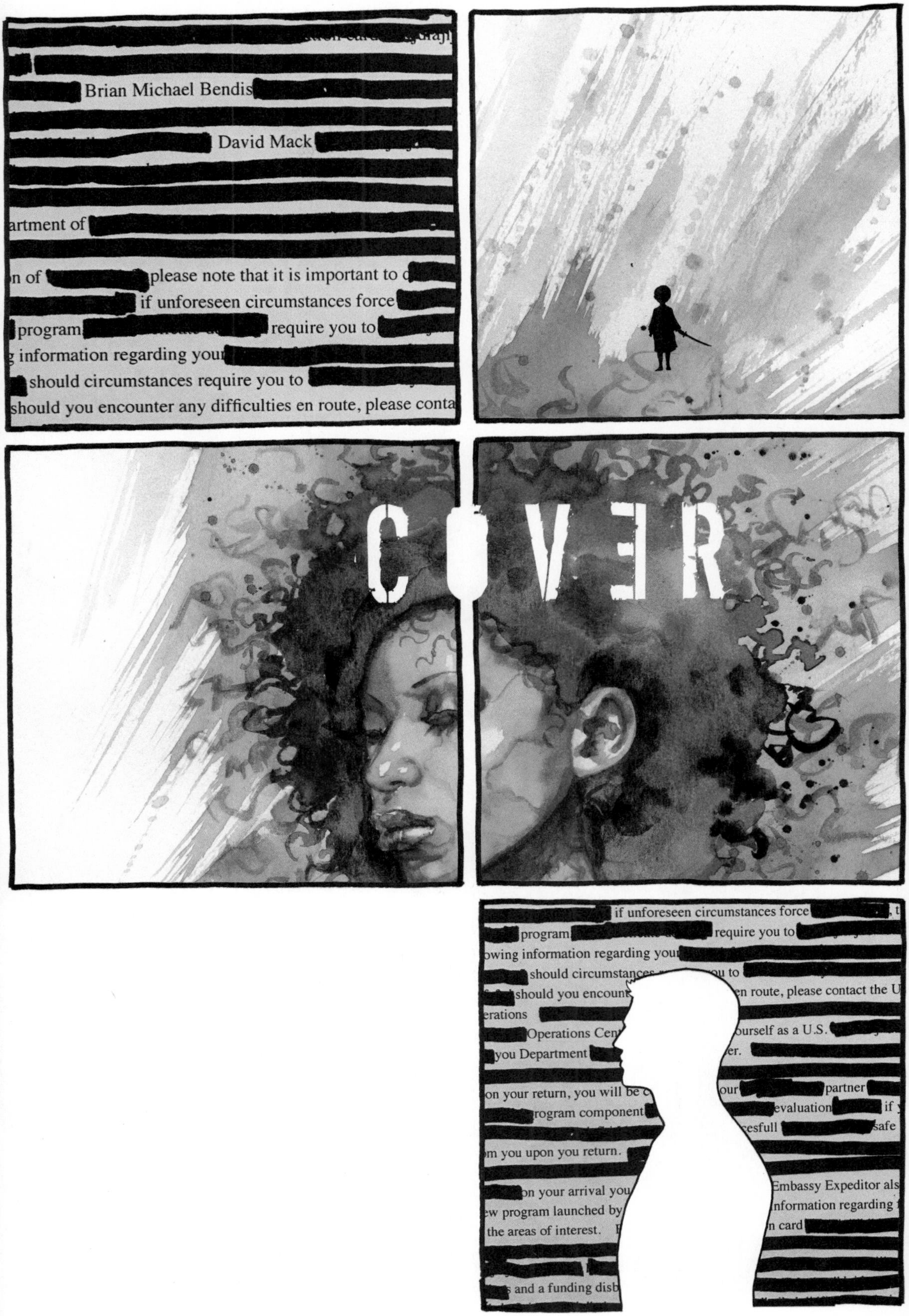

[redacted]
[redacted] Brian Michael Bendis [redacted]
[redacted] David Mack [redacted]
artment of [redacted]
n of [redacted] please note that it is important to [redacted]
[redacted] if unforeseen circumstances force [redacted]
program [redacted] require you to [redacted]
information regarding your [redacted]
[redacted] should circumstances require you to [redacted]
should you encounter any difficulties en route, please conta
COVER
[redacted] if unforeseen circumstances force [redacted]
[redacted] program [redacted] require you to [redacted]
owing information regarding your [redacted]
[redacted] should circumstances you to [redacted]
[redacted] should you encount en route, please contact the U
erations [redacted]
[redacted] Operations Cen ourself as a U.S. [redacted]
[redacted] you Department [redacted] er. [redacted]
on your return, you will be c our [redacted] partner [redacted]
[redacted] rogram component evaluation [redacted] if y
cesfull [redacted] safe
m you upon you return. [redacted]
[redacted] on your arrival you Embassy Expeditor als
ew program launched by Information regarding
the areas of interest. n card [redacted]
[redacted]
s and a funding disb

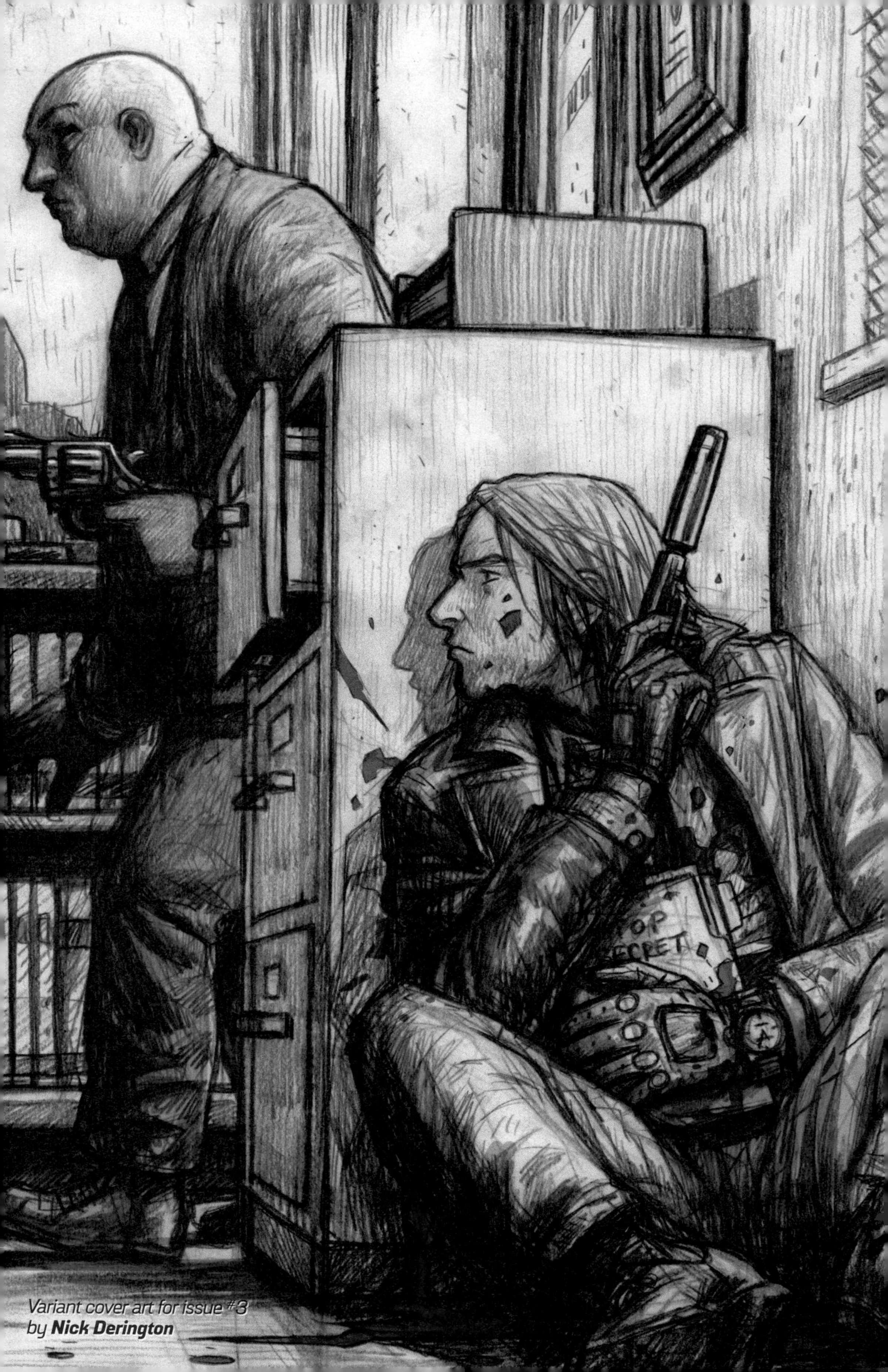

Variant cover art for issue #3
by **Nick Derington**

I took after
my father.

I worked for the
swordmaker,
as my father did.

Slipping in between
the battle lines.
Gathering information,
running errands unseen.

I can't talk about
what I did.

Occasionally I caught
an arrow or two.

But soon they passed
through me with no fixed
soul to get stuck on.

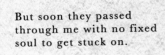

I learned archery
in reverse.

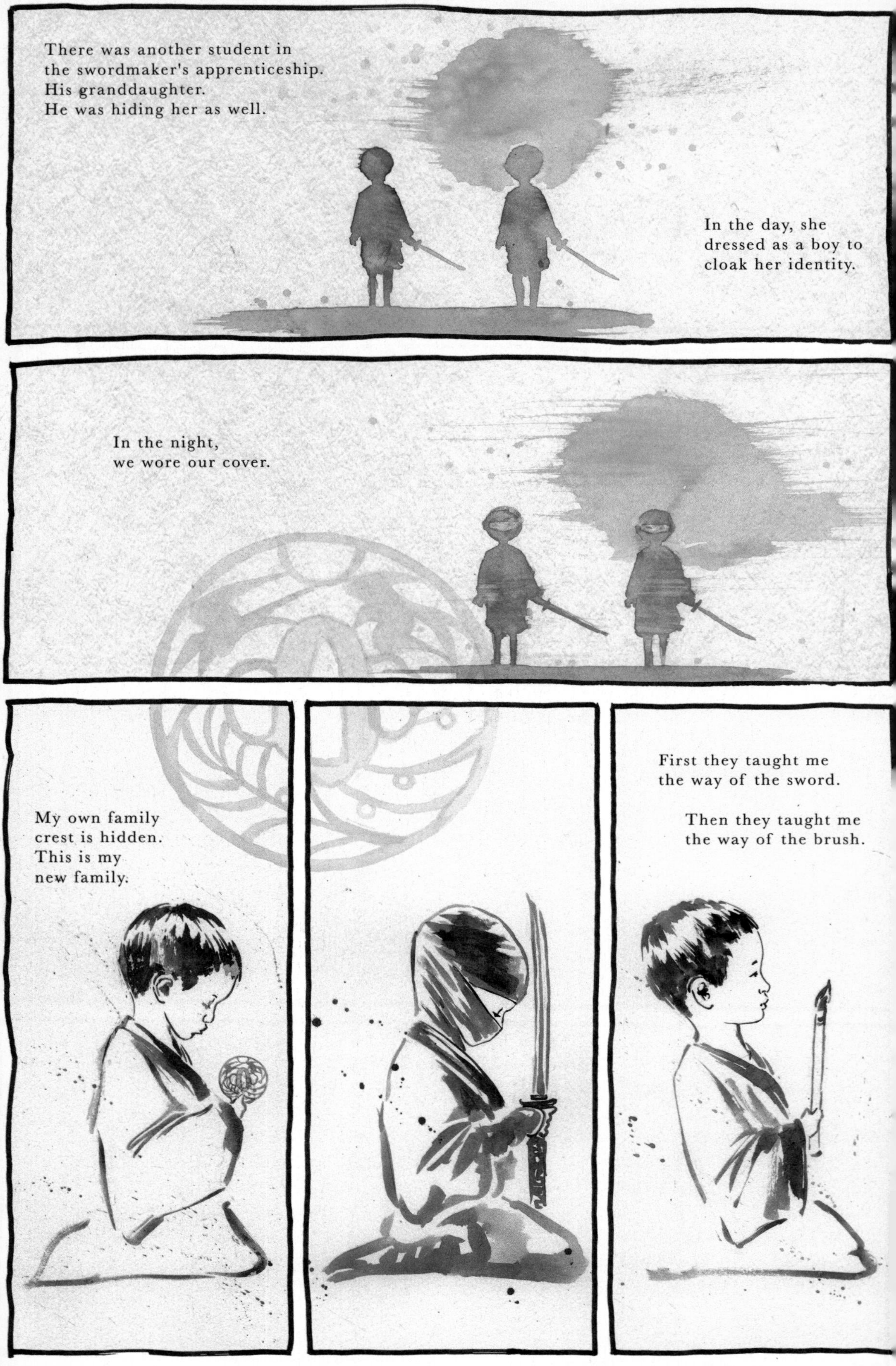
There was another student in the swordmaker's apprenticeship. His granddaughter. He was hiding her as well.
In the day, she dressed as a boy to cloak her identity.
In the night, we wore our cover.
My own family crest is hidden. This is my new family.
First they taught me the way of the sword.
Then they taught me the way of the brush.

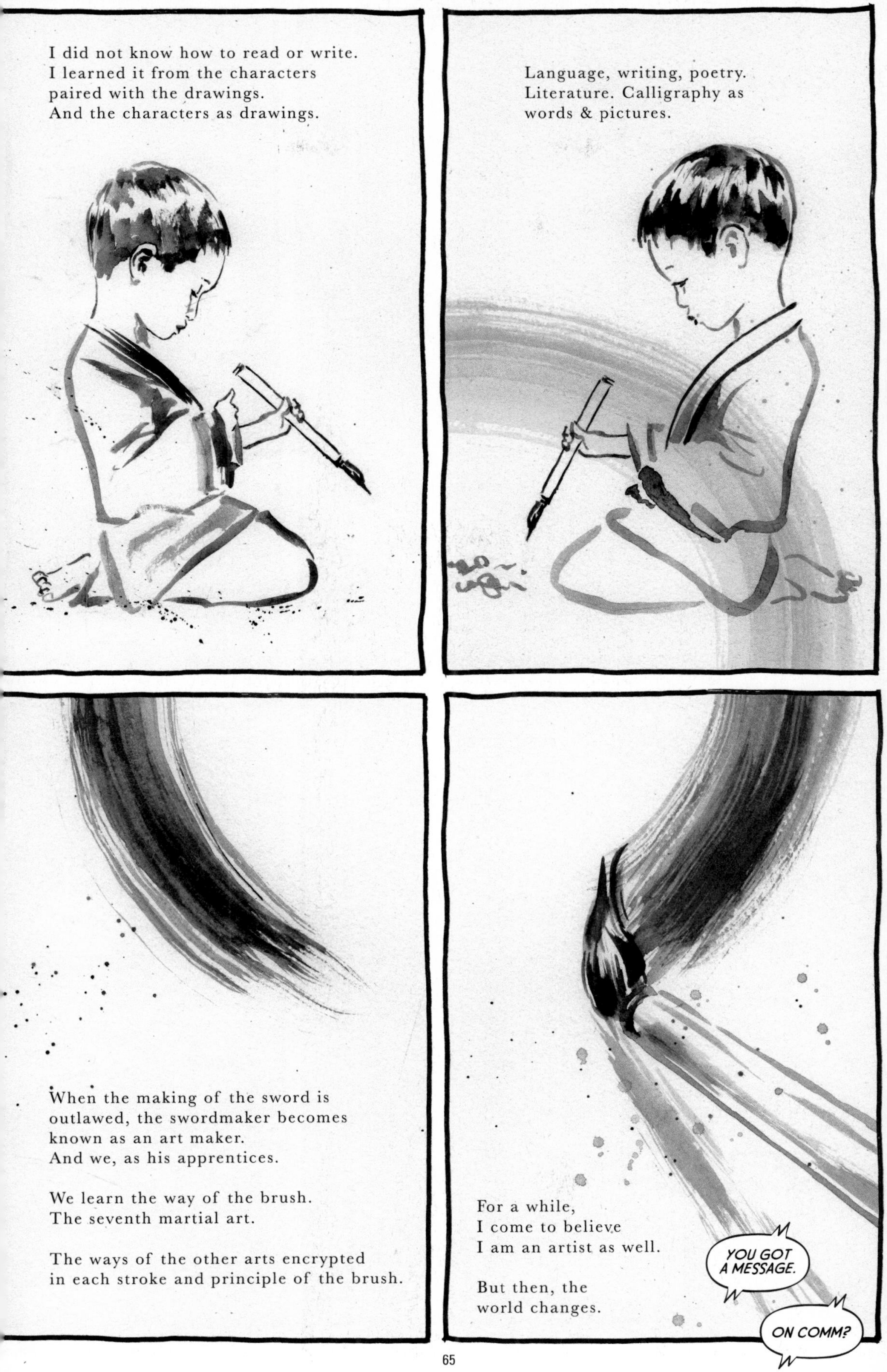
I did not know how to read or write.
I learned it from the characters
paired with the drawings.
And the characters as drawings.
Language, writing, poetry.
Literature. Calligraphy as
words & pictures.
When the making of the sword is
outlawed, the swordmaker becomes
known as an art maker.
And we, as his apprentices.
We learn the way of the brush.
The seventh martial art.
The ways of the other arts encrypted
in each stroke and principle of the brush.
For a while,
I come to believe
I am an artist as well.
But then, the
world changes.
YOU GOT A MESSAGE.
ON COMM?

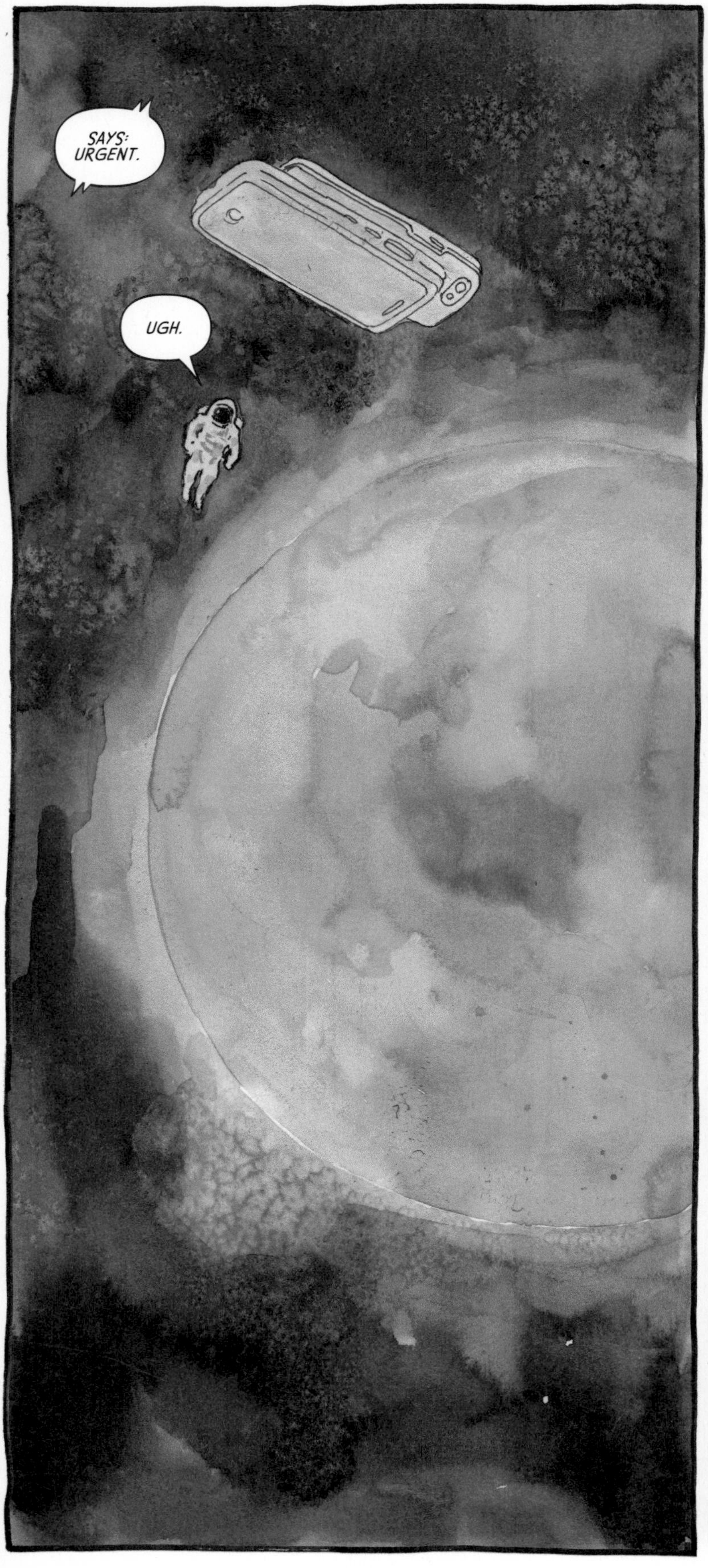
SAYS: URGENT.
UGH.

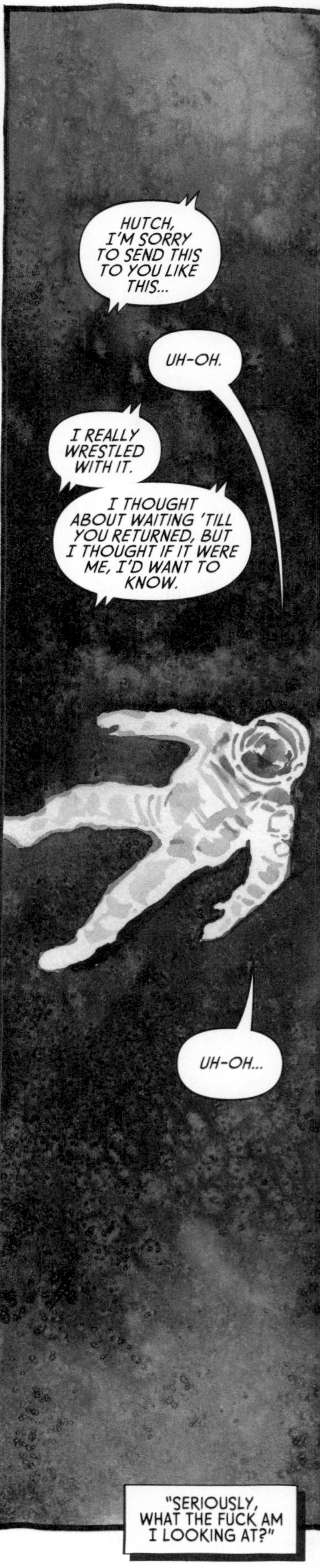
HUTCH, I'M SORRY TO SEND THIS TO YOU LIKE THIS...
UH-OH.
I REALLY WRESTLED WITH IT.
I THOUGHT ABOUT WAITING 'TILL YOU RETURNED, BUT I THOUGHT IF IT WERE ME, I'D WANT TO KNOW.
UH-OH...
"SERIOUSLY, WHAT THE FUCK AM I LOOKING AT?"

SWEETIE, MY DARLING...

UGH, THIS IS HARD.

YOUR FATHER--

OH NO...

HE DIED, SWEETIE.

HE'S GONE.

HE WAS HIT BY A DRUNK DRIVER.

IT'S SO NOT FAIR.

HE WAS HERE...AND THEN HE DIDN'T COME HOME, AND THEN I GOT A CALL.

OH GOD...

I'M SORRY, SWEETIE.

I KNOW YOU'D BE SO MAD IF YOU CAME ALL THE WAY HOME AND I DIDN'T--WELL, I'M SORRY.

BUT YOU KNOW--YOU **KNOW** HOW INSANELY PROUD OF YOU HE WAS.

"OH MY FUCKING GOD."

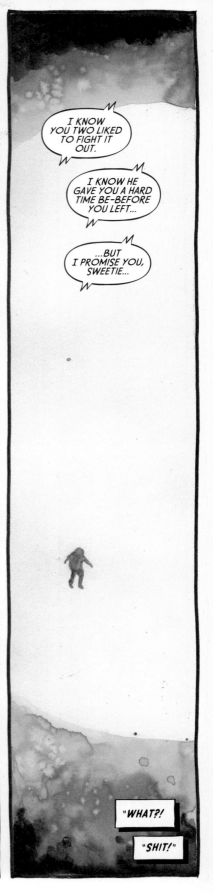

I KNOW YOU TWO LIKED TO FIGHT IT OUT.

I KNOW HE GAVE YOU A HARD TIME BE-BEFORE YOU LEFT...

...BUT I PROMISE YOU, SWEETIE...

"*WHAT?!*"

"*SHIT!*"

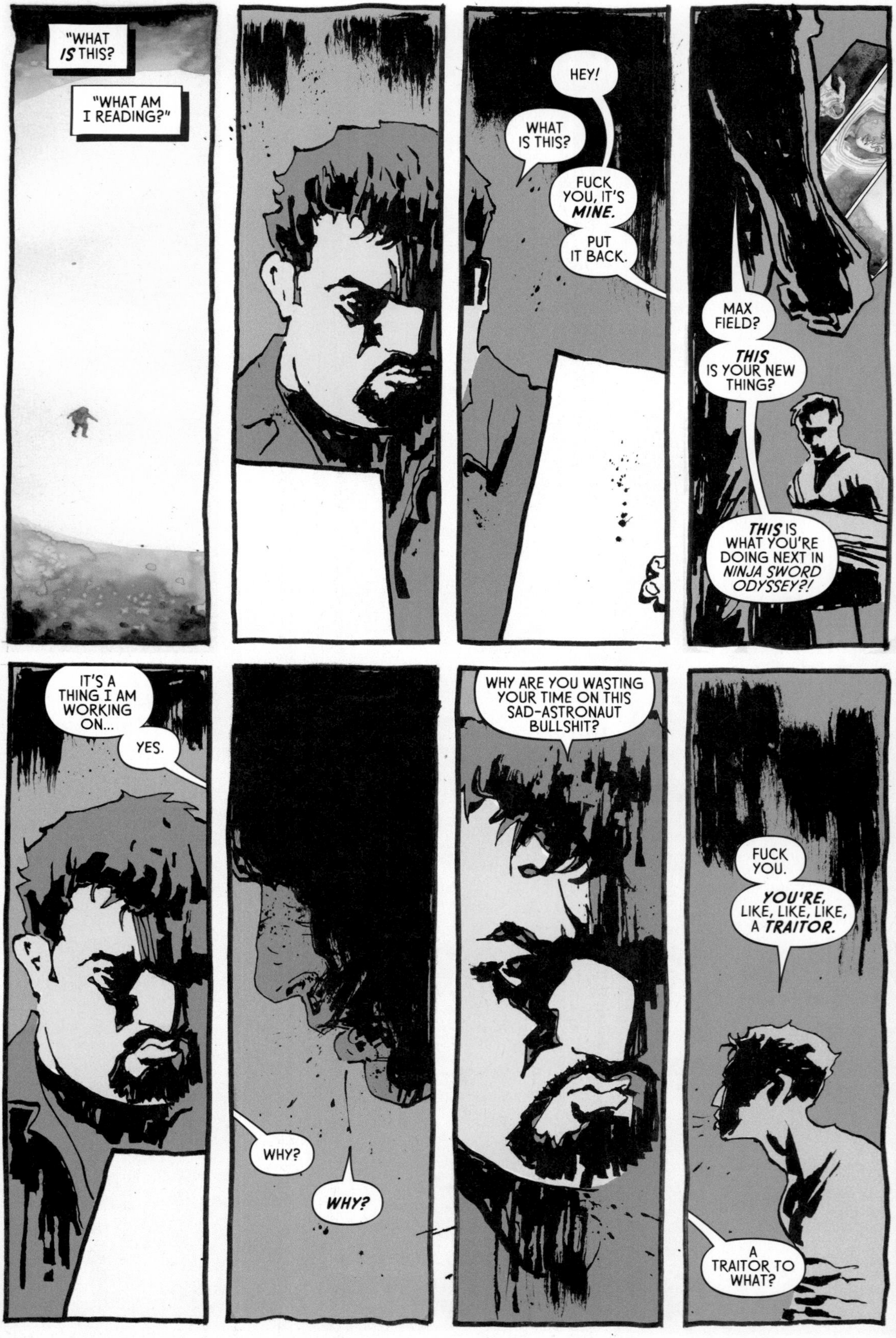

"WHAT *IS* THIS?
"WHAT AM I READING?"
HEY!
WHAT IS THIS?
FUCK YOU, IT'S *MINE.*
PUT IT BACK.
MAX FIELD?
THIS IS YOUR NEW THING?
THIS IS WHAT YOU'RE DOING NEXT IN *NINJA SWORD ODYSSEY?!*
IT'S A THING I AM WORKING ON...
YES.
WHY?
WHY?
WHY ARE YOU WASTING YOUR TIME ON THIS SAD-ASTRONAUT BULLSHIT?
FUCK YOU.
YOU'RE, LIKE, LIKE, LIKE, A *TRAITOR.*
A TRAITOR TO WHAT?

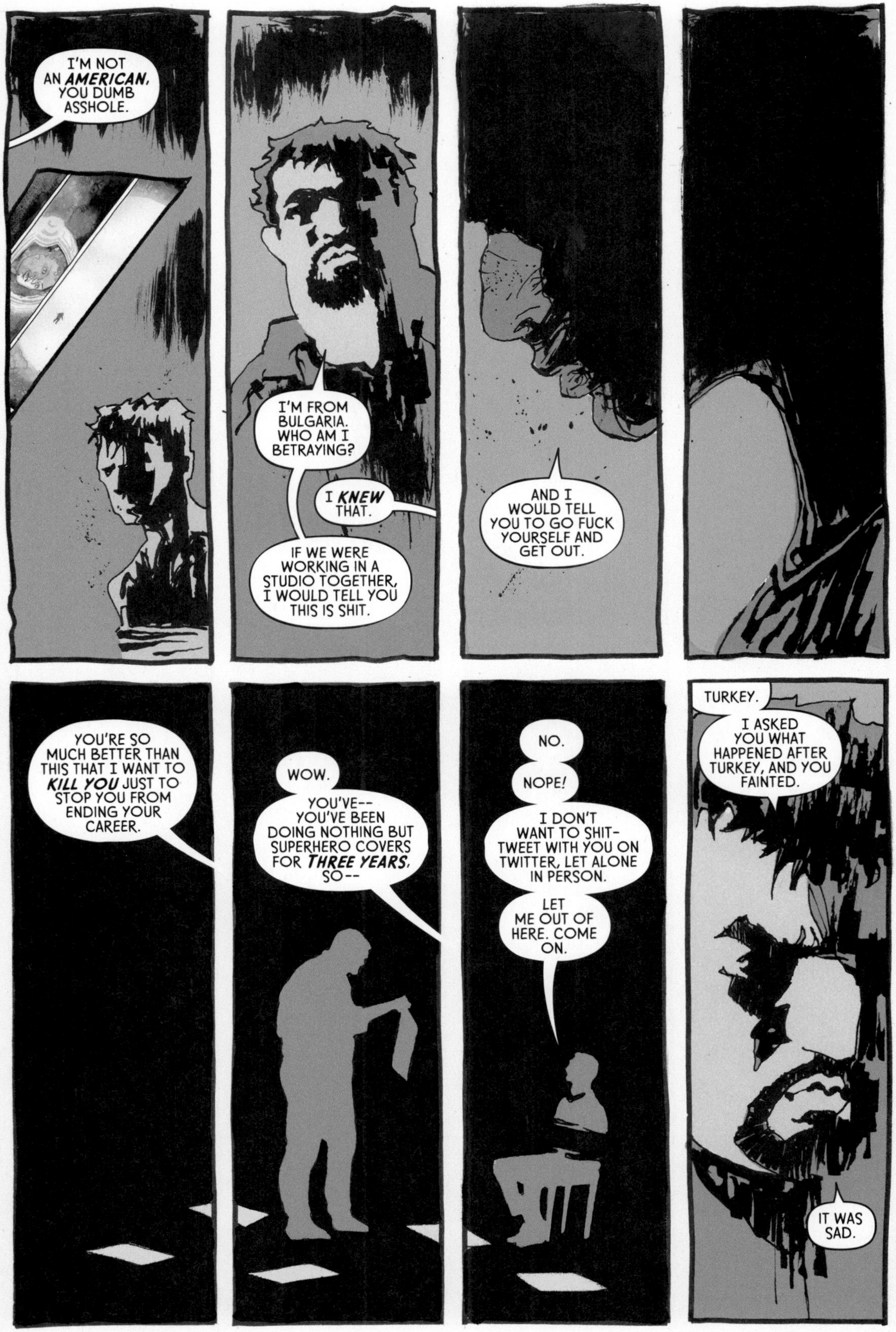
I'M NOT AN *AMERICAN,* YOU DUMB ASSHOLE.
I'M FROM BULGARIA. WHO AM I BETRAYING?
I *KNEW* THAT.
IF WE WERE WORKING IN A STUDIO TOGETHER, I WOULD TELL YOU THIS IS SHIT.
AND I WOULD TELL YOU TO GO FUCK YOURSELF AND GET OUT.
YOU'RE SO MUCH BETTER THAN THIS THAT I WANT TO *KILL YOU* JUST TO STOP YOU FROM ENDING YOUR CAREER.
WOW.
YOU'VE-- YOU'VE BEEN DOING NOTHING BUT SUPERHERO COVERS FOR *THREE YEARS,* SO--
NO.
NOPE!
I DON'T WANT TO SHIT-TWEET WITH YOU ON TWITTER, LET ALONE IN PERSON.
LET ME OUT OF HERE. COME ON.
TURKEY.
I ASKED YOU WHAT HAPPENED AFTER TURKEY, AND YOU FAINTED.
IT WAS SAD.

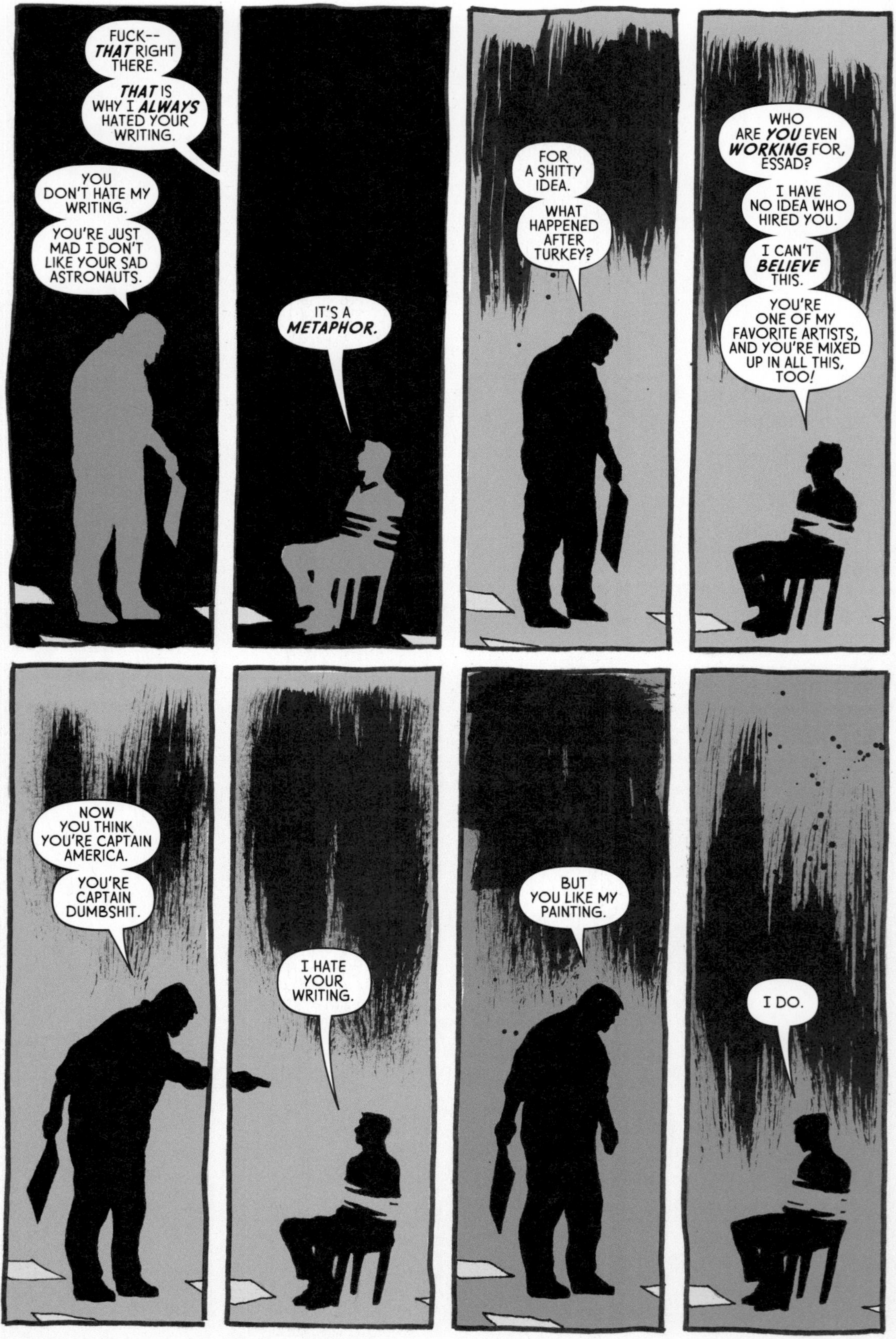
FUCK-- THAT RIGHT THERE.
THAT IS WHY I ALWAYS HATED YOUR WRITING.
YOU DON'T HATE MY WRITING.
YOU'RE JUST MAD I DON'T LIKE YOUR SAD ASTRONAUTS.
IT'S A METAPHOR.
FOR A SHITTY IDEA.
WHAT HAPPENED AFTER TURKEY?
WHO ARE YOU EVEN WORKING FOR, ESSAD?
I HAVE NO IDEA WHO HIRED YOU.
I CAN'T BELIEVE THIS.
YOU'RE ONE OF MY FAVORITE ARTISTS, AND YOU'RE MIXED UP IN ALL THIS, TOO!
NOW YOU THINK YOU'RE CAPTAIN AMERICA.
YOU'RE CAPTAIN DUMBSHIT.
I HATE YOUR WRITING.
BUT YOU LIKE MY PAINTING.
I DO.

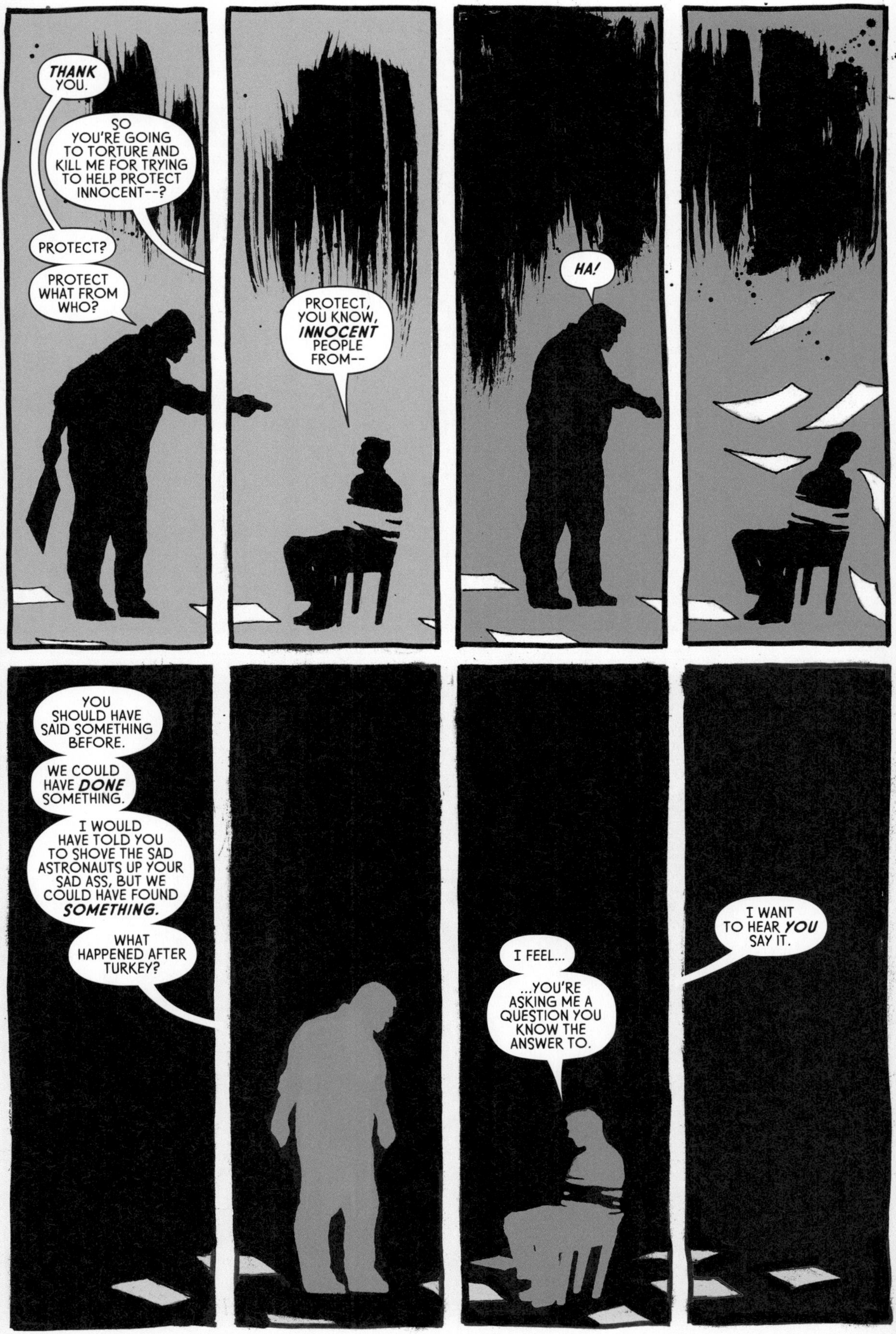
THANK YOU.
SO YOU'RE GOING TO TORTURE AND KILL ME FOR TRYING TO HELP PROTECT INNOCENT--?
PROTECT?
PROTECT WHAT FROM WHO?
PROTECT, YOU KNOW, INNOCENT PEOPLE FROM--
HA!
YOU SHOULD HAVE SAID SOMETHING BEFORE.
WE COULD HAVE DONE SOMETHING.
I WOULD HAVE TOLD YOU TO SHOVE THE SAD ASTRONAUTS UP YOUR SAD ASS, BUT WE COULD HAVE FOUND SOMETHING.
WHAT HAPPENED AFTER TURKEY?
I FEEL...
...YOU'RE ASKING ME A QUESTION YOU KNOW THE ANSWER TO.
I WANT TO HEAR YOU SAY IT.

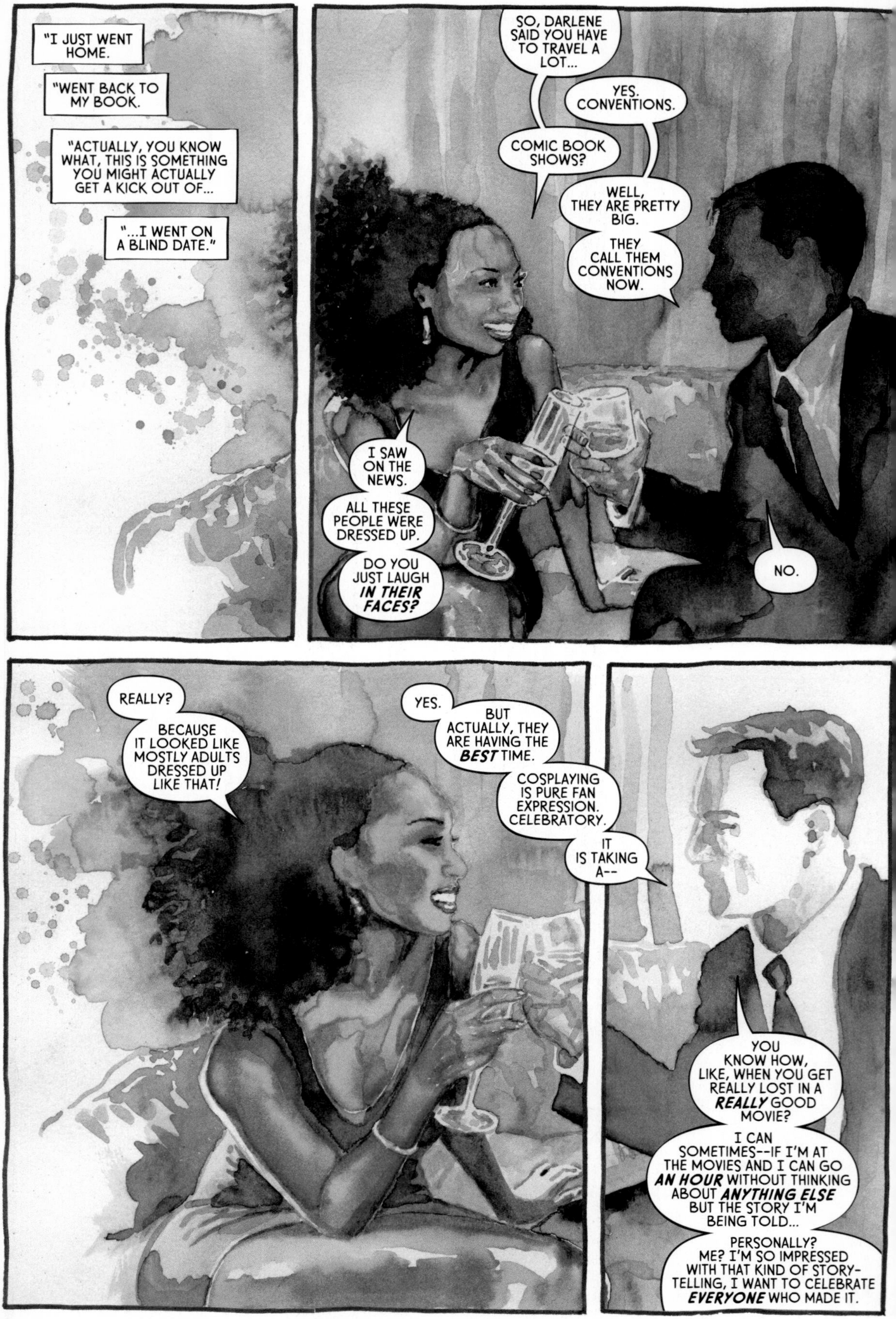
"I JUST WENT HOME.
"WENT BACK TO MY BOOK.
"ACTUALLY, YOU KNOW WHAT, THIS IS SOMETHING YOU MIGHT ACTUALLY GET A KICK OUT OF...
"...I WENT ON A BLIND DATE."
SO, DARLENE SAID YOU HAVE TO TRAVEL A LOT...
YES. CONVENTIONS.
COMIC BOOK SHOWS?
WELL, THEY ARE PRETTY BIG.
THEY CALL THEM CONVENTIONS NOW.
I SAW ON THE NEWS.
ALL THESE PEOPLE WERE DRESSED UP.
DO YOU JUST LAUGH ***IN THEIR FACES?***
NO.
REALLY?
BECAUSE IT LOOKED LIKE MOSTLY ADULTS DRESSED UP LIKE THAT!
YES.
BUT ACTUALLY, THEY ARE HAVING THE ***BEST*** TIME.
COSPLAYING IS PURE FAN EXPRESSION. CELEBRATORY.
IT IS TAKING A--
YOU KNOW HOW, LIKE, WHEN YOU GET REALLY LOST IN A ***REALLY*** GOOD MOVIE?
I CAN SOMETIMES--IF I'M AT THE MOVIES AND I CAN GO ***AN HOUR*** WITHOUT THINKING ABOUT ***ANYTHING ELSE*** BUT THE STORY I'M BEING TOLD...
PERSONALLY? ME? I'M SO IMPRESSED WITH THAT KIND OF STORY-TELLING, I WANT TO CELEBRATE ***EVERYONE*** WHO MADE IT.

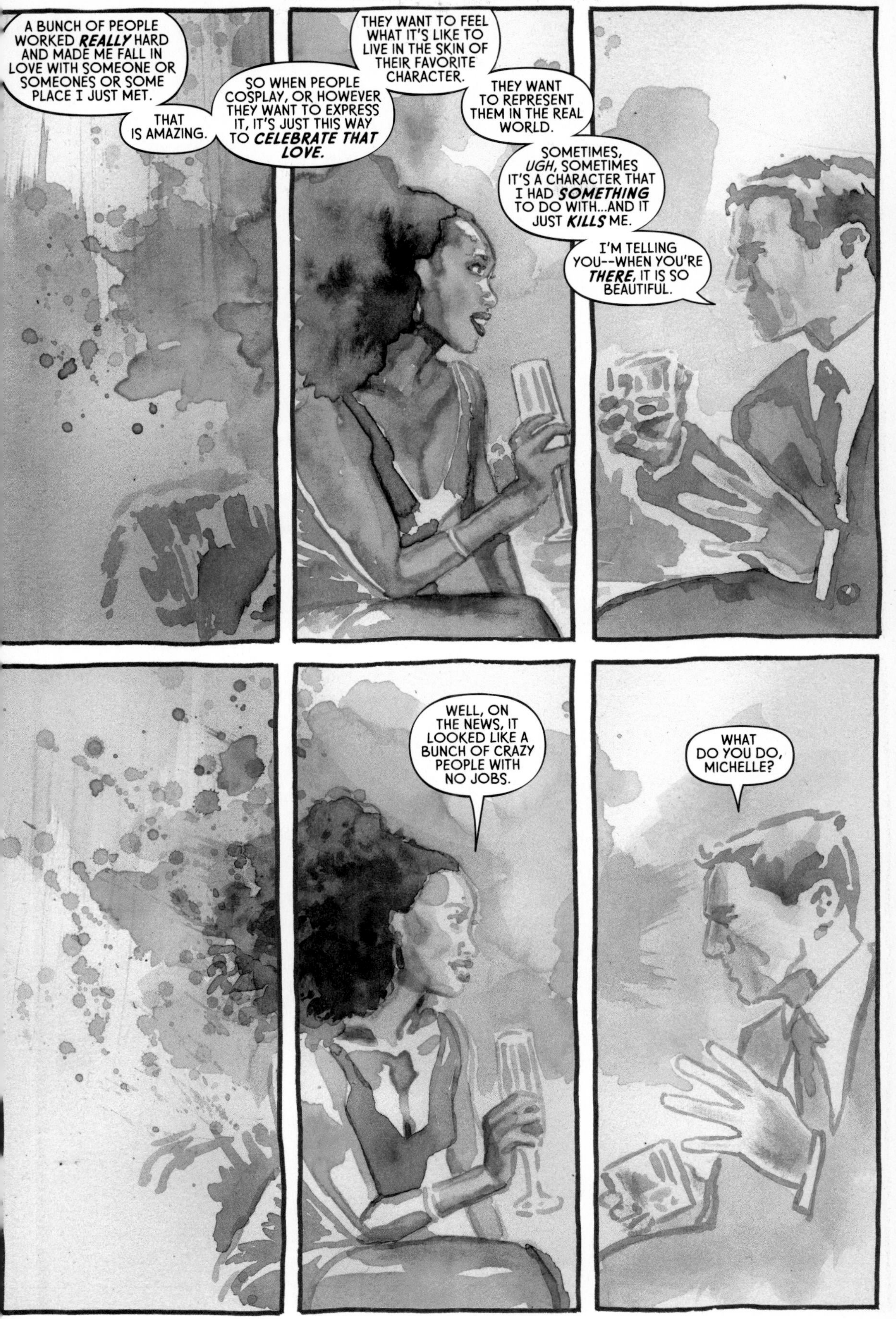
A BUNCH OF PEOPLE WORKED REALLY HARD AND MADE ME FALL IN LOVE WITH SOMEONE OR SOMEONES OR SOME PLACE I JUST MET.
THAT IS AMAZING.
SO WHEN PEOPLE COSPLAY, OR HOWEVER THEY WANT TO EXPRESS IT, IT'S JUST THIS WAY TO CELEBRATE THAT LOVE.
THEY WANT TO FEEL WHAT IT'S LIKE TO LIVE IN THE SKIN OF THEIR FAVORITE CHARACTER.
THEY WANT TO REPRESENT THEM IN THE REAL WORLD.
SOMETIMES, UGH, SOMETIMES IT'S A CHARACTER THAT I HAD SOMETHING TO DO WITH...AND IT JUST KILLS ME.
I'M TELLING YOU--WHEN YOU'RE THERE, IT IS SO BEAUTIFUL.
WELL, ON THE NEWS, IT LOOKED LIKE A BUNCH OF CRAZY PEOPLE WITH NO JOBS.
WHAT DO YOU DO, MICHELLE?

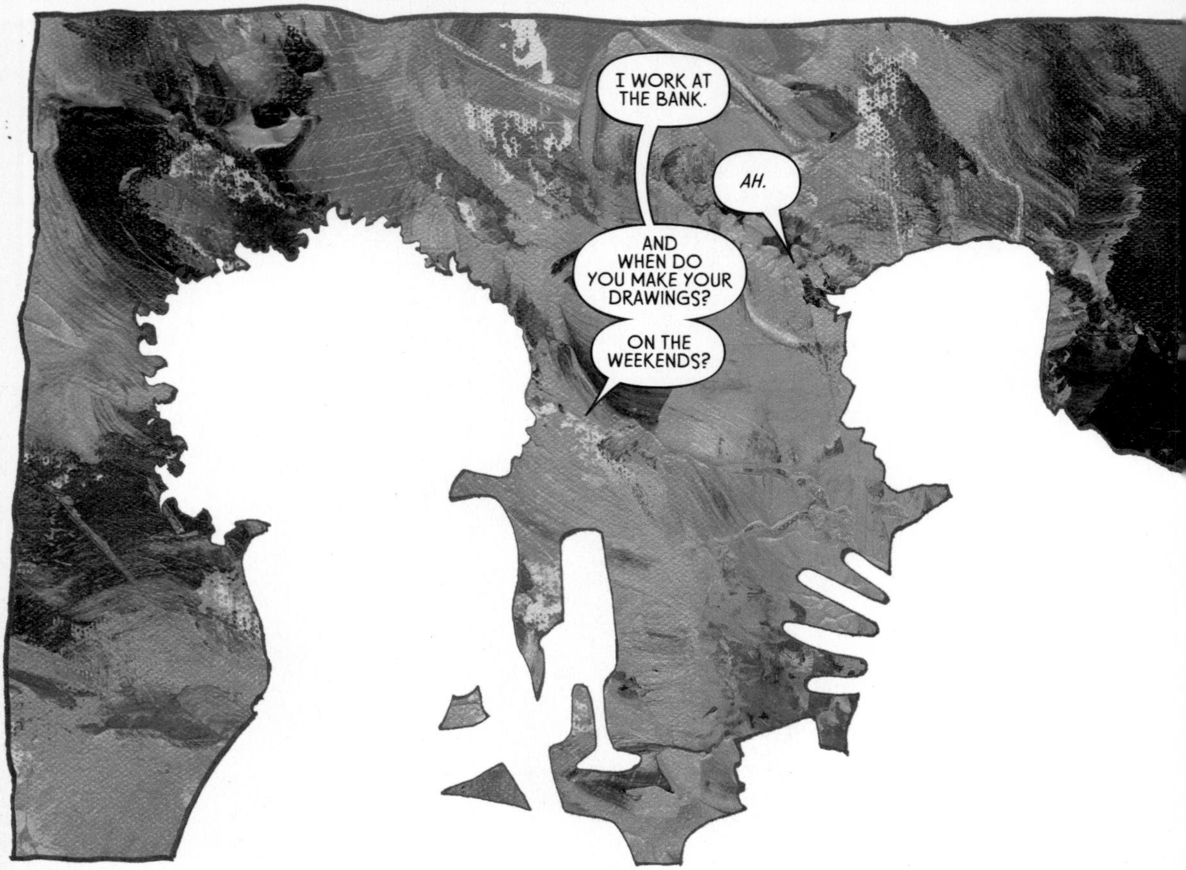
I WORK AT THE BANK.
AH.
AND WHEN DO YOU MAKE YOUR DRAWINGS?
ON THE WEEKENDS?

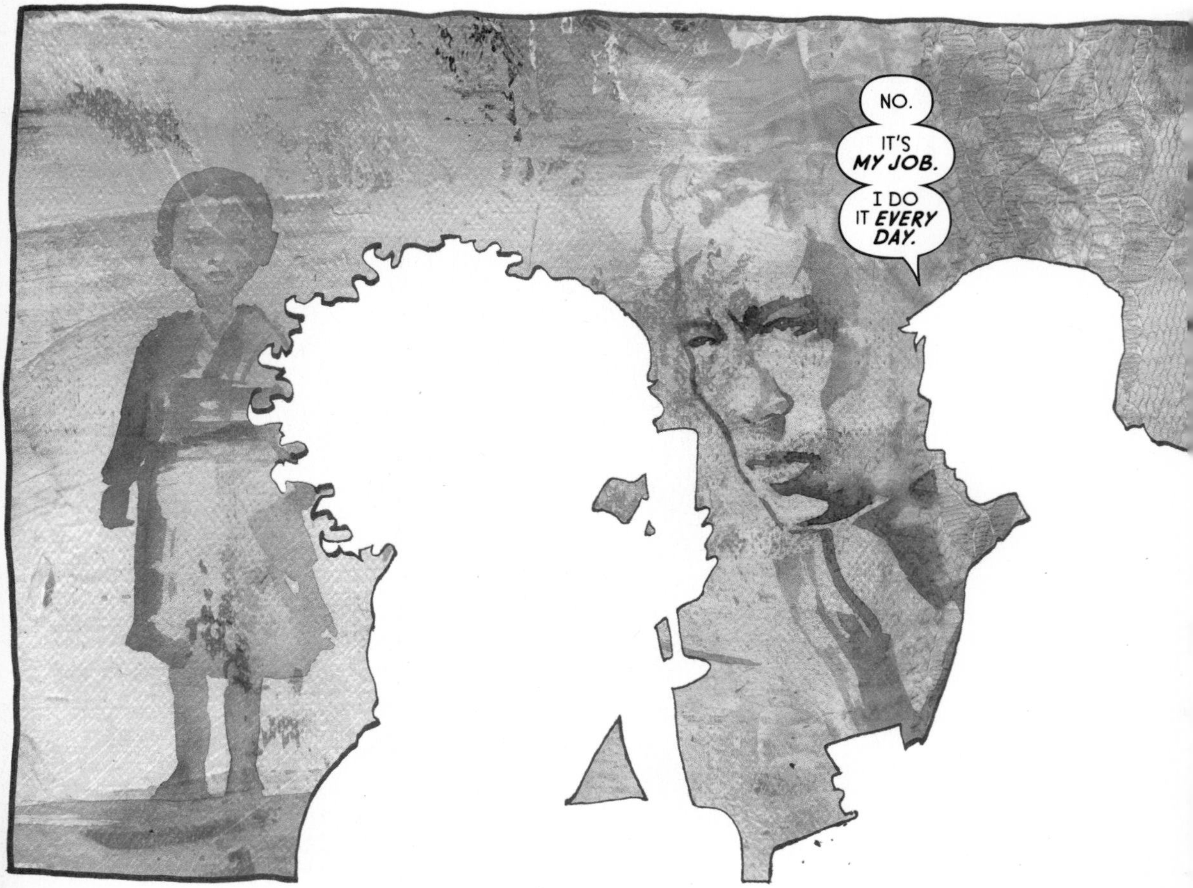
NO.
IT'S *MY JOB.*
I DO IT *EVERY DAY.*

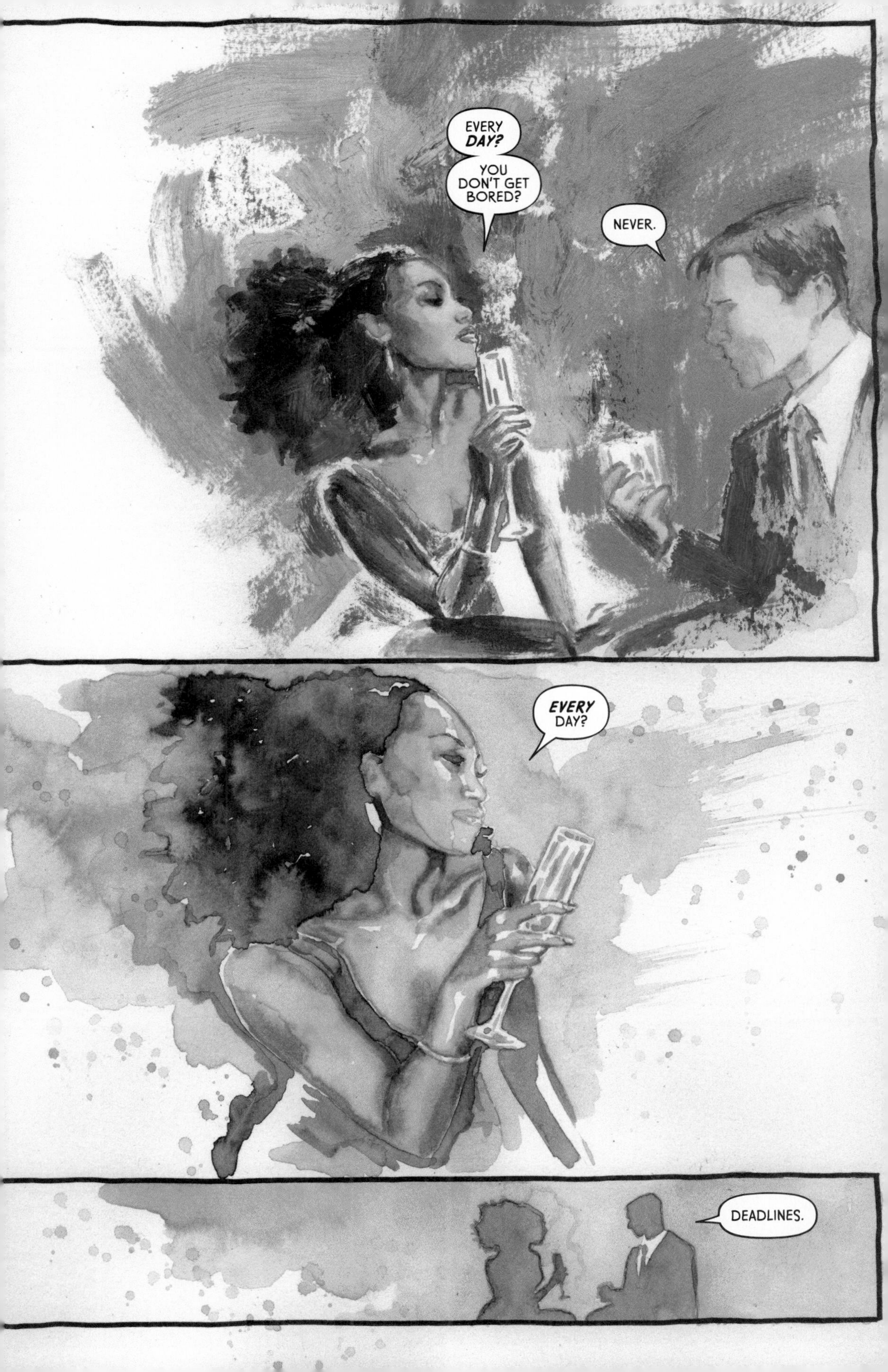
EVERY DAY?
YOU DON'T GET BORED?
NEVER.
EVERY DAY?
DEADLINES.

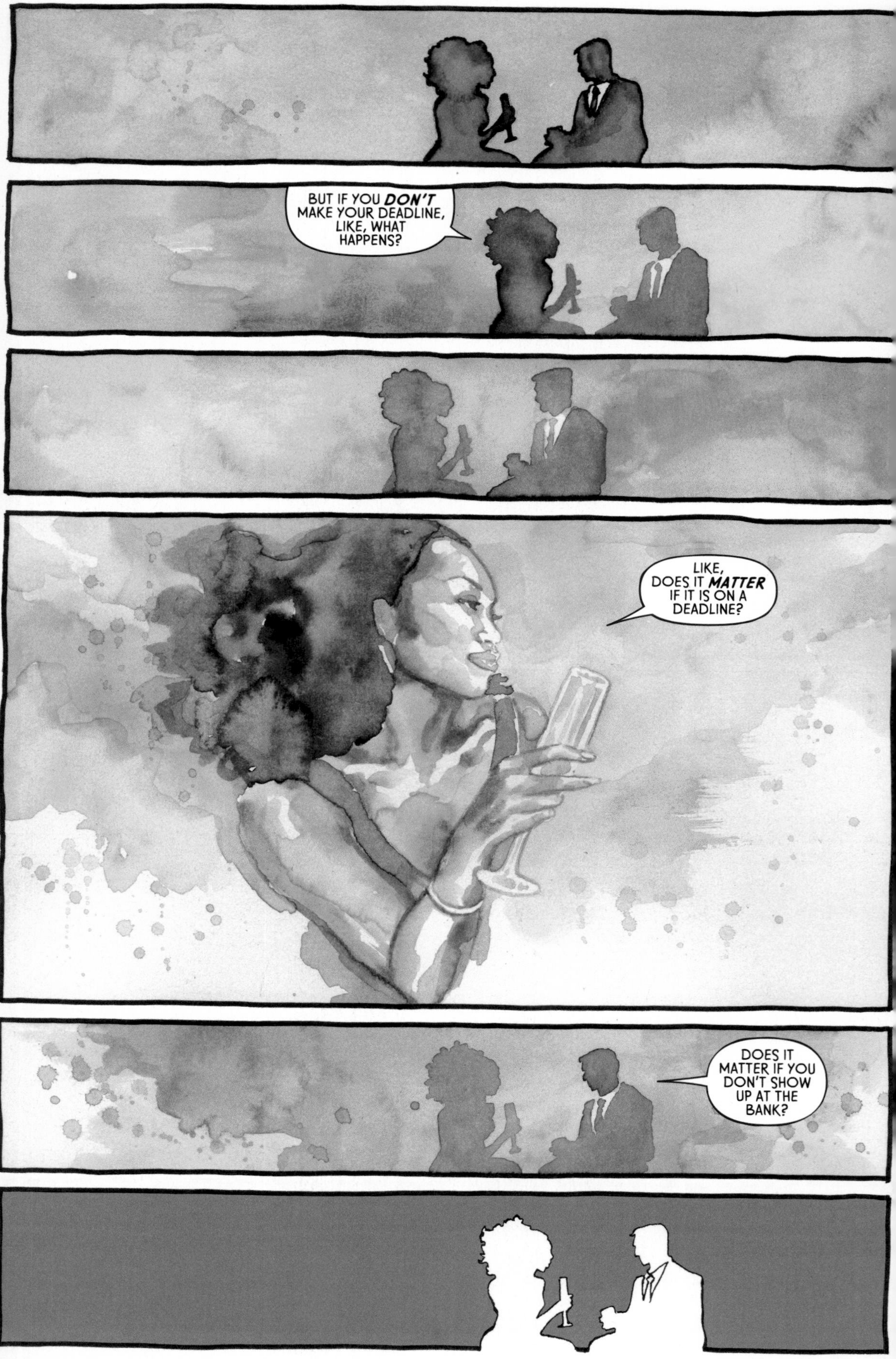
BUT IF YOU *DON'T* MAKE YOUR DEADLINE, LIKE, WHAT HAPPENS?
LIKE, DOES IT *MATTER* IF IT IS ON A DEADLINE?
DOES IT MATTER IF YOU DON'T SHOW UP AT THE BANK?

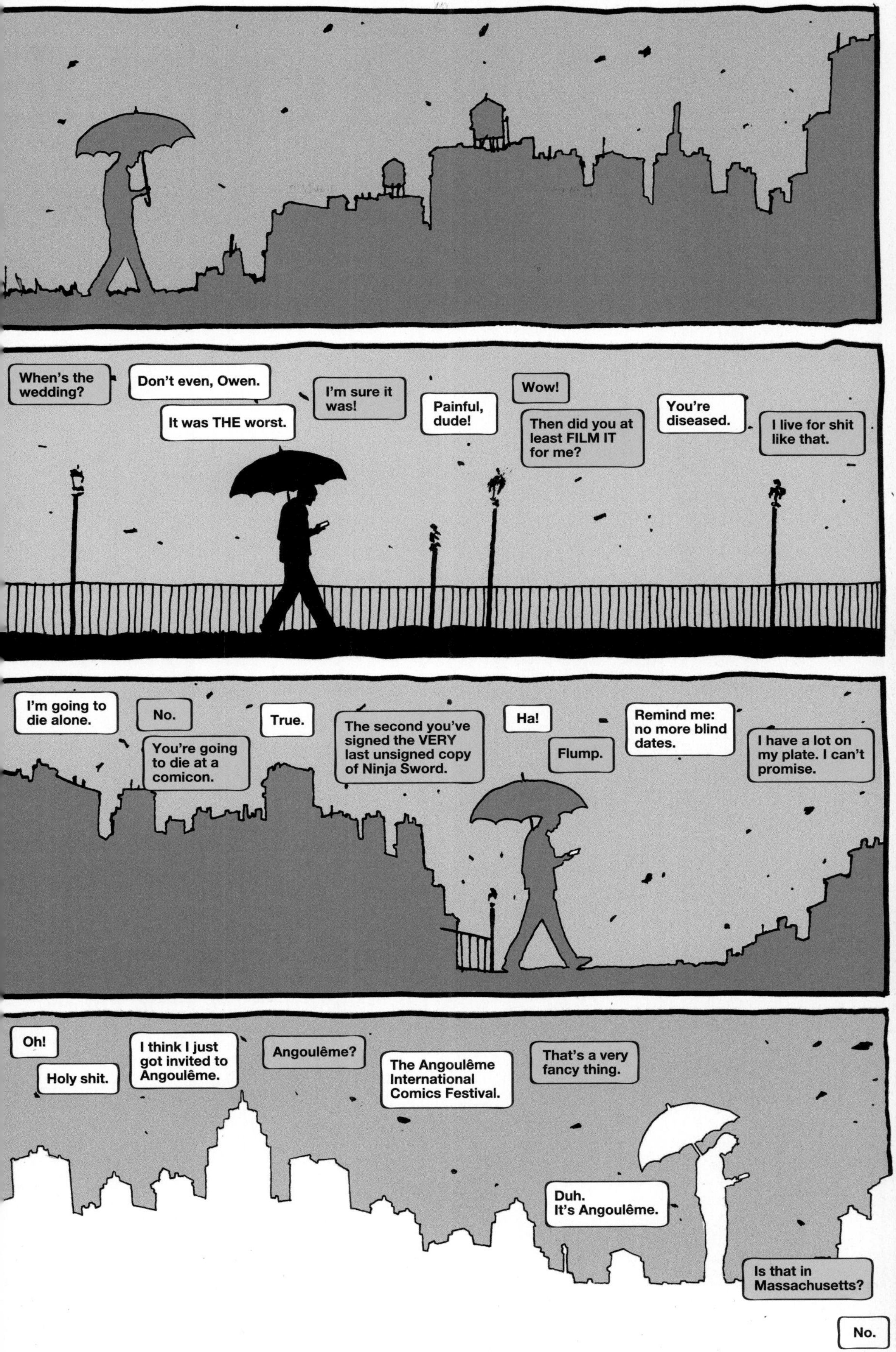
When's the wedding?
Don't even, Owen.
It was THE worst.
I'm sure it was!
Painful, dude!
Wow!
Then did you at least FILM IT for me?
You're diseased.
I live for shit like that.
I'm going to die alone.
No.
You're going to die at a comicon.
True.
The second you've signed the VERY last unsigned copy of Ninja Sword.
Ha!
Flump.
Remind me: no more blind dates.
I have a lot on my plate. I can't promise.
Oh!
Holy shit.
I think I just got invited to Angoulême.
Angoulême?
The Angoulême International Comics Festival.
That's a very fancy thing.
Duh. It's Angoulême.
Is that in Massachusetts?
No.

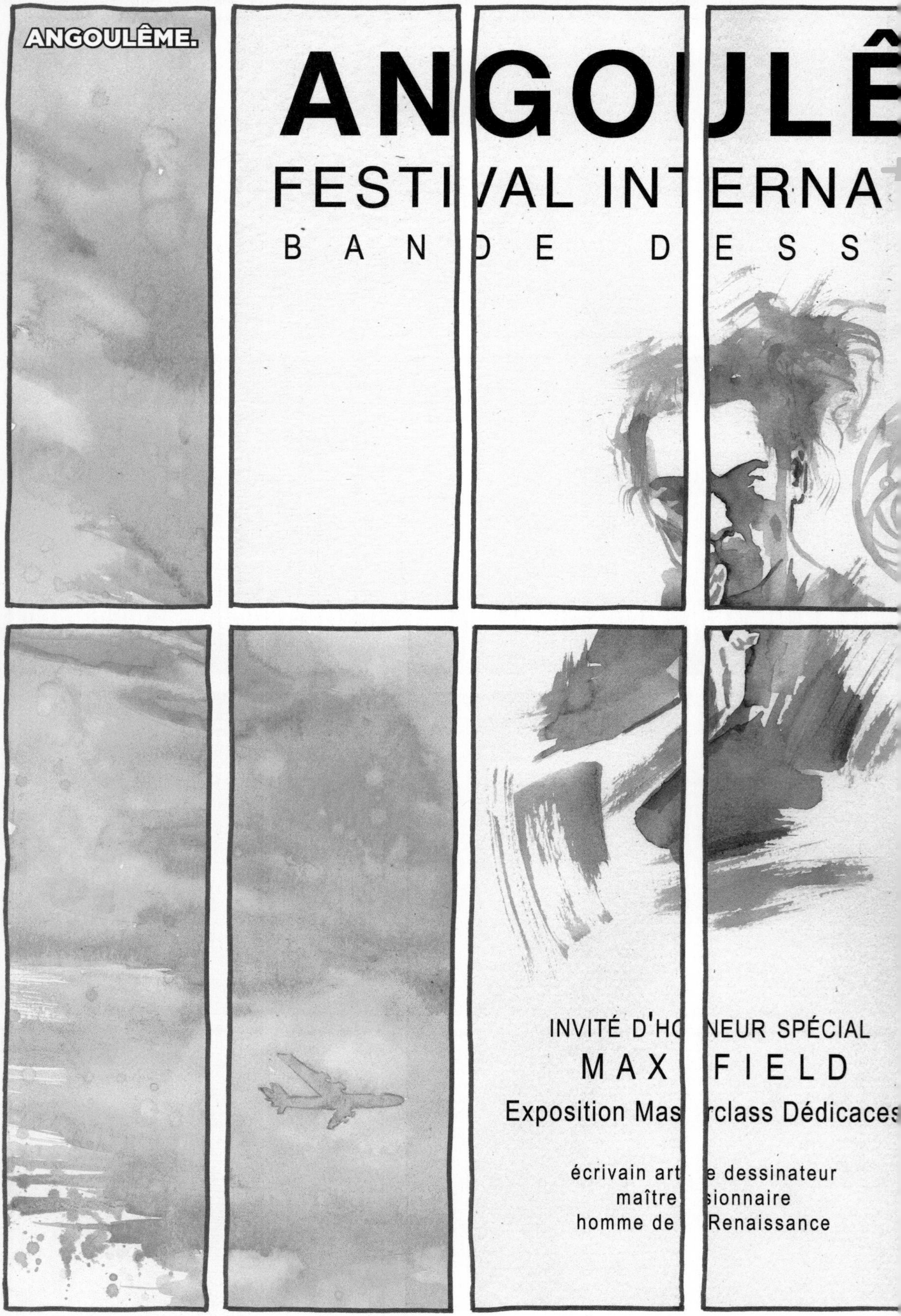
ANGOULÊME.
ANGOULÊ
FESTIVAL INTERNA
B A N D E D E S S
INVITÉ D'HO NEUR SPÉCIAL
M A X FIELD
Exposition Mas rclass Dédicaces
écrivain art e dessinateur
maître sionnaire
homme de Renaissance

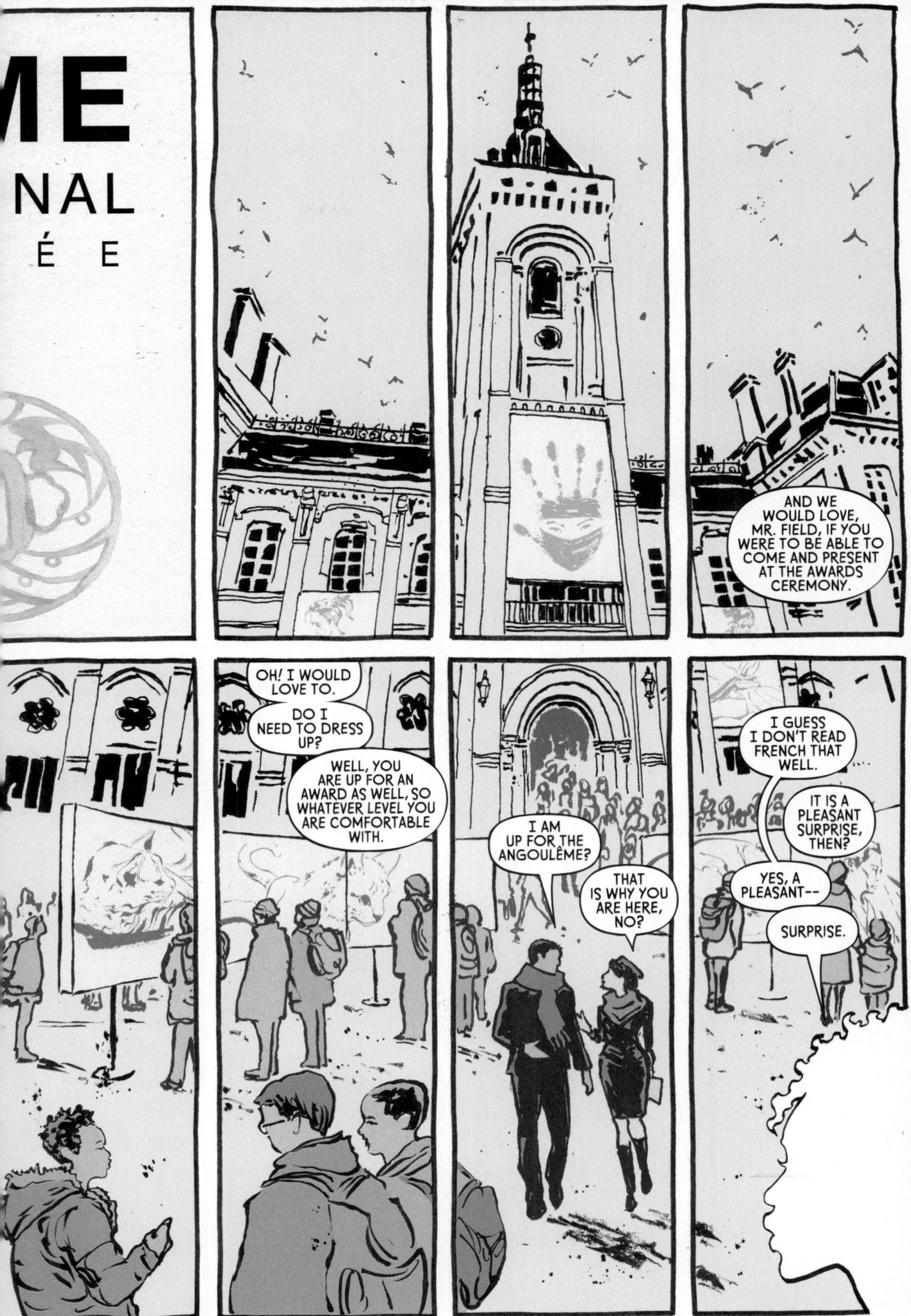
ME
NAL
É E
AND WE WOULD LOVE, MR. FIELD, IF YOU WERE TO BE ABLE TO COME AND PRESENT AT THE AWARDS CEREMONY.
OH! I WOULD LOVE TO.
DO I NEED TO DRESS UP?
WELL, YOU ARE UP FOR AN AWARD AS WELL, SO WHATEVER LEVEL YOU ARE COMFORTABLE WITH.
I AM UP FOR THE ANGOULÊME?
THAT IS WHY YOU ARE HERE, NO?
I GUESS I DON'T READ FRENCH THAT WELL.
IT IS A PLEASANT SURPRISE, THEN?
YES, A PLEASANT--
SURPRISE.

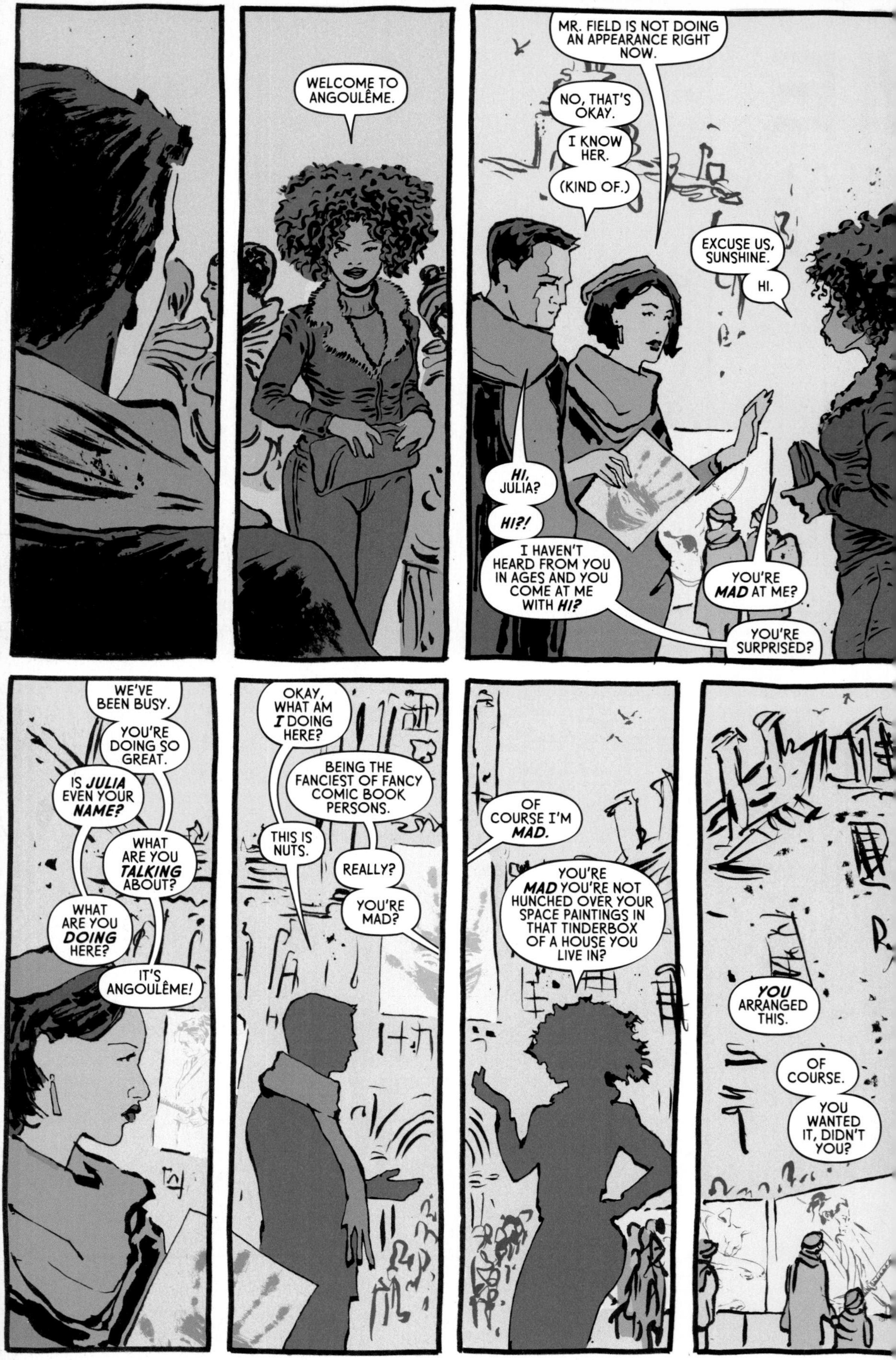
WELCOME TO ANGOULÊME.
MR. FIELD IS NOT DOING AN APPEARANCE RIGHT NOW.
NO, THAT'S OKAY.
I KNOW HER.
(KIND OF.)
EXCUSE US, SUNSHINE.
HI.
HI, JULIA?
HI?!
I HAVEN'T HEARD FROM YOU IN AGES AND YOU COME AT ME WITH HI?
YOU'RE MAD AT ME?
YOU'RE SURPRISED?
WE'VE BEEN BUSY.
YOU'RE DOING SO GREAT.
IS JULIA EVEN YOUR NAME?
WHAT ARE YOU TALKING ABOUT?
WHAT ARE YOU DOING HERE?
IT'S ANGOULÊME!
OKAY, WHAT AM I DOING HERE?
BEING THE FANCIEST OF FANCY COMIC BOOK PERSONS.
THIS IS NUTS.
REALLY?
YOU'RE MAD?
OF COURSE I'M MAD.
YOU'RE MAD YOU'RE NOT HUNCHED OVER YOUR SPACE PAINTINGS IN THAT TINDERBOX OF A HOUSE YOU LIVE IN?
YOU ARRANGED THIS.
OF COURSE.
YOU WANTED IT, DIDN'T YOU?

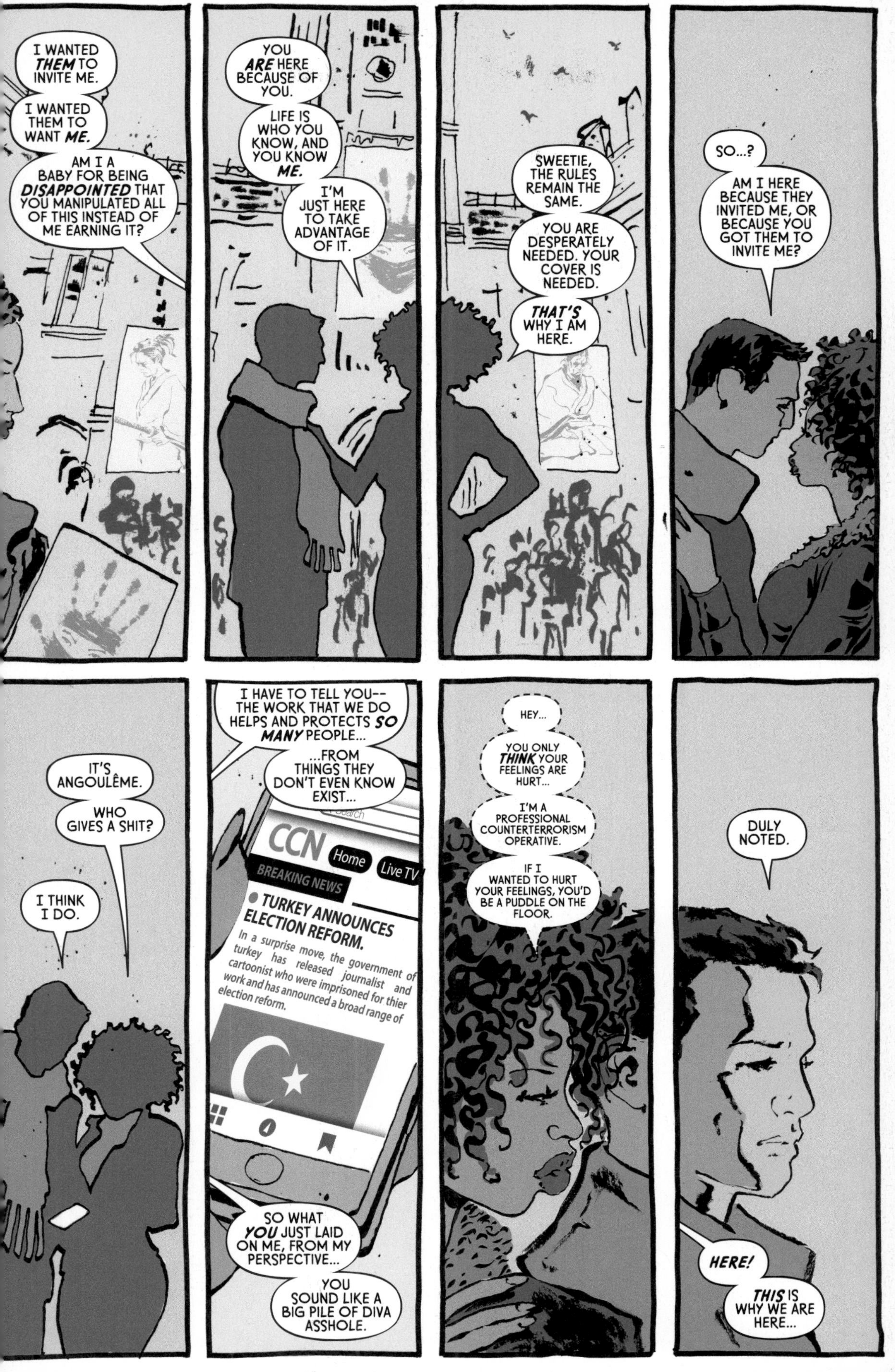
I WANTED *THEM* TO INVITE ME.
I WANTED THEM TO WANT *ME.*
AM I A BABY FOR BEING *DISAPPOINTED* THAT YOU MANIPULATED ALL OF THIS INSTEAD OF ME EARNING IT?
YOU *ARE* HERE BECAUSE OF YOU.
LIFE IS WHO YOU KNOW, AND YOU KNOW *ME.*
I'M JUST HERE TO TAKE ADVANTAGE OF IT.
SWEETIE, THE RULES REMAIN THE SAME.
YOU ARE DESPERATELY NEEDED. YOUR COVER IS NEEDED.
THAT'S WHY I AM HERE.
SO...?
AM I HERE BECAUSE THEY INVITED ME, OR BECAUSE YOU GOT THEM TO INVITE ME?
IT'S ANGOULÊME.
WHO GIVES A SHIT?
I THINK I DO.
I HAVE TO TELL YOU-- THE WORK THAT WE DO HELPS AND PROTECTS *SO MANY* PEOPLE...
...FROM THINGS THEY DON'T EVEN KNOW EXIST...
CCN
Home
Live TV
BREAKING NEWS
TURKEY ANNOUNCES ELECTION REFORM.
In a surprise move, the government of turkey has released journalist and cartoonist who were imprisoned for thier work and has announced a broad range of election reform.
SO WHAT *YOU* JUST LAID ON ME, FROM MY PERSPECTIVE...
YOU SOUND LIKE A BIG PILE OF DIVA ASSHOLE.
HEY...
YOU ONLY *THINK* YOUR FEELINGS ARE HURT...
I'M A PROFESSIONAL COUNTERTERRORISM OPERATIVE.
IF I WANTED TO HURT YOUR FEELINGS, YOU'D BE A PUDDLE ON THE FLOOR.
DULY NOTED.
HERE!
THIS IS WHY WE ARE HERE...

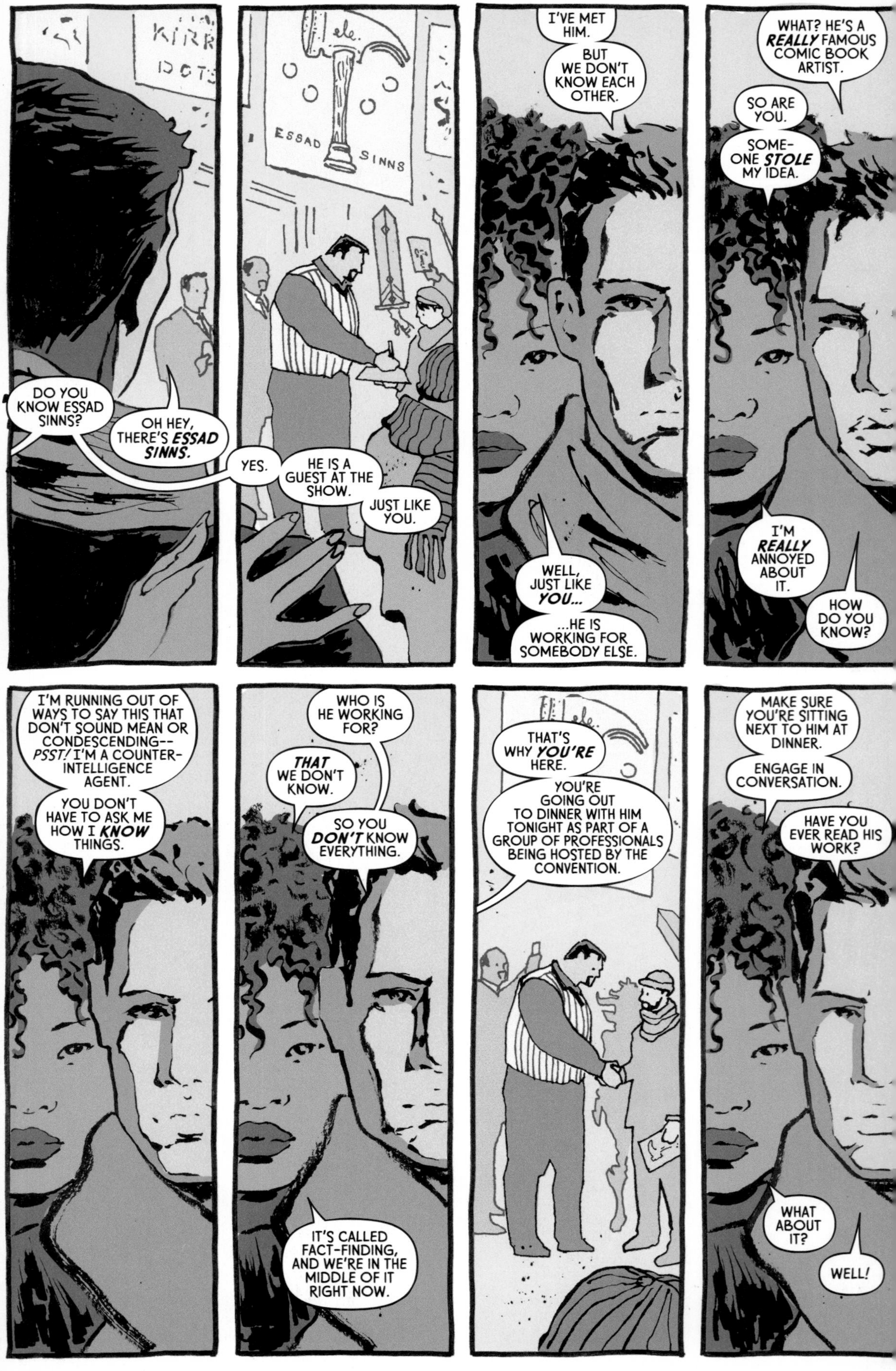
DO YOU KNOW ESSAD SINNS?
OH HEY, THERE'S ESSAD SINNS.
YES.
HE IS A GUEST AT THE SHOW.
JUST LIKE YOU.
I'VE MET HIM.
BUT WE DON'T KNOW EACH OTHER.
WELL, JUST LIKE YOU...
...HE IS WORKING FOR SOMEBODY ELSE.
WHAT? HE'S A REALLY FAMOUS COMIC BOOK ARTIST.
SO ARE YOU.
SOME-ONE STOLE MY IDEA.
I'M REALLY ANNOYED ABOUT IT.
HOW DO YOU KNOW?
I'M RUNNING OUT OF WAYS TO SAY THIS THAT DON'T SOUND MEAN OR CONDESCENDING-- PSST! I'M A COUNTER-INTELLIGENCE AGENT.
YOU DON'T HAVE TO ASK ME HOW I KNOW THINGS.
WHO IS HE WORKING FOR?
THAT WE DON'T KNOW.
SO YOU DON'T KNOW EVERYTHING.
IT'S CALLED FACT-FINDING, AND WE'RE IN THE MIDDLE OF IT RIGHT NOW.
THAT'S WHY YOU'RE HERE.
YOU'RE GOING OUT TO DINNER WITH HIM TONIGHT AS PART OF A GROUP OF PROFESSIONALS BEING HOSTED BY THE CONVENTION.
MAKE SURE YOU'RE SITTING NEXT TO HIM AT DINNER.
ENGAGE IN CONVERSATION.
HAVE YOU EVER READ HIS WORK?
WHAT ABOUT IT?
WELL!

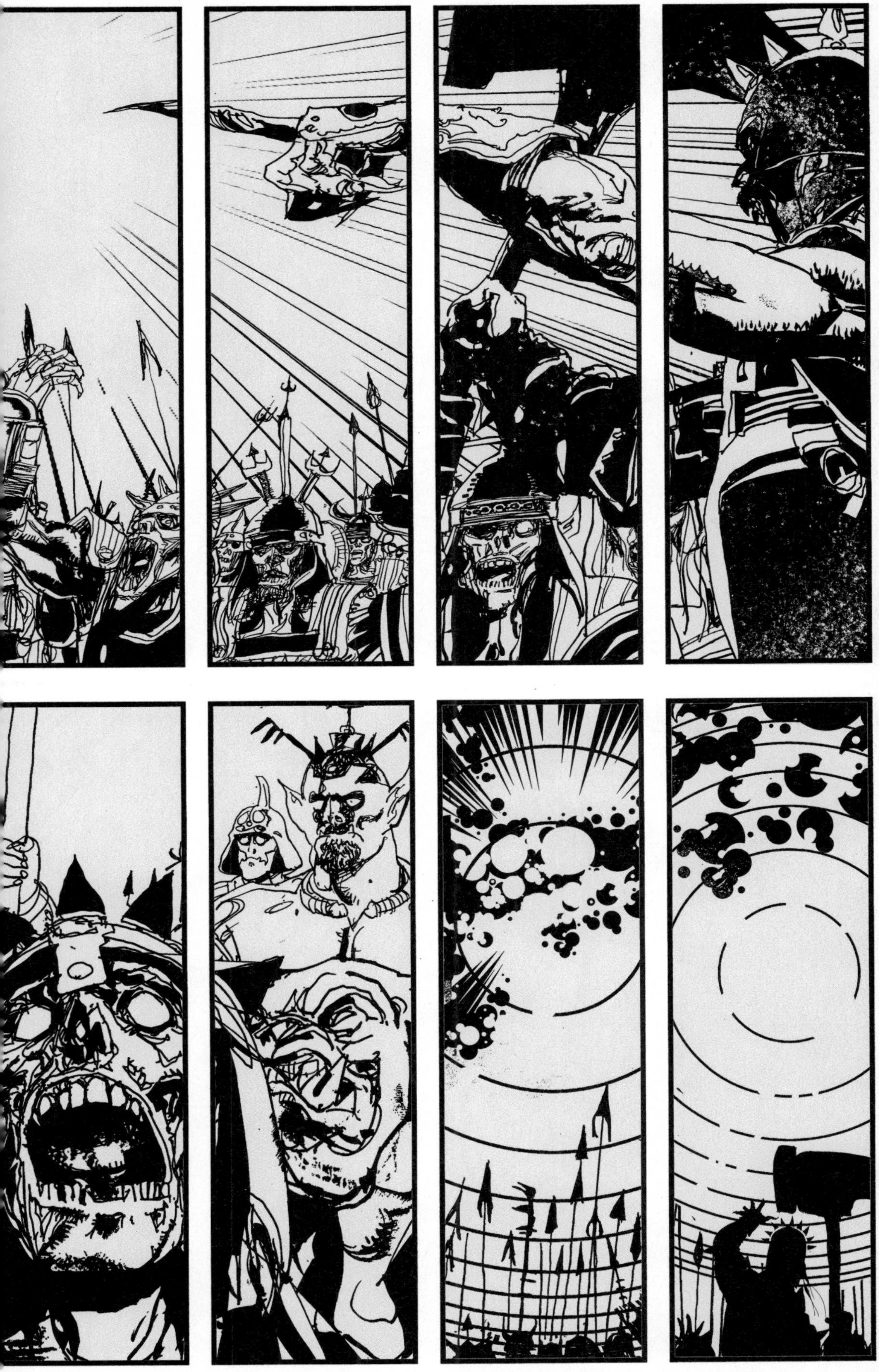

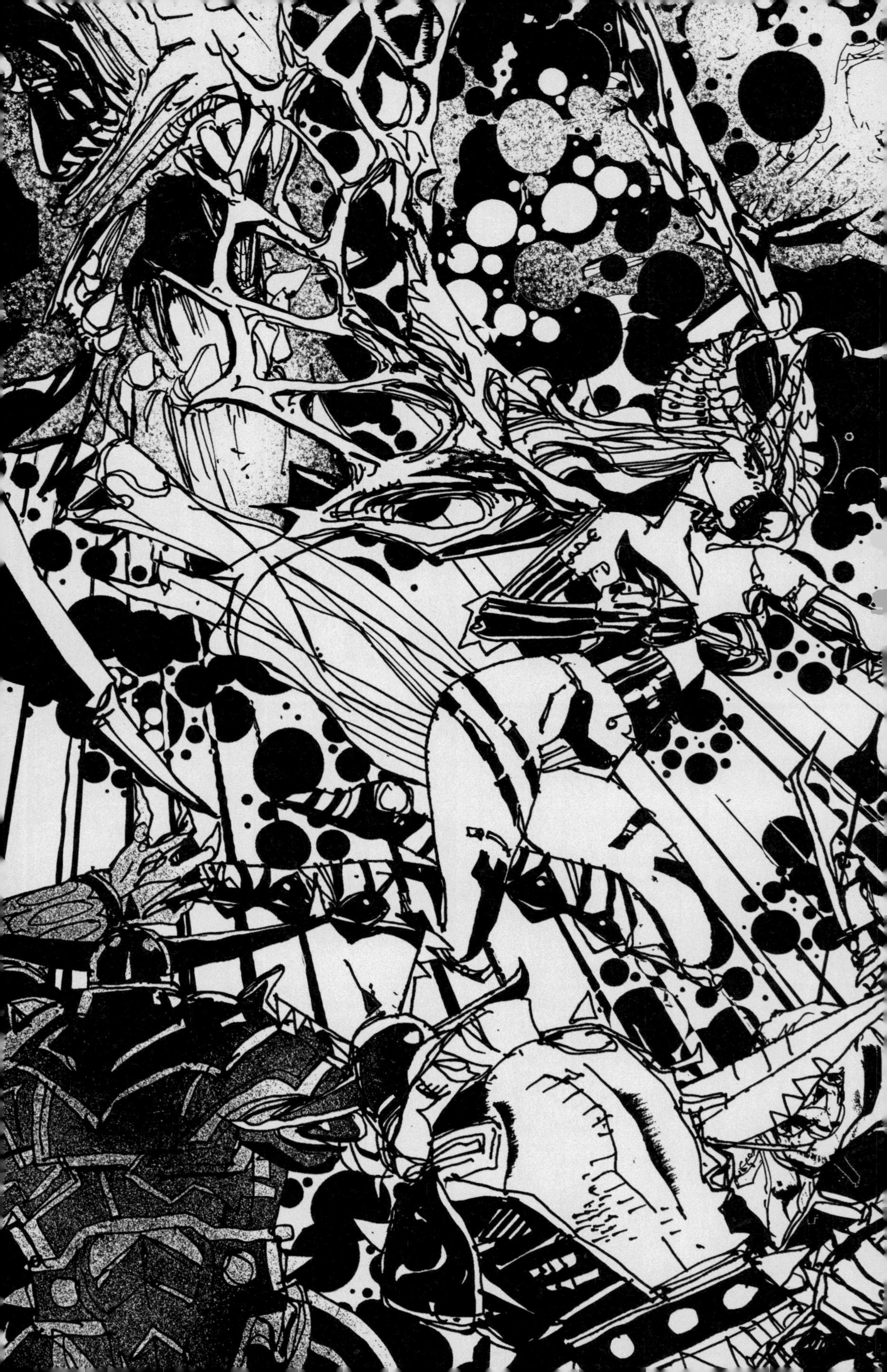

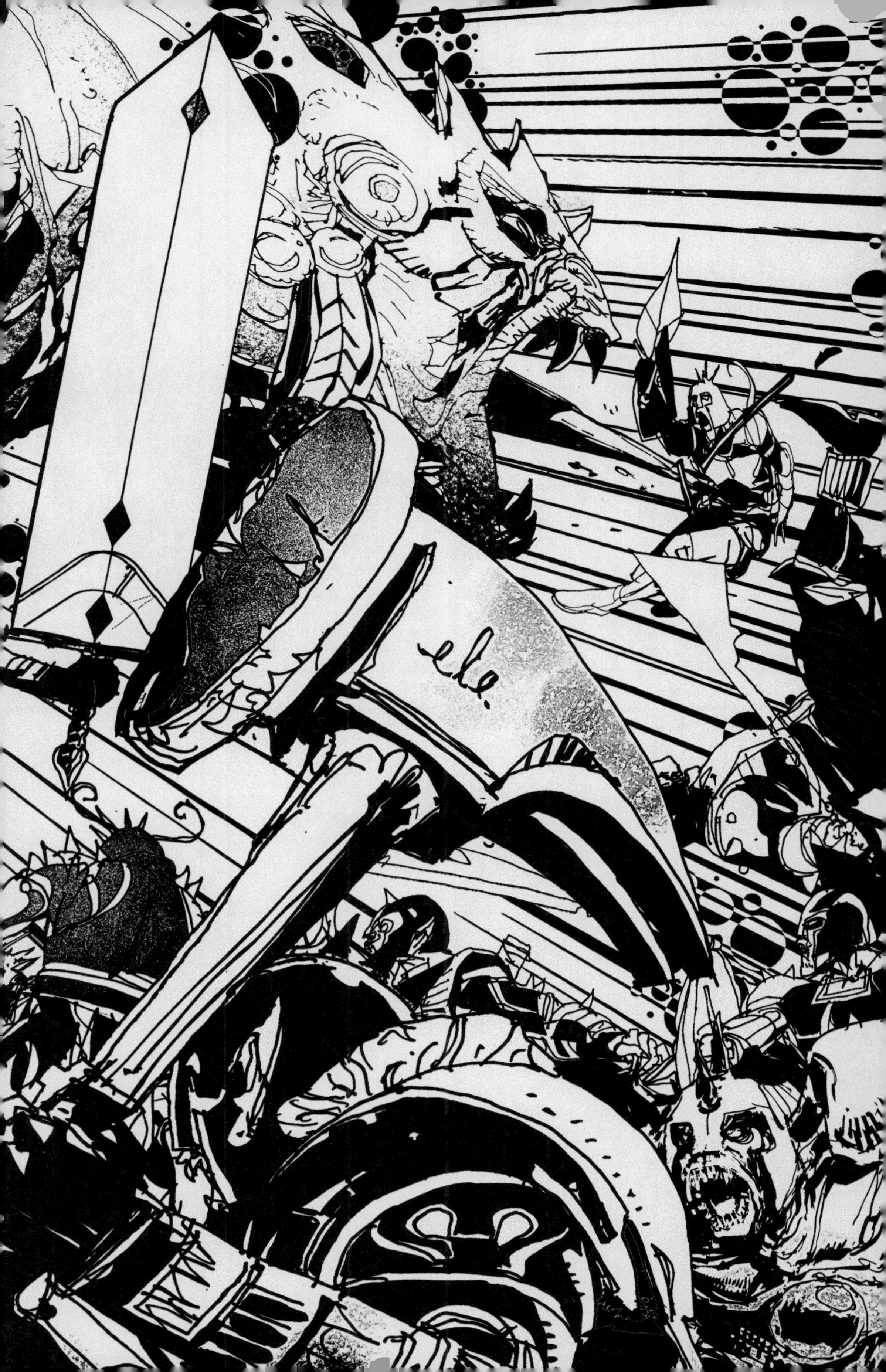

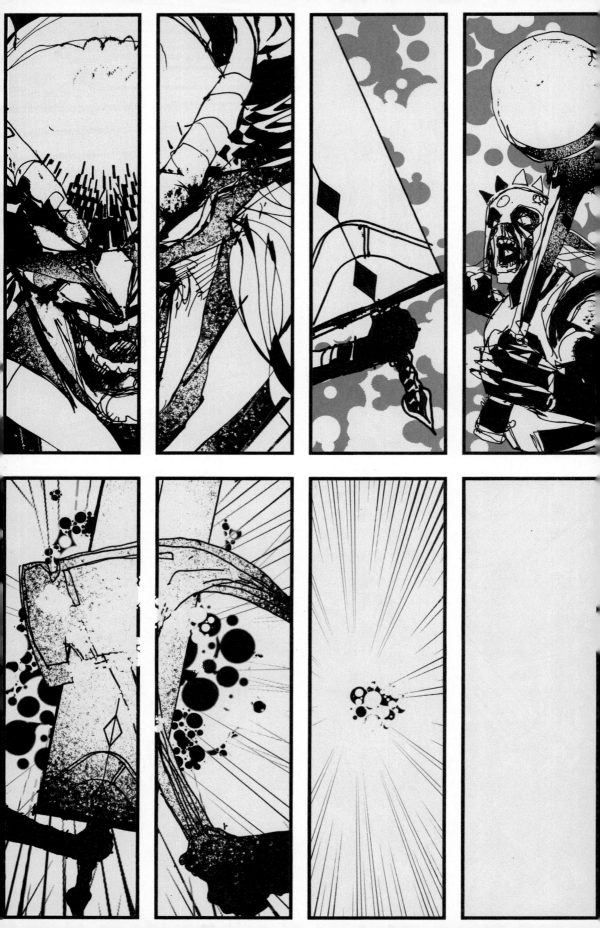

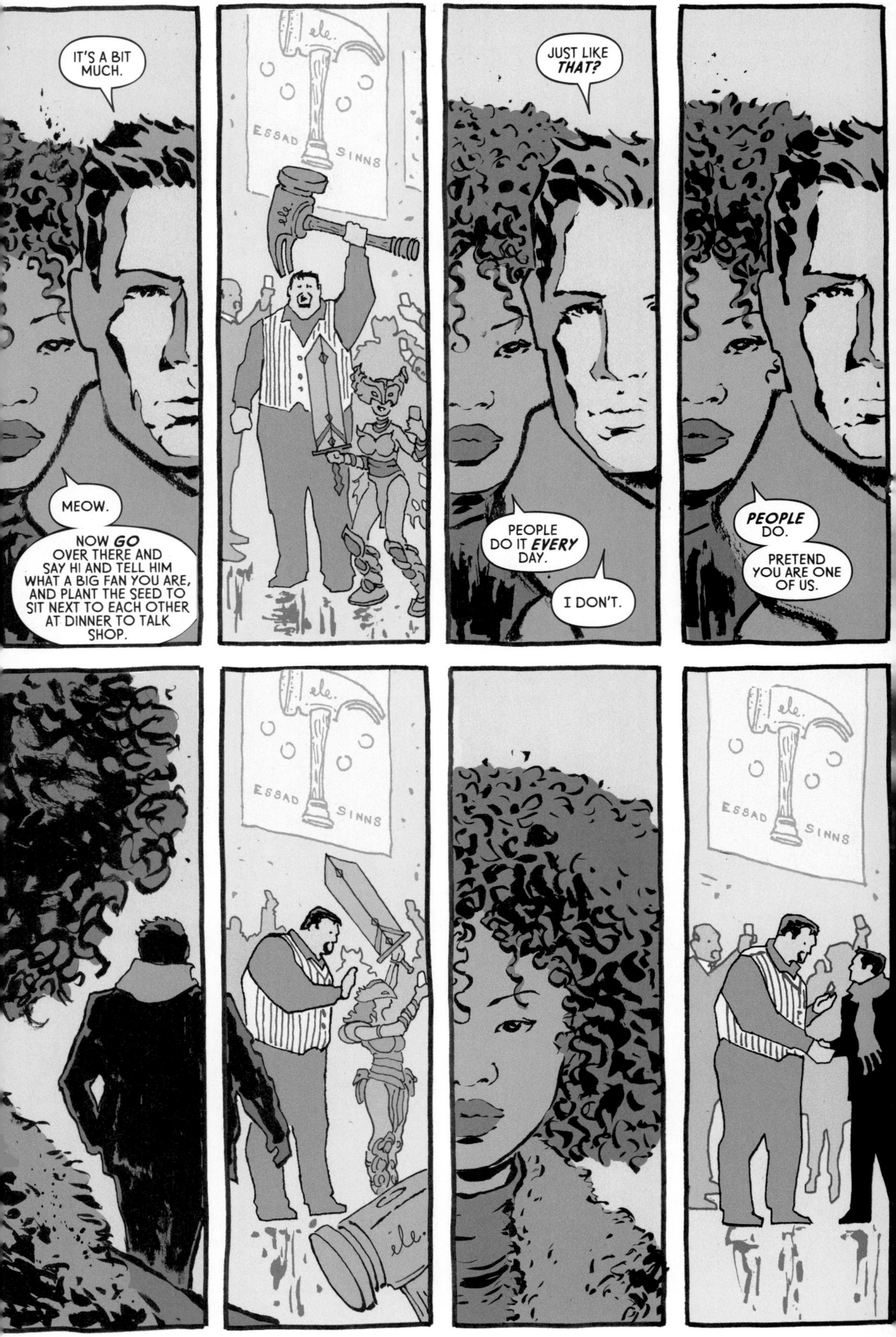
IT'S A BIT MUCH.
MEOW.
NOW GO OVER THERE AND SAY HI AND TELL HIM WHAT A BIG FAN YOU ARE, AND PLANT THE SEED TO SIT NEXT TO EACH OTHER AT DINNER TO TALK SHOP.
ele.
ESSAD SINNS
JUST LIKE THAT?
PEOPLE DO IT EVERY DAY.
I DON'T.
PEOPLE DO.
PRETEND YOU ARE ONE OF US.
ESSAD SINNS
ESSAD SINNS

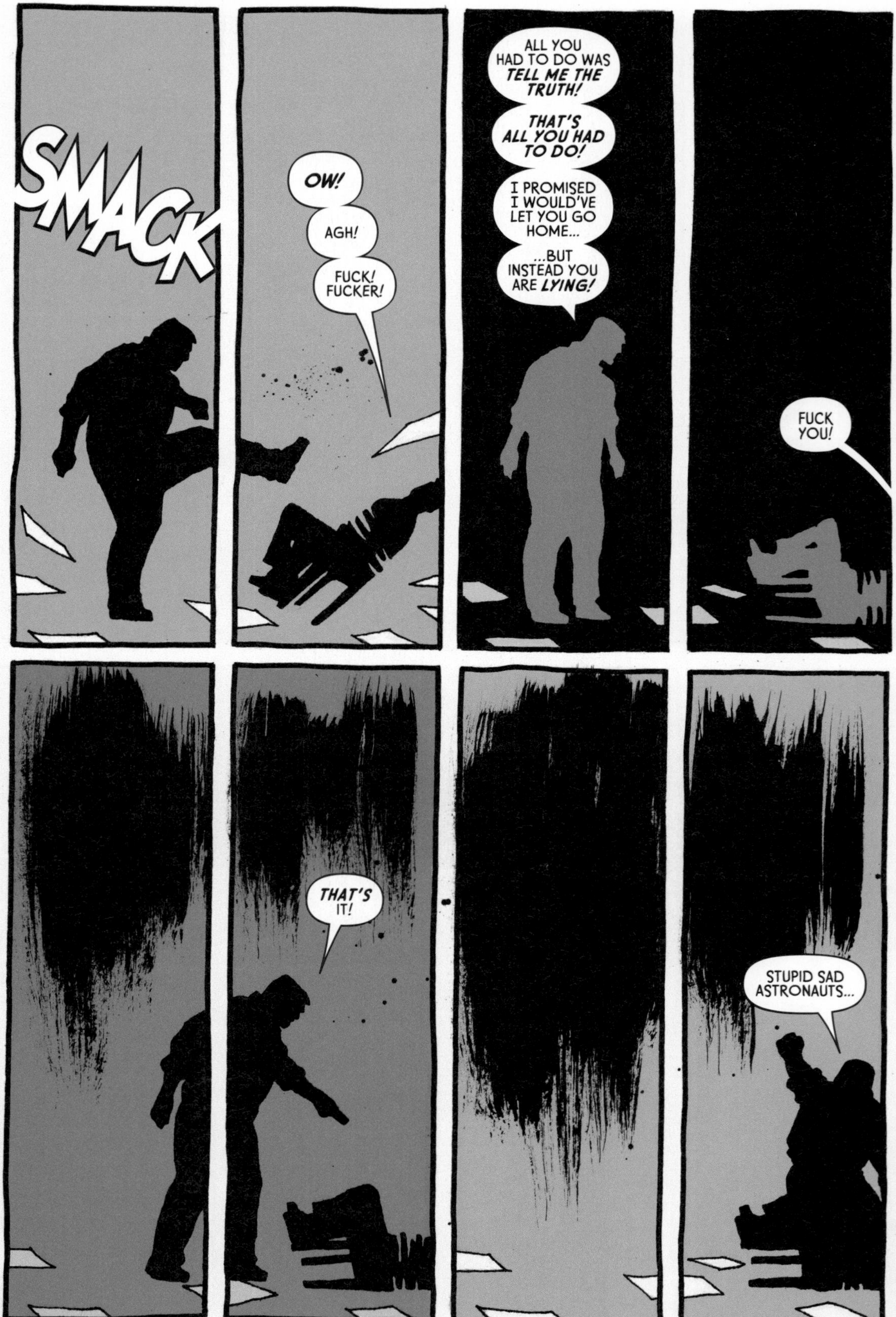
SMACK
OW!
AGH!
FUCK! FUCKER!
ALL YOU HAD TO DO WAS TELL ME THE TRUTH!
THAT'S ALL YOU HAD TO DO!
I PROMISED I WOULD'VE LET YOU GO HOME...
...BUT INSTEAD YOU ARE LYING!
FUCK YOU!
THAT'S IT!
STUPID SAD ASTRONAUTS...

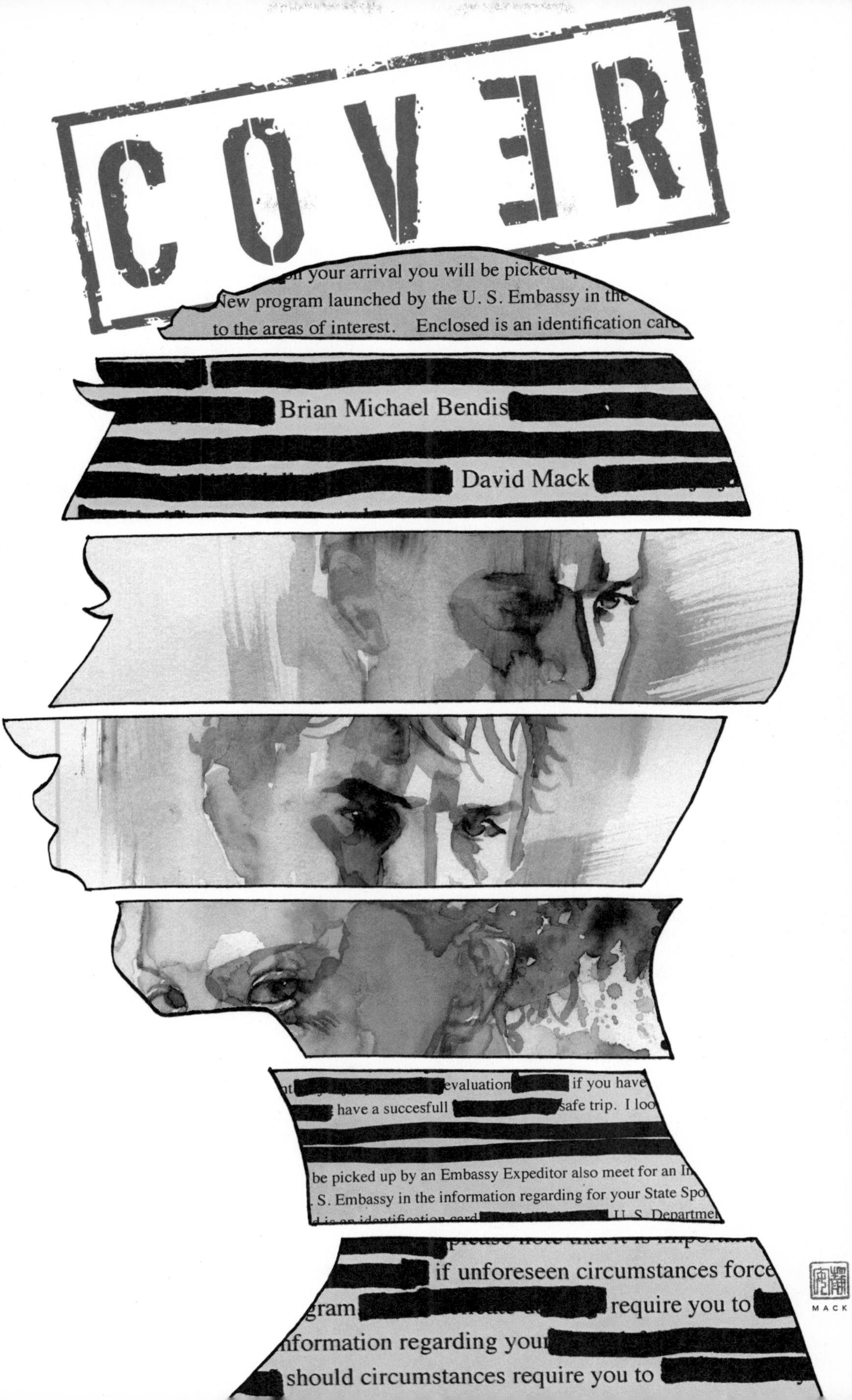
COVER
your arrival you will be picked
New program launched by the U. S. Embassy in the
to the areas of interest. Enclosed is an identification
[redacted] Brian Michael Bendis [redacted]
[redacted] David Mack [redacted]
[redacted] evaluation [redacted] if you have
[redacted] have a succesfull [redacted] safe trip.
[redacted]
be picked up by an Embassy Expeditor also meet for an
S. Embassy in the information regarding for your State
[redacted] U. S.
[redacted] if unforeseen circumstances force
gram [redacted] require you to [redacted]
regarding your [redacted]
[redacted] should circumstances require you to [redacted]
MACK

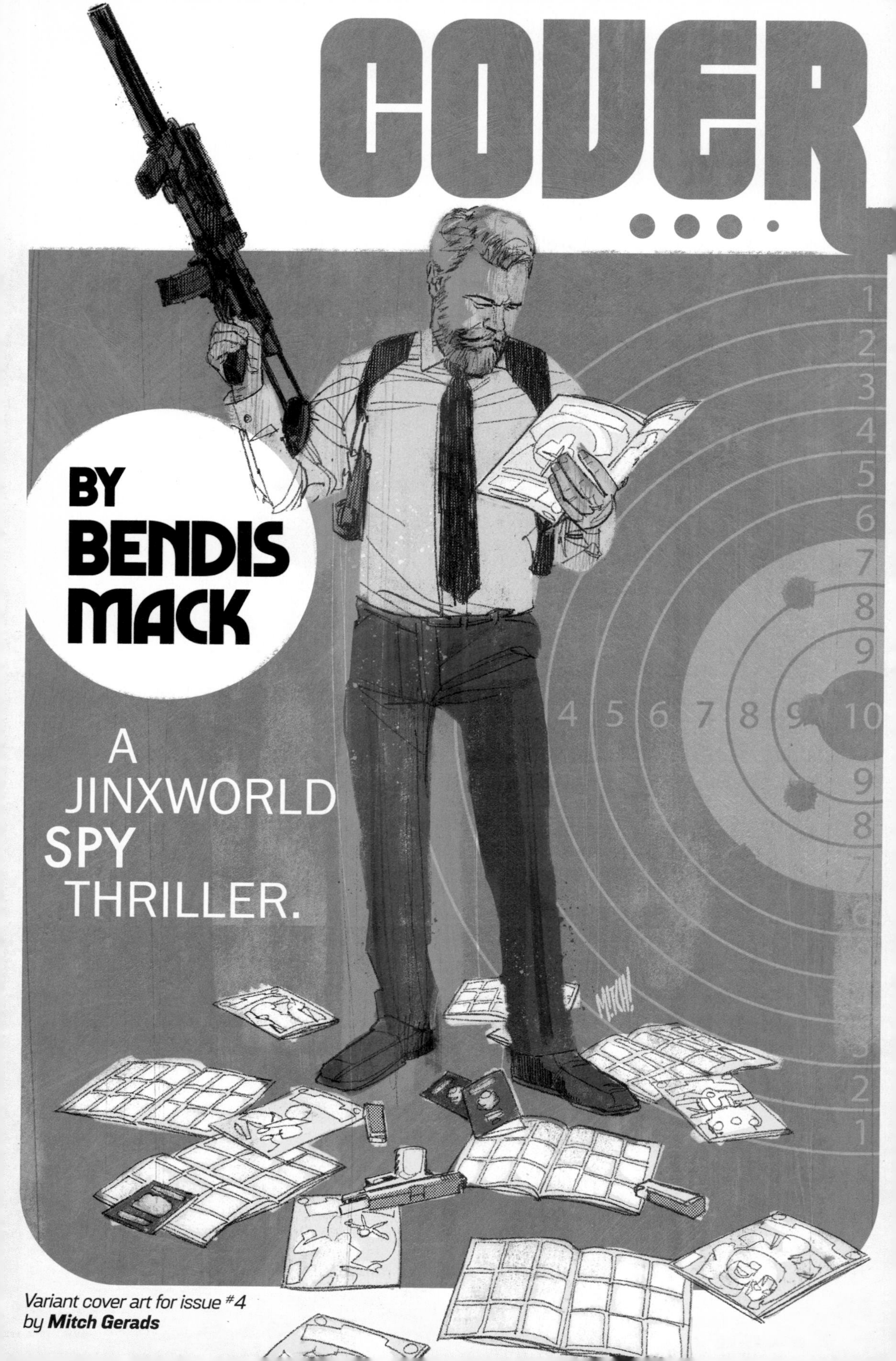
COVER
BY
BENDIS
MACK
A
JINXWORLD
SPY
THRILLER.

Variant cover art for issue #4
by ***Mitch Gerads***

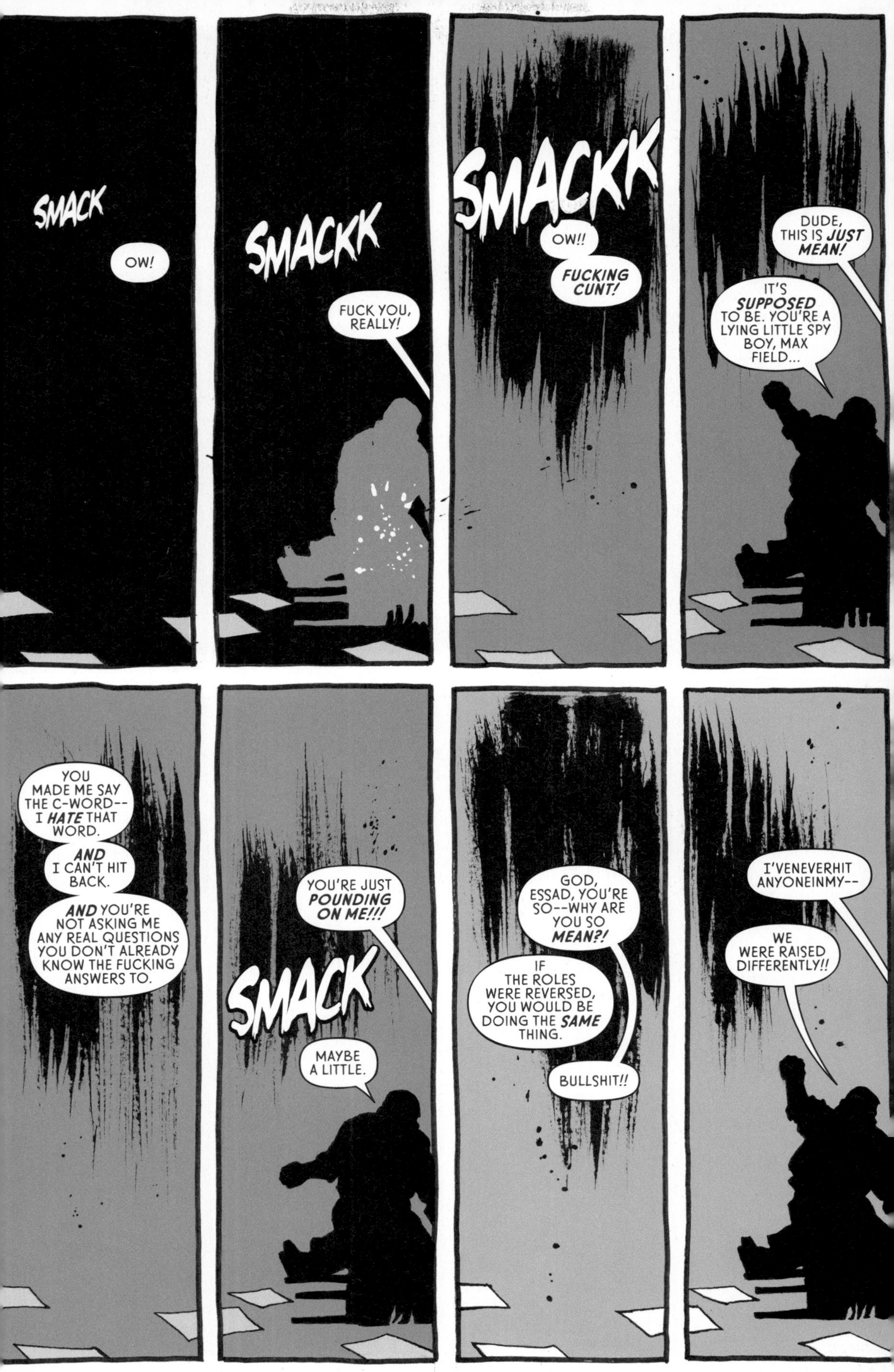
SMACK
OW!
SMACKK
FUCK YOU, REALLY!
SMACKK
OW!!
FUCKING CUNT!
DUDE, THIS IS JUST MEAN!
IT'S SUPPOSED TO BE. YOU'RE A LYING LITTLE SPY BOY, MAX FIELD...
YOU MADE ME SAY THE C-WORD-- I HATE THAT WORD.
AND I CAN'T HIT BACK.
AND YOU'RE NOT ASKING ME ANY REAL QUESTIONS YOU DON'T ALREADY KNOW THE FUCKING ANSWERS TO.
YOU'RE JUST POUNDING ON ME!!!
SMACK
MAYBE A LITTLE.
GOD, ESSAD, YOU'RE SO--WHY ARE YOU SO MEAN?!
IF THE ROLES WERE REVERSED, YOU WOULD BE DOING THE SAME THING.
BULLSHIT!!
I'VENEVERHIT ANYONEINMY--
WE WERE RAISED DIFFERENTLY!!

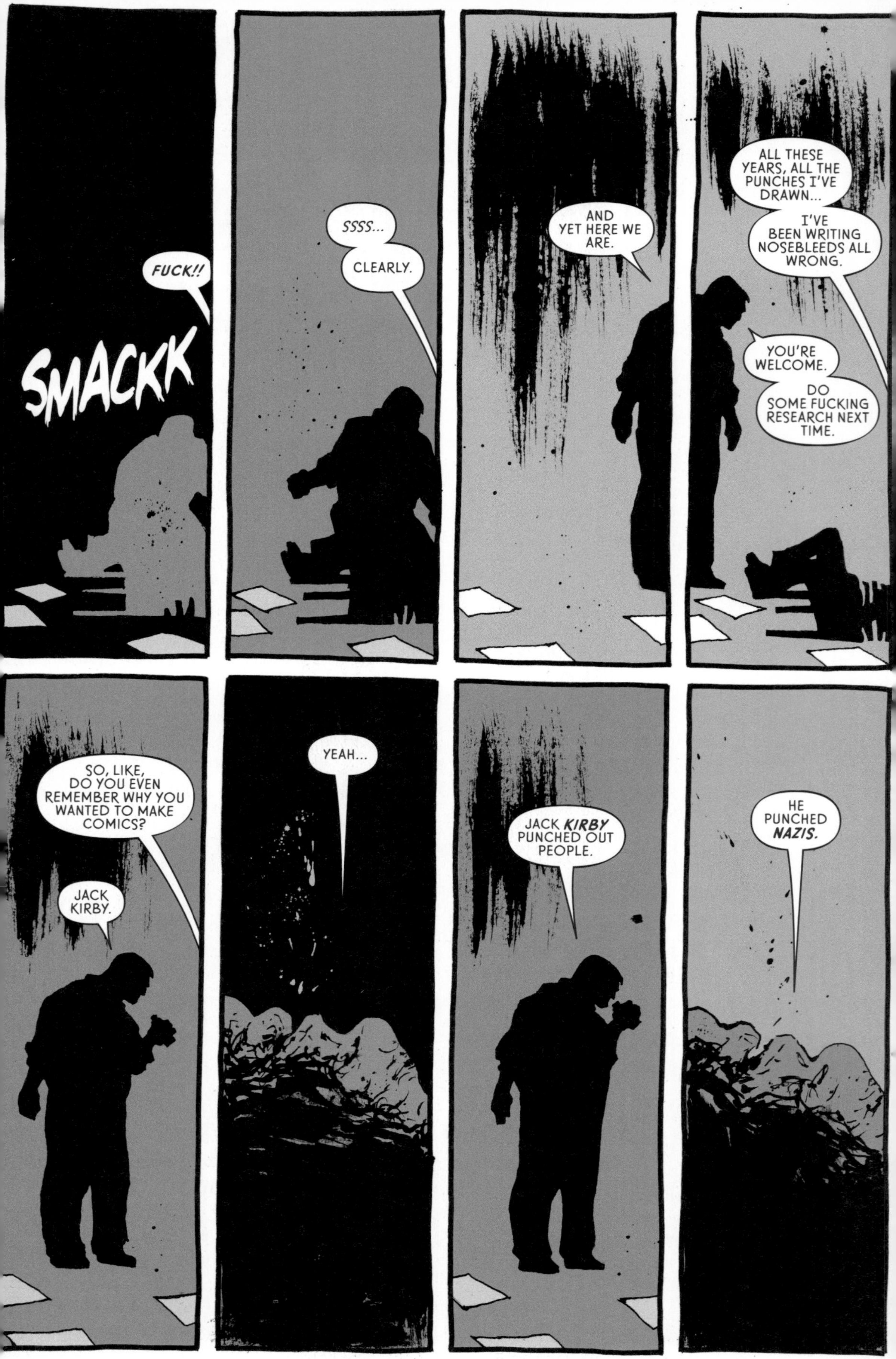
FUCK!!
SMACKK
SSSS...
CLEARLY.
AND YET HERE WE ARE.
ALL THESE YEARS, ALL THE PUNCHES I'VE DRAWN...
I'VE BEEN WRITING NOSEBLEEDS ALL WRONG.
YOU'RE WELCOME.
DO SOME FUCKING RESEARCH NEXT TIME.
SO, LIKE, DO YOU EVEN REMEMBER WHY YOU WANTED TO MAKE COMICS?
JACK KIRBY.
YEAH...
JACK KIRBY PUNCHED OUT PEOPLE.
HE PUNCHED NAZIS.

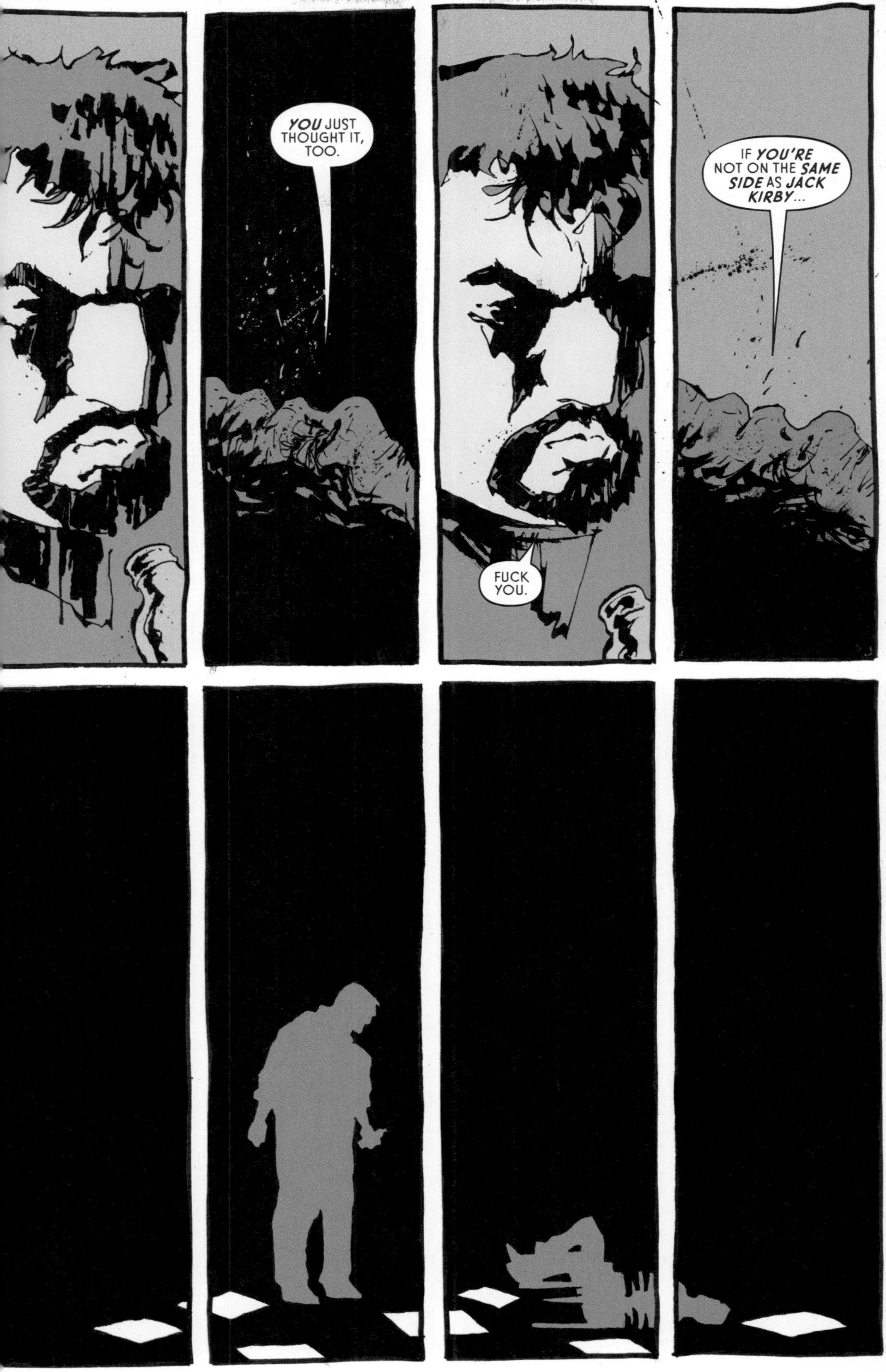
YOU JUST THOUGHT IT, TOO.
FUCK YOU.
IF YOU'RE NOT ON THE SAME SIDE AS JACK KIRBY...

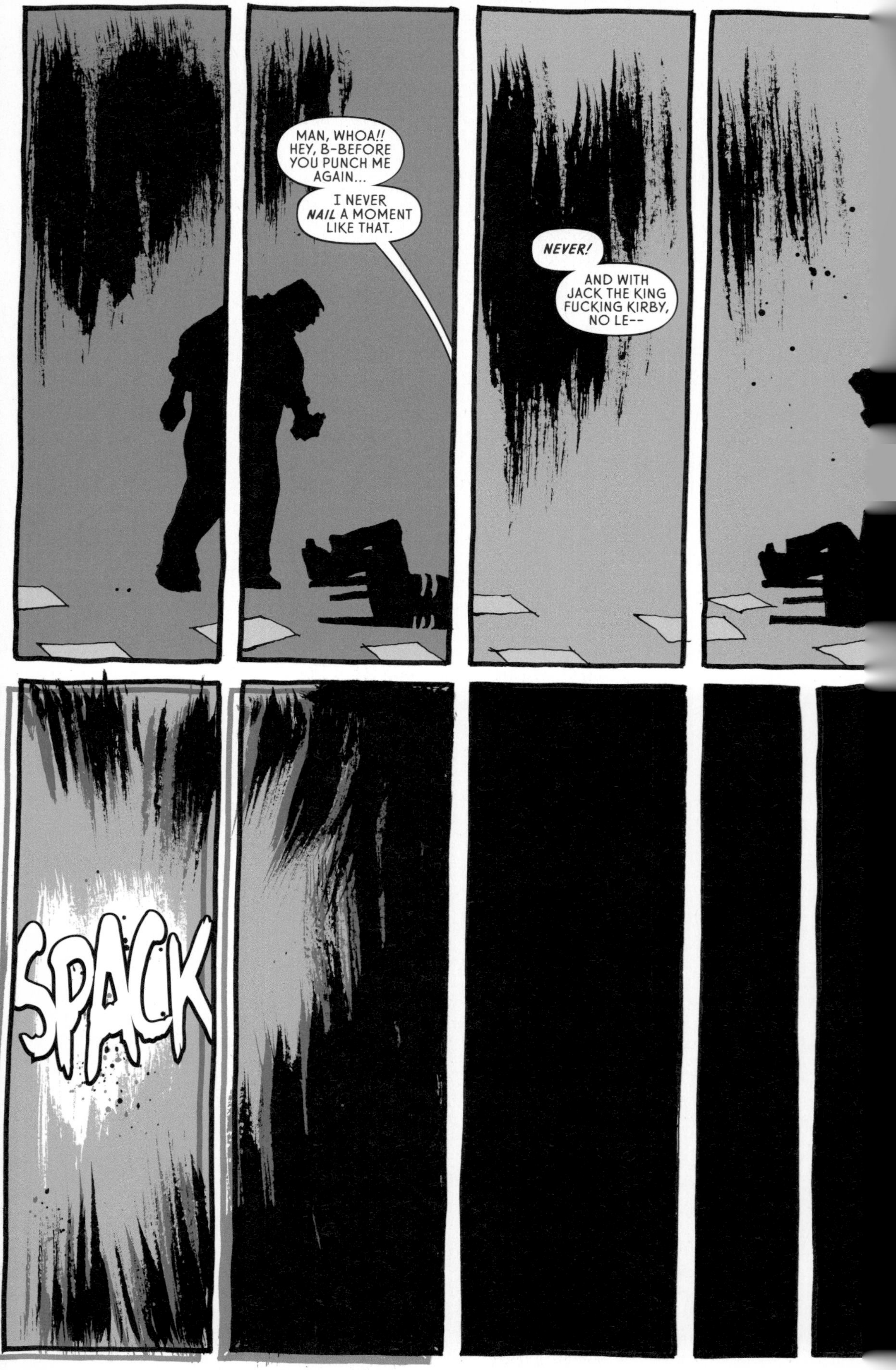
MAN, WHOA!! HEY, B-BEFORE YOU PUNCH ME AGAIN...
I NEVER *NAIL* A MOMENT LIKE THAT.
NEVER!
AND WITH JACK THE KING FUCKING KIRBY, NO LE--
SPACK

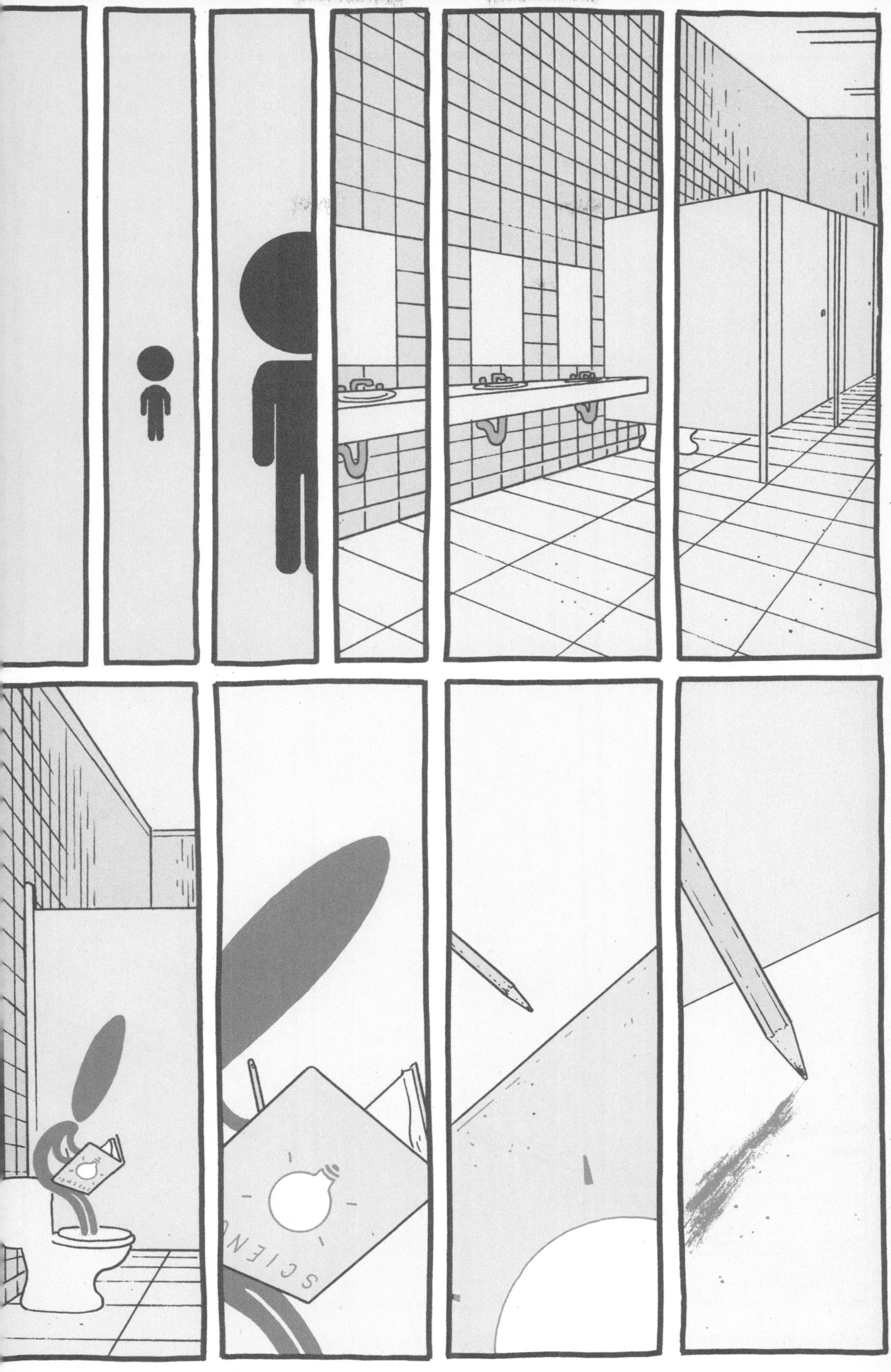
SCIENC

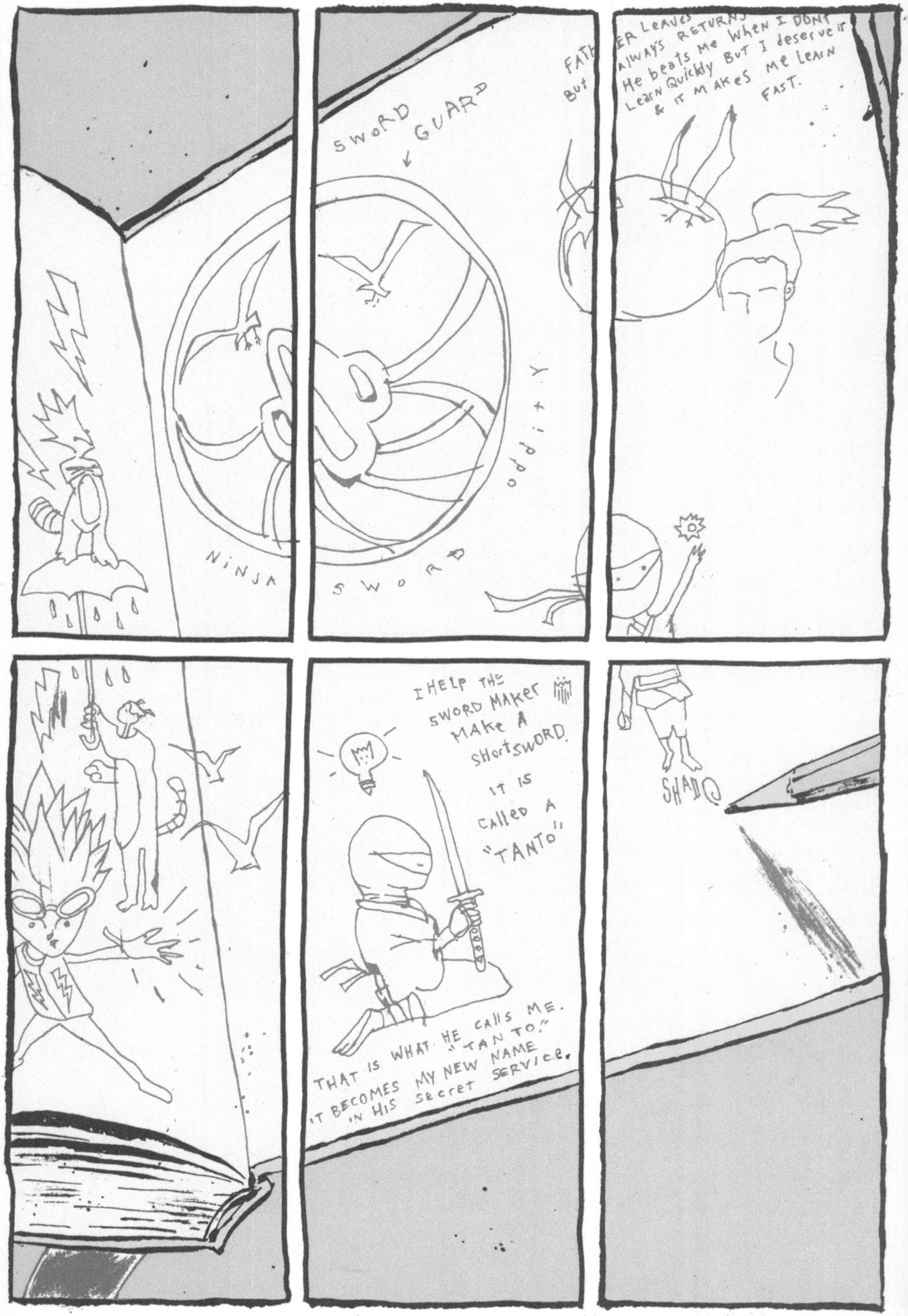

SWORD GUARD
NINJA SWORD
oddity
FATHER LEAVES
But ALWAYS RETURNS
He beats me when I DONT Learn Quickly But I deserve it & IT MAKES me Learn FAST.
I HELP THE SWORD MAKER MAKE A SHORTSWORD. IT IS CALLED A "TANTO"
THAT IS WHAT HE CALLS ME. "TAN TO."
IT BECOMES MY NEW NAME IN HIS secret SERVICE.
SHAD

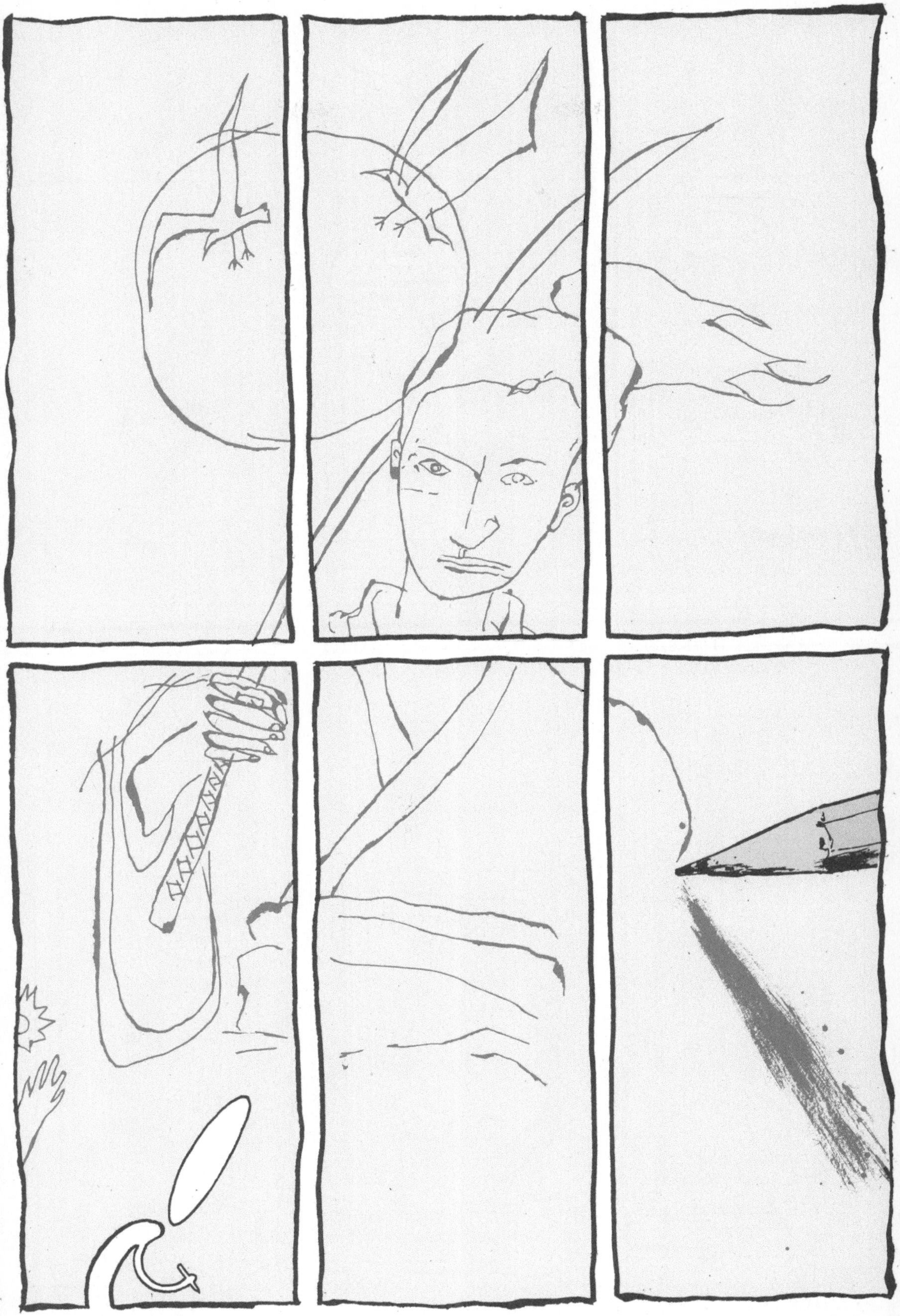

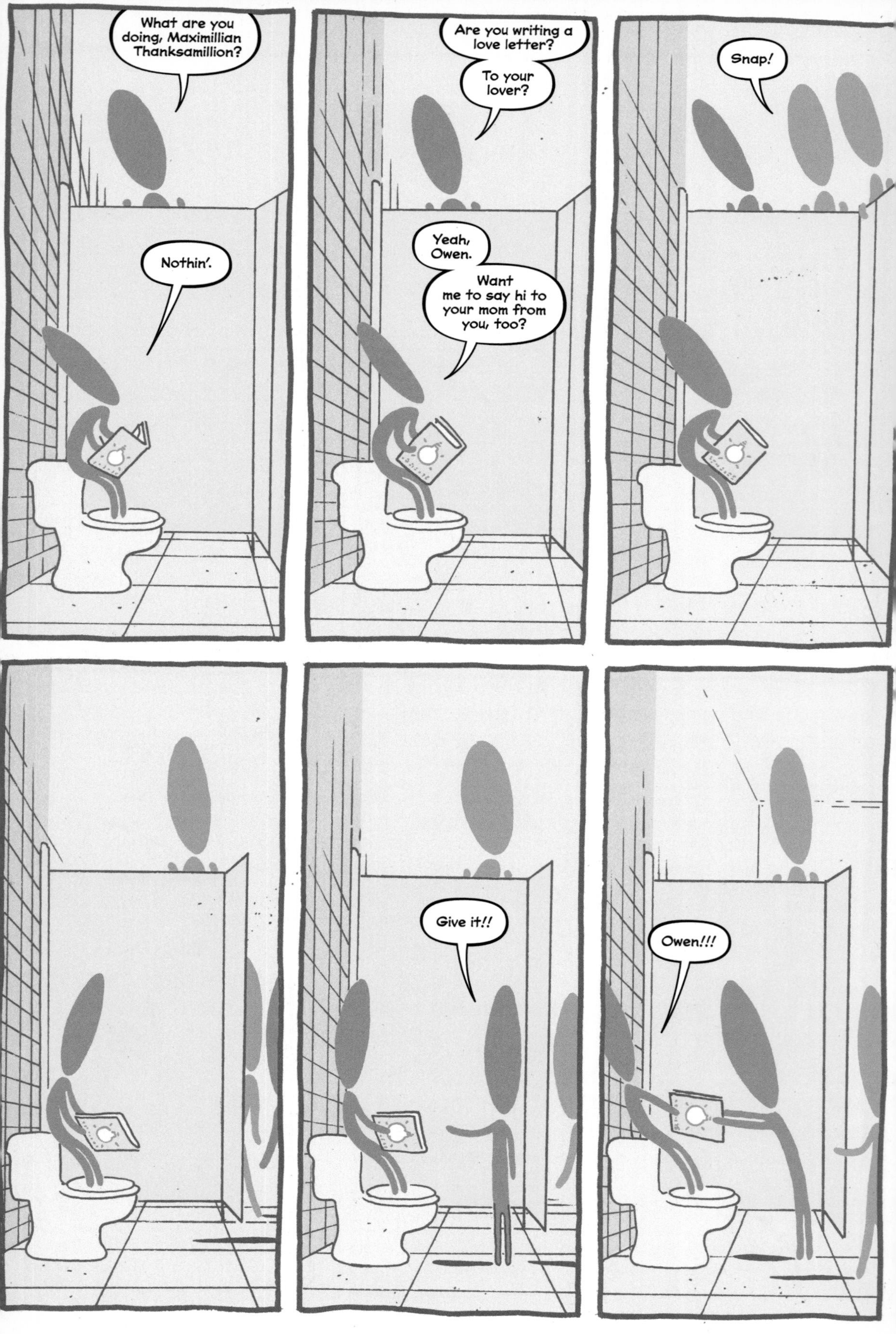
What are you doing, Maximillian Thanksamillion?
Nothin'.
Are you writing a love letter?
To your lover?
Yeah, Owen.
Want me to say hi to your mom from you, too?
Snap!
Give it!!
Owen!!!

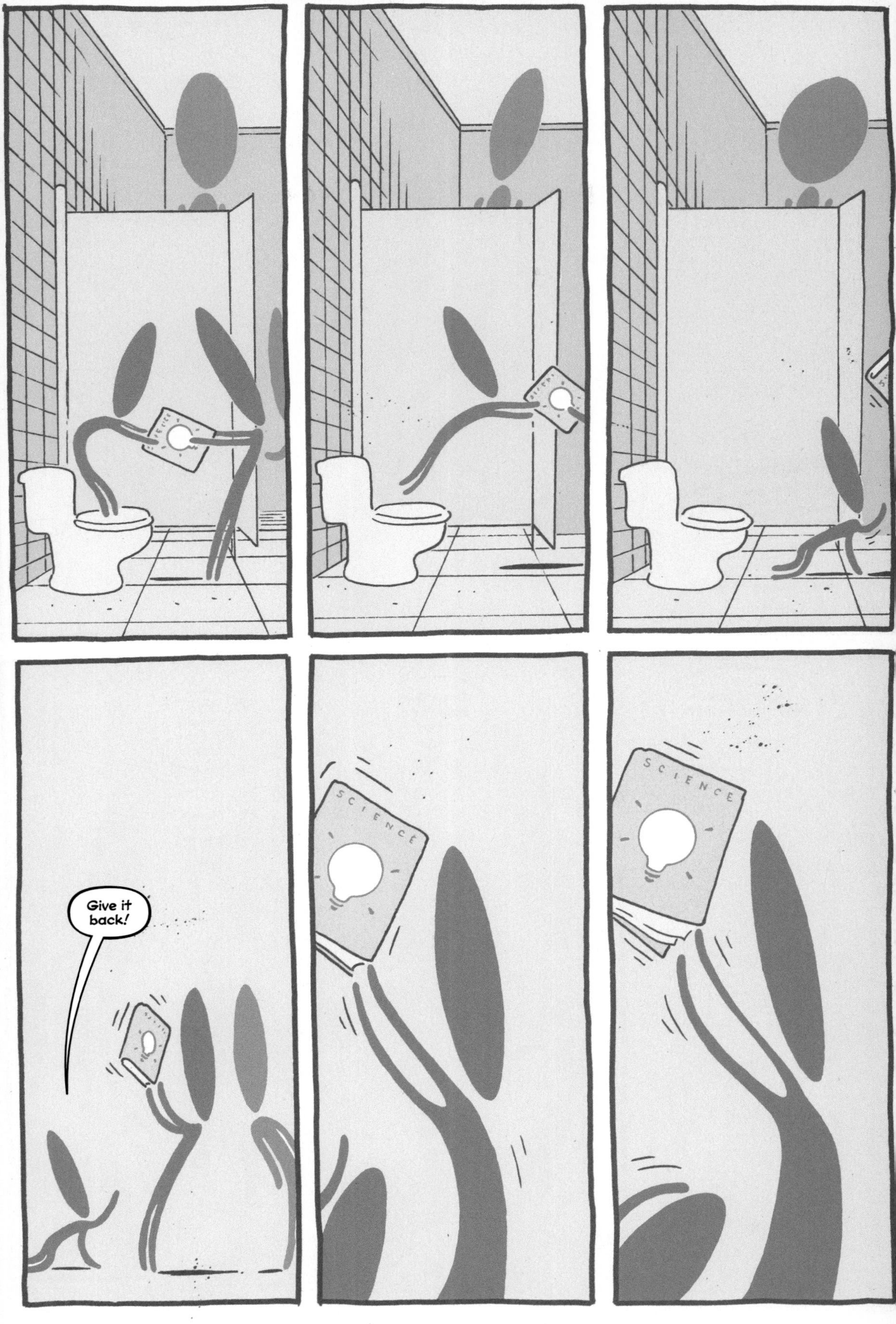

Give it back!
SCIENCE
SCIENCE

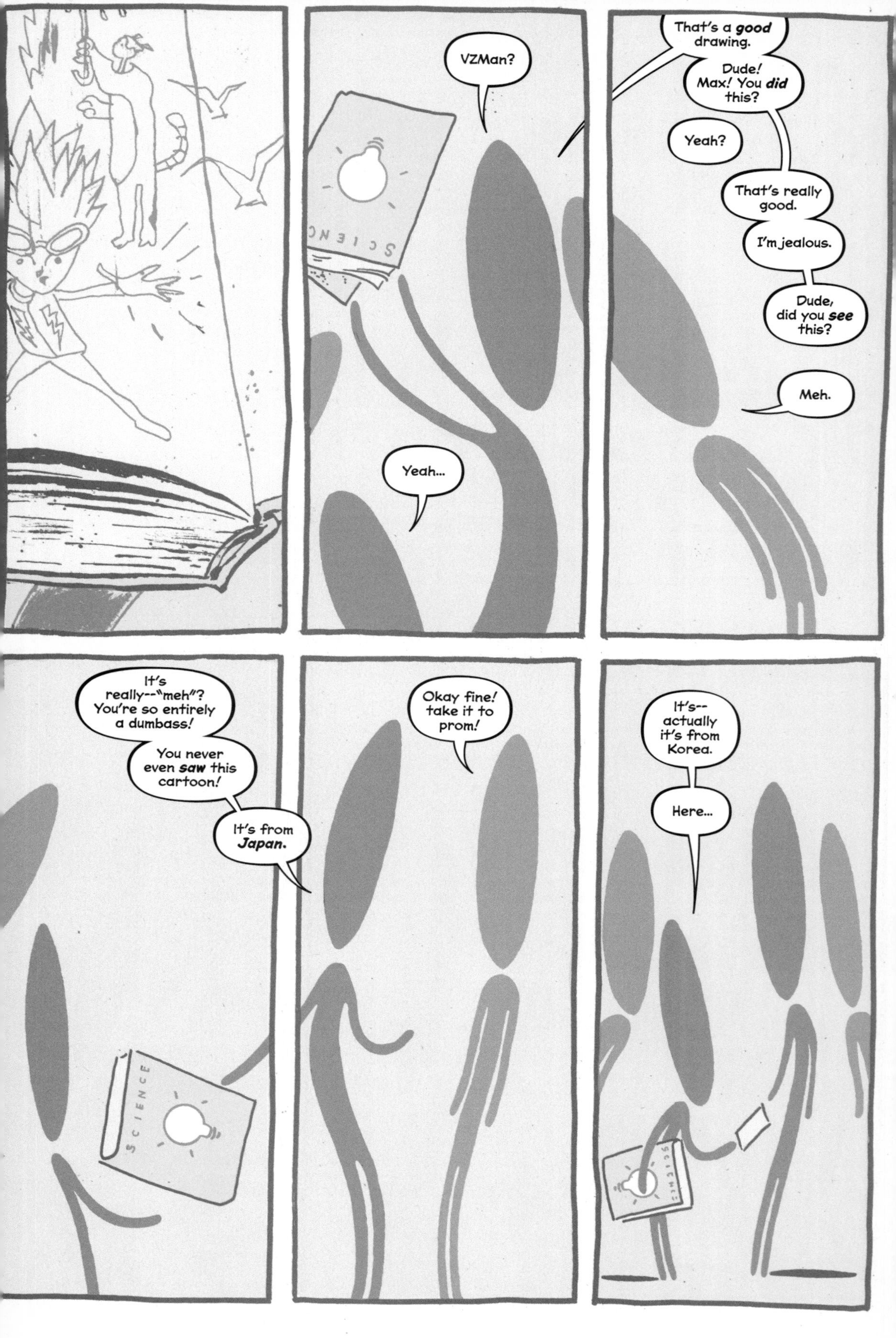
VZMan?
Yeah...
That's a good drawing.
Dude! Max! You did this?
Yeah?
That's really good.
I'm jealous.
Dude, did you see this?
Meh.
SCIENCE
It's really--"meh"? You're so entirely a dumbass!
You never even saw this cartoon!
It's from Japan.
Okay fine! take it to prom!
It's-- actually it's from Korea.
Here...

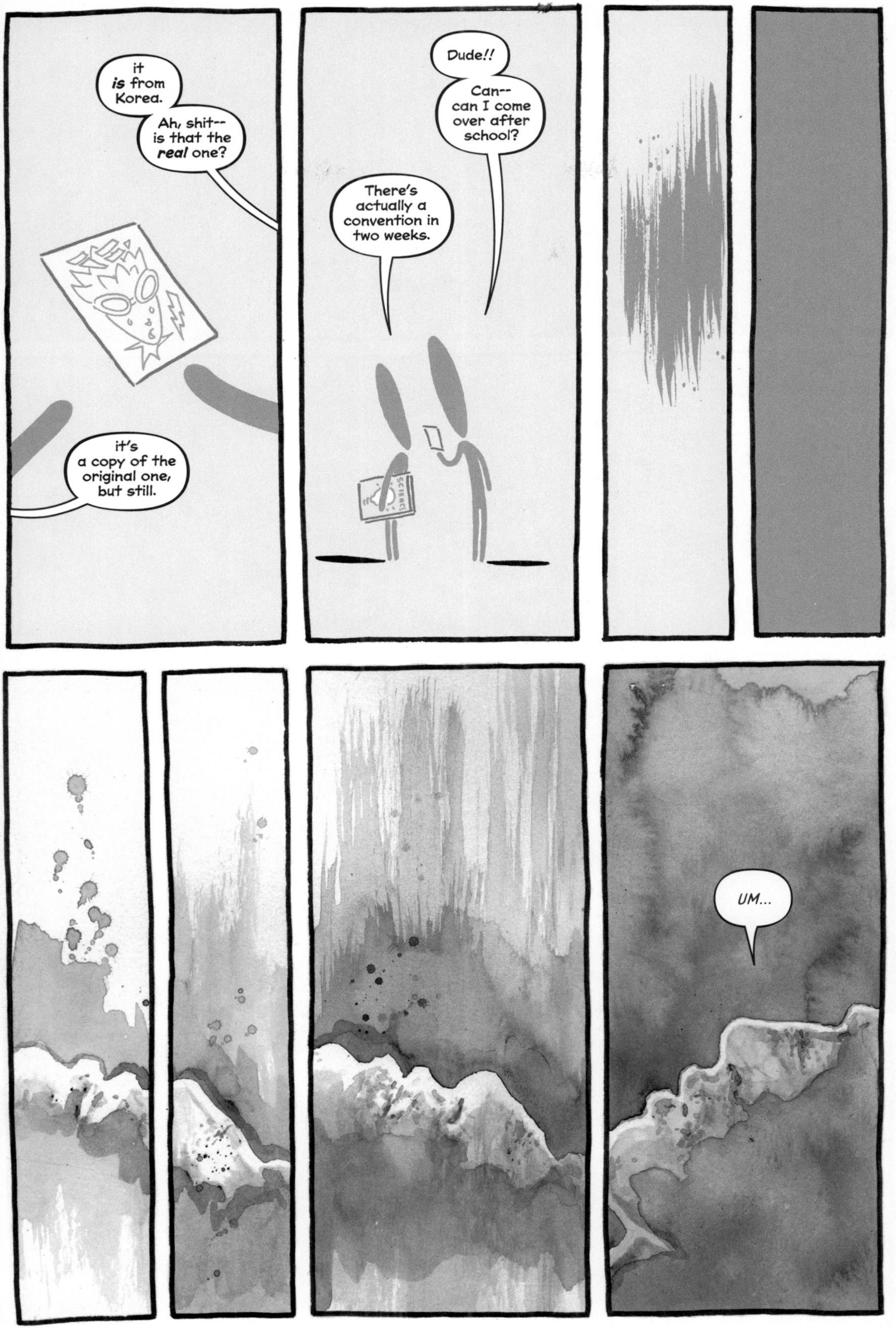
it is from Korea.
Ah, shit-- is that the real one?
it's a copy of the original one, but still.
Dude!!
Can-- can I come over after school?
There's actually a convention in two weeks.
SCIENCE
UM...

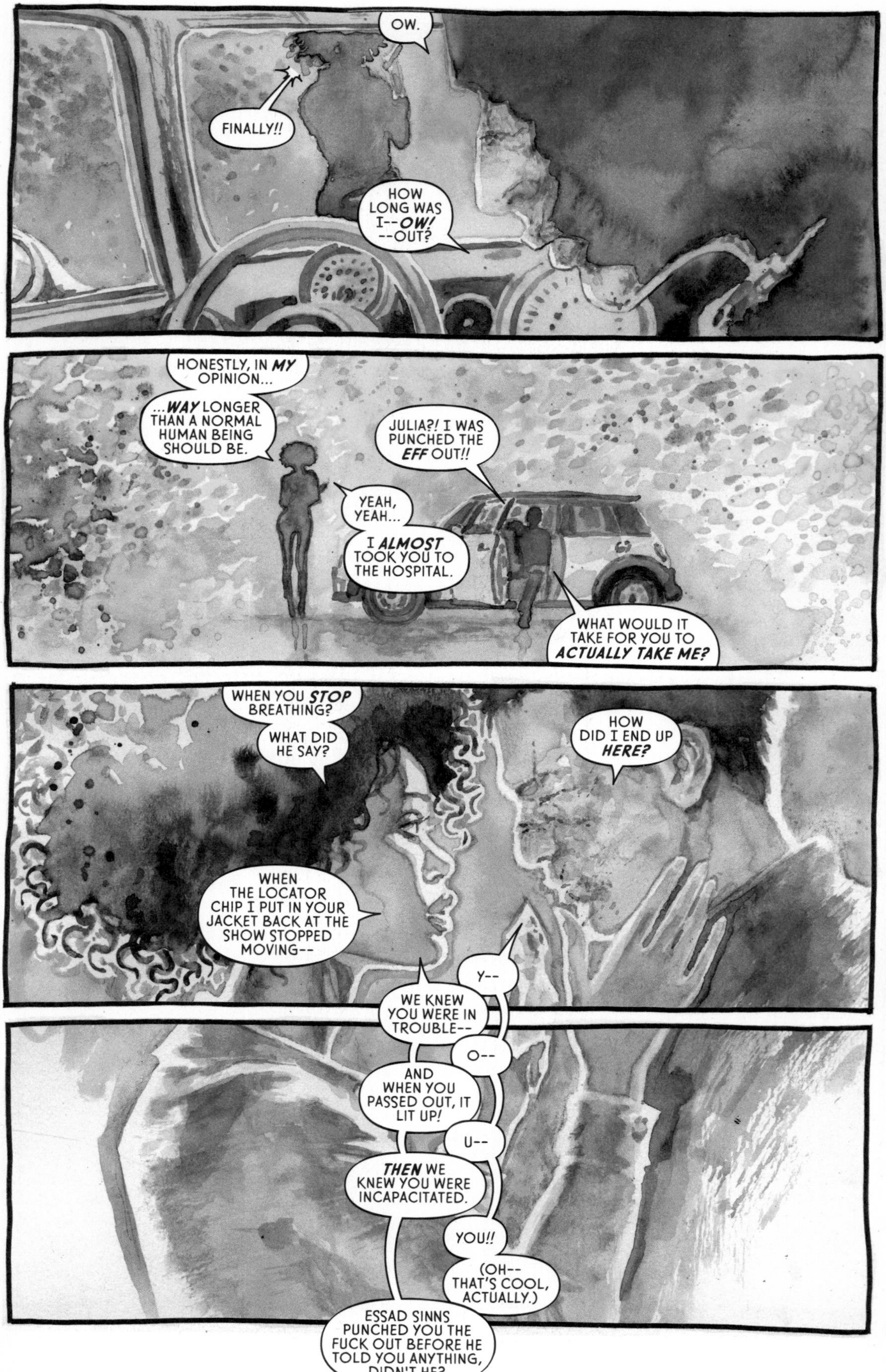

OW.
FINALLY!!
HOW LONG WAS I--OW! --OUT?
HONESTLY, IN MY OPINION...
...WAY LONGER THAN A NORMAL HUMAN BEING SHOULD BE.
JULIA?! I WAS PUNCHED THE EFF OUT!!
YEAH, YEAH...
I ALMOST TOOK YOU TO THE HOSPITAL.
WHAT WOULD IT TAKE FOR YOU TO ACTUALLY TAKE ME?
WHEN YOU STOP BREATHING?
WHAT DID HE SAY?
HOW DID I END UP HERE?
WHEN THE LOCATOR CHIP I PUT IN YOUR JACKET BACK AT THE SHOW STOPPED MOVING--
Y--
WE KNEW YOU WERE IN TROUBLE--
O--
AND WHEN YOU PASSED OUT, IT LIT UP!
U--
THEN WE KNEW YOU WERE INCAPACITATED.
YOU!!
(OH-- THAT'S COOL, ACTUALLY.)
ESSAD SINNS PUNCHED YOU THE FUCK OUT BEFORE HE TOLD YOU ANYTHING, DIDN'T HE?

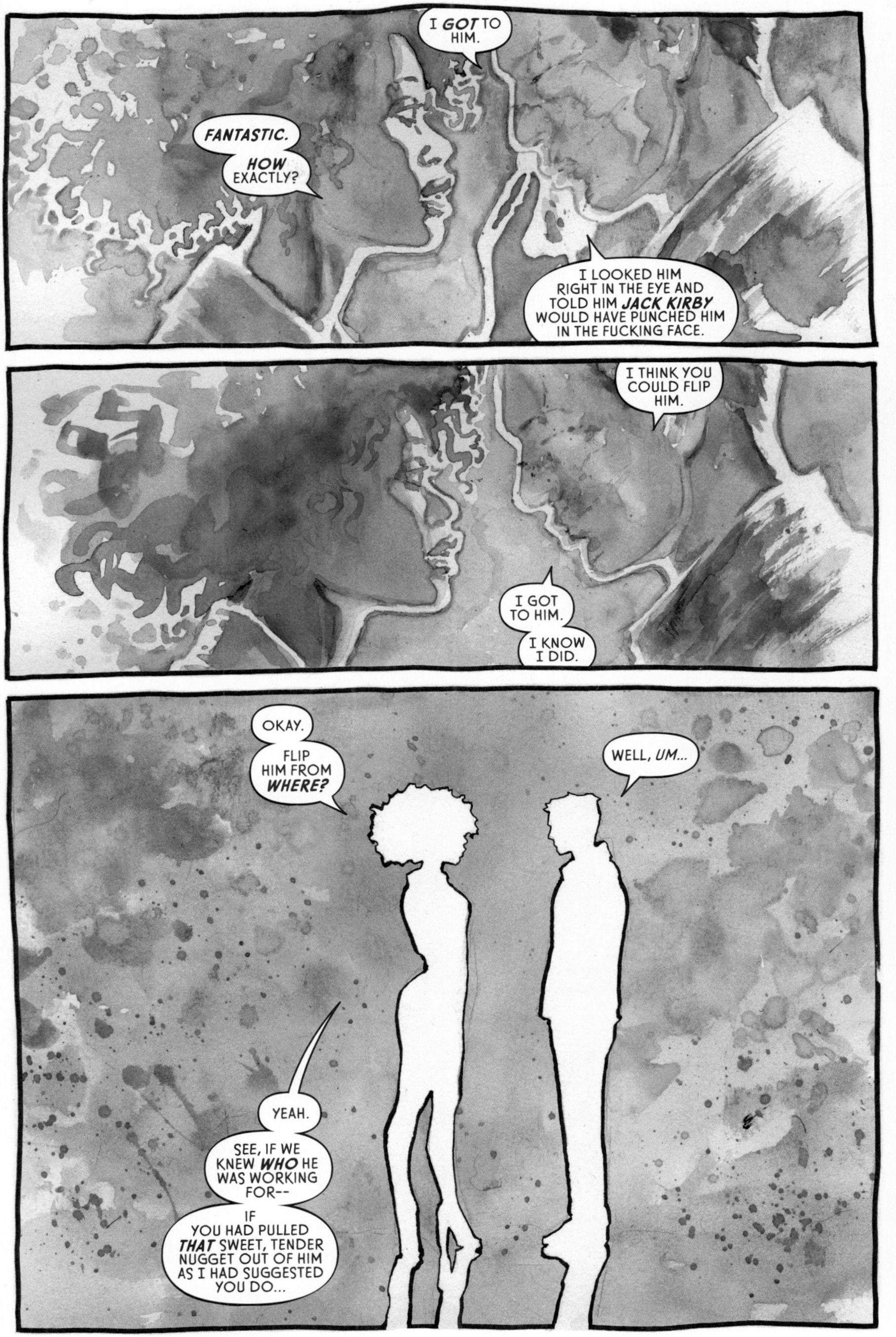
I **GOT** TO HIM.
FANTASTIC.
HOW EXACTLY?
I LOOKED HIM RIGHT IN THE EYE AND TOLD HIM **JACK KIRBY** WOULD HAVE PUNCHED HIM IN THE FUCKING FACE.
I THINK YOU COULD FLIP HIM.
I GOT TO HIM.
I KNOW I DID.
OKAY.
FLIP HIM FROM **WHERE?**
WELL, *UM*...
YEAH.
SEE, IF WE KNEW **WHO** HE WAS WORKING FOR--
IF YOU HAD PULLED **THAT** SWEET, TENDER NUGGET OUT OF HIM AS I HAD SUGGESTED YOU DO...

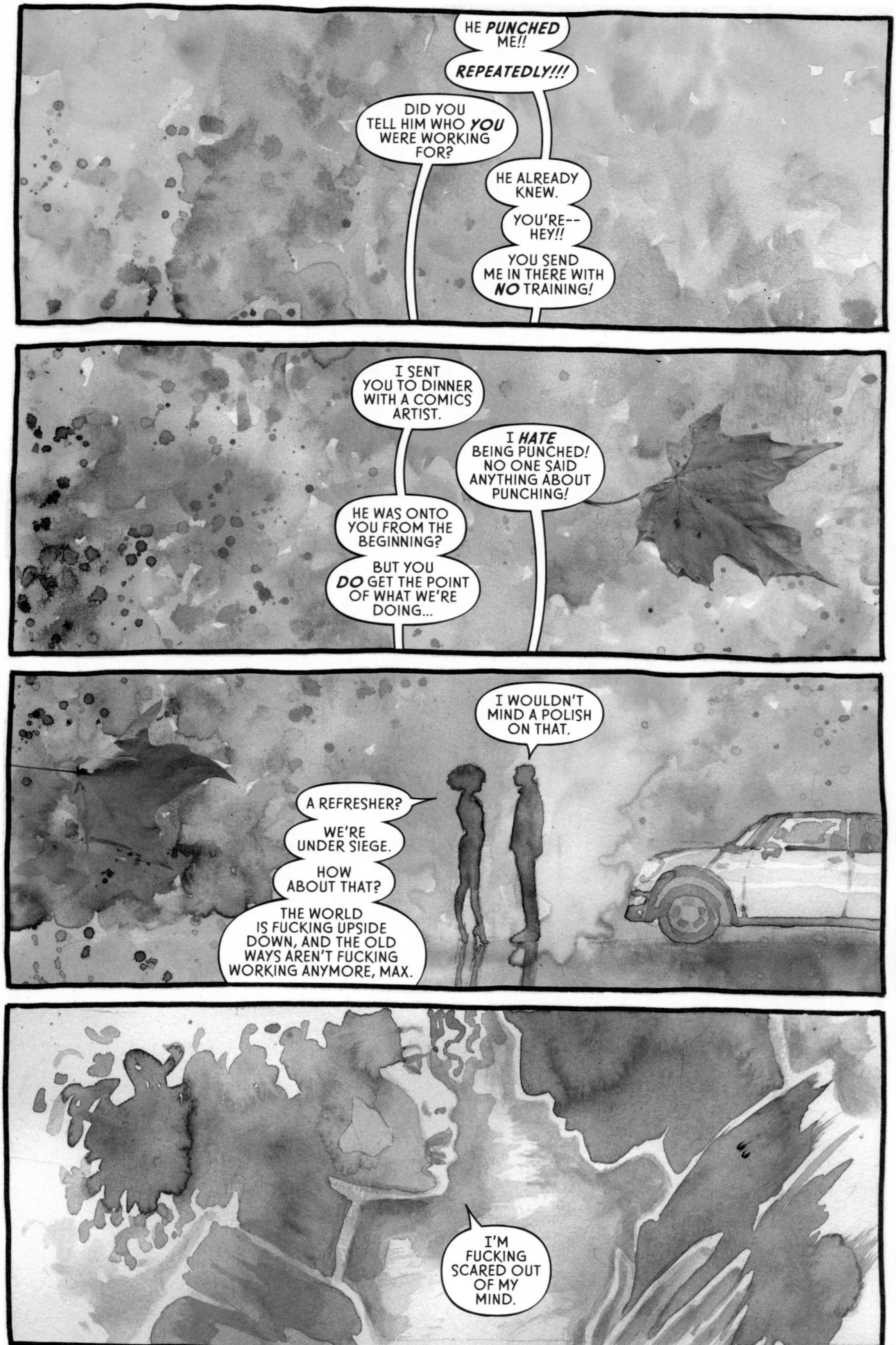

HE *PUNCHED* ME!!
REPEATEDLY!!!
DID YOU TELL HIM WHO *YOU* WERE WORKING FOR?
HE ALREADY KNEW.
YOU'RE-- HEY!!
YOU SEND ME IN THERE WITH *NO* TRAINING!
I SENT YOU TO DINNER WITH A COMICS ARTIST.
I *HATE* BEING PUNCHED! NO ONE SAID ANYTHING ABOUT PUNCHING!
HE WAS ONTO YOU FROM THE BEGINNING?
BUT YOU *DO* GET THE POINT OF WHAT WE'RE DOING...
I WOULDN'T MIND A POLISH ON THAT.
A REFRESHER?
WE'RE UNDER SIEGE.
HOW ABOUT THAT?
THE WORLD IS FUCKING UPSIDE DOWN, AND THE OLD WAYS AREN'T FUCKING WORKING ANYMORE, MAX.
I'M FUCKING SCARED OUT OF MY MIND.

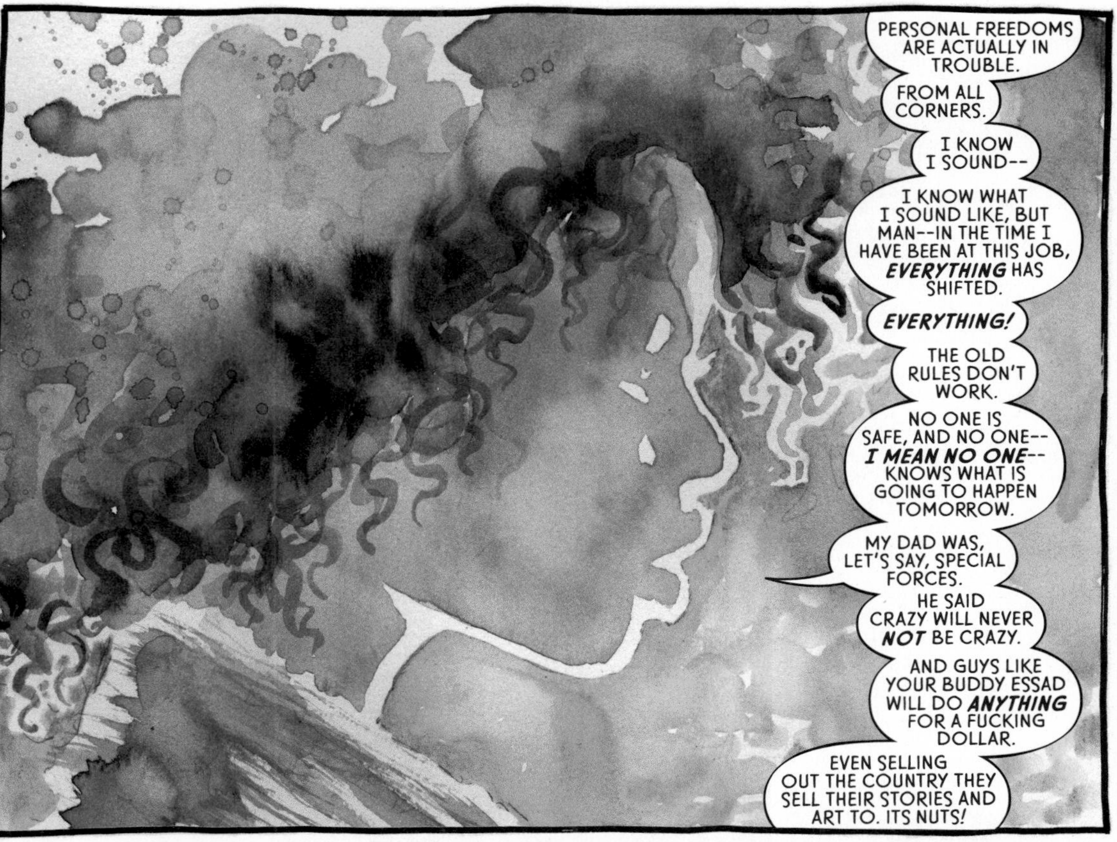
PERSONAL FREEDOMS ARE ACTUALLY IN TROUBLE.
FROM ALL CORNERS.
I KNOW I SOUND--
I KNOW WHAT I SOUND LIKE, BUT MAN--IN THE TIME I HAVE BEEN AT THIS JOB, *EVERYTHING* HAS SHIFTED.
EVERYTHING!
THE OLD RULES DON'T WORK.
NO ONE IS SAFE, AND NO ONE-- *I MEAN NO ONE*-- KNOWS WHAT IS GOING TO HAPPEN TOMORROW.
MY DAD WAS, LET'S SAY, SPECIAL FORCES.
HE SAID CRAZY WILL NEVER *NOT* BE CRAZY.
AND GUYS LIKE YOUR BUDDY ESSAD WILL DO *ANYTHING* FOR A FUCKING DOLLAR.
EVEN SELLING OUT THE COUNTRY THEY SELL THEIR STORIES AND ART TO. ITS NUTS!

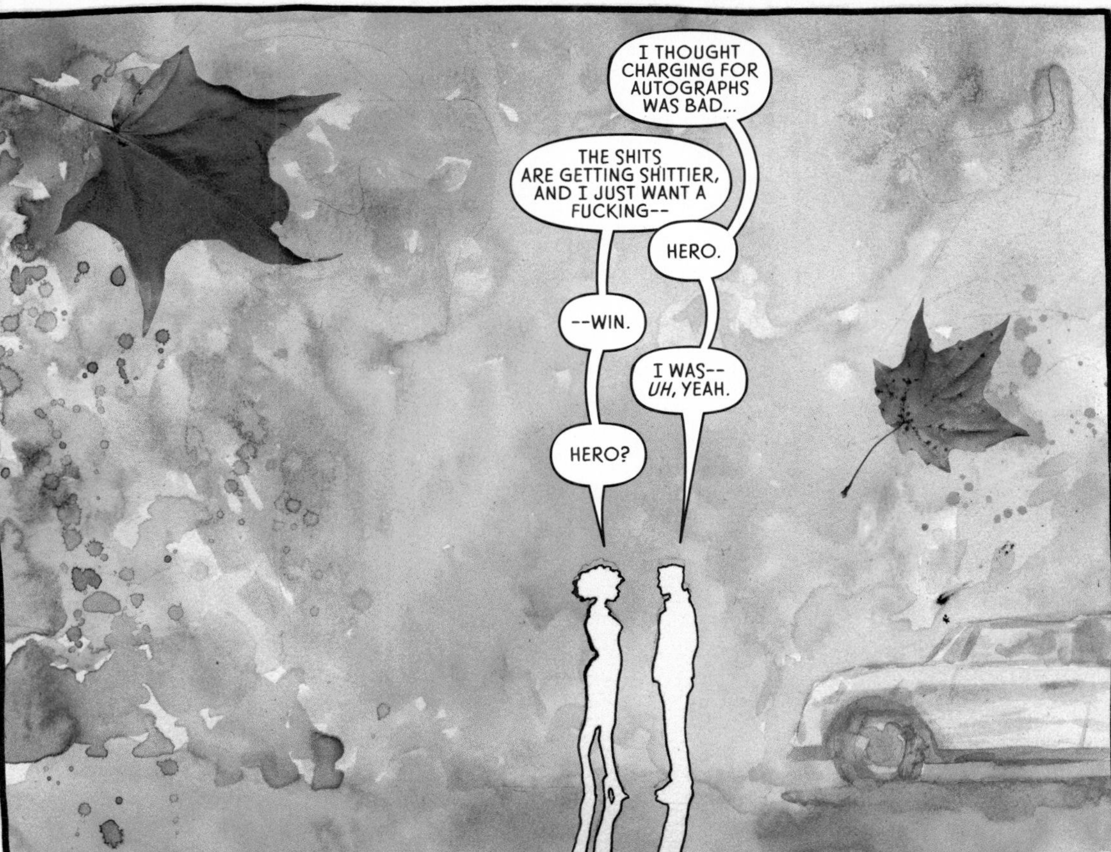
I THOUGHT CHARGING FOR AUTOGRAPHS WAS BAD...
THE SHITS ARE GETTING SHITTIER, AND I JUST WANT A FUCKING--
HERO.
--WIN.
I WAS-- *UH*, YEAH.
HERO?

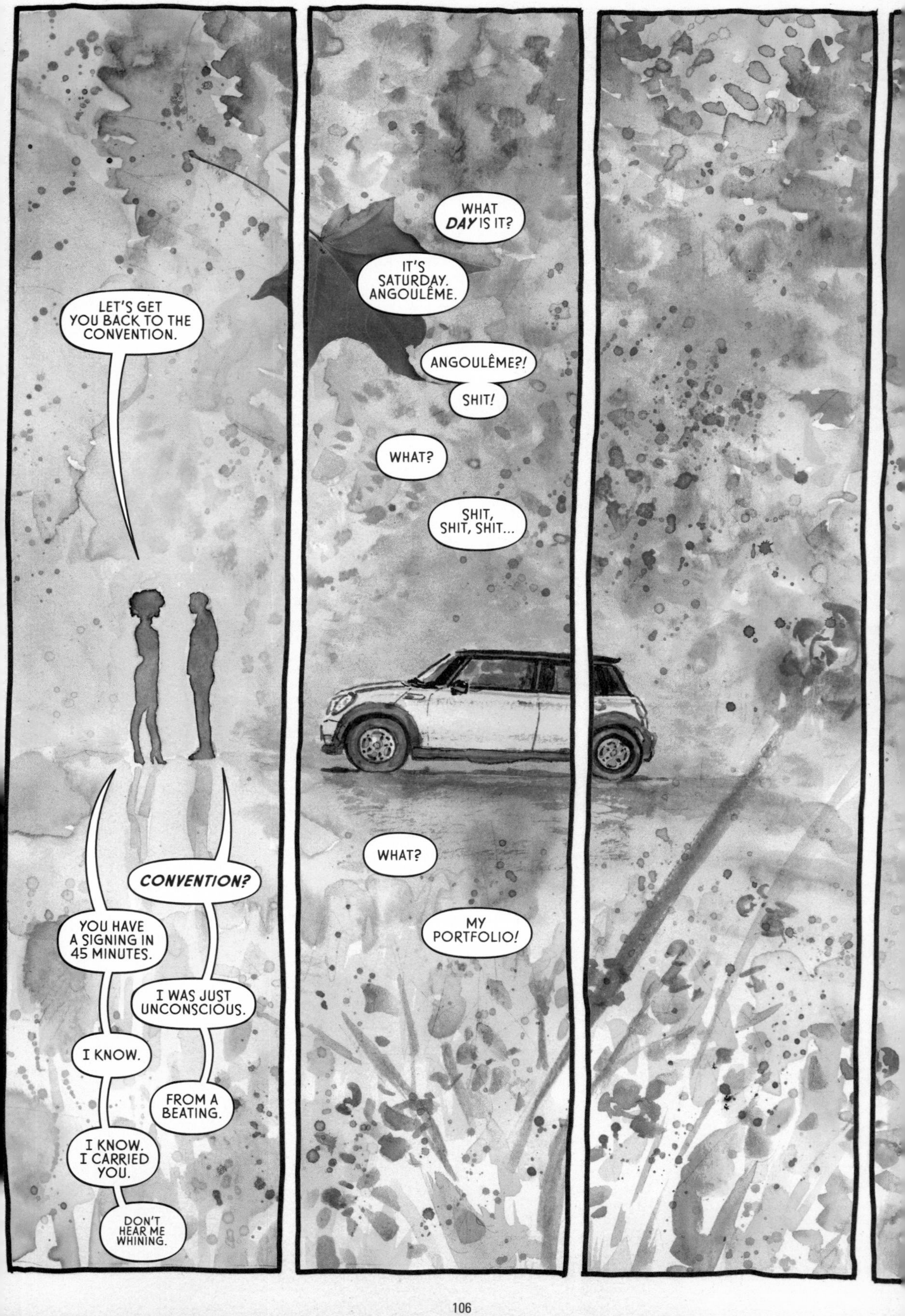
LET'S GET YOU BACK TO THE CONVENTION.
CONVENTION?
YOU HAVE A SIGNING IN 45 MINUTES.
I WAS JUST UNCONSCIOUS.
I KNOW.
FROM A BEATING.
I KNOW. I CARRIED YOU.
DON'T HEAR ME WHINING.
WHAT DAY IS IT?
IT'S SATURDAY. ANGOULÊME.
ANGOULÊME?!
SHIT!
WHAT?
SHIT, SHIT, SHIT...
WHAT?
MY PORTFOLIO!

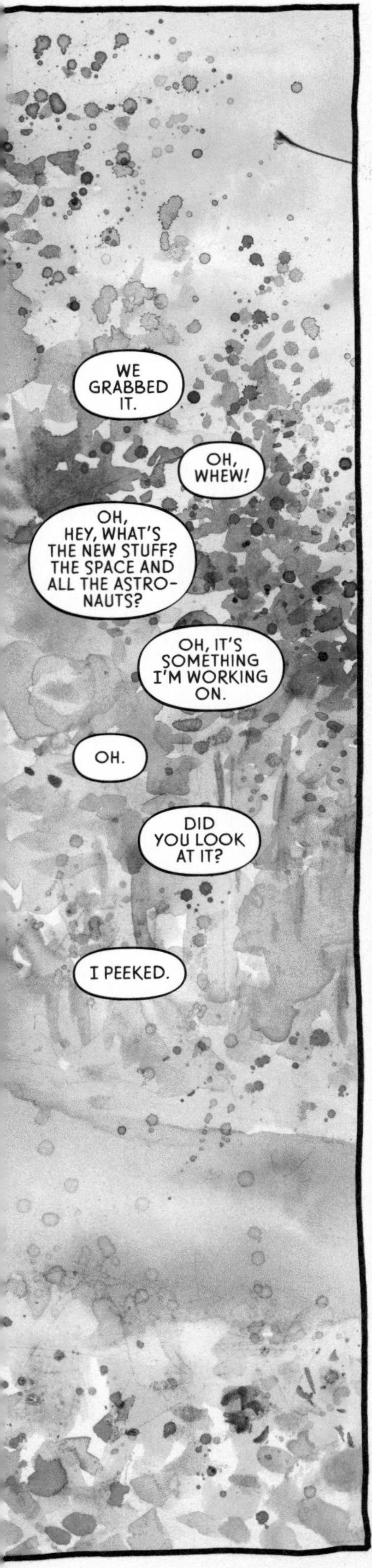
WE GRABBED IT.
OH, WHEW!
OH, HEY, WHAT'S THE NEW STUFF? THE SPACE AND ALL THE ASTRO-NAUTS?
OH, IT'S SOMETHING I'M WORKING ON.
OH.
DID YOU LOOK AT IT?
I PEEKED.

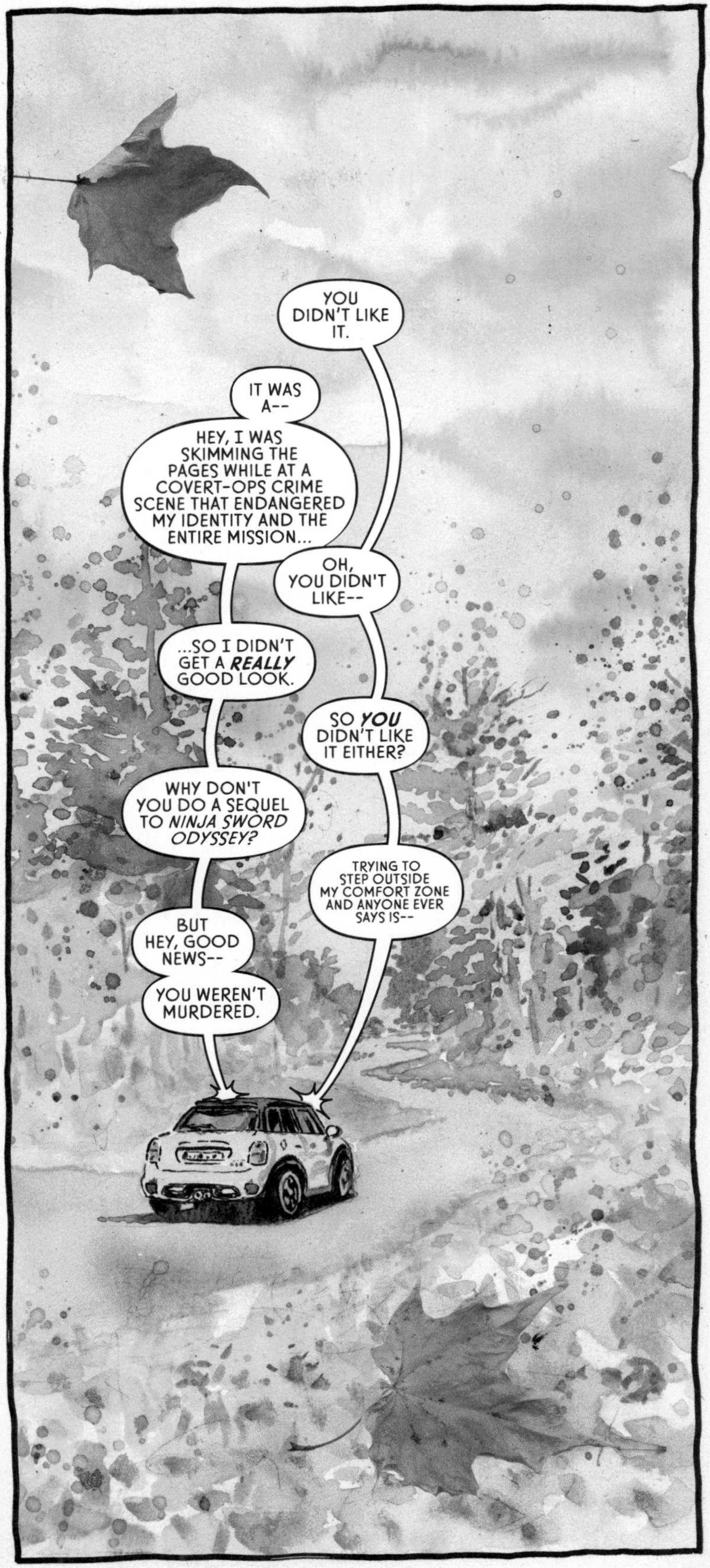
YOU DIDN'T LIKE IT.
IT WAS A--
HEY, I WAS SKIMMING THE PAGES WHILE AT A COVERT-OPS CRIME SCENE THAT ENDANGERED MY IDENTITY AND THE ENTIRE MISSION...
OH, YOU DIDN'T LIKE--
...SO I DIDN'T GET A ***REALLY*** GOOD LOOK.
SO ***YOU*** DIDN'T LIKE IT EITHER?
WHY DON'T YOU DO A SEQUEL TO *NINJA SWORD ODYSSEY?*
TRYING TO STEP OUTSIDE MY COMFORT ZONE AND ANYONE EVER SAYS IS--
BUT HEY, GOOD NEWS--
YOU WEREN'T MURDERED.

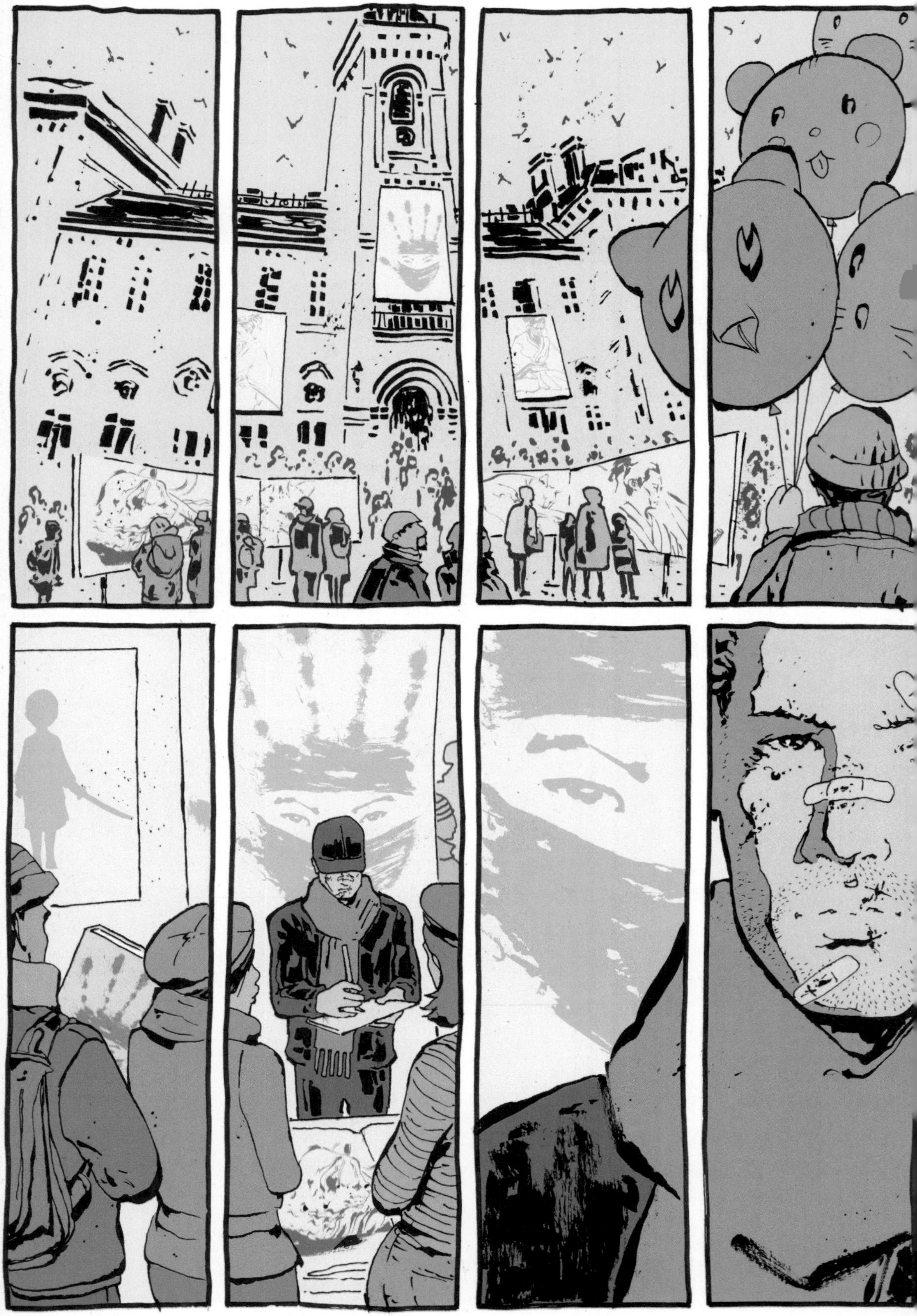

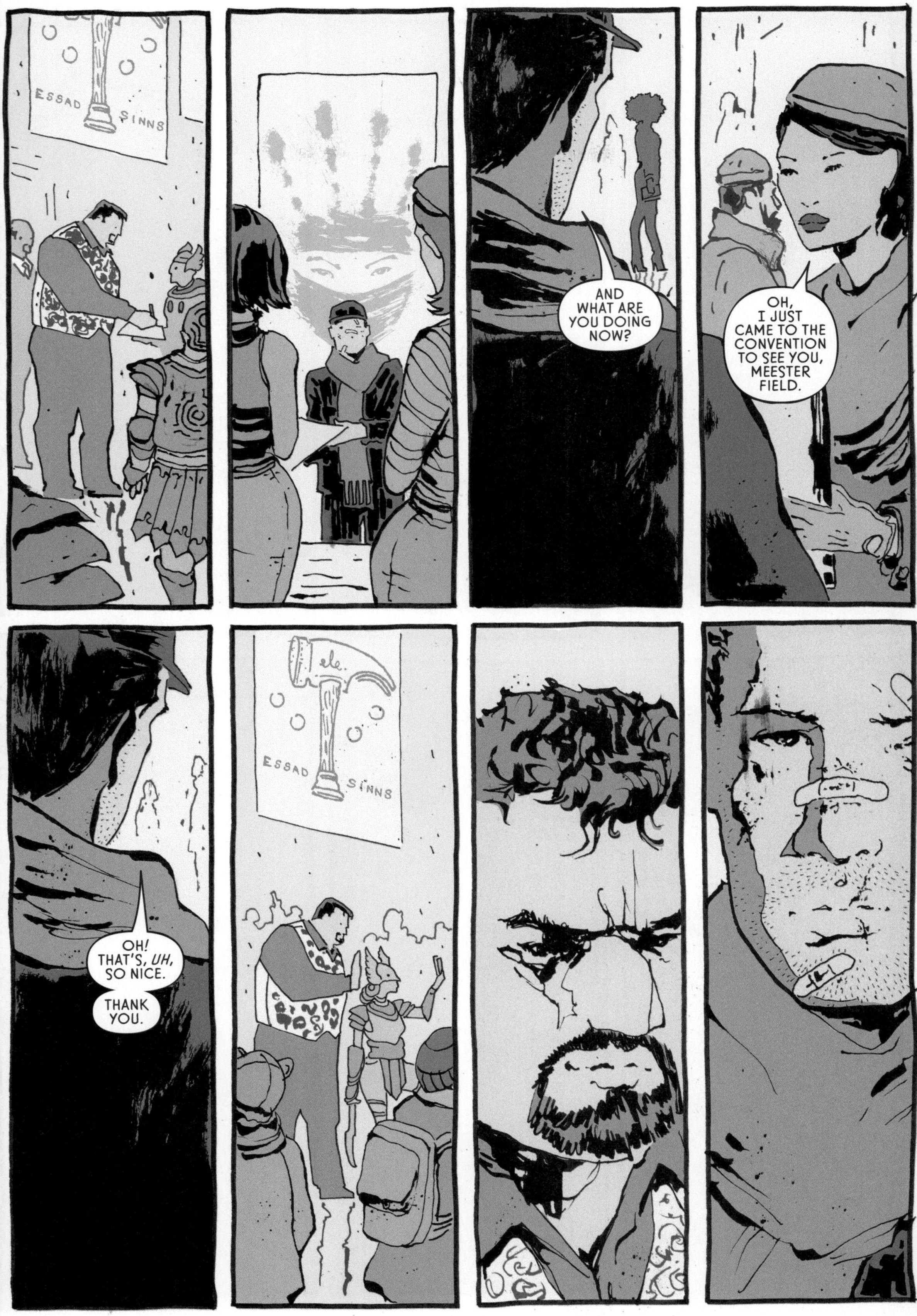
ESSAD
SINNS
AND WHAT ARE YOU DOING NOW?
OH, I JUST CAME TO THE CONVENTION TO SEE YOU, MEESTER FIELD.
OH! THAT'S, *UH,* SO NICE.
THANK YOU.
ESSAD
SINNS

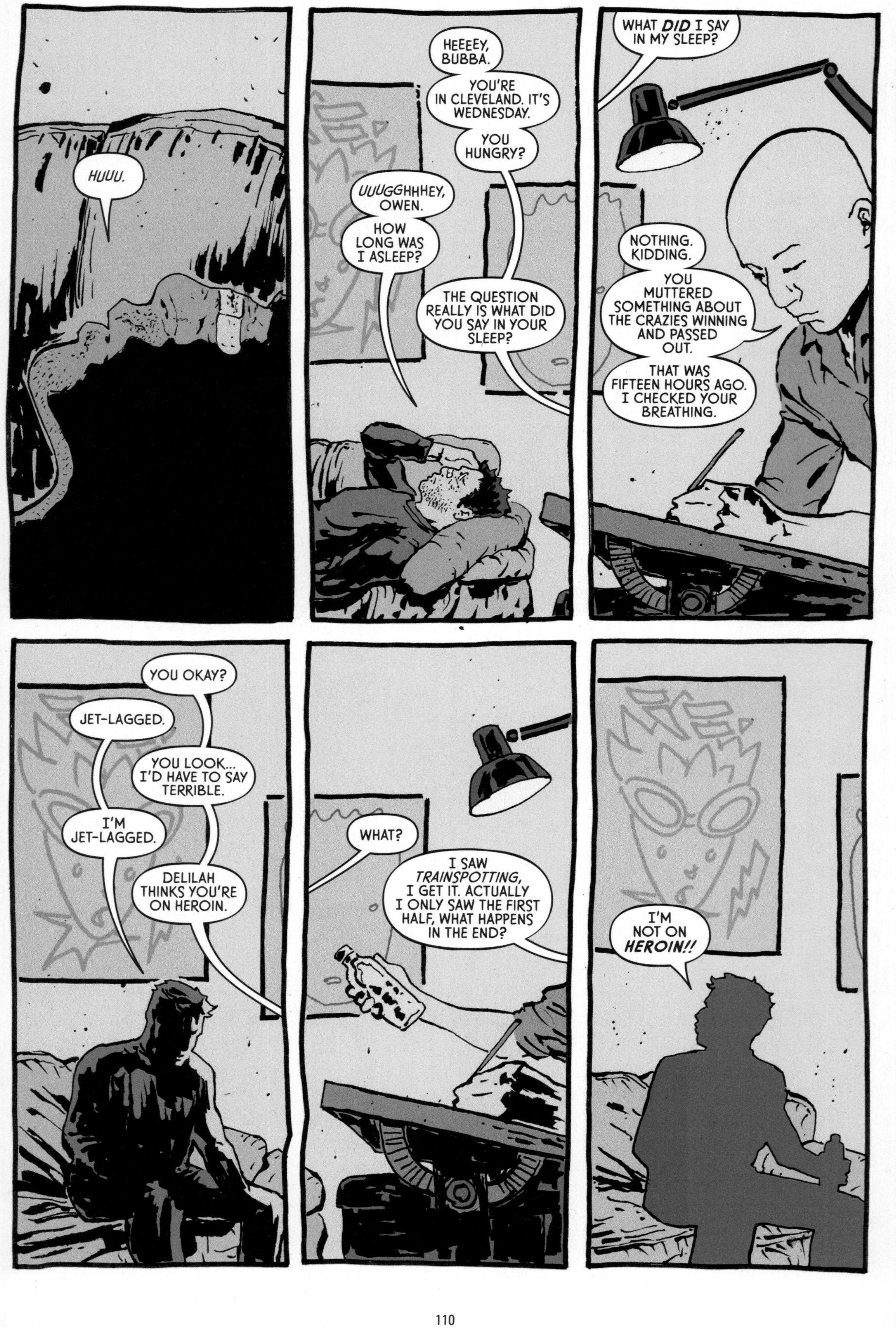
HUUU.
HEEEEY, BUBBA.
YOU'RE IN CLEVELAND. IT'S WEDNESDAY.
YOU HUNGRY?
UUUGGHHHEY, OWEN.
HOW LONG WAS I ASLEEP?
THE QUESTION REALLY IS WHAT DID YOU SAY IN YOUR SLEEP?
WHAT DID I SAY IN MY SLEEP?
NOTHING. KIDDING.
YOU MUTTERED SOMETHING ABOUT THE CRAZIES WINNING AND PASSED OUT.
THAT WAS FIFTEEN HOURS AGO. I CHECKED YOUR BREATHING.
YOU OKAY?
JET-LAGGED.
YOU LOOK... I'D HAVE TO SAY TERRIBLE.
I'M JET-LAGGED.
DELILAH THINKS YOU'RE ON HEROIN.
WHAT?
I SAW TRAINSPOTTING, I GET IT. ACTUALLY I ONLY SAW THE FIRST HALF, WHAT HAPPENS IN THE END?
I'M NOT ON HEROIN!!

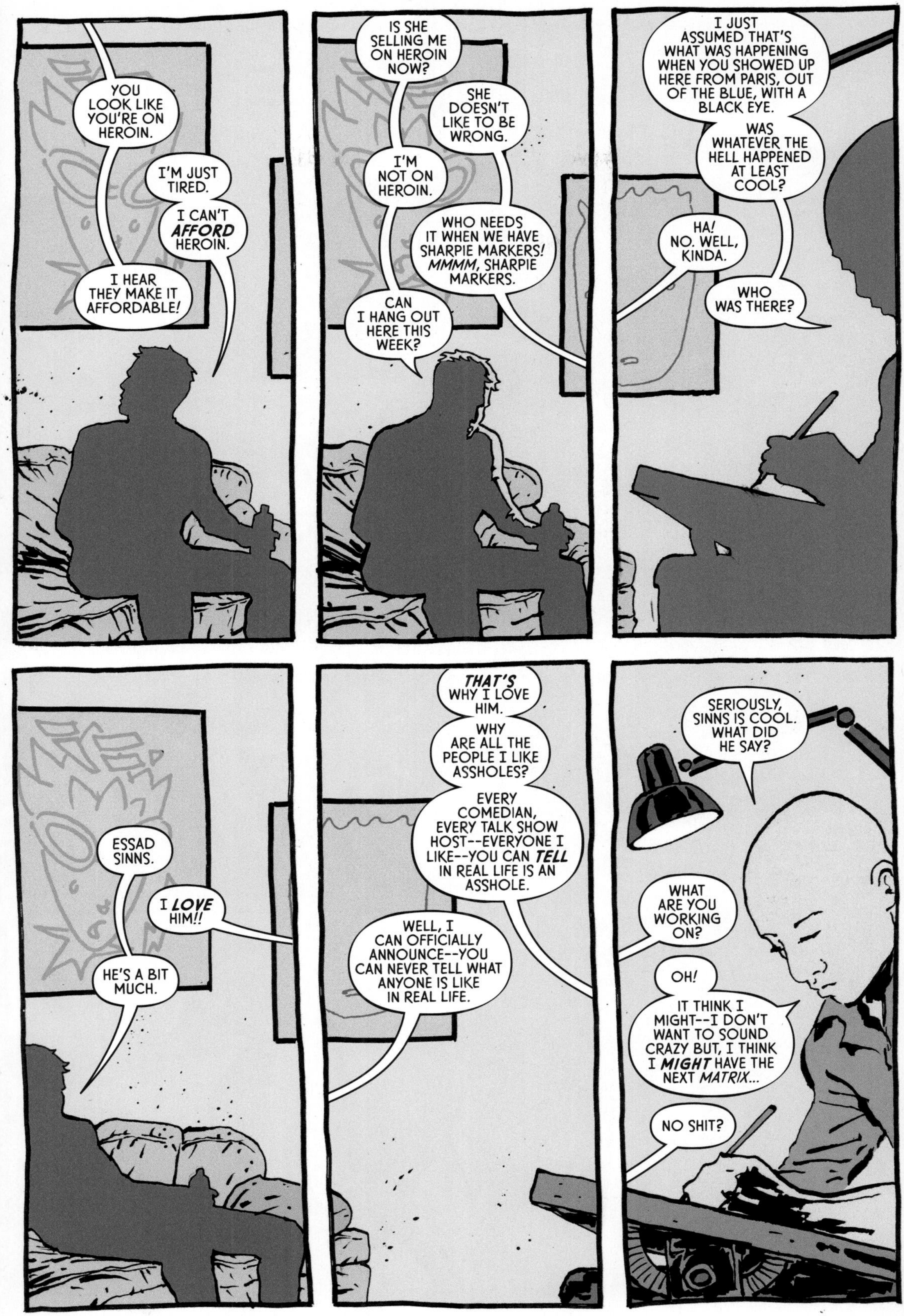
YOU LOOK LIKE YOU'RE ON HEROIN.
I'M JUST TIRED.
I CAN'T AFFORD HEROIN.
I HEAR THEY MAKE IT AFFORDABLE!
IS SHE SELLING ME ON HEROIN NOW?
SHE DOESN'T LIKE TO BE WRONG.
I'M NOT ON HEROIN.
WHO NEEDS IT WHEN WE HAVE SHARPIE MARKERS! MMMM, SHARPIE MARKERS.
CAN I HANG OUT HERE THIS WEEK?
I JUST ASSUMED THAT'S WHAT WAS HAPPENING WHEN YOU SHOWED UP HERE FROM PARIS, OUT OF THE BLUE, WITH A BLACK EYE.
WAS WHATEVER THE HELL HAPPENED AT LEAST COOL?
HA! NO. WELL, KINDA.
WHO WAS THERE?
ESSAD SINNS.
I LOVE HIM!!
HE'S A BIT MUCH.
THAT'S WHY I LOVE HIM.
WHY ARE ALL THE PEOPLE I LIKE ASSHOLES?
EVERY COMEDIAN, EVERY TALK SHOW HOST--EVERYONE I LIKE--YOU CAN TELL IN REAL LIFE IS AN ASSHOLE.
WELL, I CAN OFFICIALLY ANNOUNCE--YOU CAN NEVER TELL WHAT ANYONE IS LIKE IN REAL LIFE.
SERIOUSLY, SINNS IS COOL. WHAT DID HE SAY?
WHAT ARE YOU WORKING ON?
OH!
IT THINK I MIGHT--I DON'T WANT TO SOUND CRAZY BUT, I THINK I MIGHT HAVE THE NEXT MATRIX...
NO SHIT?

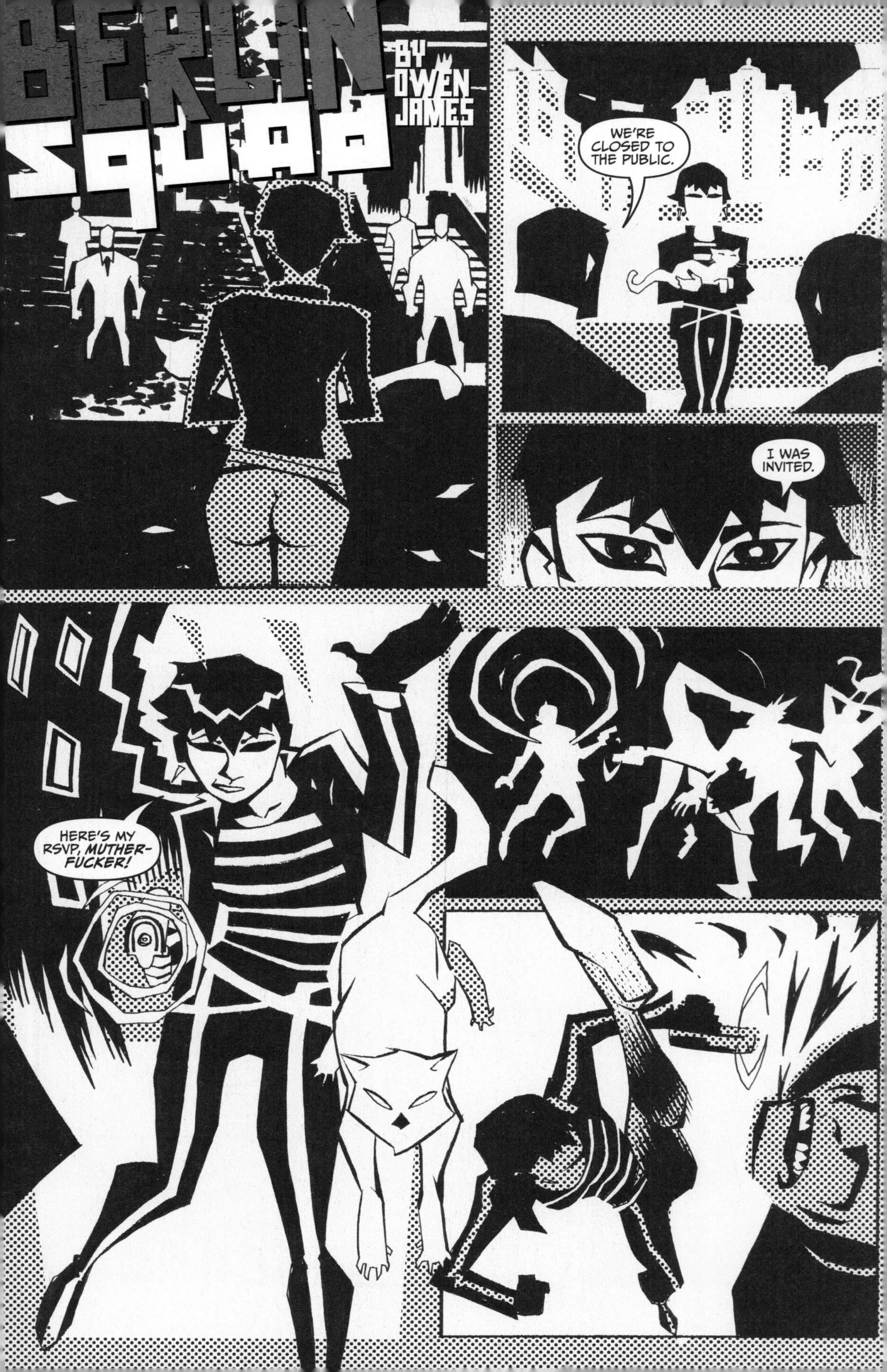

BERLIN SQUAD
BY OWEN JAMES
WE'RE CLOSED TO THE PUBLIC.
I WAS INVITED.
HERE'S MY RSVP, MUTHER-FUCKER!

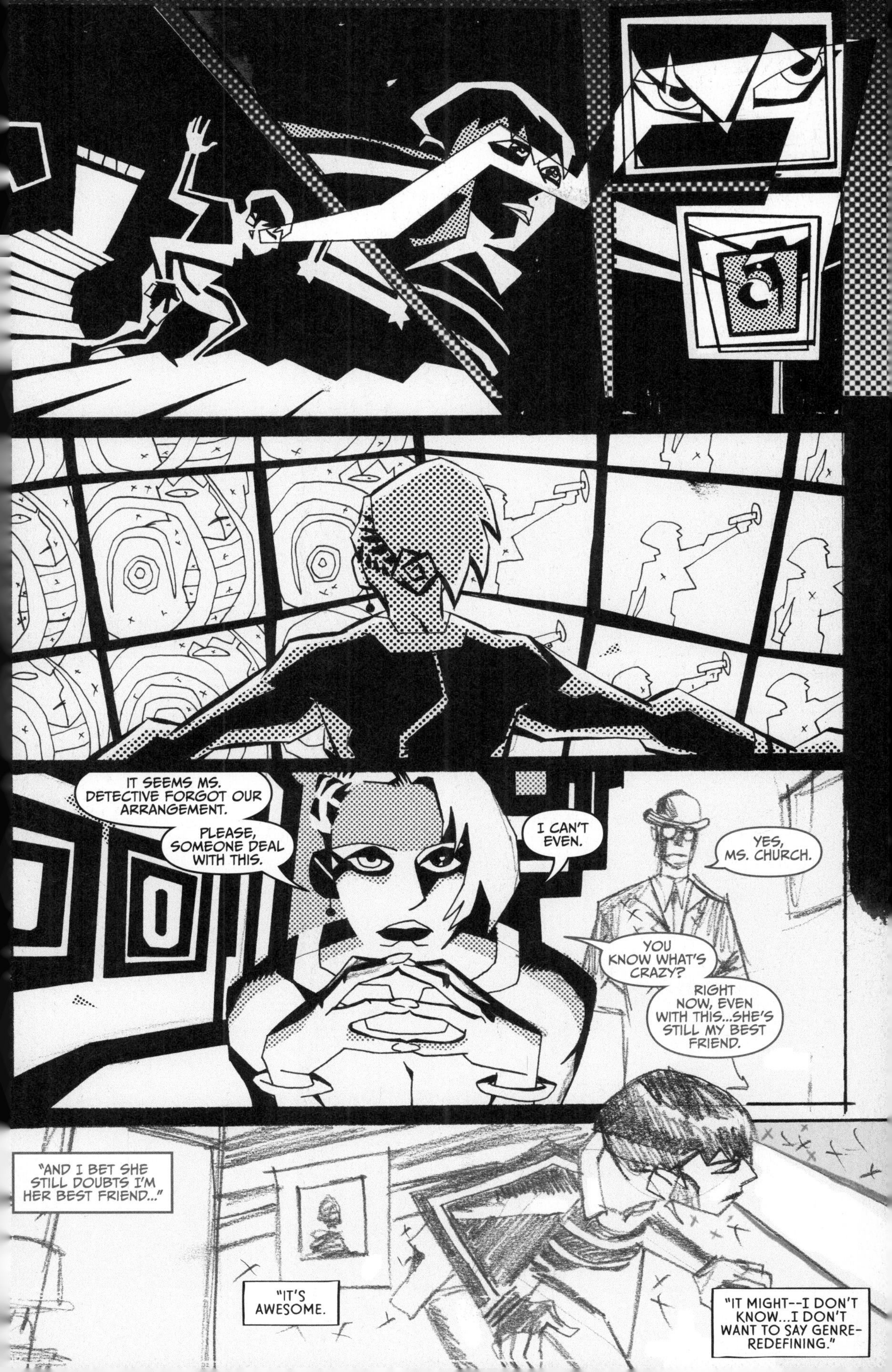
IT SEEMS MS. DETECTIVE FORGOT OUR ARRANGEMENT.
PLEASE, SOMEONE DEAL WITH THIS.
I CAN'T EVEN.
YES, MS. CHURCH.
YOU KNOW WHAT'S CRAZY?
RIGHT NOW, EVEN WITH THIS...SHE'S STILL MY BEST FRIEND.
"AND I BET SHE STILL DOUBTS I'M HER BEST FRIEND..."
"IT'S AWESOME.
"IT MIGHT--I DON'T KNOW...I DON'T WANT TO SAY GENRE-REDEFINING."

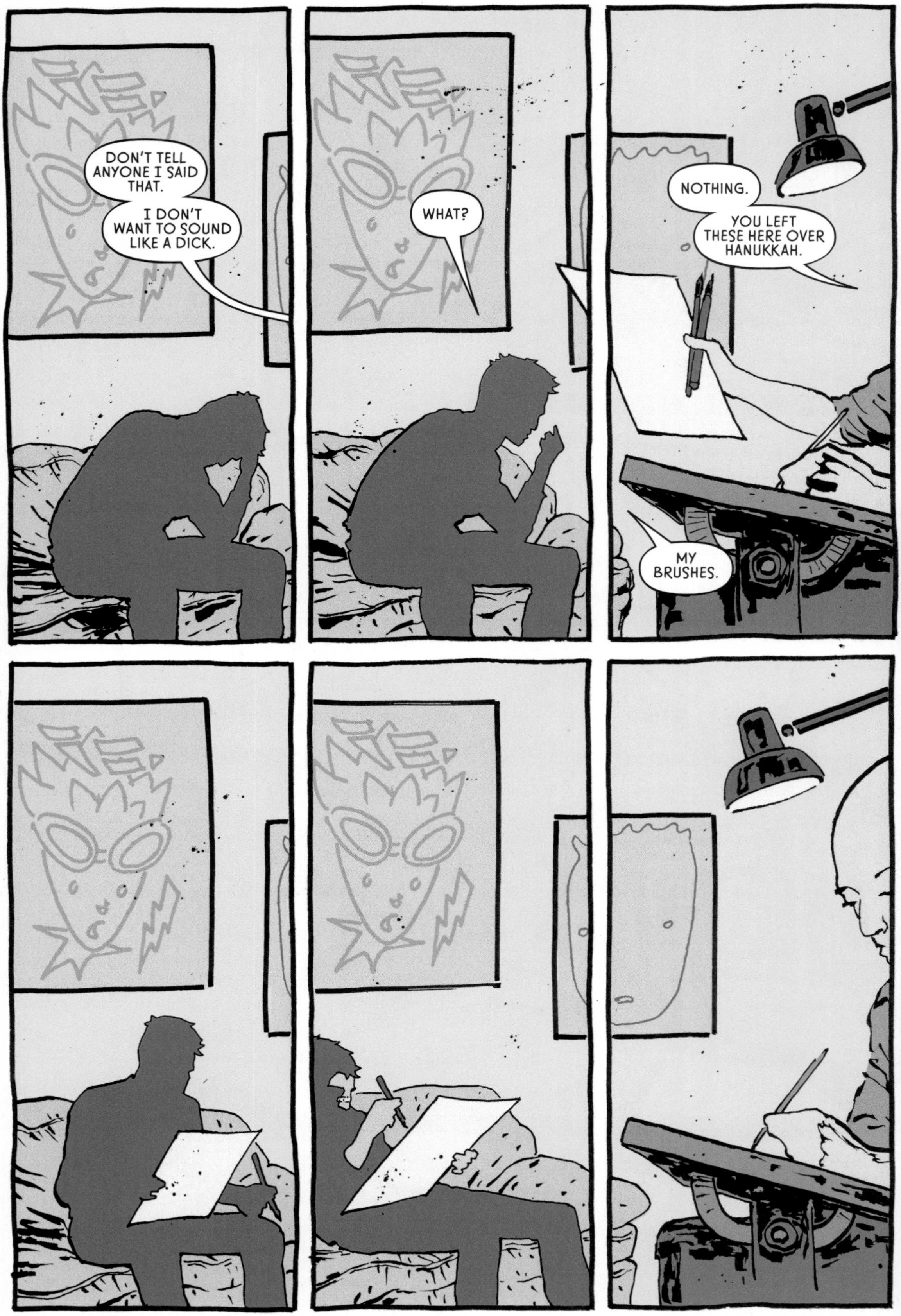
DON'T TELL ANYONE I SAID THAT.
I DON'T WANT TO SOUND LIKE A DICK.
WHAT?
NOTHING.
YOU LEFT THESE HERE OVER HANUKKAH.
MY BRUSHES.

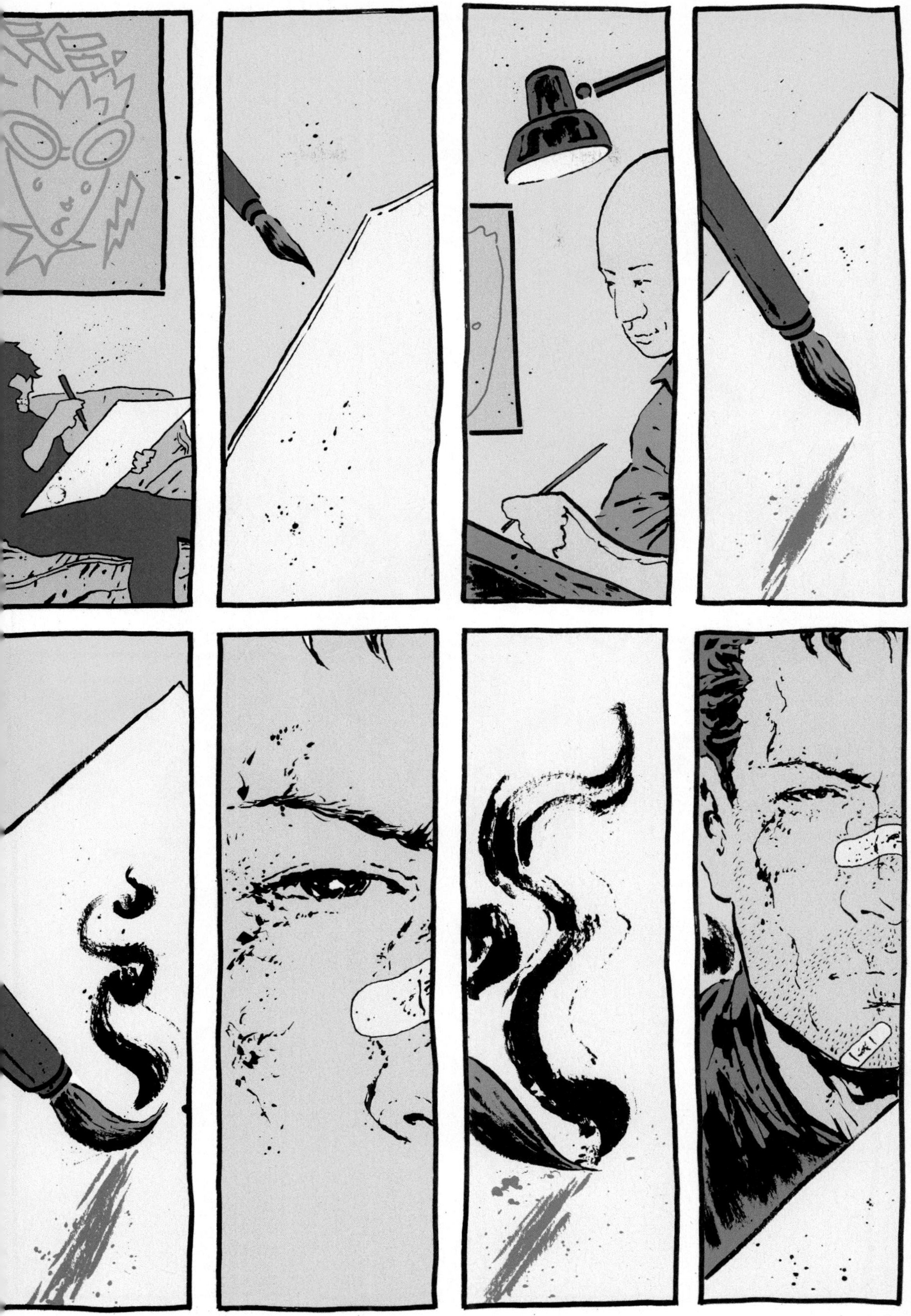

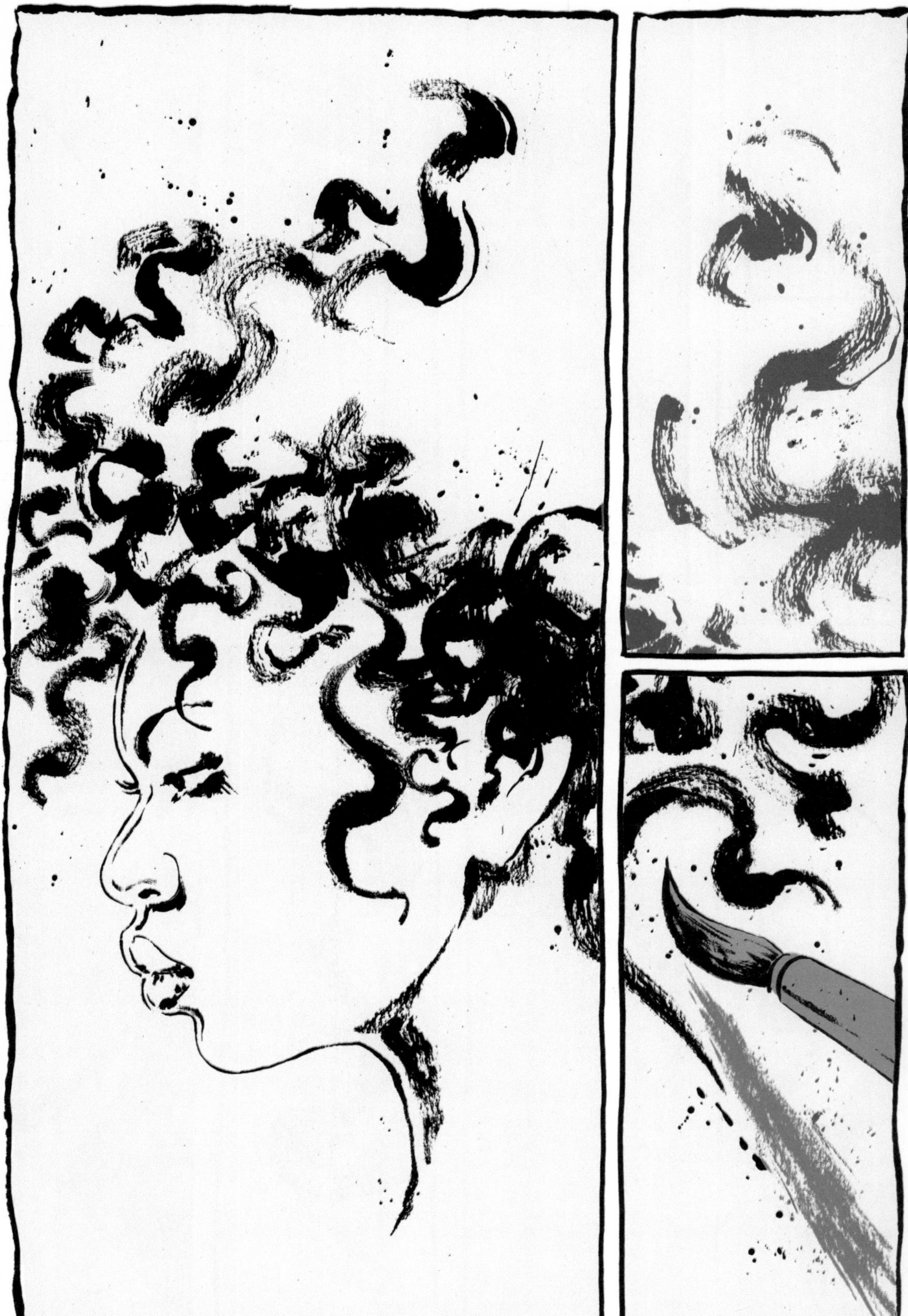

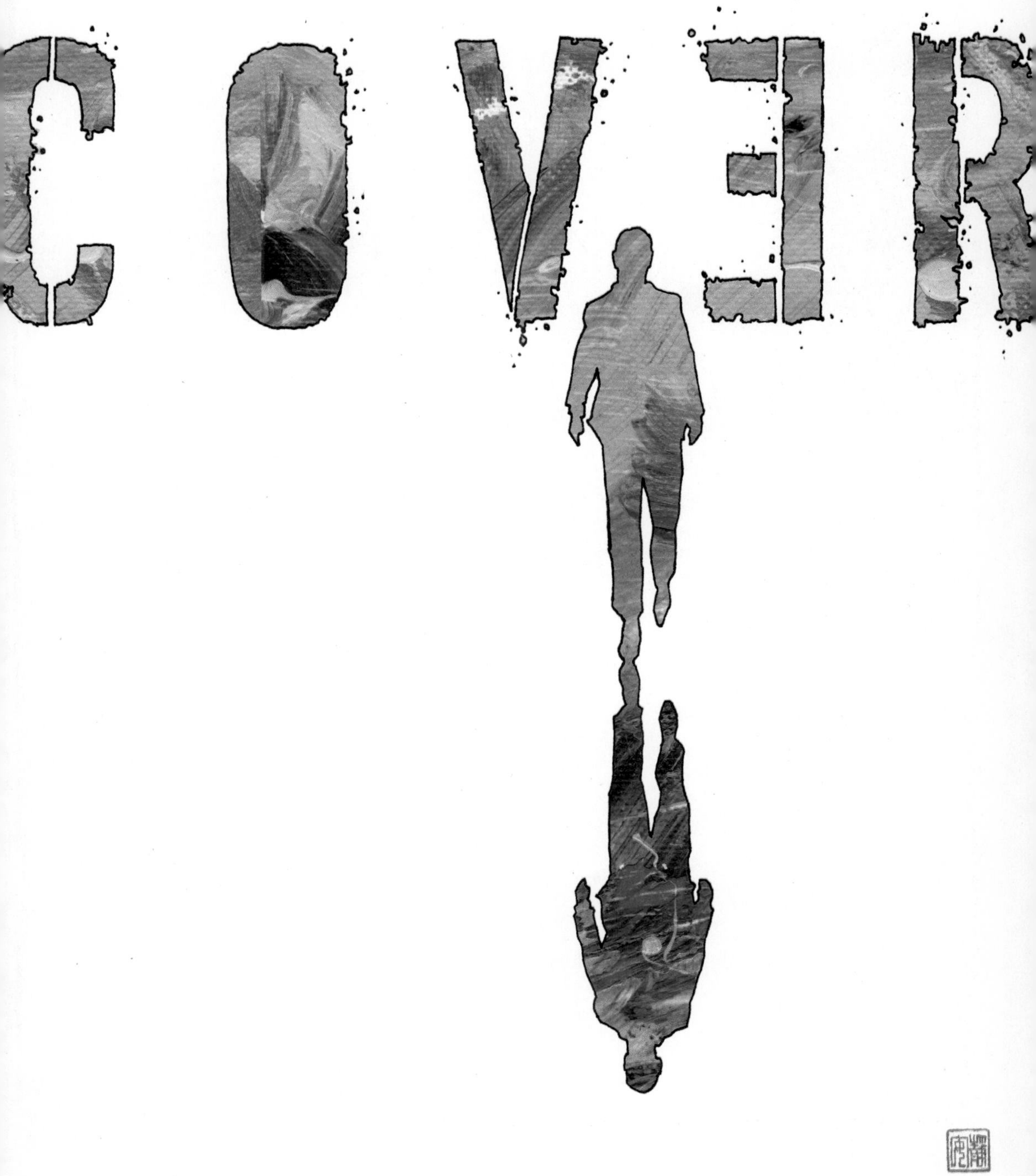
COVER
MACK

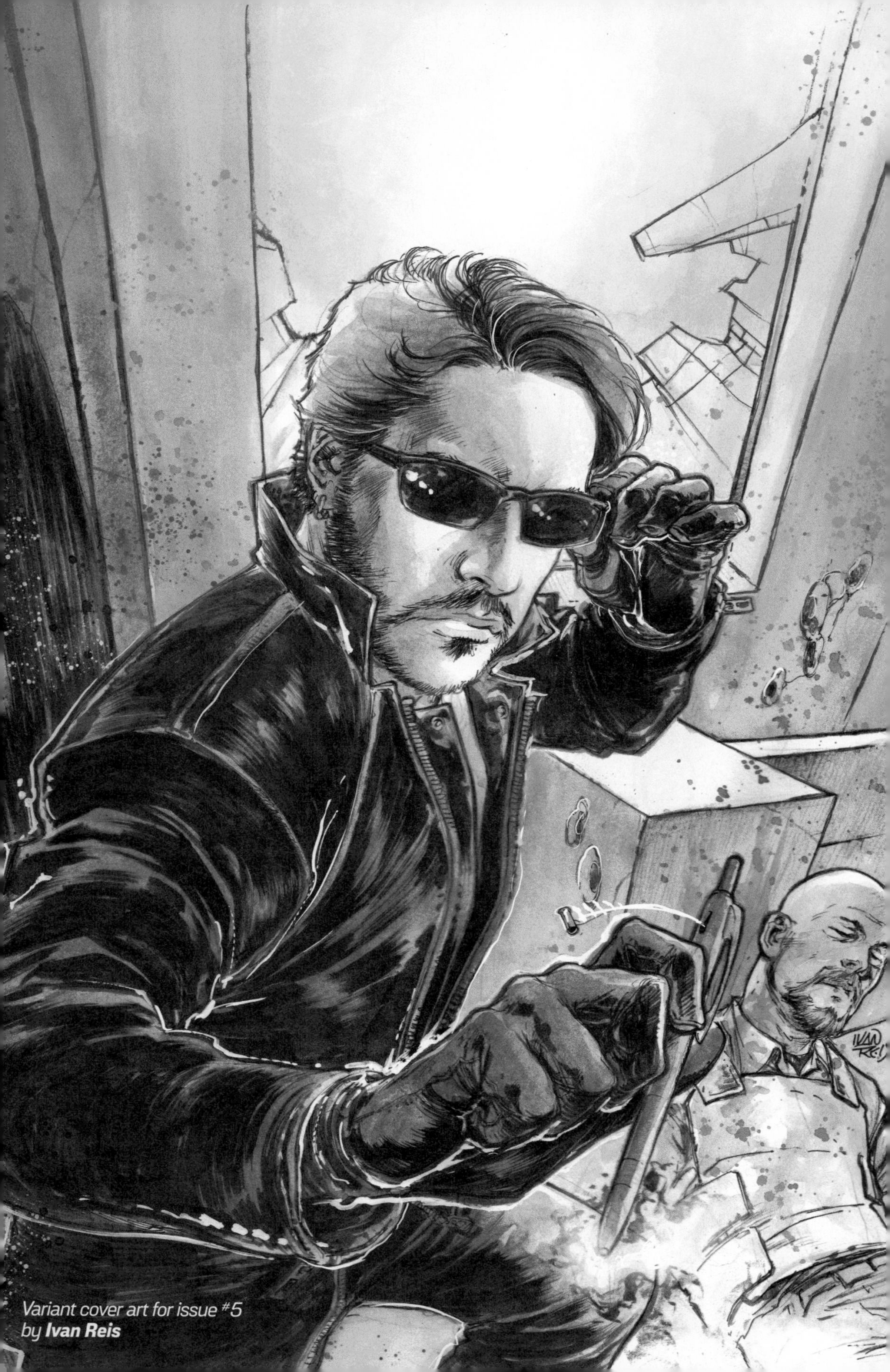

Variant cover art for issue #5
by ***Ivan Reis***

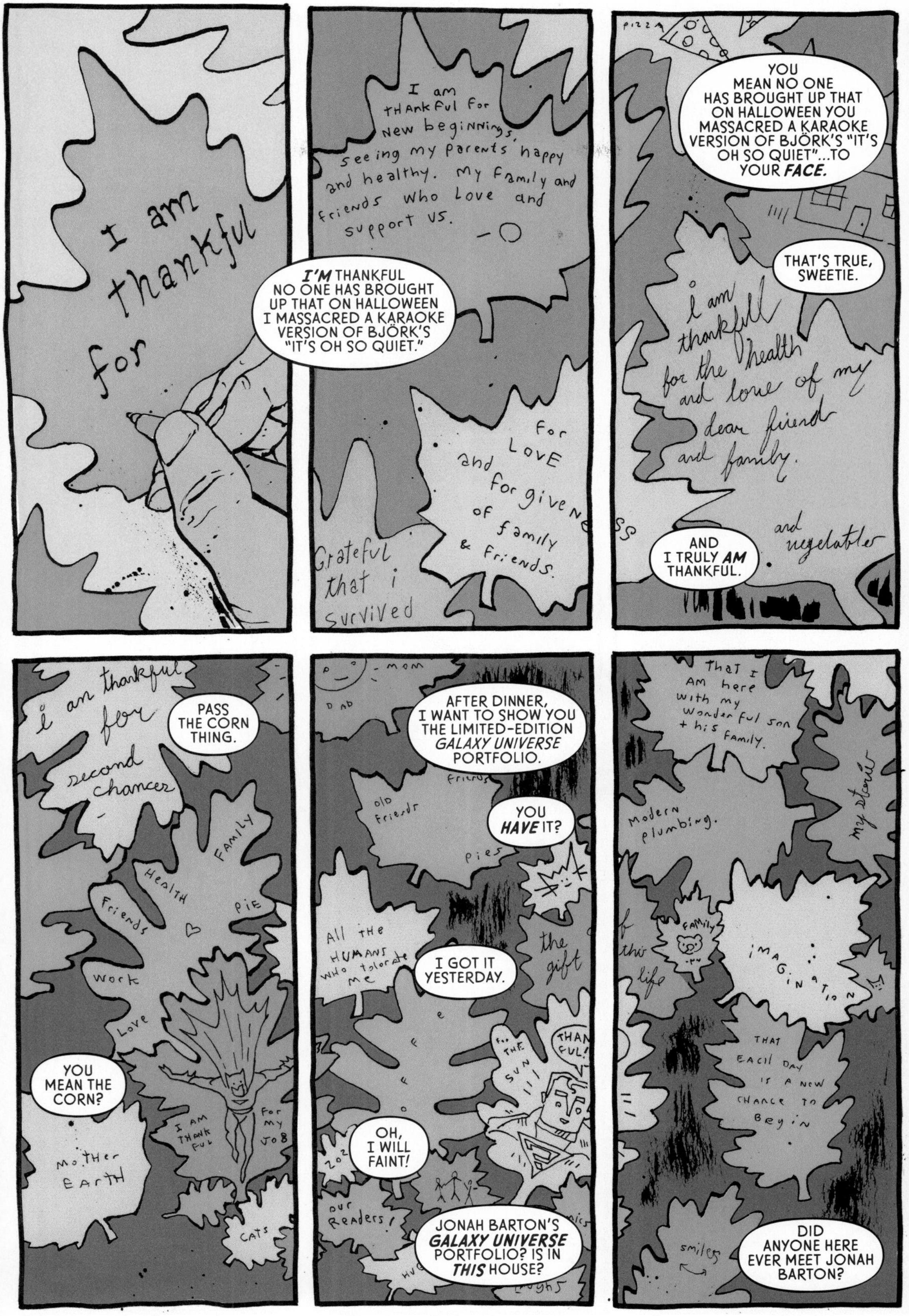
I am thankful for
I am thankful for new beginnings, seeing my parents happy and healthy. My family and friends who love and support us.
I'M THANKFUL NO ONE HAS BROUGHT UP THAT ON HALLOWEEN I MASSACRED A KARAOKE VERSION OF BJÖRK'S "IT'S OH SO QUIET."
For LOVE and forgiveness of family & Friends.
Grateful that i survived
PIZZA
YOU MEAN NO ONE HAS BROUGHT UP THAT ON HALLOWEEN YOU MASSACRED A KARAOKE VERSION OF BJÖRK'S "IT'S OH SO QUIET"...TO YOUR FACE.
THAT'S TRUE, SWEETIE.
i am thankfull for the health and love of my dear friends and family.
AND I TRULY AM THANKFUL.
and vegetables
i am thankful for second chances
PASS THE CORN THING.
FAMILY
Health
Friends
PIE
Work
Love
YOU MEAN THE CORN?
I AM THANKFUL
For my JOB
Mother EARTH
CATS
MOM
DAD
AFTER DINNER, I WANT TO SHOW YOU THE LIMITED-EDITION GALAXY UNIVERSE PORTFOLIO.
old friends
YOU HAVE IT?
pies
All the HUMANS who tolerate me
I GOT IT YESTERDAY.
the gift
For THE SUN
THANKFUL!
OH, I WILL FAINT!
our Readers!
JONAH BARTON'S GALAXY UNIVERSE PORTFOLIO? IS IN THIS HOUSE?
That I AM here with my Wonderful son + his family.
Modern plumbing.
my stories
FAMILY
of this life
IMAGINATION
THAT EACH DAY IS A NEW CHANCE TO Begin
smiles
DID ANYONE HERE EVER MEET JONAH BARTON?

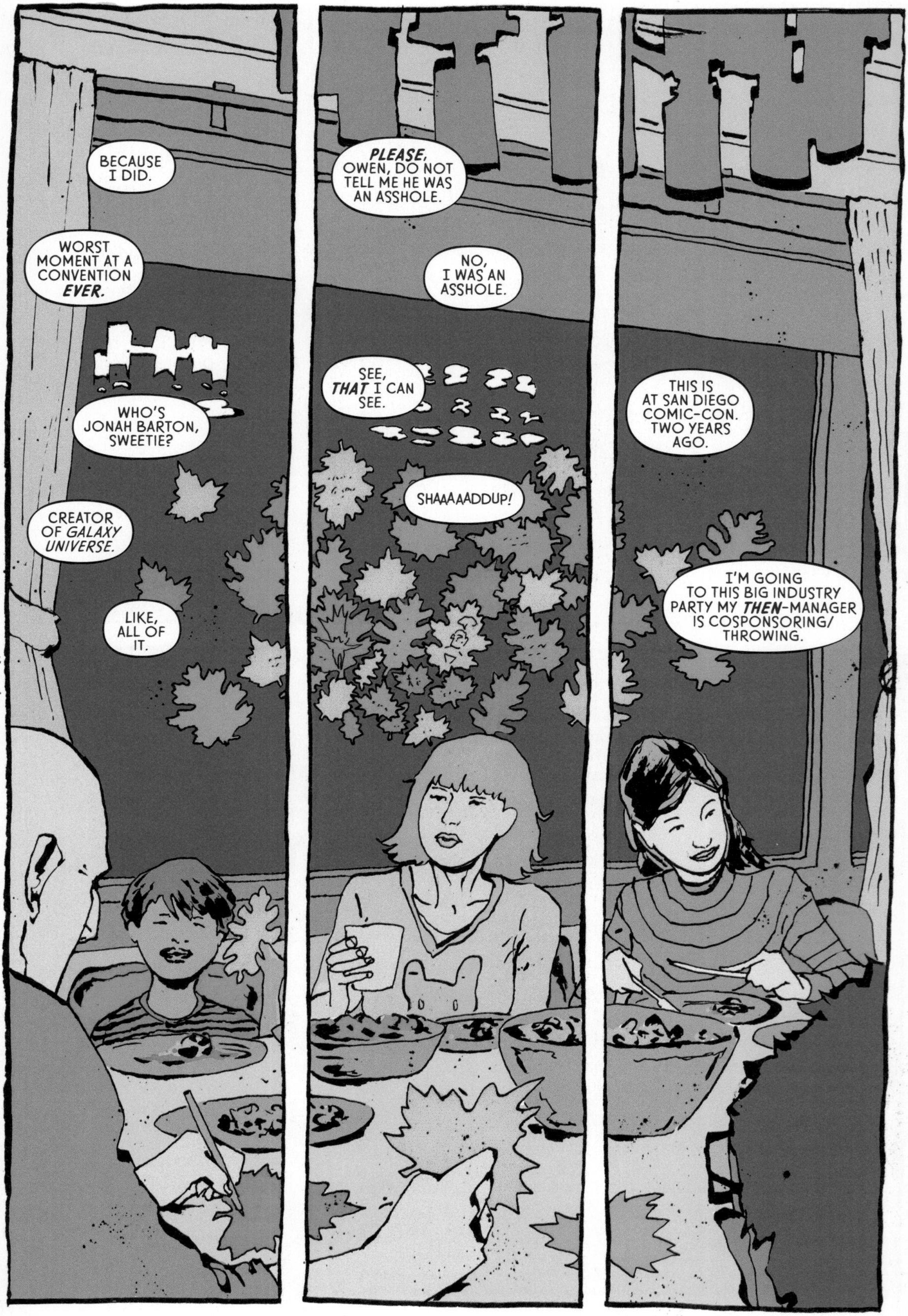
BECAUSE I DID.
WORST MOMENT AT A CONVENTION *EVER.*
WHO'S JONAH BARTON, SWEETIE?
CREATOR OF *GALAXY UNIVERSE.*
LIKE, ALL OF IT.
PLEASE, OWEN, DO NOT TELL ME HE WAS AN ASSHOLE.
NO, I WAS AN ASSHOLE.
SEE, *THAT* I CAN SEE.
SHAAAAADDUP!
THIS IS AT SAN DIEGO COMIC-CON. TWO YEARS AGO.
I'M GOING TO THIS BIG INDUSTRY PARTY MY *THEN*-MANAGER IS COSPONSORING/ THROWING.

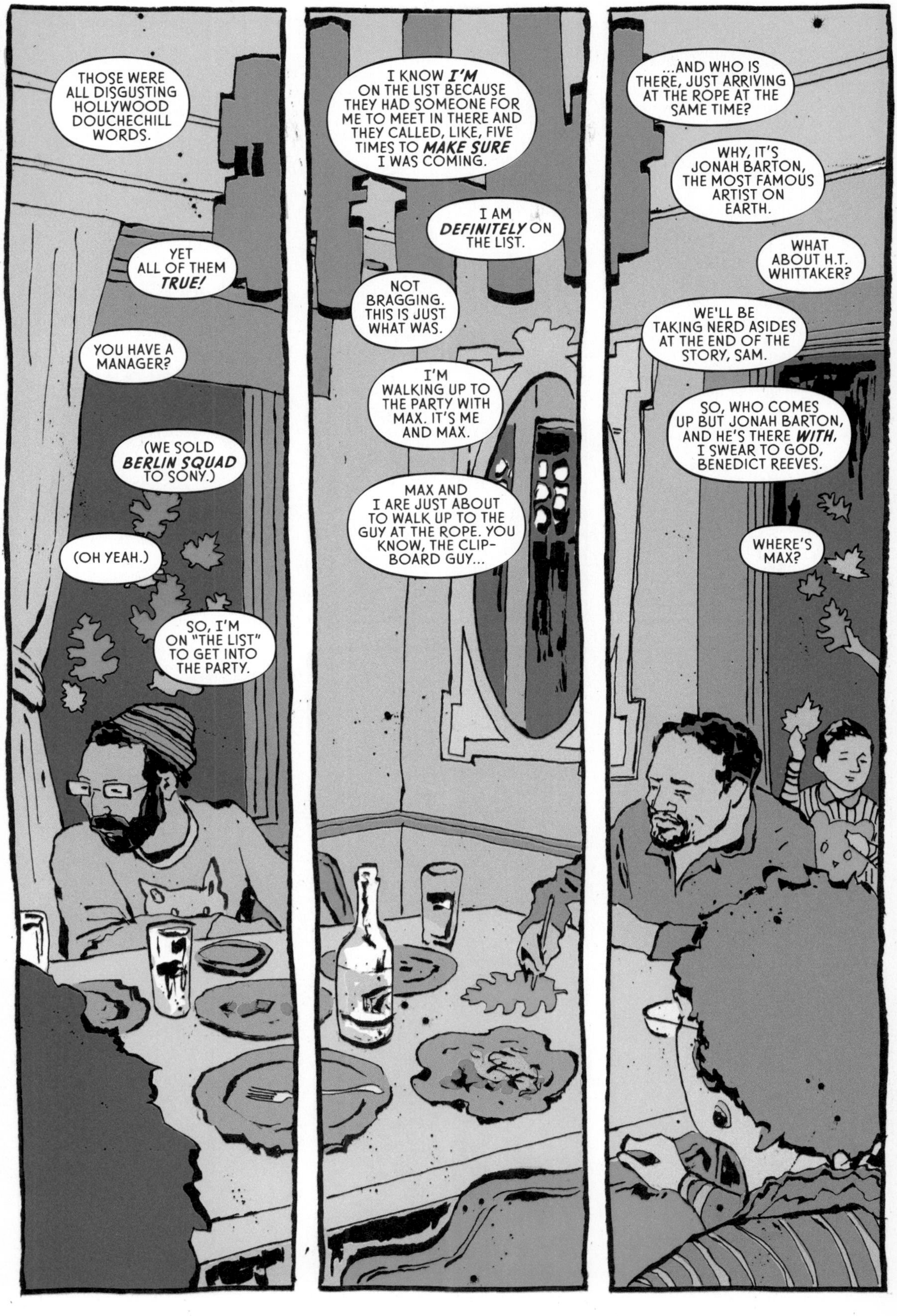
THOSE WERE ALL DISGUSTING HOLLYWOOD DOUCHECHILL WORDS.
YET ALL OF THEM TRUE!
YOU HAVE A MANAGER?
(WE SOLD BERLIN SQUAD TO SONY.)
(OH YEAH.)
SO, I'M ON "THE LIST" TO GET INTO THE PARTY.
I KNOW I'M ON THE LIST BECAUSE THEY HAD SOMEONE FOR ME TO MEET IN THERE AND THEY CALLED, LIKE, FIVE TIMES TO MAKE SURE I WAS COMING.
I AM DEFINITELY ON THE LIST.
NOT BRAGGING. THIS IS JUST WHAT WAS.
I'M WALKING UP TO THE PARTY WITH MAX. IT'S ME AND MAX.
MAX AND I ARE JUST ABOUT TO WALK UP TO THE GUY AT THE ROPE. YOU KNOW, THE CLIP-BOARD GUY...
...AND WHO IS THERE, JUST ARRIVING AT THE ROPE AT THE SAME TIME?
WHY, IT'S JONAH BARTON, THE MOST FAMOUS ARTIST ON EARTH.
WHAT ABOUT H.T. WHITTAKER?
WE'LL BE TAKING NERD ASIDES AT THE END OF THE STORY, SAM.
SO, WHO COMES UP BUT JONAH BARTON, AND HE'S THERE WITH, I SWEAR TO GOD, BENEDICT REEVES.
WHERE'S MAX?

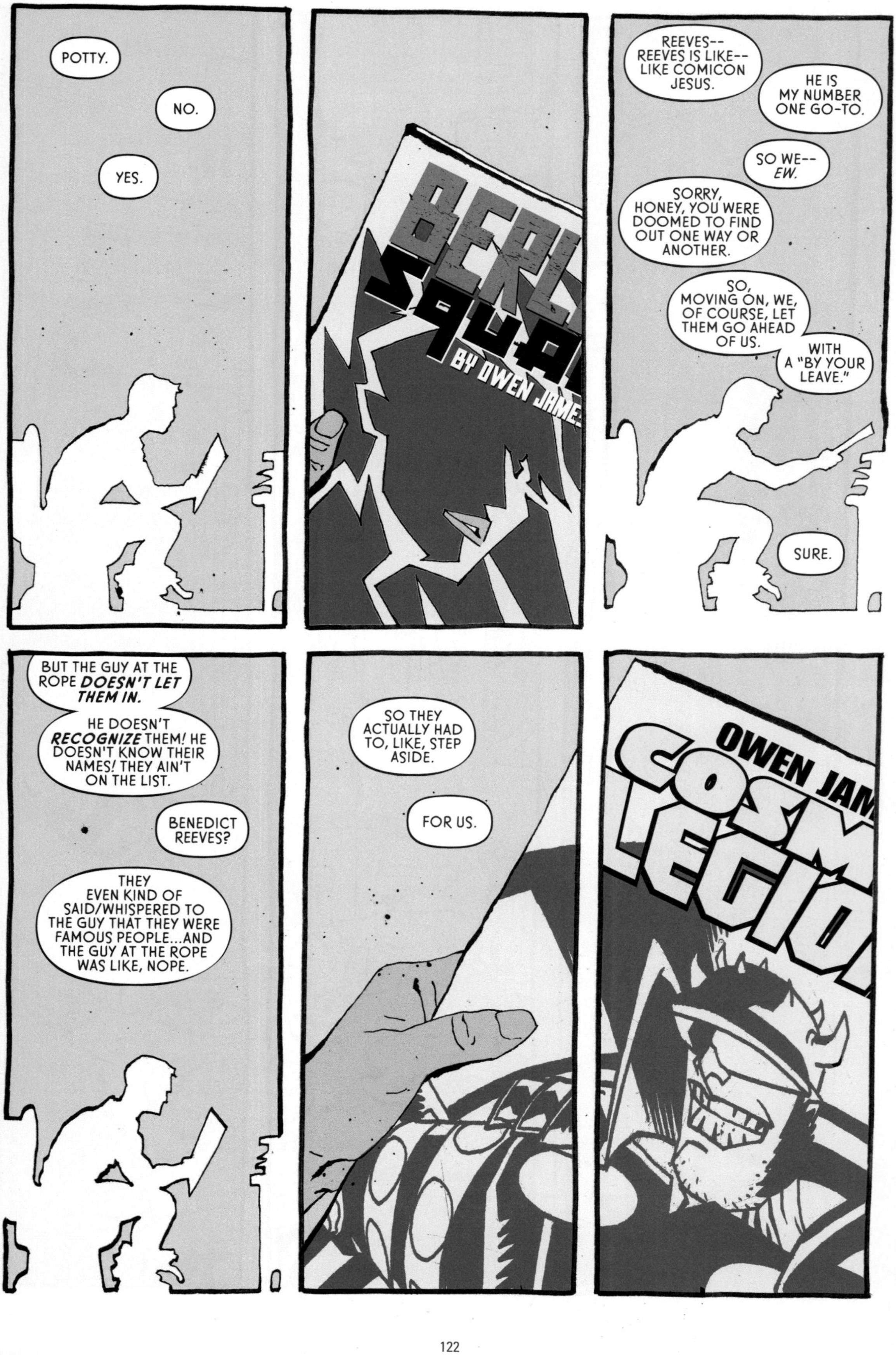
POTTY.
NO.
YES.
BERL
SQUA
BY OWEN JAME
REEVES-- REEVES IS LIKE-- LIKE COMICON JESUS.
HE IS MY NUMBER ONE GO-TO.
SO WE-- *EW.*
SORRY, HONEY, YOU WERE DOOMED TO FIND OUT ONE WAY OR ANOTHER.
SO, MOVING ON, WE, OF COURSE, LET THEM GO AHEAD OF US.
WITH A "BY YOUR LEAVE."
SURE.
BUT THE GUY AT THE ROPE ***DOESN'T LET THEM IN.***
HE DOESN'T ***RECOGNIZE*** THEM! HE DOESN'T KNOW THEIR NAMES! THEY AIN'T ON THE LIST.
BENEDICT REEVES?
THEY EVEN KIND OF SAID/WHISPERED TO THE GUY THAT THEY WERE FAMOUS PEOPLE...AND THE GUY AT THE ROPE WAS LIKE, NOPE.
SO THEY ACTUALLY HAD TO, LIKE, STEP ASIDE.
FOR US.
OWEN JAM
COSM
LEGIO

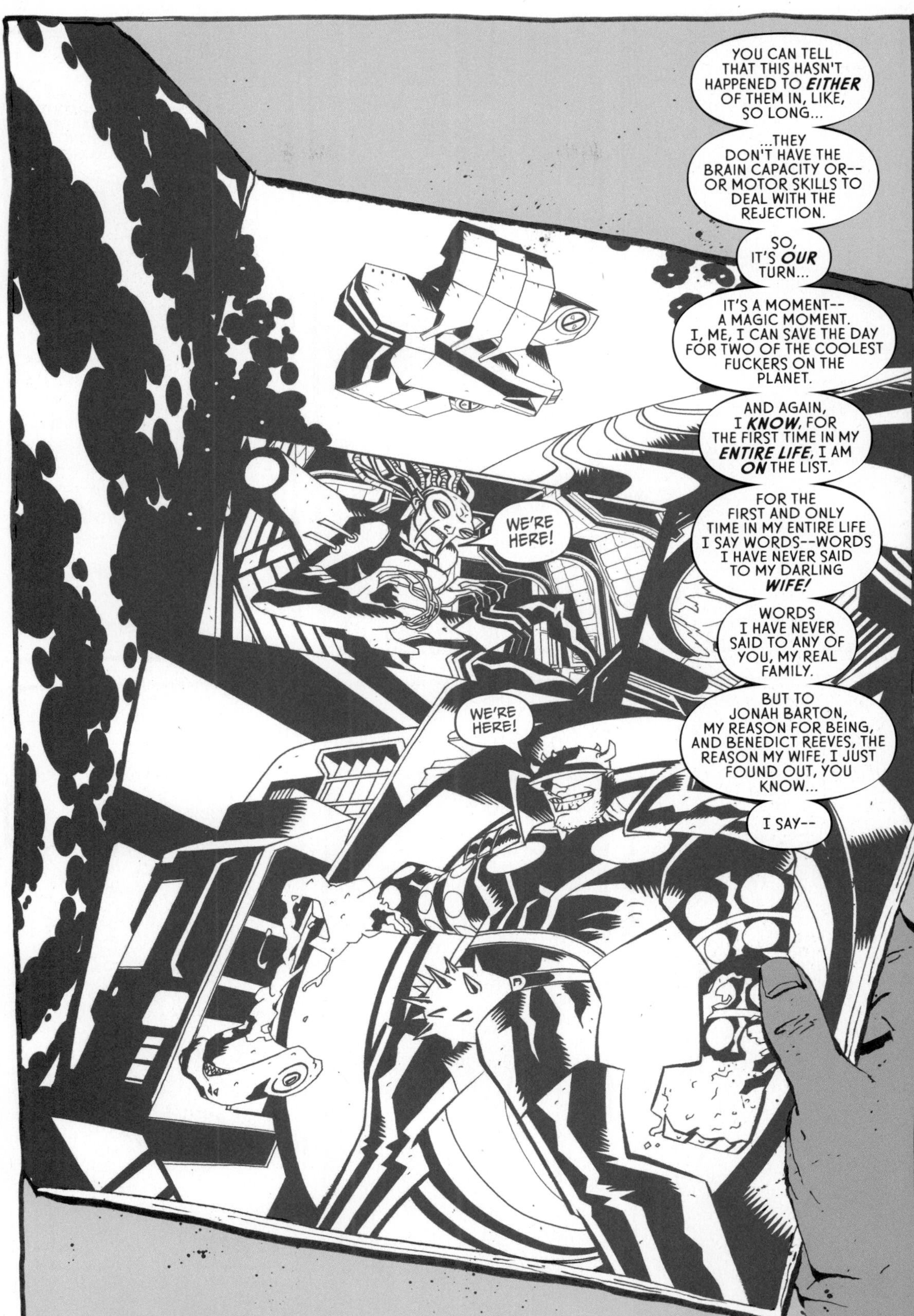
YOU CAN TELL THAT THIS HASN'T HAPPENED TO EITHER OF THEM IN, LIKE, SO LONG...
...THEY DON'T HAVE THE BRAIN CAPACITY OR-- OR MOTOR SKILLS TO DEAL WITH THE REJECTION.
SO, IT'S OUR TURN...
IT'S A MOMENT-- A MAGIC MOMENT. I, ME, I CAN SAVE THE DAY FOR TWO OF THE COOLEST FUCKERS ON THE PLANET.
AND AGAIN, I KNOW, FOR THE FIRST TIME IN MY ENTIRE LIFE, I AM ON THE LIST.
WE'RE HERE!
FOR THE FIRST AND ONLY TIME IN MY ENTIRE LIFE I SAY WORDS--WORDS I HAVE NEVER SAID TO MY DARLING WIFE!
WORDS I HAVE NEVER SAID TO ANY OF YOU, MY REAL FAMILY.
WE'RE HERE!
BUT TO JONAH BARTON, MY REASON FOR BEING, AND BENEDICT REEVES, THE REASON MY WIFE, I JUST FOUND OUT, YOU KNOW...
I SAY--

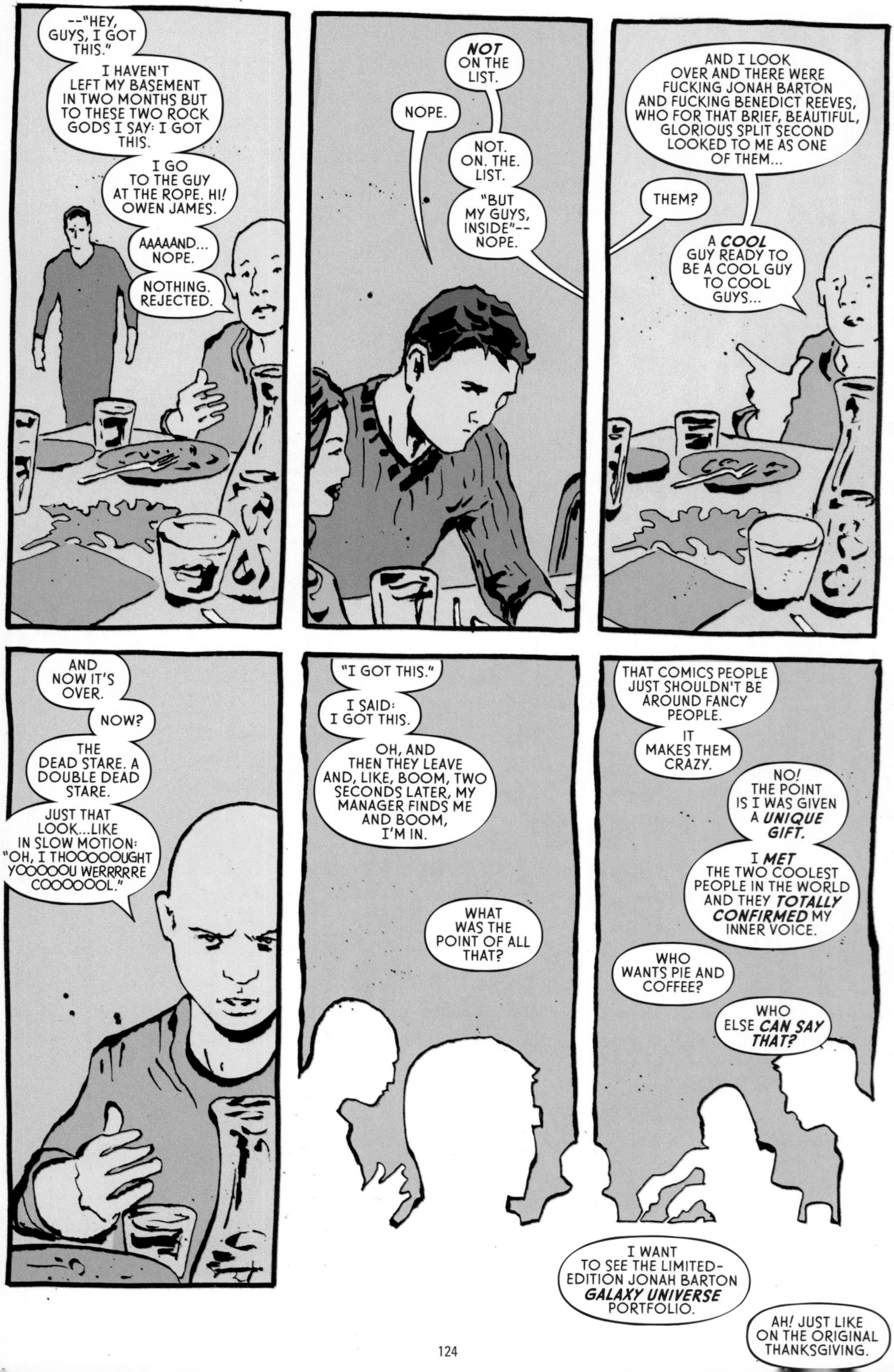

--"HEY, GUYS, I GOT THIS."
I HAVEN'T LEFT MY BASEMENT IN TWO MONTHS BUT TO THESE TWO ROCK GODS I SAY: I GOT THIS.
I GO TO THE GUY AT THE ROPE. HI! OWEN JAMES.
AAAAAND... NOPE.
NOTHING. REJECTED.
NOPE.
NOT ON THE LIST.
NOT. ON. THE. LIST.
"BUT MY GUYS, INSIDE"-- NOPE.
AND I LOOK OVER AND THERE WERE FUCKING JONAH BARTON AND FUCKING BENEDICT REEVES, WHO FOR THAT BRIEF, BEAUTIFUL, GLORIOUS SPLIT SECOND LOOKED TO ME AS ONE OF THEM...
THEM?
A COOL GUY READY TO BE A COOL GUY TO COOL GUYS...
AND NOW IT'S OVER.
NOW?
THE DEAD STARE. A DOUBLE DEAD STARE.
JUST THAT LOOK...LIKE IN SLOW MOTION: "OH, I THOOOOOUGHT YOOOOOU WERRRRRE COOOOOOL."
"I GOT THIS."
I SAID: I GOT THIS.
OH, AND THEN THEY LEAVE AND, LIKE, BOOM, TWO SECONDS LATER, MY MANAGER FINDS ME AND BOOM, I'M IN.
WHAT WAS THE POINT OF ALL THAT?
THAT COMICS PEOPLE JUST SHOULDN'T BE AROUND FANCY PEOPLE.
IT MAKES THEM CRAZY.
NO! THE POINT IS I WAS GIVEN A UNIQUE GIFT.
I MET THE TWO COOLEST PEOPLE IN THE WORLD AND THEY TOTALLY CONFIRMED MY INNER VOICE.
WHO WANTS PIE AND COFFEE?
WHO ELSE CAN SAY THAT?
I WANT TO SEE THE LIMITED-EDITION JONAH BARTON GALAXY UNIVERSE PORTFOLIO.
AH! JUST LIKE ON THE ORIGINAL THANKSGIVING.

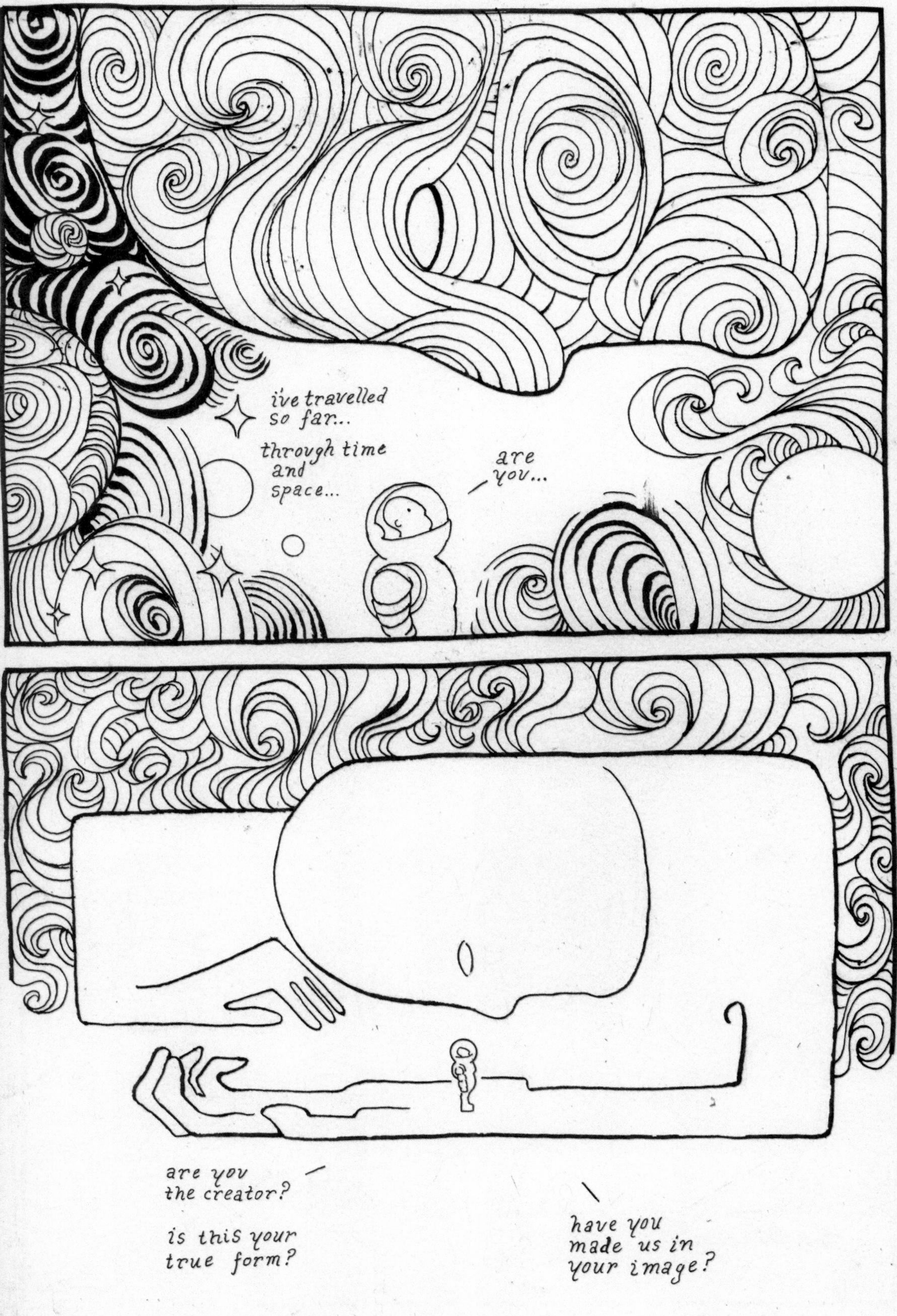
i've travelled so far...
through time and space...
are you...
are you the creator?
is this your true form?
have you made us in your image?

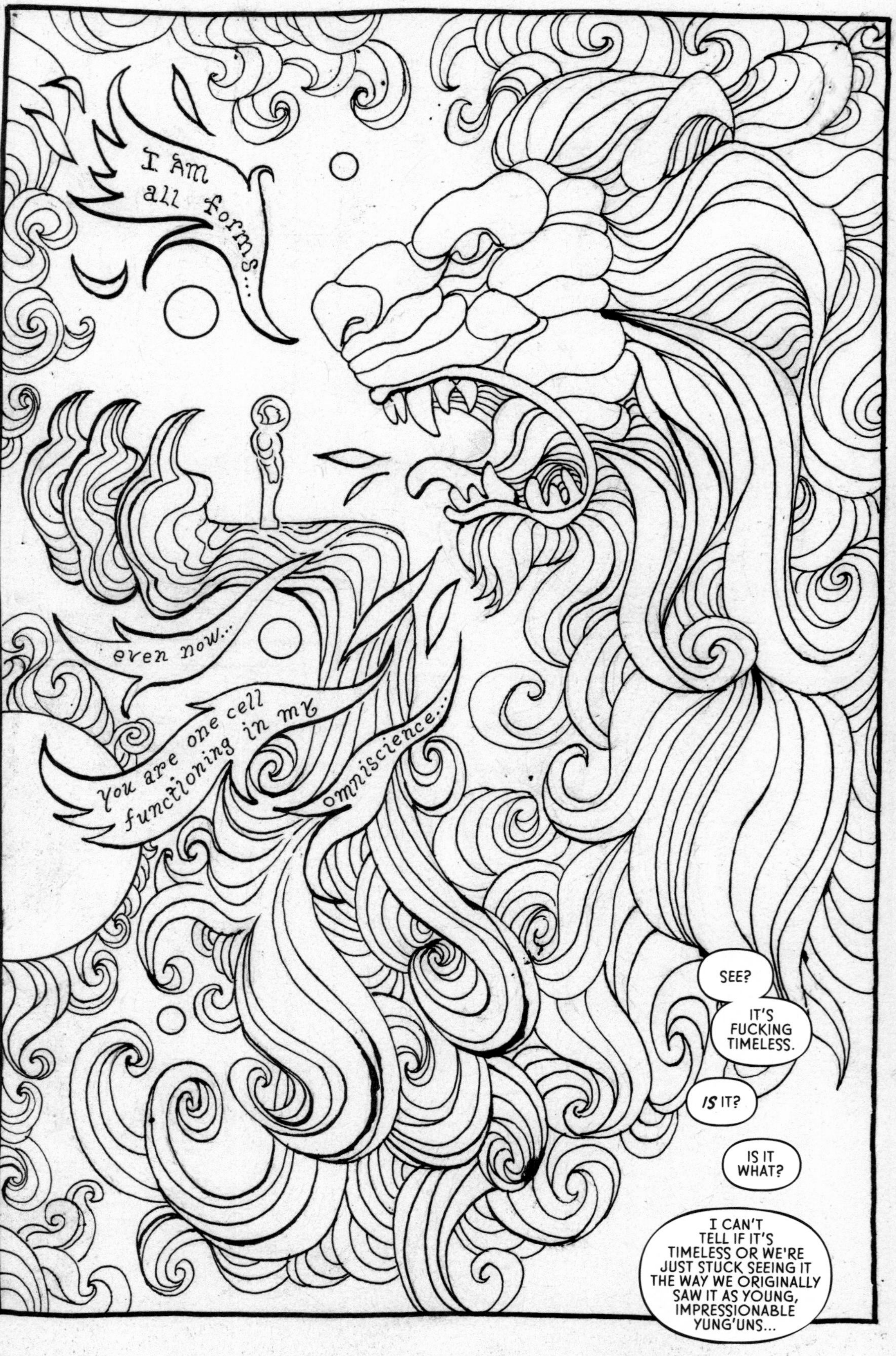
I am all forms...
even now...
you are one cell functioning in my omniscience...
SEE?
IT'S FUCKING TIMELESS.
IS IT?
IS IT WHAT?
I CAN'T TELL IF IT'S TIMELESS OR WE'RE JUST STUCK SEEING IT THE WAY WE ORIGINALLY SAW IT AS YOUNG, IMPRESSIONABLE YUNG'UNS...

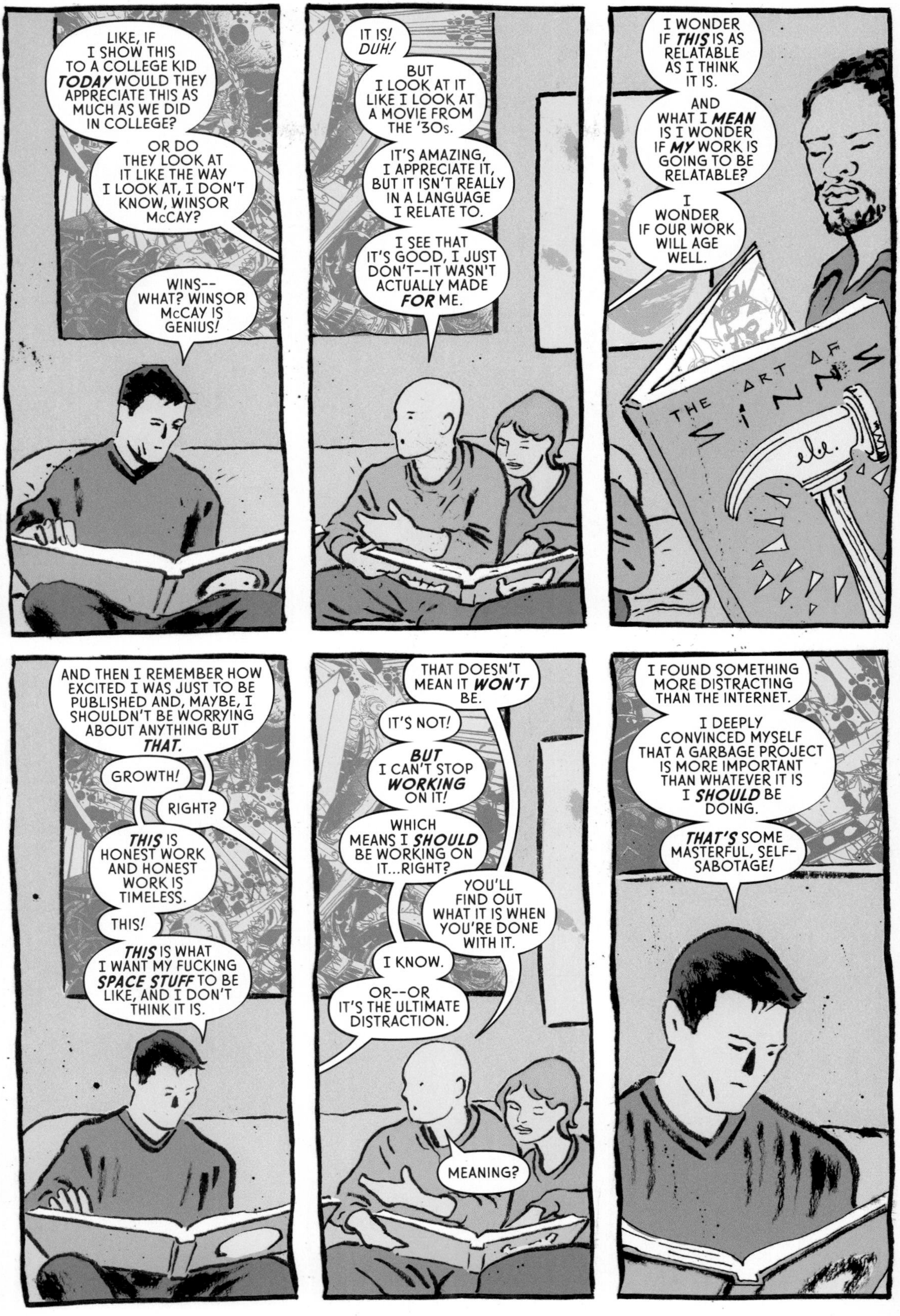

LIKE, IF I SHOW THIS TO A COLLEGE KID **TODAY** WOULD THEY APPRECIATE THIS AS MUCH AS WE DID IN COLLEGE?
OR DO THEY LOOK AT IT LIKE THE WAY I LOOK AT, I DON'T KNOW, WINSOR McCAY?
WINS--WHAT? WINSOR McCAY IS GENIUS!
IT IS! *DUH!*
BUT I LOOK AT IT LIKE I LOOK AT A MOVIE FROM THE '30s.
IT'S AMAZING, I APPRECIATE IT, BUT IT ISN'T REALLY IN A LANGUAGE I RELATE TO.
I SEE THAT IT'S GOOD, I JUST DON'T--IT WASN'T ACTUALLY MADE **FOR** ME.
I WONDER IF **THIS** IS AS RELATABLE AS I THINK IT IS.
AND WHAT I **MEAN** IS I WONDER IF **MY** WORK IS GOING TO BE RELATABLE?
I WONDER IF OUR WORK WILL AGE WELL.
THE ART OF SINNS
AND THEN I REMEMBER HOW EXCITED I WAS JUST TO BE PUBLISHED AND, MAYBE, I SHOULDN'T BE WORRYING ABOUT ANYTHING BUT **THAT.**
GROWTH!
RIGHT?
THIS IS HONEST WORK AND HONEST WORK IS TIMELESS.
THIS!
THIS IS WHAT I WANT MY FUCKING **SPACE STUFF** TO BE LIKE, AND I DON'T THINK IT IS.
THAT DOESN'T MEAN IT **WON'T** BE.
IT'S NOT!
BUT I CAN'T STOP **WORKING** ON IT!
WHICH MEANS I **SHOULD** BE WORKING ON IT...RIGHT?
YOU'LL FIND OUT WHAT IT IS WHEN YOU'RE DONE WITH IT.
I KNOW.
OR--OR IT'S THE ULTIMATE DISTRACTION.
MEANING?
I FOUND SOMETHING MORE DISTRACTING THAN THE INTERNET.
I DEEPLY CONVINCED MYSELF THAT A GARBAGE PROJECT IS MORE IMPORTANT THAN WHATEVER IT IS I **SHOULD** BE DOING.
THAT'S SOME MASTERFUL, SELF-SABOTAGE!

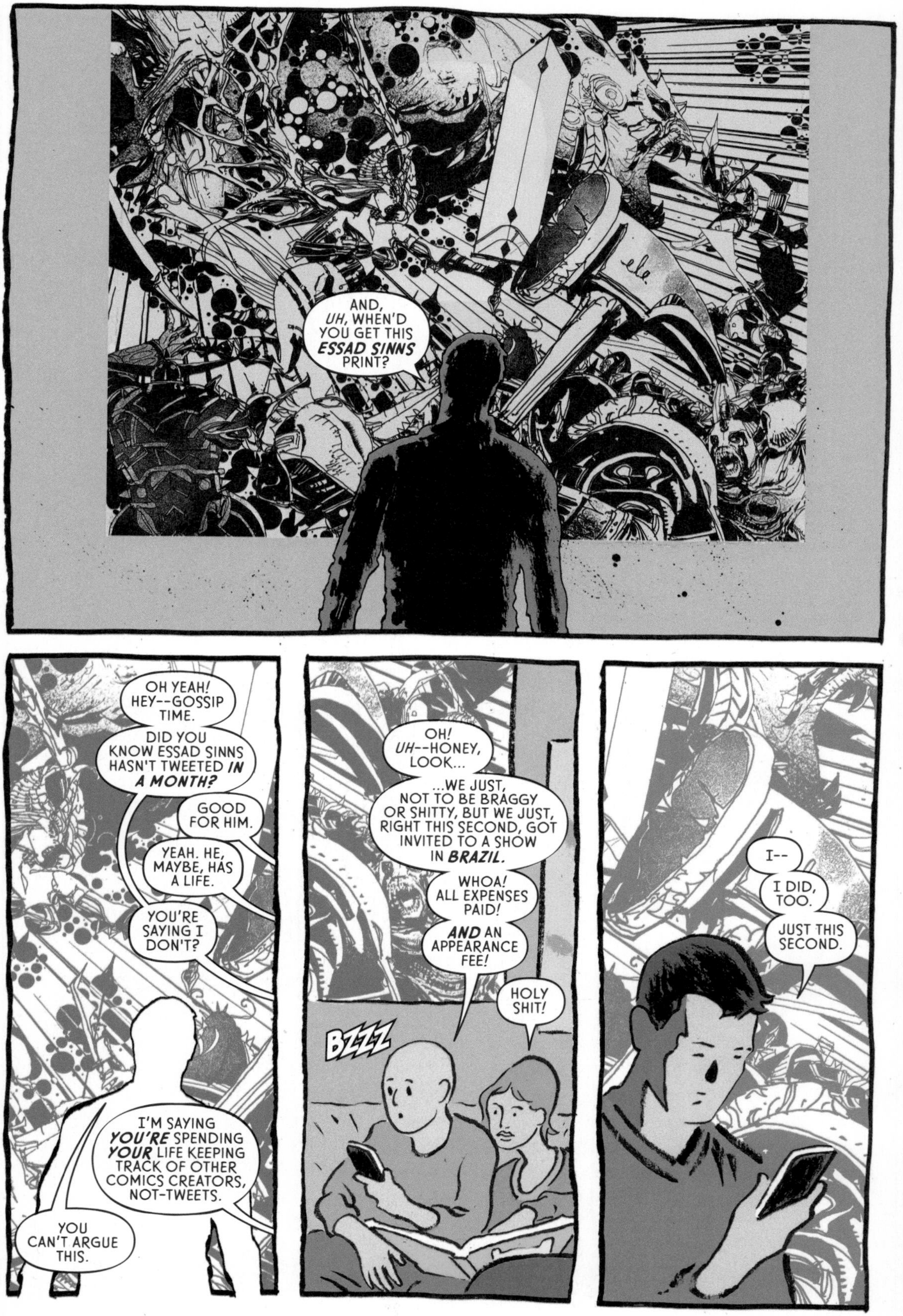
AND, UH, WHEN'D YOU GET THIS ESSAD SINNS PRINT?
OH YEAH! HEY--GOSSIP TIME.
DID YOU KNOW ESSAD SINNS HASN'T TWEETED IN A MONTH?
GOOD FOR HIM.
YEAH. HE, MAYBE, HAS A LIFE.
YOU'RE SAYING I DON'T?
I'M SAYING YOU'RE SPENDING YOUR LIFE KEEPING TRACK OF OTHER COMICS CREATORS, NOT-TWEETS.
YOU CAN'T ARGUE THIS.
OH! UH--HONEY, LOOK...
...WE JUST, NOT TO BE BRAGGY OR SHITTY, BUT WE JUST, RIGHT THIS SECOND, GOT INVITED TO A SHOW IN BRAZIL.
WHOA! ALL EXPENSES PAID!
AND AN APPEARANCE FEE!
HOLY SHIT!
BZZZ
I--
I DID, TOO.
JUST THIS SECOND.

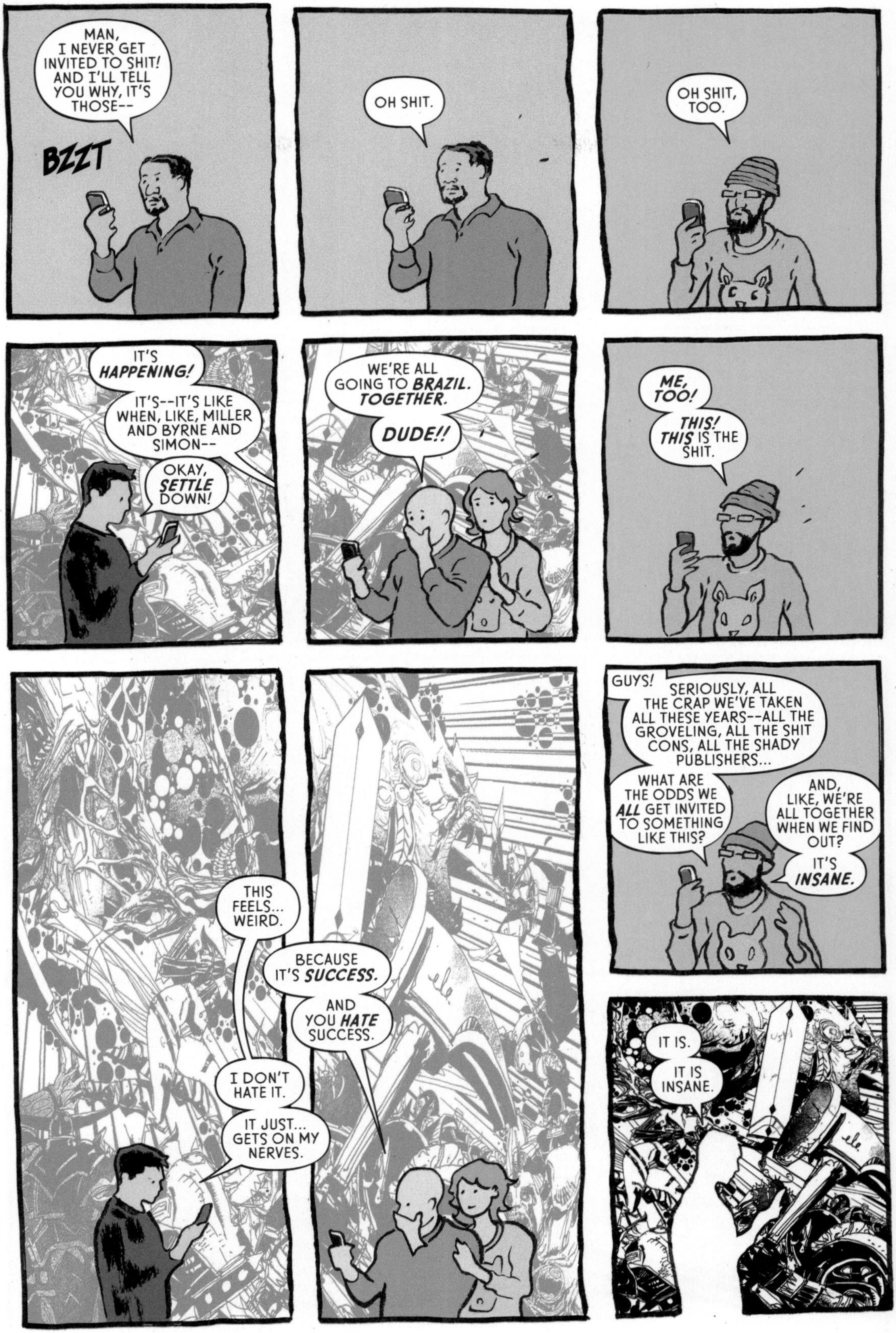
MAN, I NEVER GET INVITED TO SHIT! AND I'LL TELL YOU WHY, IT'S THOSE--
BZZT
OH SHIT.
OH SHIT, TOO.
IT'S *HAPPENING!*
IT'S--IT'S LIKE WHEN, LIKE, MILLER AND BYRNE AND SIMON--
OKAY, *SETTLE* DOWN!
WE'RE ALL GOING TO *BRAZIL. TOGETHER.*
DUDE!!
ME, TOO!
THIS! THIS IS THE SHIT.
THIS FEELS... WEIRD.
BECAUSE IT'S *SUCCESS.*
AND YOU *HATE* SUCCESS.
I DON'T HATE IT.
IT JUST... GETS ON MY NERVES.
GUYS!
SERIOUSLY, ALL THE CRAP WE'VE TAKEN ALL THESE YEARS--ALL THE GROVELING, ALL THE SHIT CONS, ALL THE SHADY PUBLISHERS...
WHAT ARE THE ODDS WE *ALL* GET INVITED TO SOMETHING LIKE THIS?
AND, LIKE, WE'RE ALL TOGETHER WHEN WE FIND OUT?
IT'S *INSANE.*
IT IS.
IT IS INSANE.

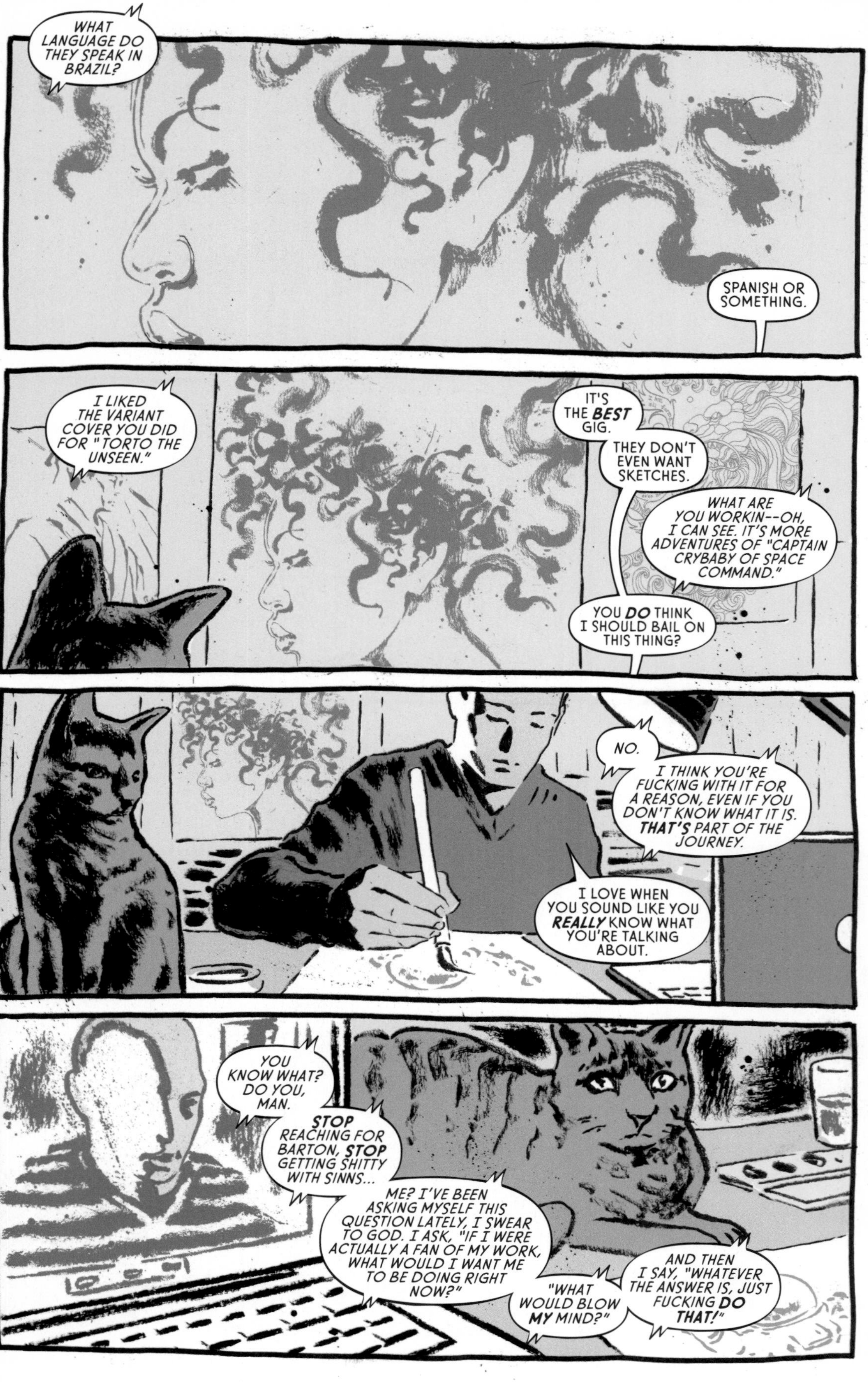
WHAT LANGUAGE DO THEY SPEAK IN BRAZIL?
SPANISH OR SOMETHING.
I LIKED THE VARIANT COVER YOU DID FOR "TORTO THE UNSEEN."
IT'S THE **BEST** GIG.
THEY DON'T EVEN WANT SKETCHES.
WHAT ARE YOU WORKIN--OH, I CAN SEE. IT'S MORE ADVENTURES OF "CAPTAIN CRYBABY OF SPACE COMMAND."
YOU **DO** THINK I SHOULD BAIL ON THIS THING?
NO.
I THINK YOU'RE FUCKING WITH IT FOR A REASON, EVEN IF YOU DON'T KNOW WHAT IT IS. **THAT'S** PART OF THE JOURNEY.
I LOVE WHEN YOU SOUND LIKE YOU **REALLY** KNOW WHAT YOU'RE TALKING ABOUT.
YOU KNOW WHAT? DO YOU, MAN.
STOP REACHING FOR BARTON, **STOP** GETTING SHITTY WITH SINNS...
ME? I'VE BEEN ASKING MYSELF THIS QUESTION LATELY, I SWEAR TO GOD. I ASK, "IF I WERE ACTUALLY A FAN OF MY WORK, WHAT WOULD I WANT ME TO BE DOING RIGHT NOW?"
"WHAT WOULD BLOW **MY** MIND?"
AND THEN I SAY, "WHATEVER THE ANSWER IS, JUST FUCKING **DO THAT!**"

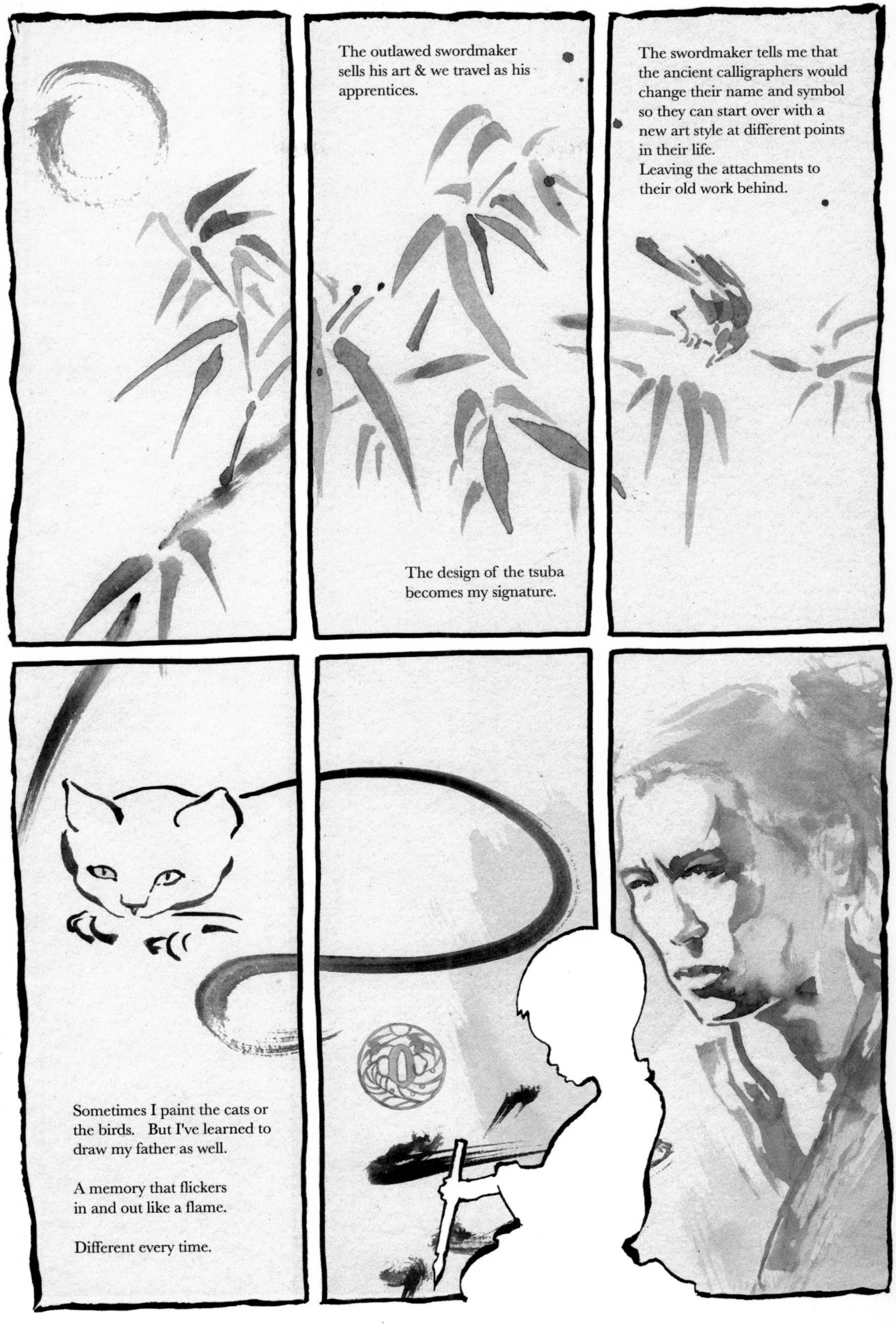

The outlawed swordmaker sells his art & we travel as his apprentices.
The swordmaker tells me that the ancient calligraphers would change their name and symbol so they can start over with a new art style at different points in their life.
Leaving the attachments to their old work behind.
The design of the tsuba becomes my signature.
Sometimes I paint the cats or the birds. But I've learned to draw my father as well.
A memory that flickers in and out like a flame.
Different every time.

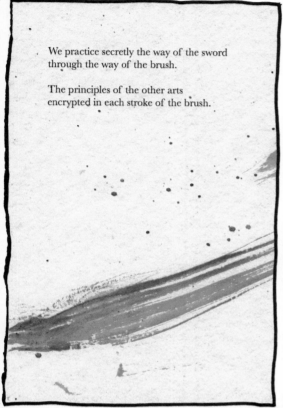

We practice secretly the way of the sword through the way of the brush.

The principles of the other arts encrypted in each stroke of the brush.

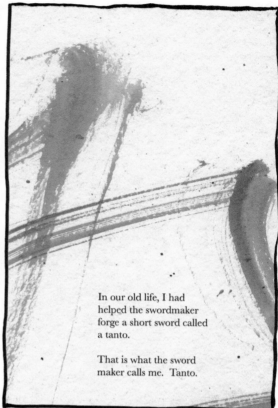

In our old life, I had helped the swordmaker forge a short sword called a tanto.

That is what the sword maker calls me. Tanto.

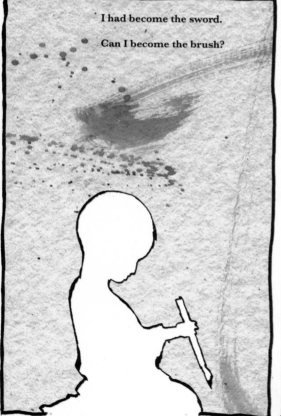

I had become the sword.

Can I become the brush?

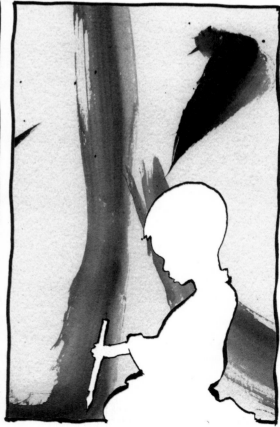

The swordmaker's granddaughter is called Kasai which means fire. She is dressed as a boy so that people think we are the same apprentice.

With this trick we can be in two places at once.

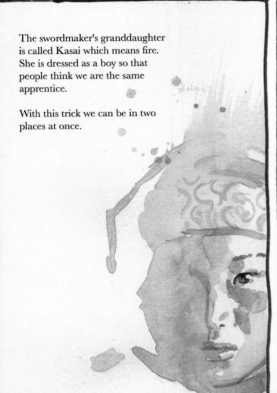

She sculpts a fox mask out of wood.   And she wears it while working.

We come to consider ourselves artists.

Our new role in life.

New rulers take over again.
New rules, new laws.
The world is liquid.

Our identity as traveling artists becomes one red stamp after another.

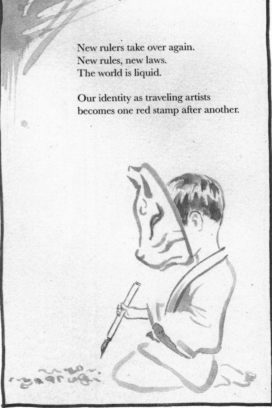

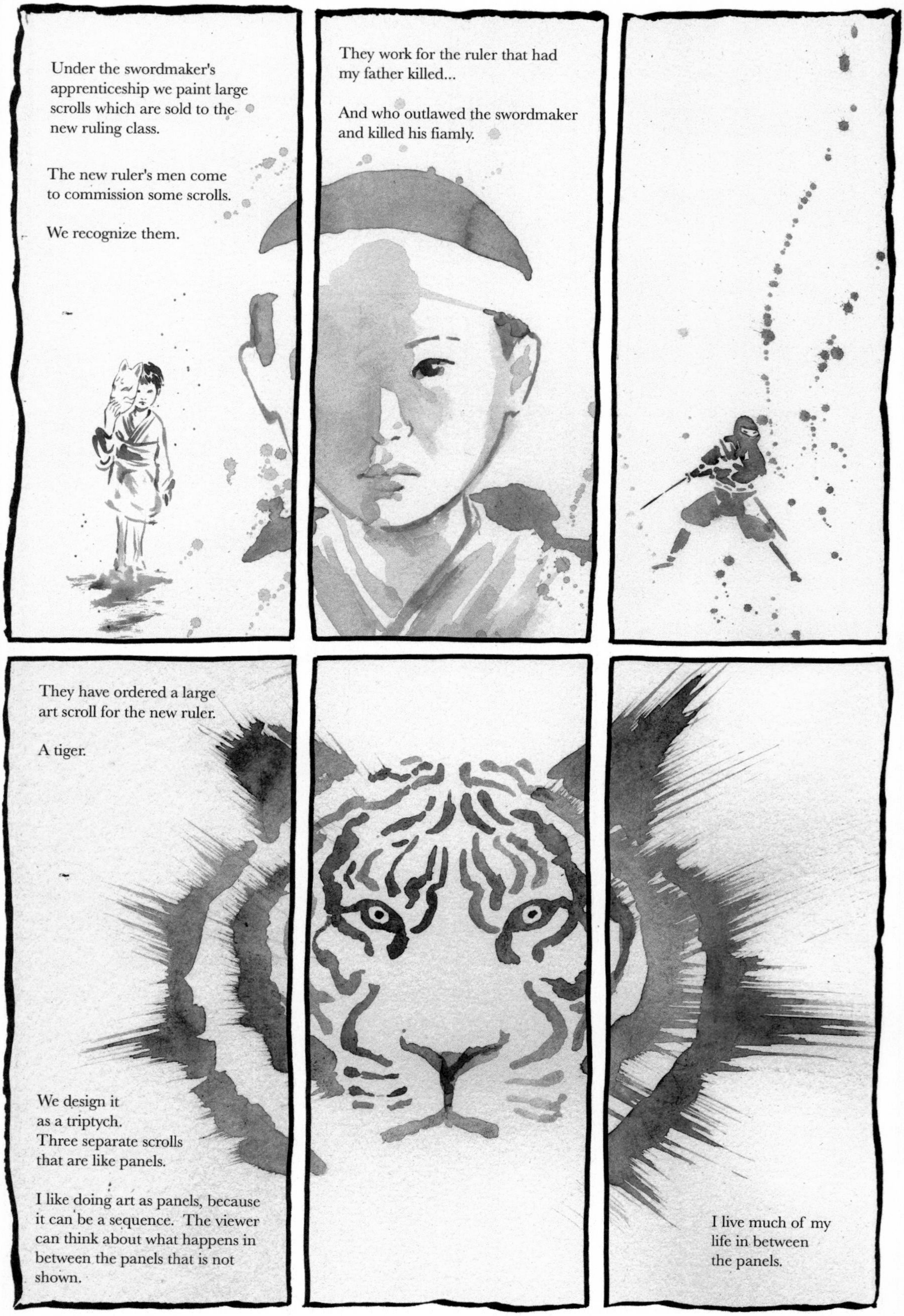
Under the swordmaker's apprenticeship we paint large scrolls which are sold to the new ruling class.
The new ruler's men come to commission some scrolls.
We recognize them.
They work for the ruler that had my father killed...
And who outlawed the swordmaker and killed his fiamly.
They have ordered a large art scroll for the new ruler.
A tiger.
We design it as a triptych. Three separate scrolls that are like panels.
I like doing art as panels, because it can be a sequence. The viewer can think about what happens in between the panels that is not shown.
I live much of my life in between the panels.

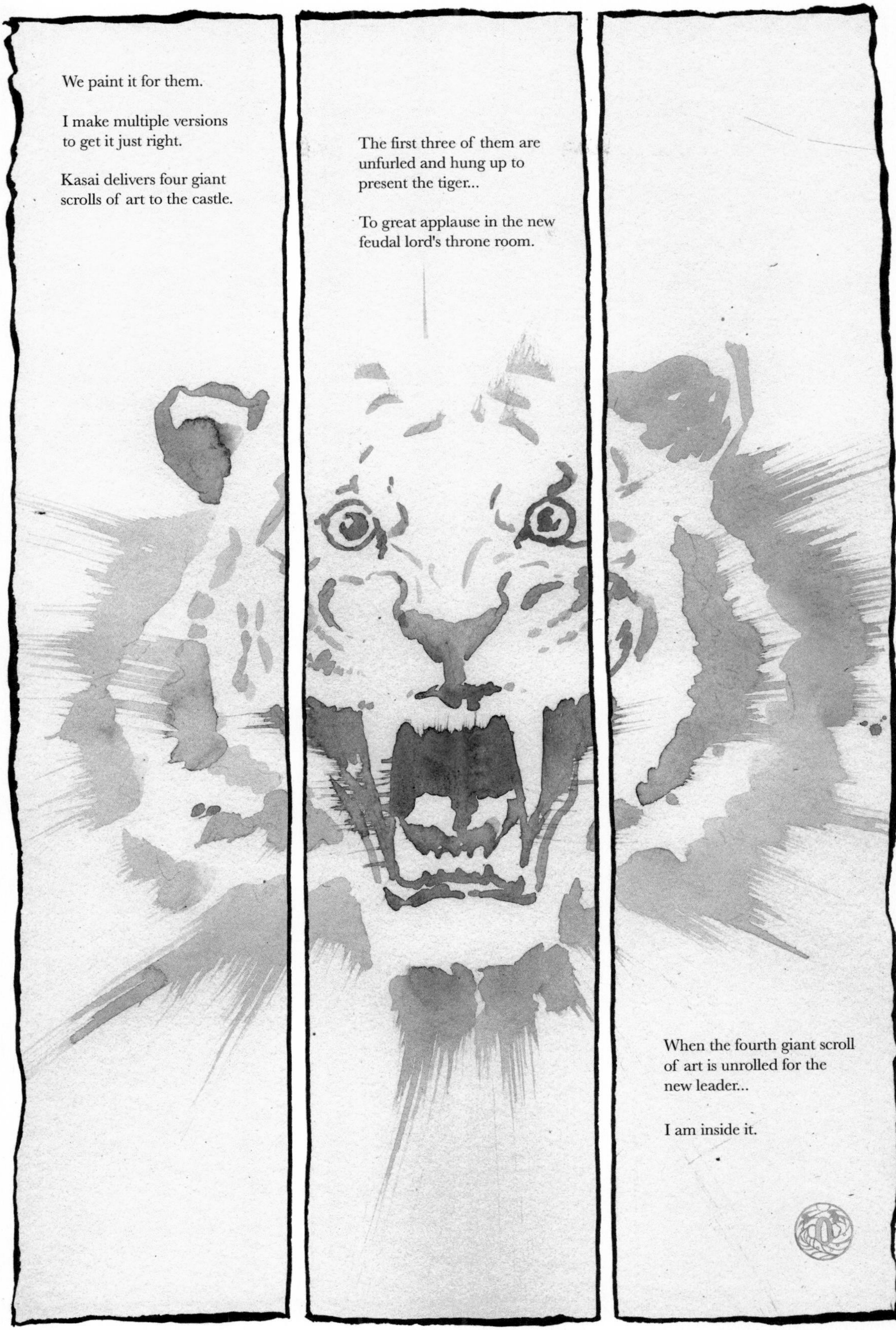
We paint it for them.
I make multiple versions to get it just right.
Kasai delivers four giant scrolls of art to the castle.
The first three of them are unfurled and hung up to present the tiger...
To great applause in the new feudal lord's throne room.
When the fourth giant scroll of art is unrolled for the new leader...
I am inside it.

There is no
making it out...

No change of
identity after this.

That is not part
of the plan.

I am archery
in reverse.

The arrow
returning
to you.

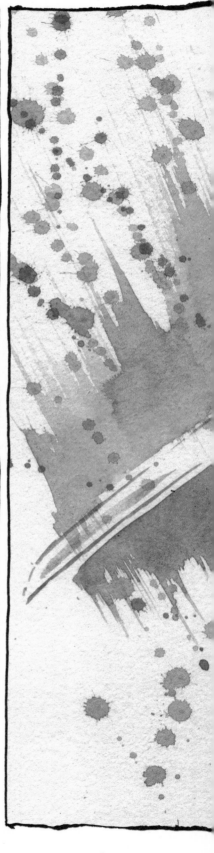

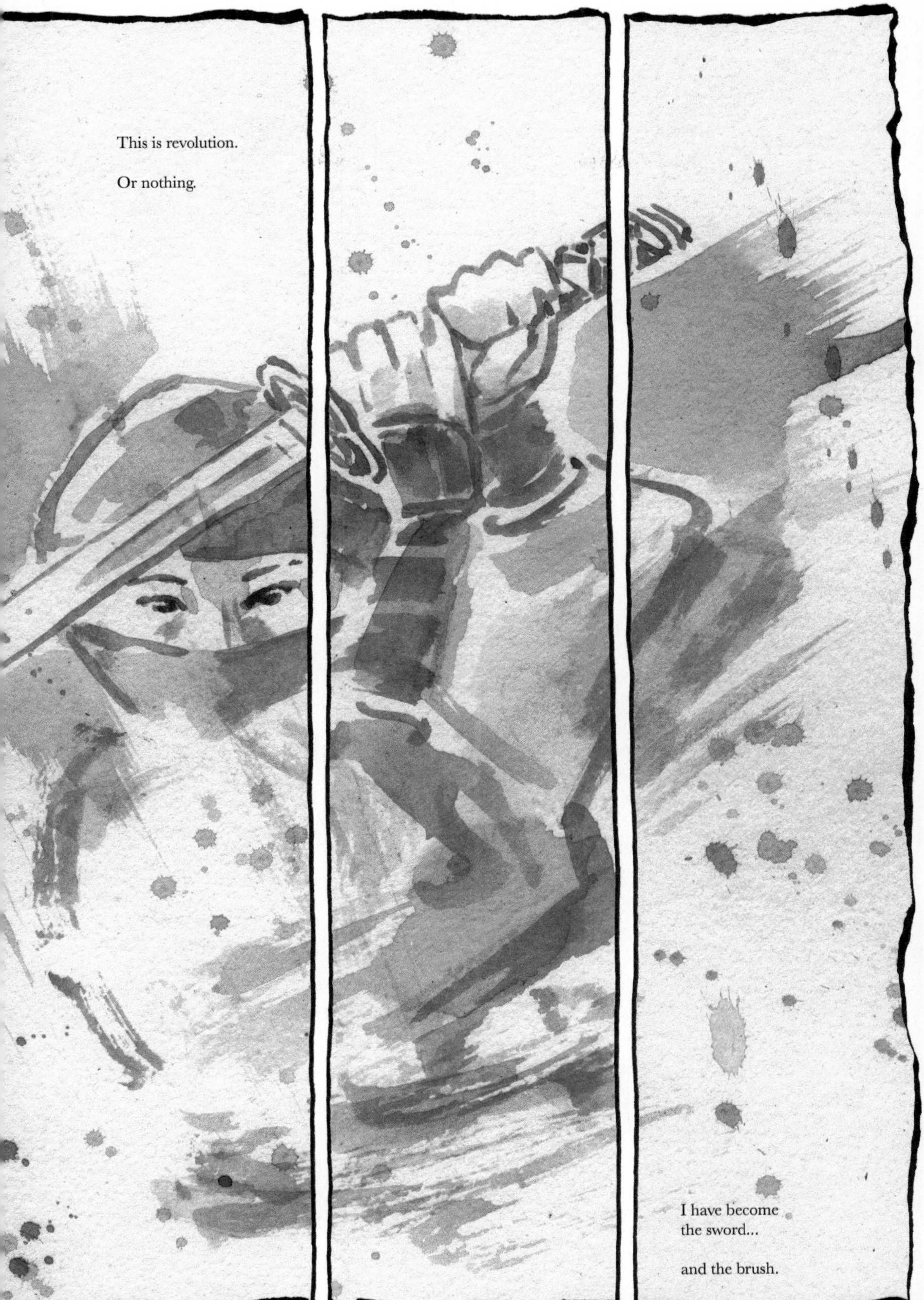
This is revolution.
Or nothing.
I have become the sword...
and the brush.

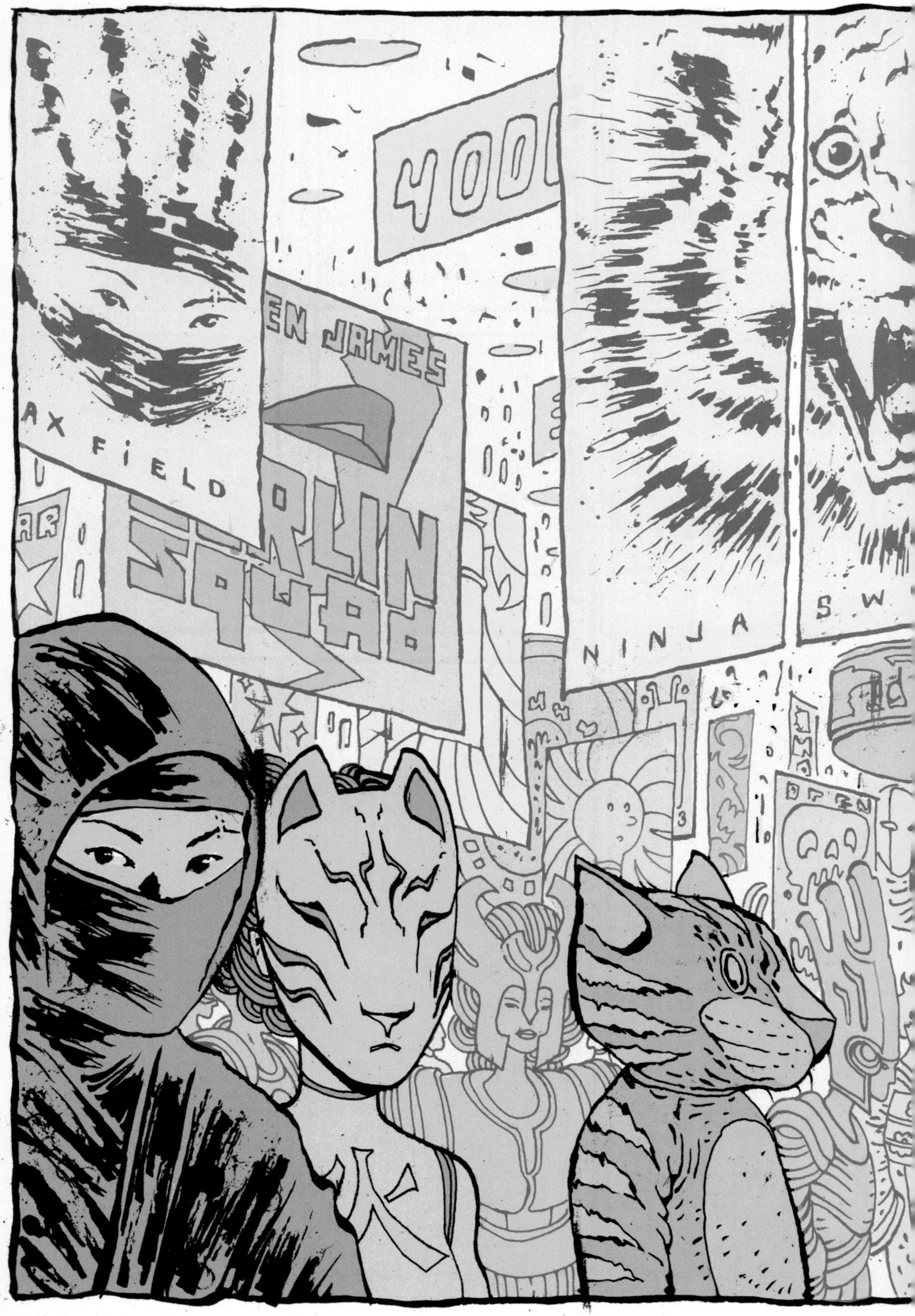
AX FIELD
EN JAMES
RLIN SQUAD
400
NINJA
S W

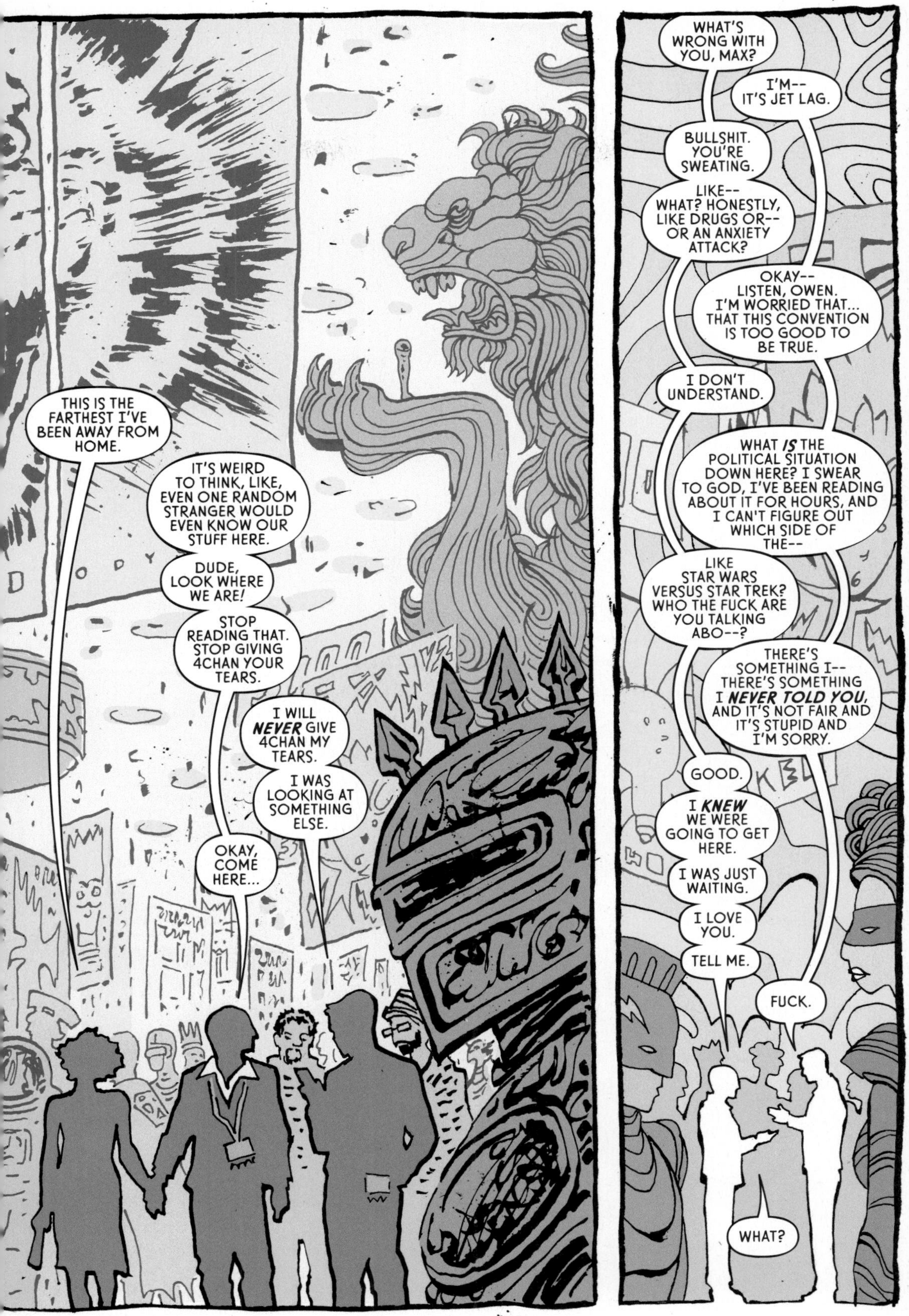
THIS IS THE FARTHEST I'VE BEEN AWAY FROM HOME.
IT'S WEIRD TO THINK, LIKE, EVEN ONE RANDOM STRANGER WOULD EVEN KNOW OUR STUFF HERE.
DUDE, LOOK WHERE WE ARE!
STOP READING THAT. STOP GIVING 4CHAN YOUR TEARS.
I WILL ***NEVER*** GIVE 4CHAN MY TEARS.
I WAS LOOKING AT SOMETHING ELSE.
OKAY, COME HERE...
WHAT'S WRONG WITH YOU, MAX?
I'M-- IT'S JET LAG.
BULLSHIT. YOU'RE SWEATING.
LIKE-- WHAT? HONESTLY, LIKE DRUGS OR-- OR AN ANXIETY ATTACK?
OKAY-- LISTEN, OWEN. I'M WORRIED THAT... THAT THIS CONVENTION IS TOO GOOD TO BE TRUE.
I DON'T UNDERSTAND.
WHAT ***IS*** THE POLITICAL SITUATION DOWN HERE? I SWEAR TO GOD, I'VE BEEN READING ABOUT IT FOR HOURS, AND I CAN'T FIGURE OUT WHICH SIDE OF THE--
LIKE STAR WARS VERSUS STAR TREK? WHO THE FUCK ARE YOU TALKING ABO--?
THERE'S SOMETHING I-- THERE'S SOMETHING I ***NEVER TOLD YOU,*** AND IT'S NOT FAIR AND IT'S STUPID AND I'M SORRY.
GOOD.
I ***KNEW*** WE WERE GOING TO GET HERE.
I WAS JUST WAITING.
I LOVE YOU.
TELL ME.
FUCK.
WHAT?

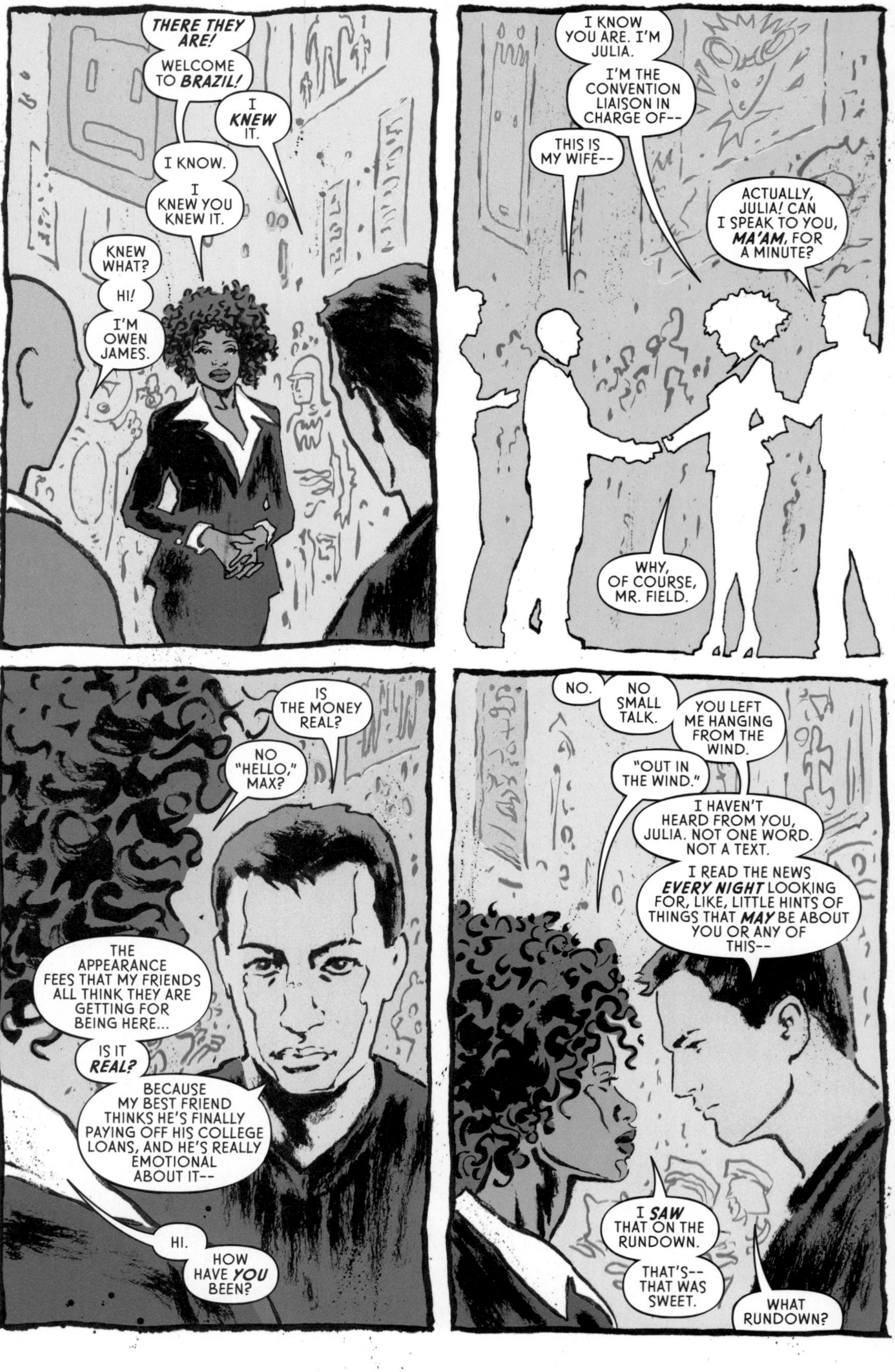
THERE THEY ARE!
WELCOME TO BRAZIL!
I KNEW IT.
I KNOW.
I KNEW YOU KNEW IT.
KNEW WHAT?
HI!
I'M OWEN JAMES.
I KNOW YOU ARE. I'M JULIA.
I'M THE CONVENTION LIAISON IN CHARGE OF--
THIS IS MY WIFE--
ACTUALLY, JULIA! CAN I SPEAK TO YOU, MA'AM, FOR A MINUTE?
WHY, OF COURSE, MR. FIELD.
IS THE MONEY REAL?
NO "HELLO," MAX?
THE APPEARANCE FEES THAT MY FRIENDS ALL THINK THEY ARE GETTING FOR BEING HERE...
IS IT REAL?
BECAUSE MY BEST FRIEND THINKS HE'S FINALLY PAYING OFF HIS COLLEGE LOANS, AND HE'S REALLY EMOTIONAL ABOUT IT--
HI.
HOW HAVE YOU BEEN?
NO.
NO SMALL TALK.
YOU LEFT ME HANGING FROM THE WIND.
"OUT IN THE WIND."
I HAVEN'T HEARD FROM YOU, JULIA. NOT ONE WORD. NOT A TEXT.
I READ THE NEWS EVERY NIGHT LOOKING FOR, LIKE, LITTLE HINTS OF THINGS THAT MAY BE ABOUT YOU OR ANY OF THIS--
I SAW THAT ON THE RUNDOWN.
THAT'S-- THAT WAS SWEET.
WHAT RUNDOWN?

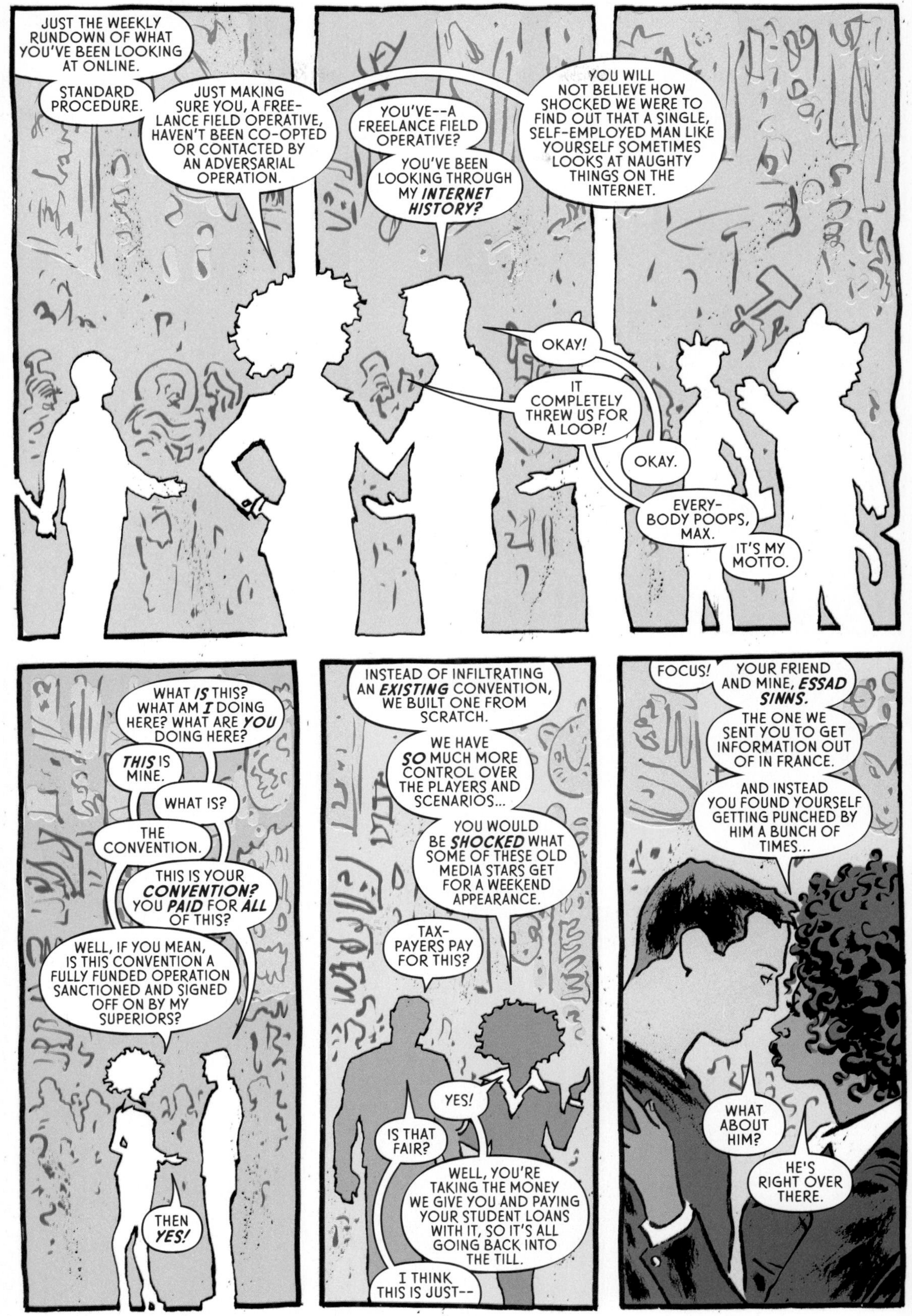

JUST THE WEEKLY RUNDOWN OF WHAT YOU'VE BEEN LOOKING AT ONLINE.
STANDARD PROCEDURE.
JUST MAKING SURE YOU, A FREE-LANCE FIELD OPERATIVE, HAVEN'T BEEN CO-OPTED OR CONTACTED BY AN ADVERSARIAL OPERATION.
YOU'VE--A FREELANCE FIELD OPERATIVE?
YOU'VE BEEN LOOKING THROUGH MY *INTERNET HISTORY?*
YOU WILL NOT BELIEVE HOW SHOCKED WE WERE TO FIND OUT THAT A SINGLE, SELF-EMPLOYED MAN LIKE YOURSELF SOMETIMES LOOKS AT NAUGHTY THINGS ON THE INTERNET.
OKAY!
IT COMPLETELY THREW US FOR A LOOP!
OKAY.
EVERY-BODY POOPS, MAX.
IT'S MY MOTTO.
WHAT *IS* THIS? WHAT AM *I* DOING HERE? WHAT ARE *YOU* DOING HERE?
THIS IS MINE.
WHAT IS?
THE CONVENTION.
THIS IS YOUR *CONVENTION?* YOU *PAID* FOR *ALL* OF THIS?
WELL, IF YOU MEAN, IS THIS CONVENTION A FULLY FUNDED OPERATION SANCTIONED AND SIGNED OFF ON BY MY SUPERIORS?
THEN *YES!*
INSTEAD OF INFILTRATING AN *EXISTING* CONVENTION, WE BUILT ONE FROM SCRATCH.
WE HAVE *SO* MUCH MORE CONTROL OVER THE PLAYERS AND SCENARIOS...
YOU WOULD BE *SHOCKED* WHAT SOME OF THESE OLD MEDIA STARS GET FOR A WEEKEND APPEARANCE.
TAX-PAYERS PAY FOR THIS?
YES!
IS THAT FAIR?
WELL, YOU'RE TAKING THE MONEY WE GIVE YOU AND PAYING YOUR STUDENT LOANS WITH IT, SO IT'S ALL GOING BACK INTO THE TILL.
I THINK THIS IS JUST--
FOCUS!
YOUR FRIEND AND MINE, *ESSAD SINNS.*
THE ONE WE SENT YOU TO GET INFORMATION OUT OF IN FRANCE.
AND INSTEAD YOU FOUND YOURSELF GETTING PUNCHED BY HIM A BUNCH OF TIMES...
WHAT ABOUT HIM?
HE'S RIGHT OVER THERE.

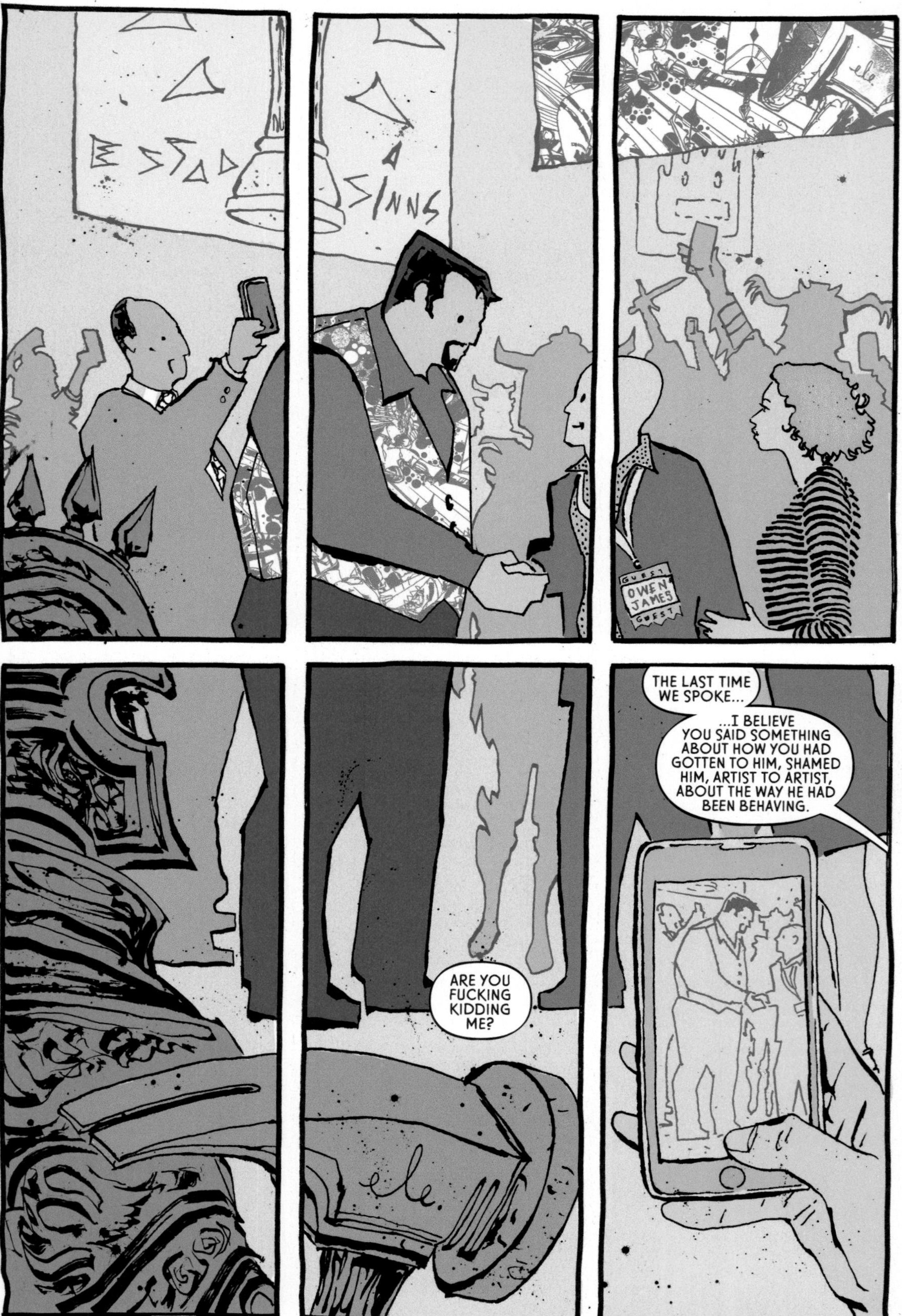
OWEN JAMES
ARE YOU FUCKING KIDDING ME?
THE LAST TIME WE SPOKE...
...I BELIEVE YOU SAID SOMETHING ABOUT HOW YOU HAD GOTTEN TO HIM, SHAMED HIM, ARTIST TO ARTIST, ABOUT THE WAY HE HAD BEEN BEHAVING.

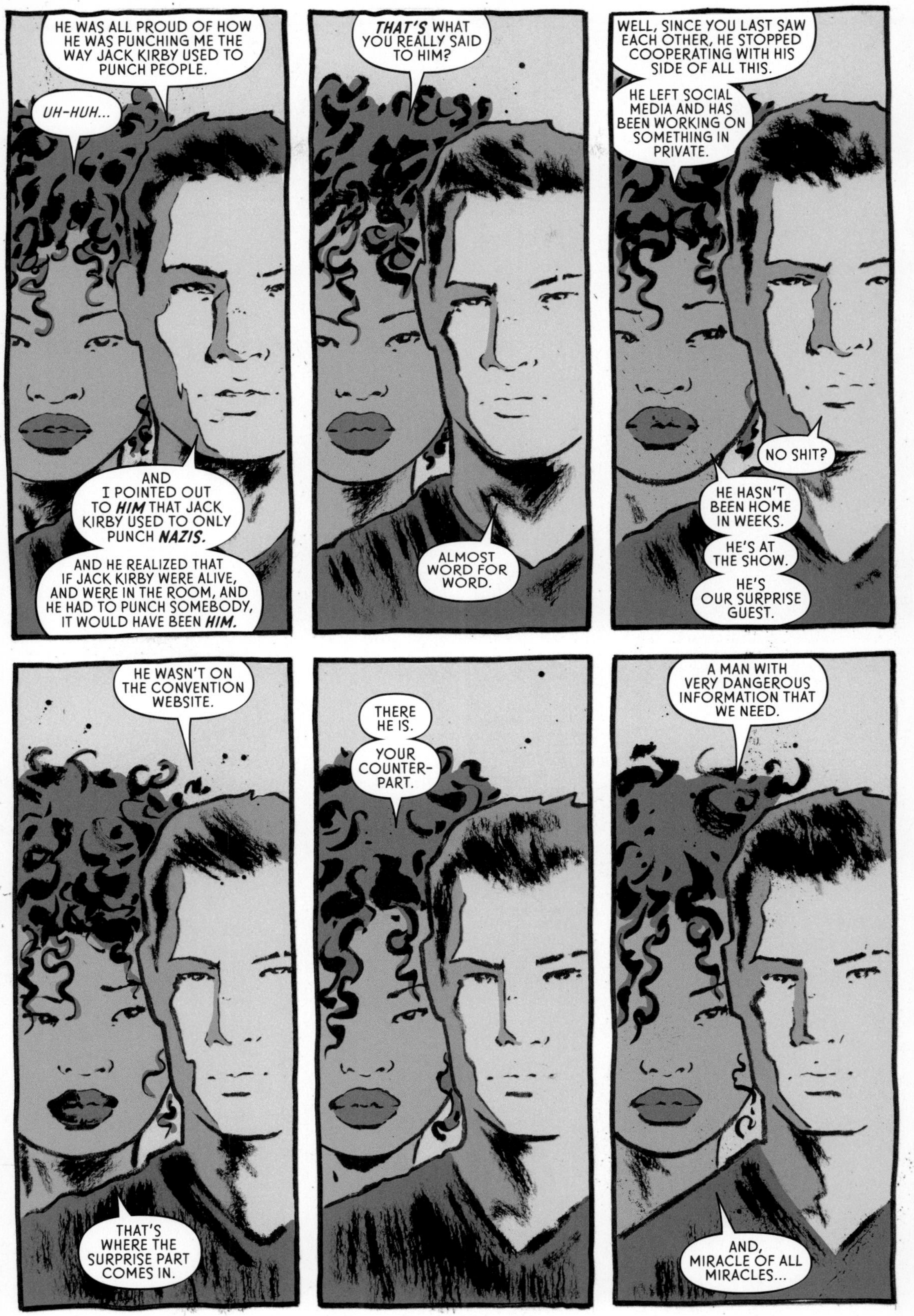
HE WAS ALL PROUD OF HOW HE WAS PUNCHING ME THE WAY JACK KIRBY USED TO PUNCH PEOPLE.
UH-HUH...
AND I POINTED OUT TO *HIM* THAT JACK KIRBY USED TO ONLY PUNCH *NAZIS.*
AND HE REALIZED THAT IF JACK KIRBY WERE ALIVE, AND WERE IN THE ROOM, AND HE HAD TO PUNCH SOMEBODY, IT WOULD HAVE BEEN *HIM.*
THAT'S WHAT YOU REALLY SAID TO HIM?
ALMOST WORD FOR WORD.
WELL, SINCE YOU LAST SAW EACH OTHER, HE STOPPED COOPERATING WITH HIS SIDE OF ALL THIS.
HE LEFT SOCIAL MEDIA AND HAS BEEN WORKING ON SOMETHING IN PRIVATE.
NO SHIT?
HE HASN'T BEEN HOME IN WEEKS.
HE'S AT THE SHOW.
HE'S OUR SURPRISE GUEST.
HE WASN'T ON THE CONVENTION WEBSITE.
THAT'S WHERE THE SURPRISE PART COMES IN.
THERE HE IS.
YOUR COUNTER-PART.
A MAN WITH VERY DANGEROUS INFORMATION THAT WE NEED.
AND, MIRACLE OF ALL MIRACLES...

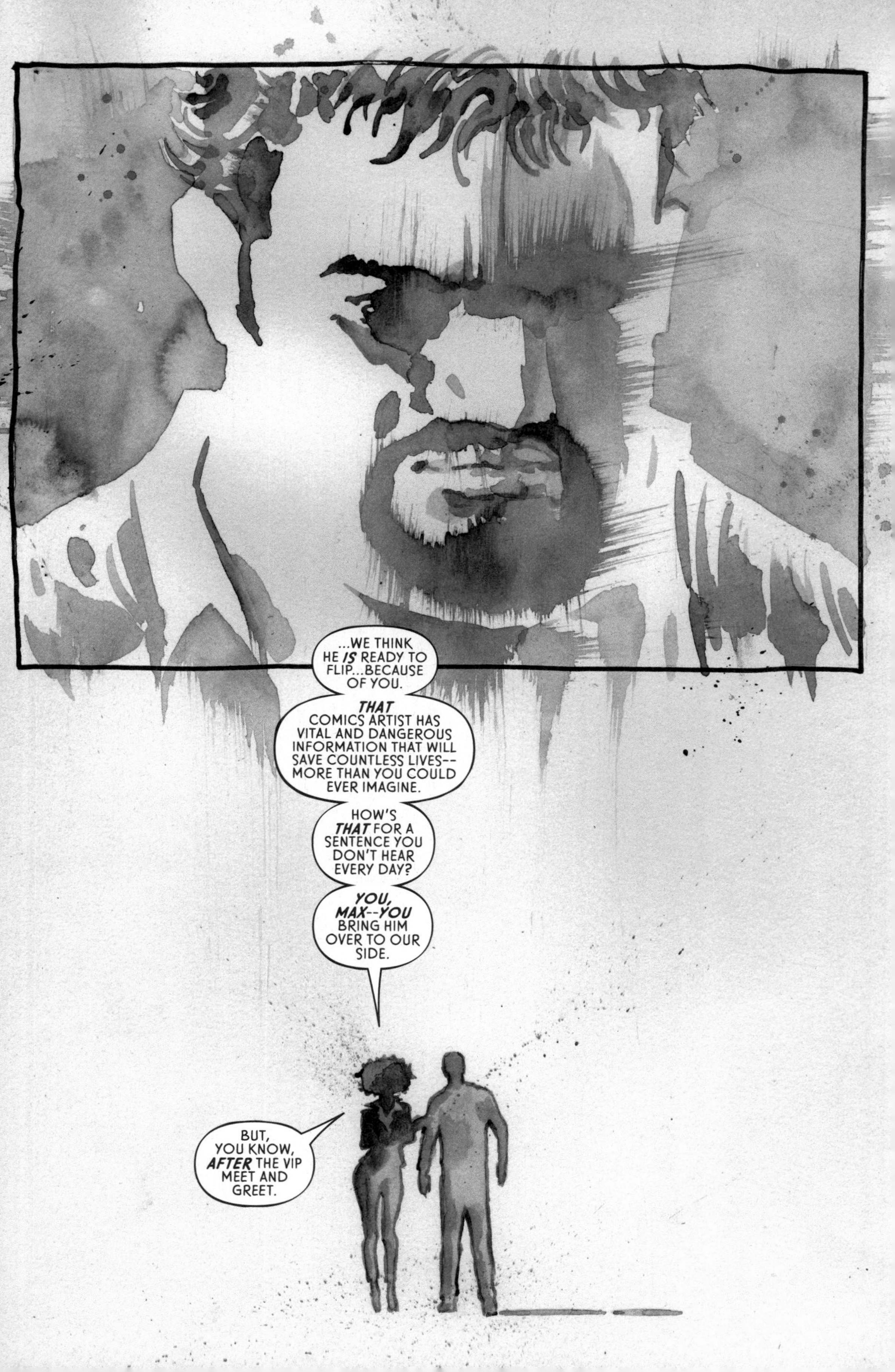
...WE THINK HE *IS* READY TO FLIP...BECAUSE OF YOU.
THAT COMICS ARTIST HAS VITAL AND DANGEROUS INFORMATION THAT WILL SAVE COUNTLESS LIVES-- MORE THAN YOU COULD EVER IMAGINE.
HOW'S *THAT* FOR A SENTENCE YOU DON'T HEAR EVERY DAY?
YOU, MAX--YOU BRING HIM OVER TO OUR SIDE.
BUT, YOU KNOW, *AFTER* THE VIP MEET AND GREET.

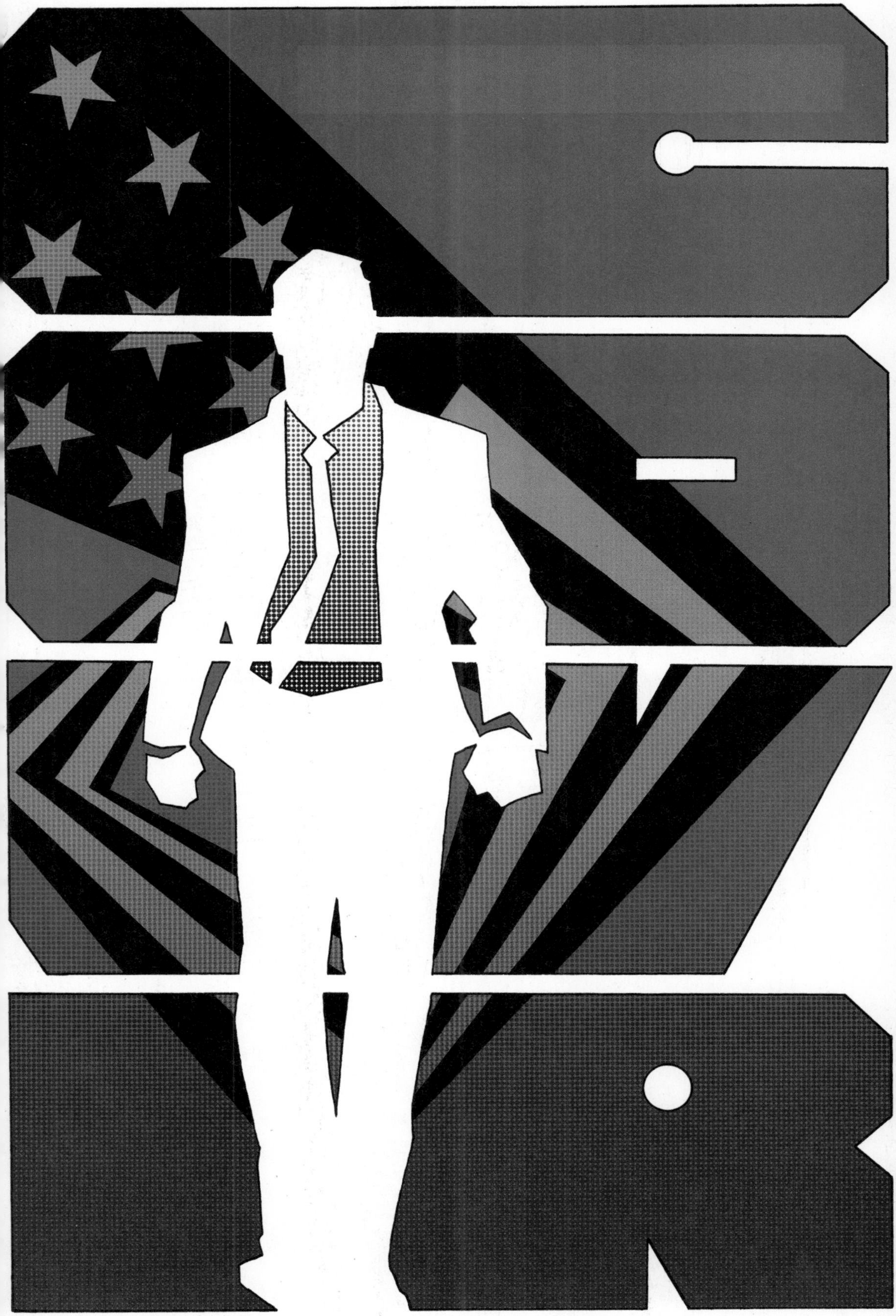

Variant cover art for issue #6
by **Jim Lee**

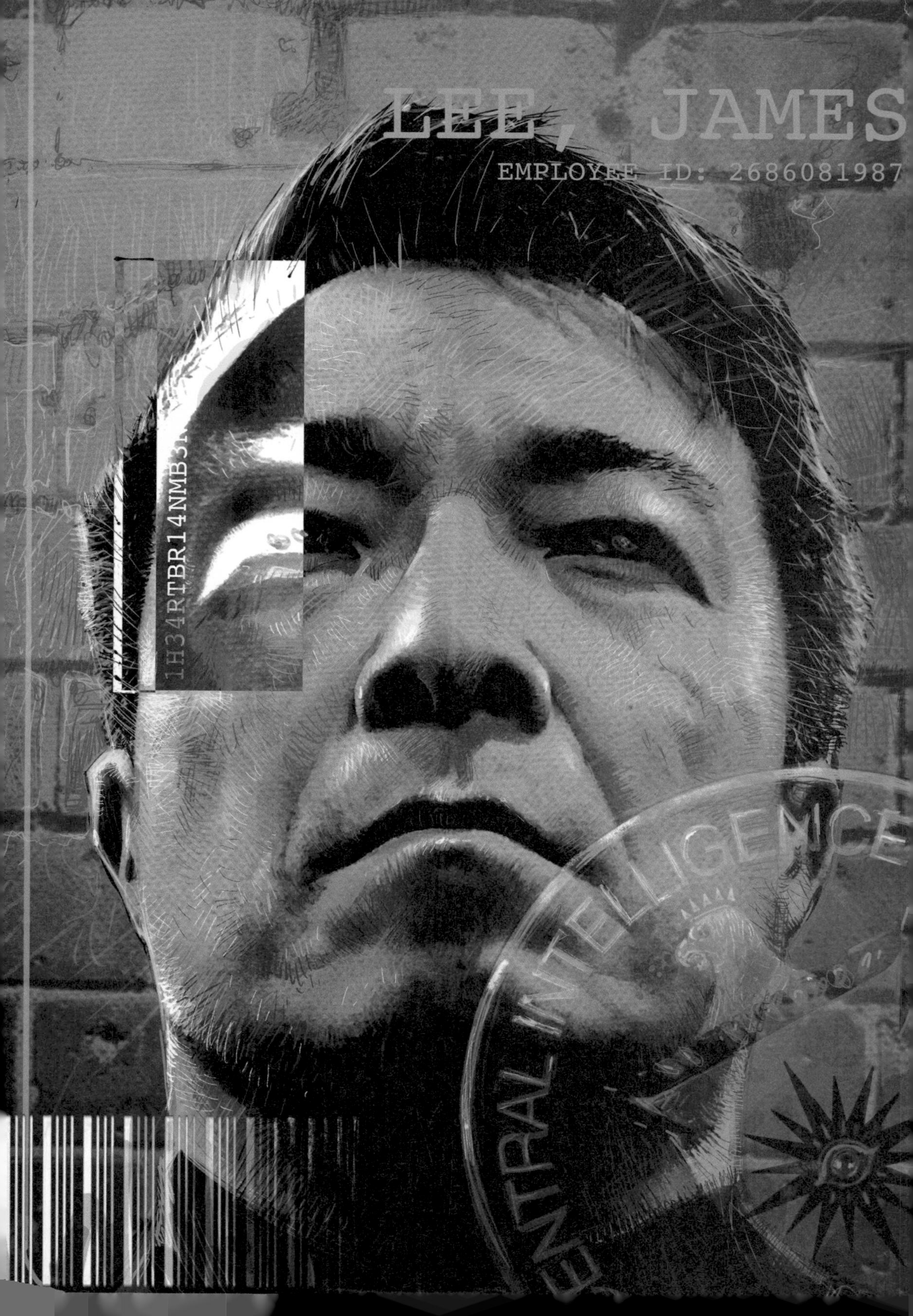
LEE, JAMES
EMPLOYEE ID: 2686081987
1H34RTBR14NMB3N
CENTRAL INTELLIGENCE

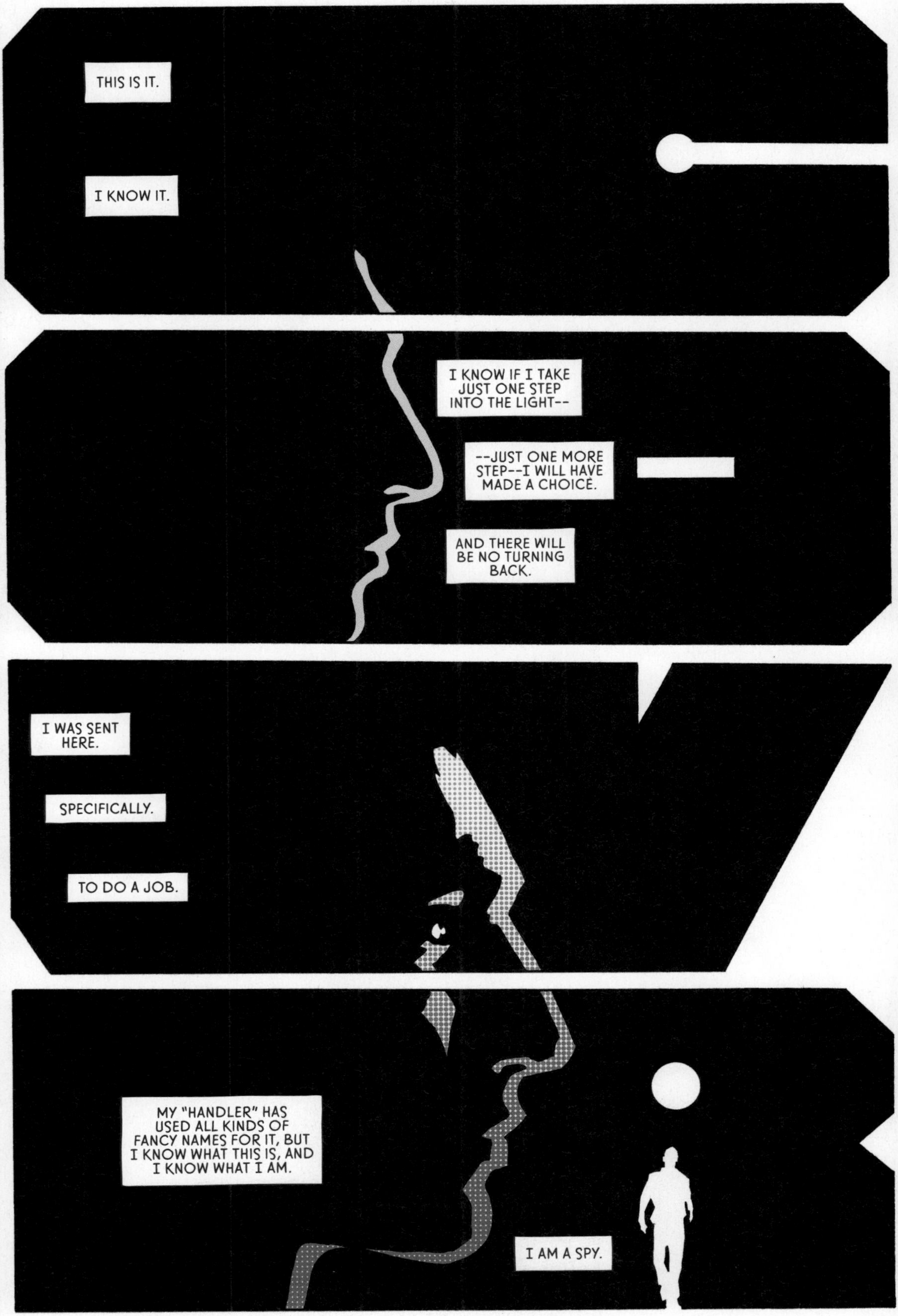
THIS IS IT.
I KNOW IT.
I KNOW IF I TAKE JUST ONE STEP INTO THE LIGHT--
--JUST ONE MORE STEP--I WILL HAVE MADE A CHOICE.
AND THERE WILL BE NO TURNING BACK.
I WAS SENT HERE.
SPECIFICALLY.
TO DO A JOB.
MY "HANDLER" HAS USED ALL KINDS OF FANCY NAMES FOR IT, BUT I KNOW WHAT THIS IS, AND I KNOW WHAT I AM.
I AM A SPY.

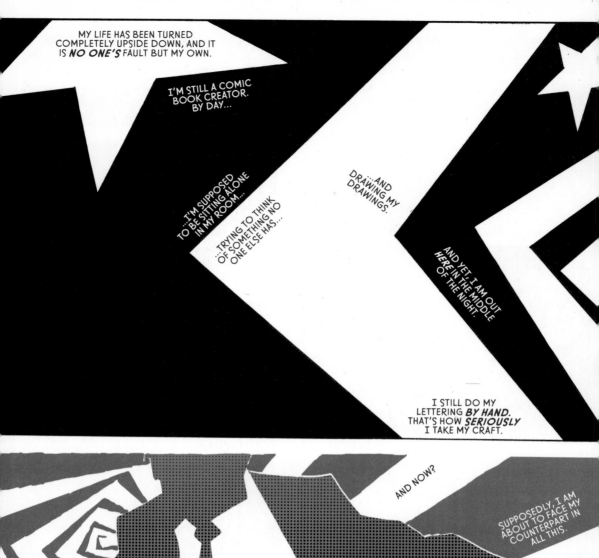

MY LIFE HAS BEEN TURNED COMPLETELY UPSIDE DOWN, AND IT IS *NO ONE'S* FAULT BUT MY OWN.

I'M STILL A COMIC BOOK CREATOR. BY DAY...

...AND DRAWING MY DRAWINGS.

...I'M SUPPOSED TO BE SITTING ALONE IN MY ROOM...

...TRYING TO THINK OF SOMETHING NO ONE ELSE HAS...

AND YET, I AM OUT *HERE* IN THE MIDDLE OF THE NIGHT.

I STILL DO MY LETTERING *BY HAND.* THAT'S HOW *SERIOUSLY* I TAKE MY CRAFT.

AND NOW?

SUPPOSEDLY, I AM ABOUT TO FACE MY COUNTERPART IN ALL THIS.

ANOTHER CREATOR. ANOTHER SPY.

ANOTHER ONE OF US SEDUCED INTO TAKING EVERY-THING HE HAD SPENT EVERY SINGLE SECOND OF HIS LIFE BUILDING TOWARD AND PREPARING FOR...

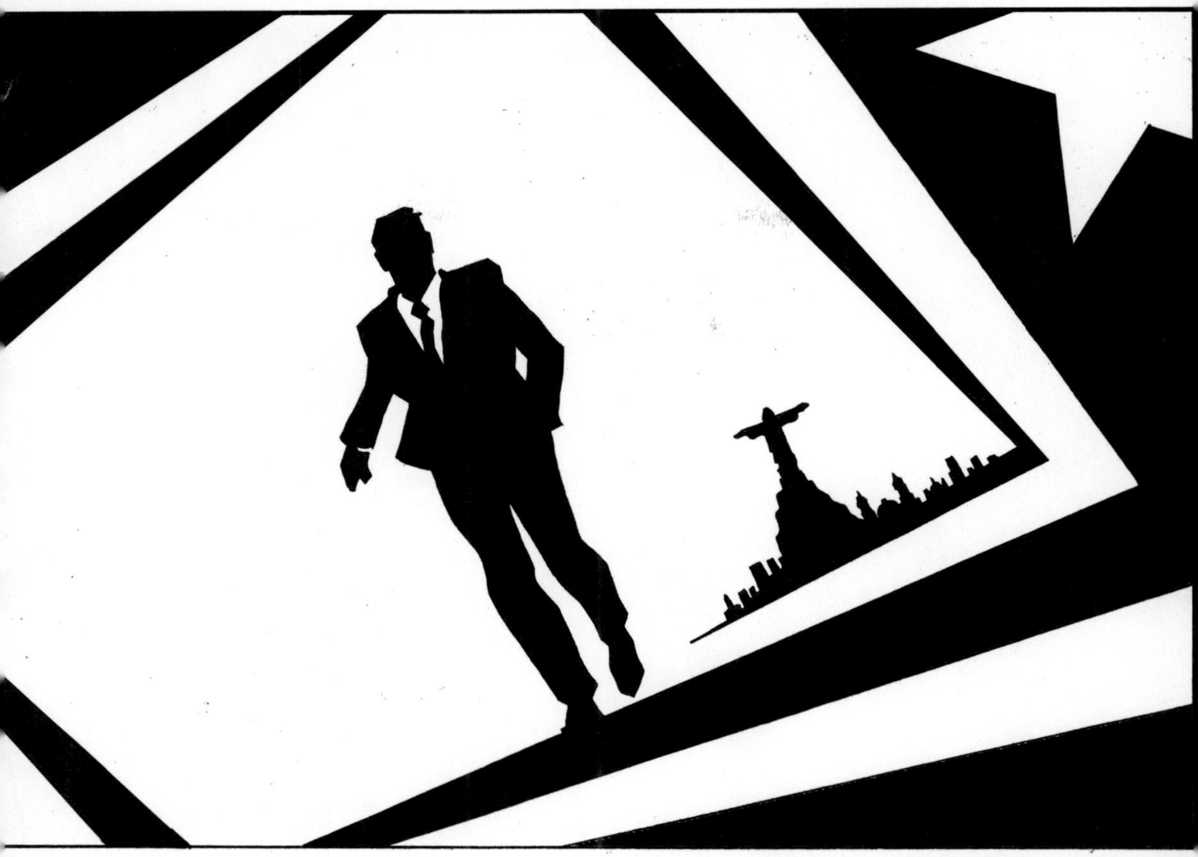

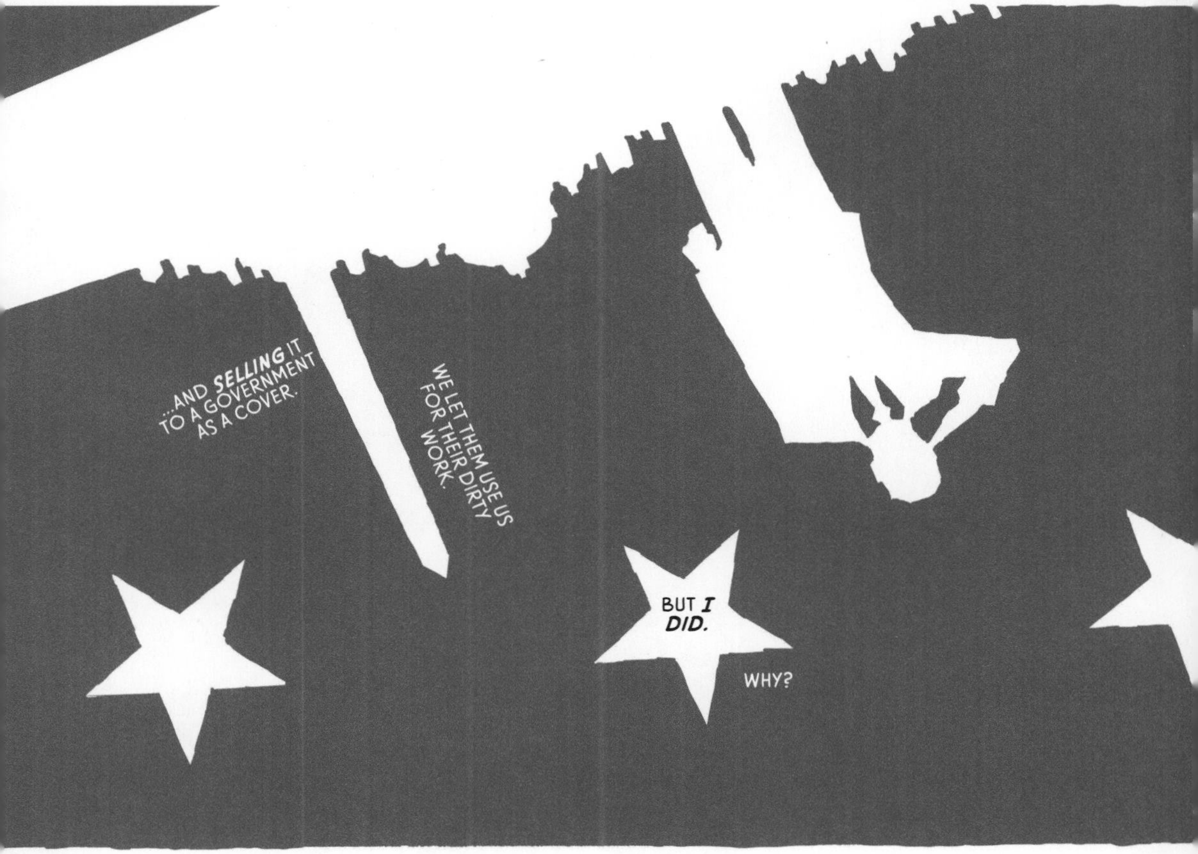

...AND **SELLING** IT TO A GOVERNMENT AS A COVER.
WE LET THEM USE US FOR THEIR DIRTY WORK.
BUT ***I DID.***
WHY?

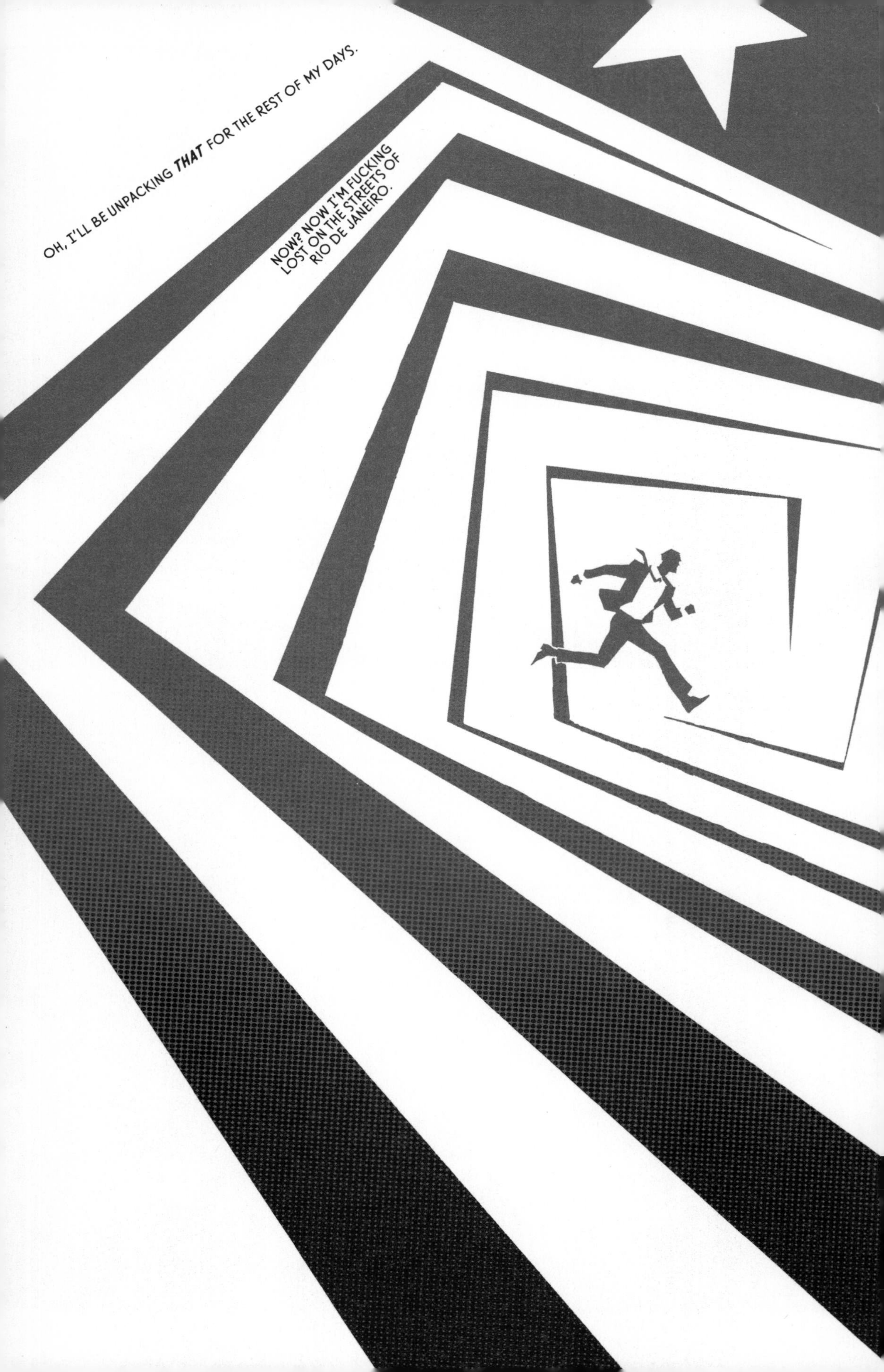

OH, I'LL BE UNPACKING THAT FOR THE REST OF MY DAYS.
NOW? NOW I'M FUCKING LOST ON THE STREETS OF RIO DE JANEIRO.

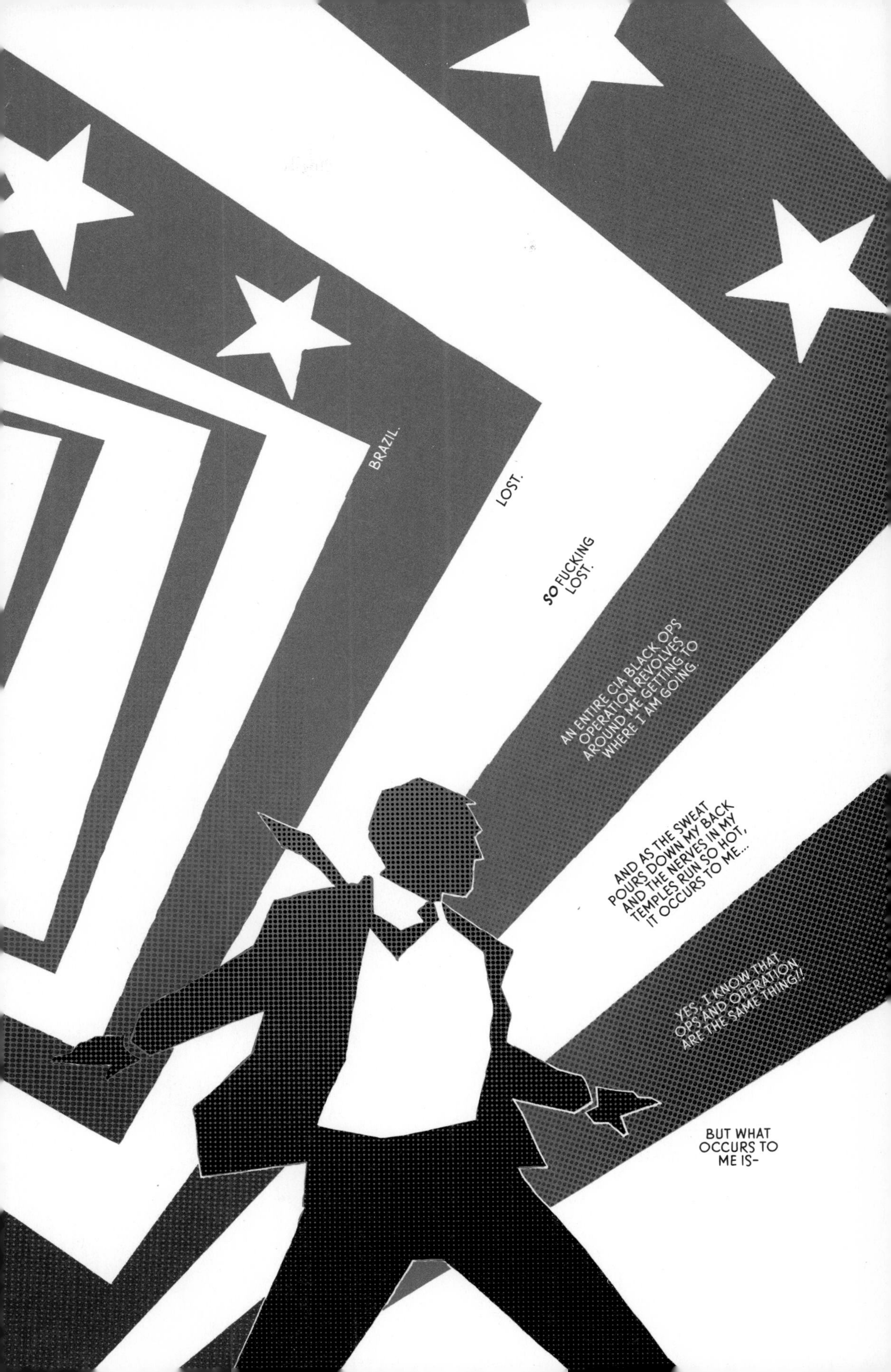

BRAZIL.
LOST.
SO FUCKING LOST.
AN ENTIRE CIA BLACK OPS OPERATION REVOLVES AROUND ME GETTING TO WHERE I AM GOING.
AND AS THE SWEAT POURS DOWN MY BACK AND THE NERVES IN MY TEMPLES RUN SO HOT, IT OCCURS TO ME...
YES, I KNOW THAT OPS AND OPERATION ARE THE SAME THING!!
BUT WHAT OCCURS TO ME IS-

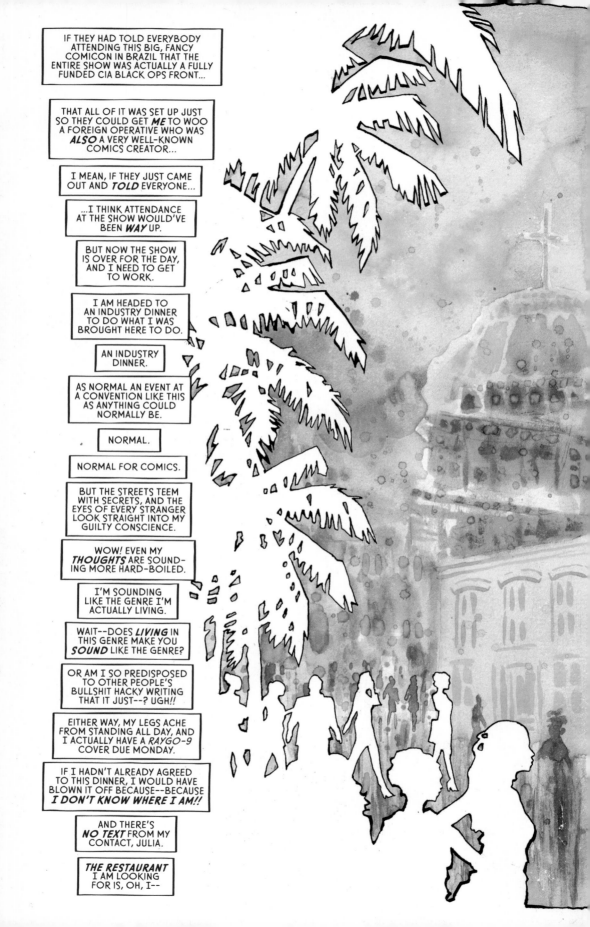

IF THEY HAD TOLD EVERYBODY ATTENDING THIS BIG, FANCY COMICON IN BRAZIL THAT THE ENTIRE SHOW WAS ACTUALLY A FULLY FUNDED CIA BLACK OPS FRONT...

THAT ALL OF IT WAS SET UP JUST SO THEY COULD GET *ME* TO WOO A FOREIGN OPERATIVE WHO WAS *ALSO* A VERY WELL-KNOWN COMICS CREATOR...

I MEAN, IF THEY JUST CAME OUT AND *TOLD* EVERYONE...

...I THINK ATTENDANCE AT THE SHOW WOULD'VE BEEN *WAY* UP.

BUT NOW THE SHOW IS OVER FOR THE DAY, AND I NEED TO GET TO WORK.

I AM HEADED TO AN INDUSTRY DINNER TO DO WHAT I WAS BROUGHT HERE TO DO.

AN INDUSTRY DINNER.

AS NORMAL AN EVENT AT A CONVENTION LIKE THIS AS ANYTHING COULD NORMALLY BE.

NORMAL.

NORMAL FOR COMICS.

BUT THE STREETS TEEM WITH SECRETS, AND THE EYES OF EVERY STRANGER LOOK STRAIGHT INTO MY GUILTY CONSCIENCE.

WOW! EVEN MY *THOUGHTS* ARE SOUND- ING MORE HARD-BOILED.

I'M SOUNDING LIKE THE GENRE I'M ACTUALLY LIVING.

WAIT--DOES *LIVING* IN THIS GENRE MAKE YOU *SOUND* LIKE THE GENRE?

OR AM I SO PREDISPOSED TO OTHER PEOPLE'S BULLSHIT HACKY WRITING THAT IT JUST--? UGH!!

EITHER WAY, MY LEGS ACHE FROM STANDING ALL DAY, AND I ACTUALLY HAVE A *RAYGO-9* COVER DUE MONDAY.

IF I HADN'T ALREADY AGREED TO THIS DINNER, I WOULD HAVE BLOWN IT OFF BECAUSE--BECAUSE *I DON'T KNOW WHERE I AM!!*

AND THERE'S *NO TEXT* FROM MY CONTACT, JULIA.

THE RESTAURANT I AM LOOKING FOR IS, OH, I--

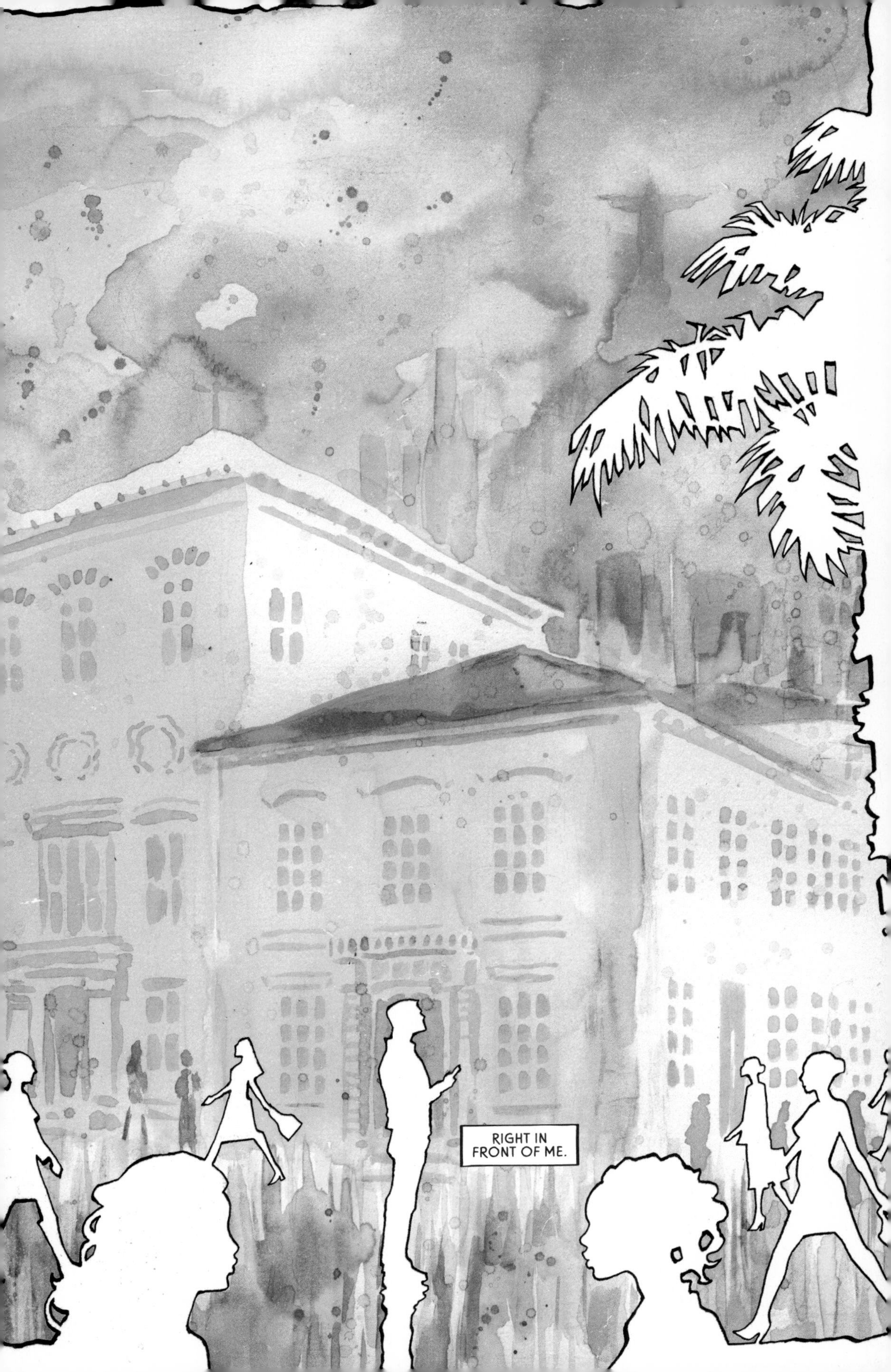

RIGHT IN
FRONT OF ME.

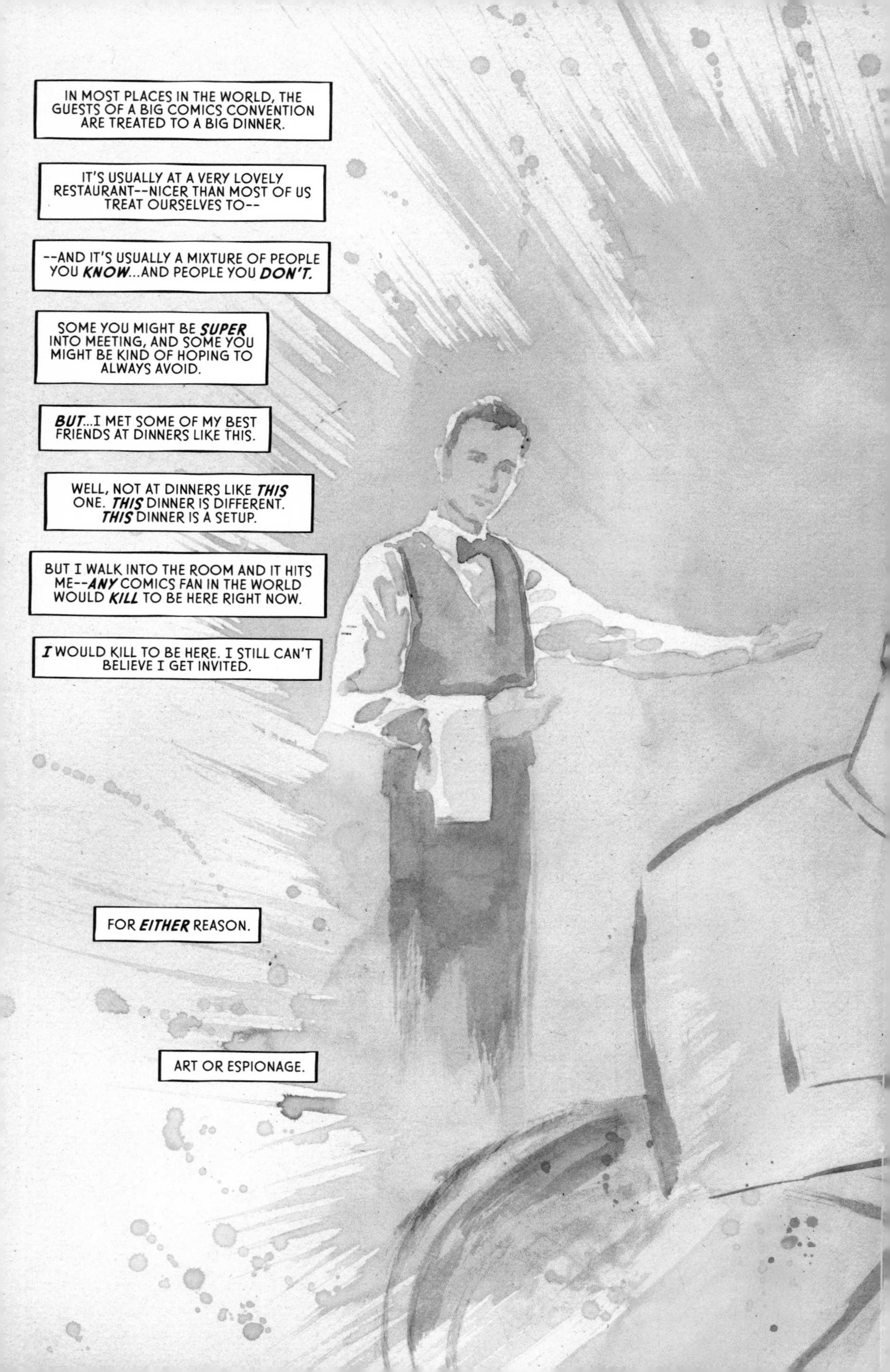
IN MOST PLACES IN THE WORLD, THE GUESTS OF A BIG COMICS CONVENTION ARE TREATED TO A BIG DINNER.
IT'S USUALLY AT A VERY LOVELY RESTAURANT--NICER THAN MOST OF US TREAT OURSELVES TO--
--AND IT'S USUALLY A MIXTURE OF PEOPLE YOU KNOW...AND PEOPLE YOU DON'T.
SOME YOU MIGHT BE SUPER INTO MEETING, AND SOME YOU MIGHT BE KIND OF HOPING TO ALWAYS AVOID.
BUT...I MET SOME OF MY BEST FRIENDS AT DINNERS LIKE THIS.
WELL, NOT AT DINNERS LIKE THIS ONE. THIS DINNER IS DIFFERENT. THIS DINNER IS A SETUP.
BUT I WALK INTO THE ROOM AND IT HITS ME--ANY COMICS FAN IN THE WORLD WOULD KILL TO BE HERE RIGHT NOW.
I WOULD KILL TO BE HERE. I STILL CAN'T BELIEVE I GET INVITED.
FOR EITHER REASON.
ART OR ESPIONAGE.

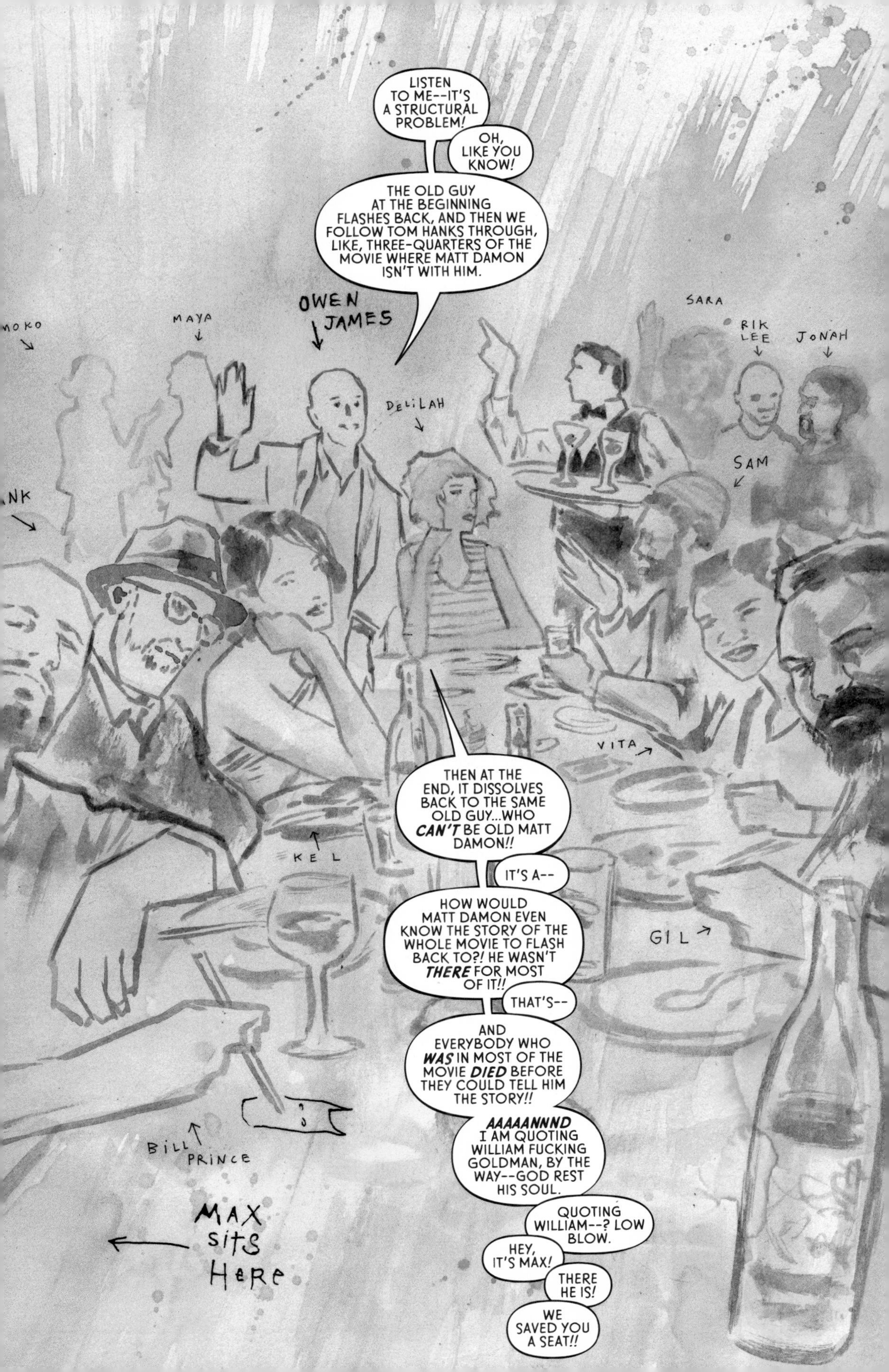
LISTEN TO ME--IT'S A STRUCTURAL PROBLEM!
OH, LIKE YOU KNOW!
THE OLD GUY AT THE BEGINNING FLASHES BACK, AND THEN WE FOLLOW TOM HANKS THROUGH, LIKE, THREE-QUARTERS OF THE MOVIE WHERE MATT DAMON ISN'T WITH HIM.
MAYA
OWEN JAMES
DELILAH
SARA
RIK LEE
JONAH
SAM
VITA
KEL
GIL
BILL
PRINCE
THEN AT THE END, IT DISSOLVES BACK TO THE SAME OLD GUY...WHO ***CAN'T*** BE OLD MATT DAMON!!
IT'S A--
HOW WOULD MATT DAMON EVEN KNOW THE STORY OF THE WHOLE MOVIE TO FLASH BACK TO?! HE WASN'T ***THERE*** FOR MOST OF IT!!
THAT'S--
AND EVERYBODY WHO ***WAS*** IN MOST OF THE MOVIE ***DIED*** BEFORE THEY COULD TELL HIM THE STORY!!
AAAAANNND I AM QUOTING WILLIAM FUCKING GOLDMAN, BY THE WAY--GOD REST HIS SOUL.
QUOTING WILLIAM--? LOW BLOW.
MAX sits Here
HEY, IT'S MAX!
THERE HE IS!
WE SAVED YOU A SEAT!!

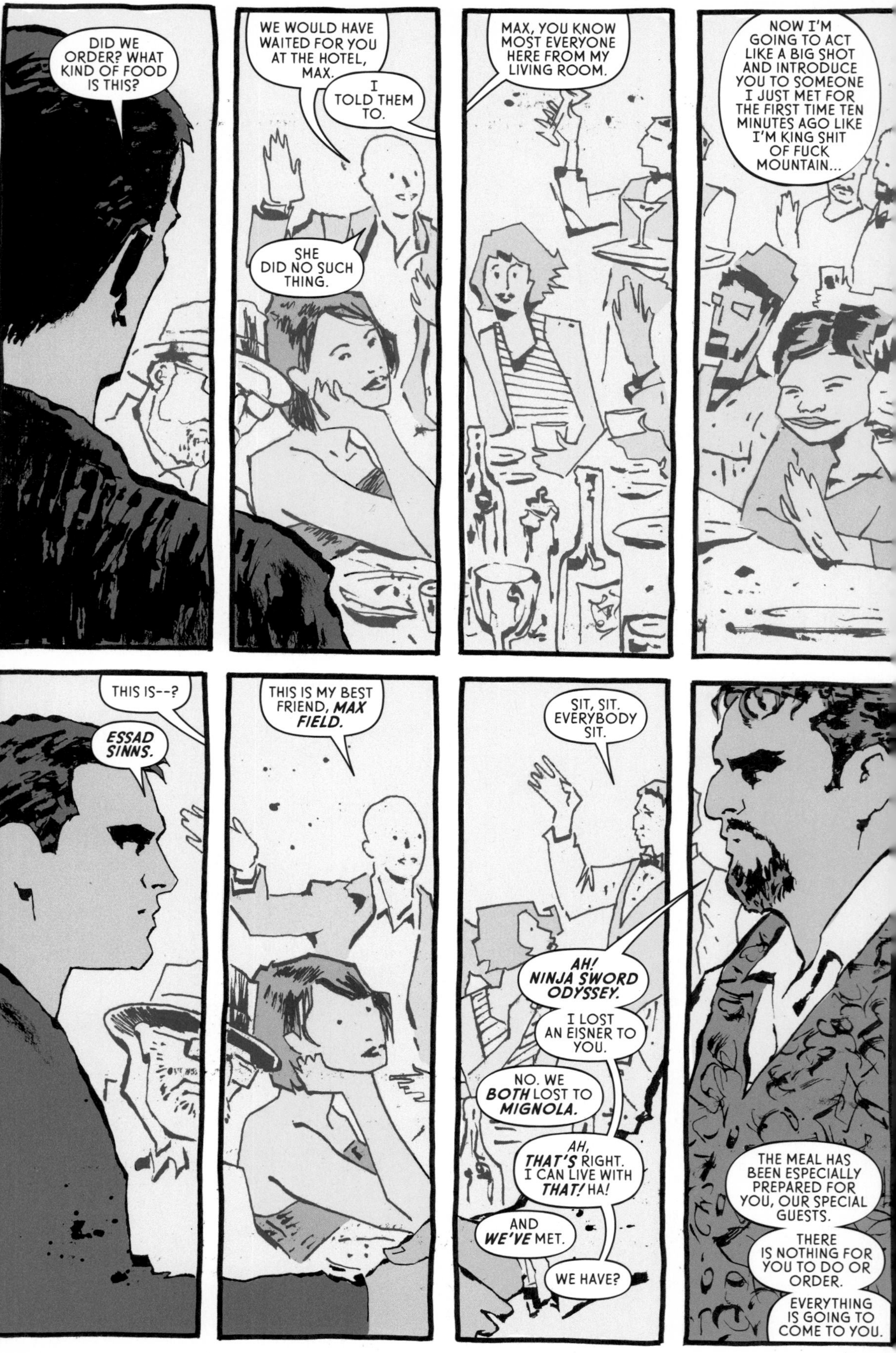
DID WE ORDER? WHAT KIND OF FOOD IS THIS?
WE WOULD HAVE WAITED FOR YOU AT THE HOTEL, MAX.
I TOLD THEM TO.
SHE DID NO SUCH THING.
MAX, YOU KNOW MOST EVERYONE HERE FROM MY LIVING ROOM.
NOW I'M GOING TO ACT LIKE A BIG SHOT AND INTRODUCE YOU TO SOMEONE I JUST MET FOR THE FIRST TIME TEN MINUTES AGO LIKE I'M KING SHIT OF FUCK MOUNTAIN...
THIS IS--?
ESSAD SINNS.
THIS IS MY BEST FRIEND, MAX FIELD.
SIT, SIT. EVERYBODY SIT.
AH! NINJA SWORD ODYSSEY.
I LOST AN EISNER TO YOU.
NO. WE BOTH LOST TO MIGNOLA.
AH, THAT'S RIGHT. I CAN LIVE WITH THAT! HA!
AND WE'VE MET.
WE HAVE?
THE MEAL HAS BEEN ESPECIALLY PREPARED FOR YOU, OUR SPECIAL GUESTS.
THERE IS NOTHING FOR YOU TO DO OR ORDER.
EVERYTHING IS GOING TO COME TO YOU.

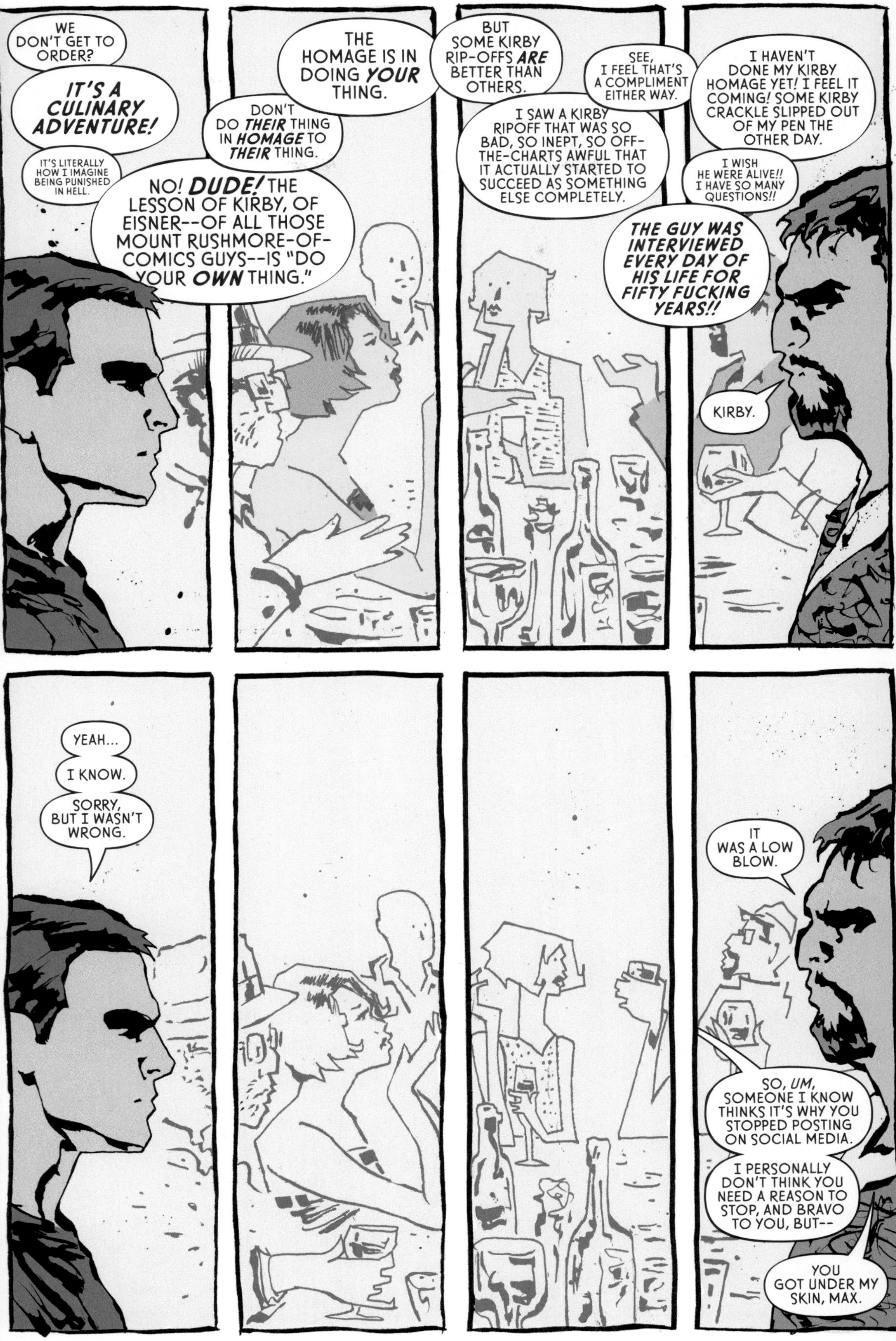
WE DON'T GET TO ORDER?
IT'S A CULINARY ADVENTURE!
IT'S LITERALLY HOW I IMAGINE BEING PUNISHED IN HELL.
NO! DUDE! THE LESSON OF KIRBY, OF EISNER--OF ALL THOSE MOUNT RUSHMORE-OF-COMICS GUYS--IS "DO YOUR OWN THING."
DON'T DO THEIR THING IN HOMAGE TO THEIR THING.
THE HOMAGE IS IN DOING YOUR THING.
BUT SOME KIRBY RIP-OFFS ARE BETTER THAN OTHERS.
I SAW A KIRBY RIPOFF THAT WAS SO BAD, SO INEPT, SO OFF-THE-CHARTS AWFUL THAT IT ACTUALLY STARTED TO SUCCEED AS SOMETHING ELSE COMPLETELY.
SEE, I FEEL THAT'S A COMPLIMENT EITHER WAY.
I HAVEN'T DONE MY KIRBY HOMAGE YET! I FEEL IT COMING! SOME KIRBY CRACKLE SLIPPED OUT OF MY PEN THE OTHER DAY.
I WISH HE WERE ALIVE!! I HAVE SO MANY QUESTIONS!!
THE GUY WAS INTERVIEWED EVERY DAY OF HIS LIFE FOR FIFTY FUCKING YEARS!!
KIRBY.
YEAH...
I KNOW.
SORRY, BUT I WASN'T WRONG.
IT WAS A LOW BLOW.
SO, UM, SOMEONE I KNOW THINKS IT'S WHY YOU STOPPED POSTING ON SOCIAL MEDIA.
I PERSONALLY DON'T THINK YOU NEED A REASON TO STOP, AND BRAVO TO YOU, BUT--
YOU GOT UNDER MY SKIN, MAX.

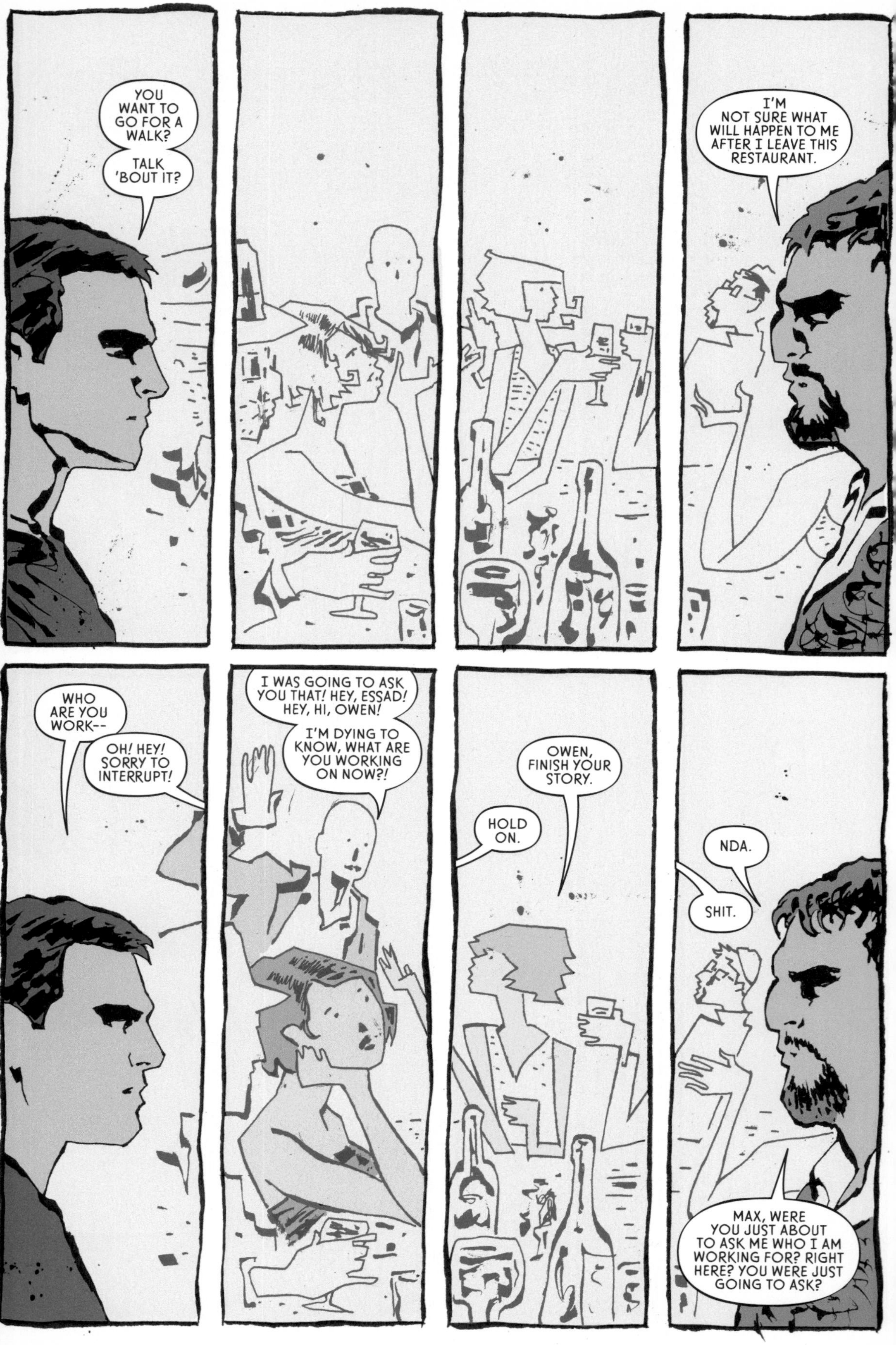
YOU WANT TO GO FOR A WALK?
TALK 'BOUT IT?
I'M NOT SURE WHAT WILL HAPPEN TO ME AFTER I LEAVE THIS RESTAURANT.
WHO ARE YOU WORK--
OH! HEY! SORRY TO INTERRUPT!
I WAS GOING TO ASK YOU THAT! HEY, ESSAD! HEY, HI, OWEN!
I'M DYING TO KNOW, WHAT ARE YOU WORKING ON NOW?!
OWEN, FINISH YOUR STORY.
HOLD ON.
NDA.
SHIT.
MAX, WERE YOU JUST ABOUT TO ASK ME WHO I AM WORKING FOR? RIGHT HERE? YOU WERE JUST GOING TO ASK?

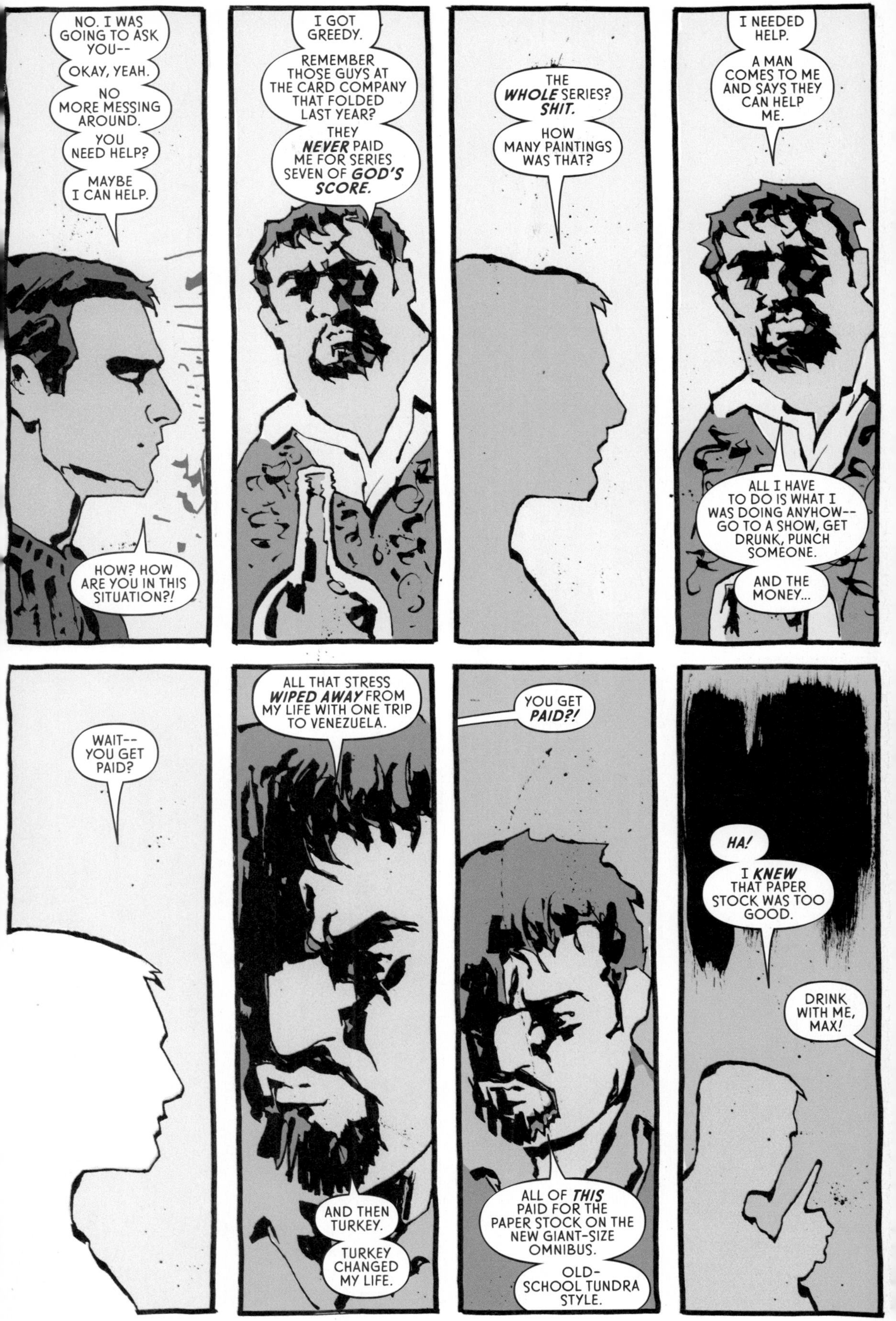
NO. I WAS GOING TO ASK YOU--
OKAY, YEAH.
NO MORE MESSING AROUND.
YOU NEED HELP?
MAYBE I CAN HELP.
HOW? HOW ARE YOU IN THIS SITUATION?!
I GOT GREEDY.
REMEMBER THOSE GUYS AT THE CARD COMPANY THAT FOLDED LAST YEAR?
THEY ***NEVER*** PAID ME FOR SERIES SEVEN OF ***GOD'S SCORE.***
THE ***WHOLE*** SERIES? ***SHIT.***
HOW MANY PAINTINGS WAS THAT?
I NEEDED HELP.
A MAN COMES TO ME AND SAYS THEY CAN HELP ME.
ALL I HAVE TO DO IS WHAT I WAS DOING ANYHOW--GO TO A SHOW, GET DRUNK, PUNCH SOMEONE.
AND THE MONEY...
WAIT--YOU GET PAID?
ALL THAT STRESS ***WIPED AWAY*** FROM MY LIFE WITH ONE TRIP TO VENEZUELA.
AND THEN TURKEY.
TURKEY CHANGED MY LIFE.
YOU GET ***PAID?!***
ALL OF ***THIS*** PAID FOR THE PAPER STOCK ON THE NEW GIANT-SIZE OMNIBUS.
OLD-SCHOOL TUNDRA STYLE.
HA!
I ***KNEW*** THAT PAPER STOCK WAS TOO GOOD.
DRINK WITH ME, MAX!

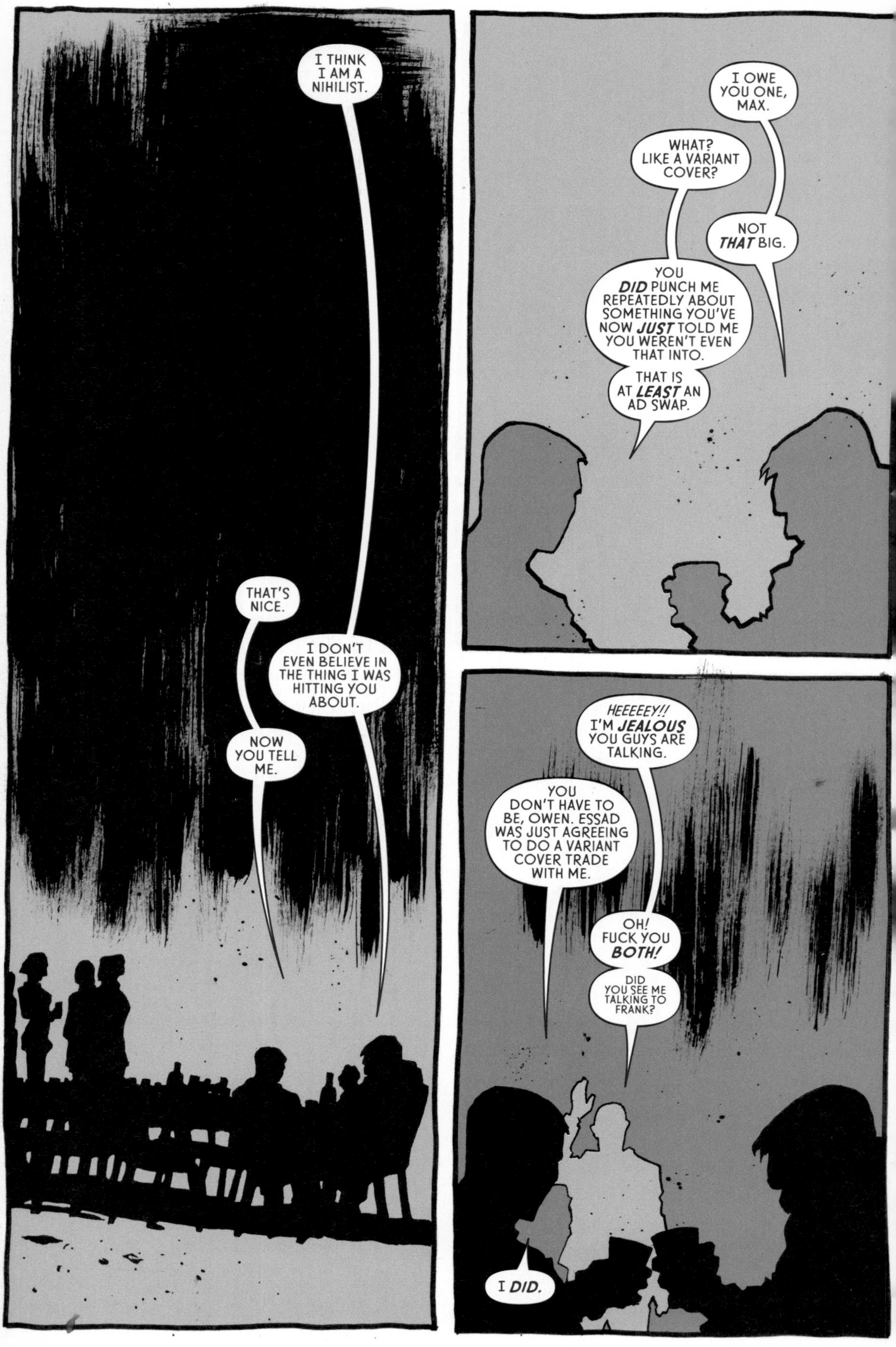
I THINK I AM A NIHILIST.
THAT'S NICE.
I DON'T EVEN BELIEVE IN THE THING I WAS HITTING YOU ABOUT.
NOW YOU TELL ME.
I OWE YOU ONE, MAX.
WHAT? LIKE A VARIANT COVER?
NOT THAT BIG.
YOU DID PUNCH ME REPEATEDLY ABOUT SOMETHING YOU'VE NOW JUST TOLD ME YOU WEREN'T EVEN THAT INTO.
THAT IS AT LEAST AN AD SWAP.
HEEEEEY!! I'M JEALOUS YOU GUYS ARE TALKING.
YOU DON'T HAVE TO BE, OWEN. ESSAD WAS JUST AGREEING TO DO A VARIANT COVER TRADE WITH ME.
OH! FUCK YOU BOTH!
DID YOU SEE ME TALKING TO FRANK?
I DID.

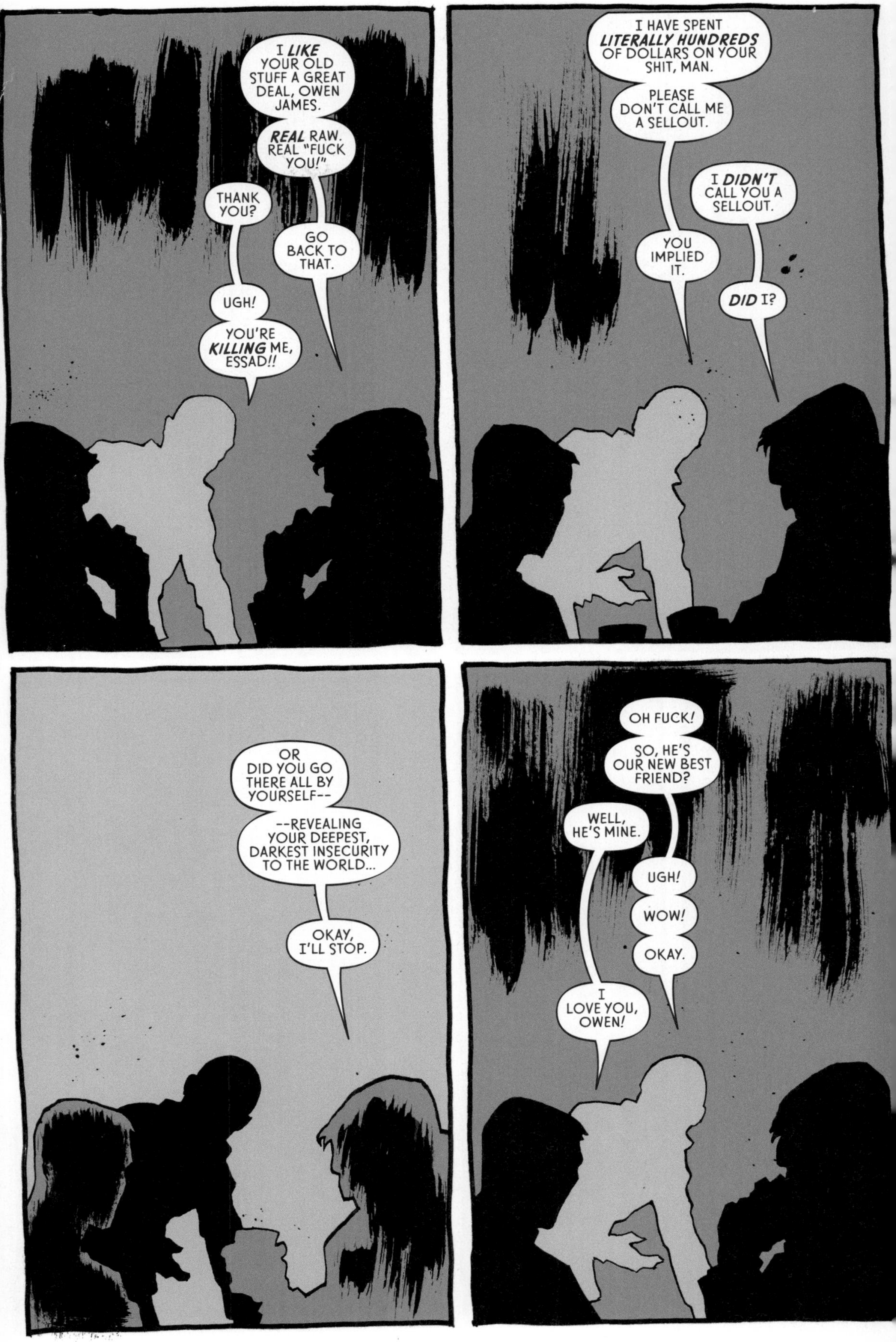
I LIKE YOUR OLD STUFF A GREAT DEAL, OWEN JAMES.
REAL RAW. REAL "FUCK YOU!"
THANK YOU?
GO BACK TO THAT.
UGH!
YOU'RE KILLING ME, ESSAD!!
I HAVE SPENT LITERALLY HUNDREDS OF DOLLARS ON YOUR SHIT, MAN.
PLEASE DON'T CALL ME A SELLOUT.
I DIDN'T CALL YOU A SELLOUT.
YOU IMPLIED IT.
DID I?
OR DID YOU GO THERE ALL BY YOURSELF--
--REVEALING YOUR DEEPEST, DARKEST INSECURITY TO THE WORLD...
OKAY, I'LL STOP.
OH FUCK!
SO, HE'S OUR NEW BEST FRIEND?
WELL, HE'S MINE.
UGH!
WOW!
OKAY.
I LOVE YOU, OWEN!

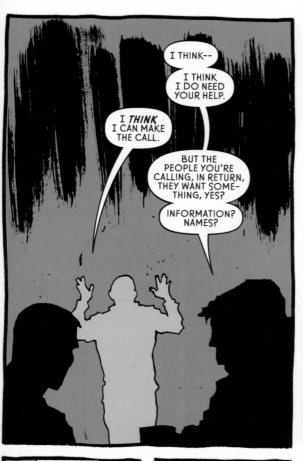

I THINK--

I THINK I DO NEED YOUR HELP.

I *THINK* I CAN MAKE THE CALL.

BUT THE PEOPLE YOU'RE CALLING, IN RETURN, THEY WANT SOMETHING, YES?

INFORMATION? NAMES?

I IMAGINE.

HONESTLY, EVERYONE IS SO VAGUE WITH ME...

BUT I *THINK* THEY THINK, LIKE, WE KNOW...

MAKE THE CALL.

BUT-- BUT ONLY YOU.

I ONLY COME TO THEM IF YOU BRING ME.

OH THANK GOD.

I WAS HAVING *SUCH GUILT* OVER ALL THE MONEY THEY SPENT ON THIS STUPID OPERATION, BUT IF IT *WORKS*...

WHAT A *LOAD* OFF.

AS LONG AS *YOU* FEEL BETTER.

THANK YOU.

NO SIGNAL.

SHOULD WE WALK?

HOTEL'S HONESTLY *RIGHT* OVER THERE.

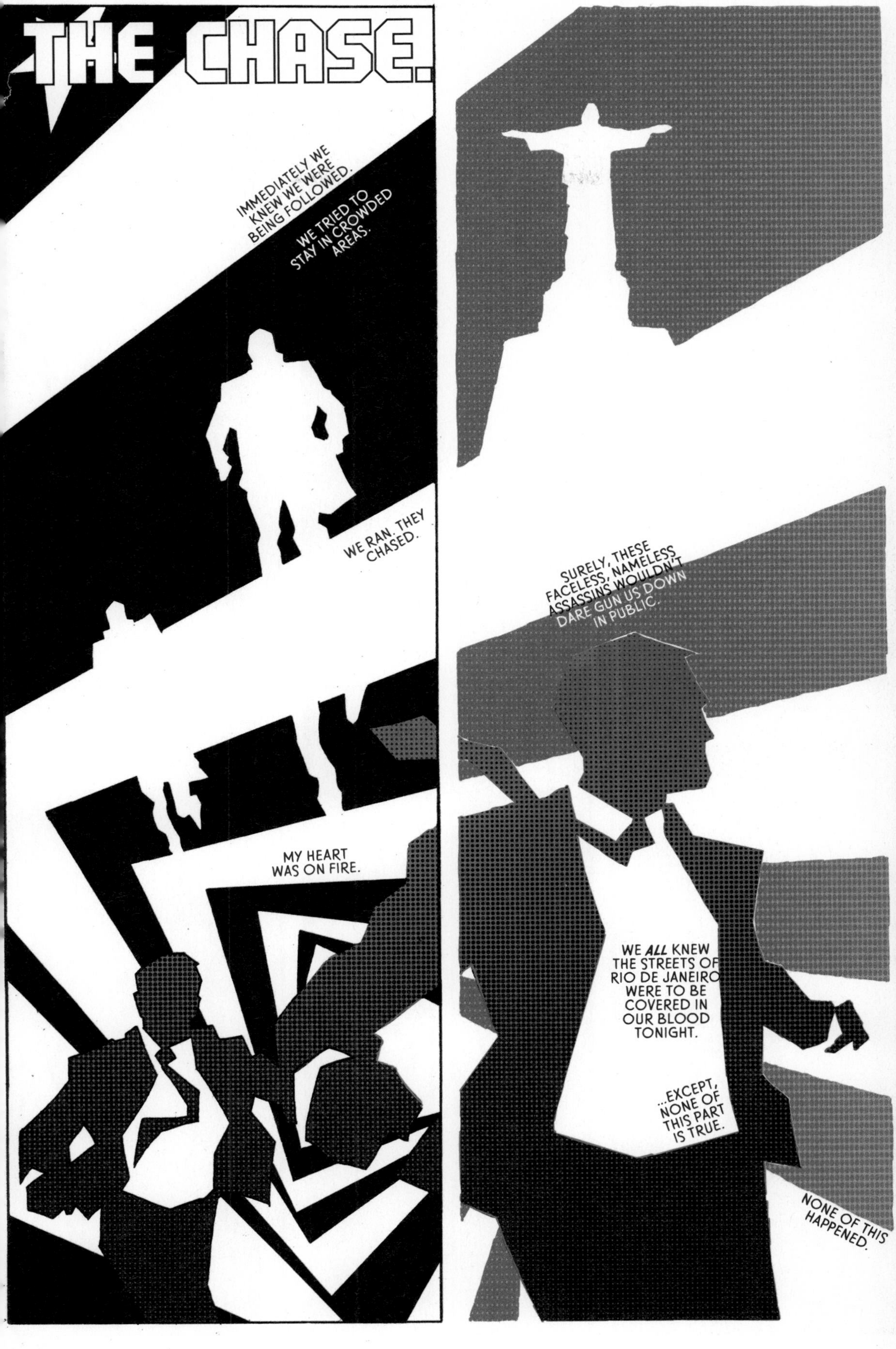
THE CHASE.
IMMEDIATELY WE KNEW WE WERE BEING FOLLOWED.
WE TRIED TO STAY IN CROWDED AREAS.
WE RAN. THEY CHASED.
MY HEART WAS ON FIRE.
SURELY, THESE FACELESS, NAMELESS ASSASSINS WOULDN'T DARE GUN US DOWN IN PUBLIC.
WE ALL KNEW THE STREETS OF RIO DE JANEIRO WERE TO BE COVERED IN OUR BLOOD TONIGHT.
...EXCEPT, NONE OF THIS PART IS TRUE.
NONE OF THIS HAPPENED.

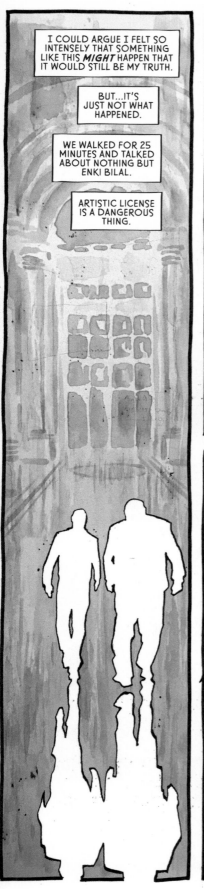

I COULD ARGUE I FELT SO INTENSELY THAT SOMETHING LIKE THIS *MIGHT* HAPPEN THAT IT WOULD STILL BE MY TRUTH.

BUT...IT'S JUST NOT WHAT HAPPENED.

WE WALKED FOR 25 MINUTES AND TALKED ABOUT NOTHING BUT ENKI BILAL.

ARTISTIC LICENSE IS A DANGEROUS THING.

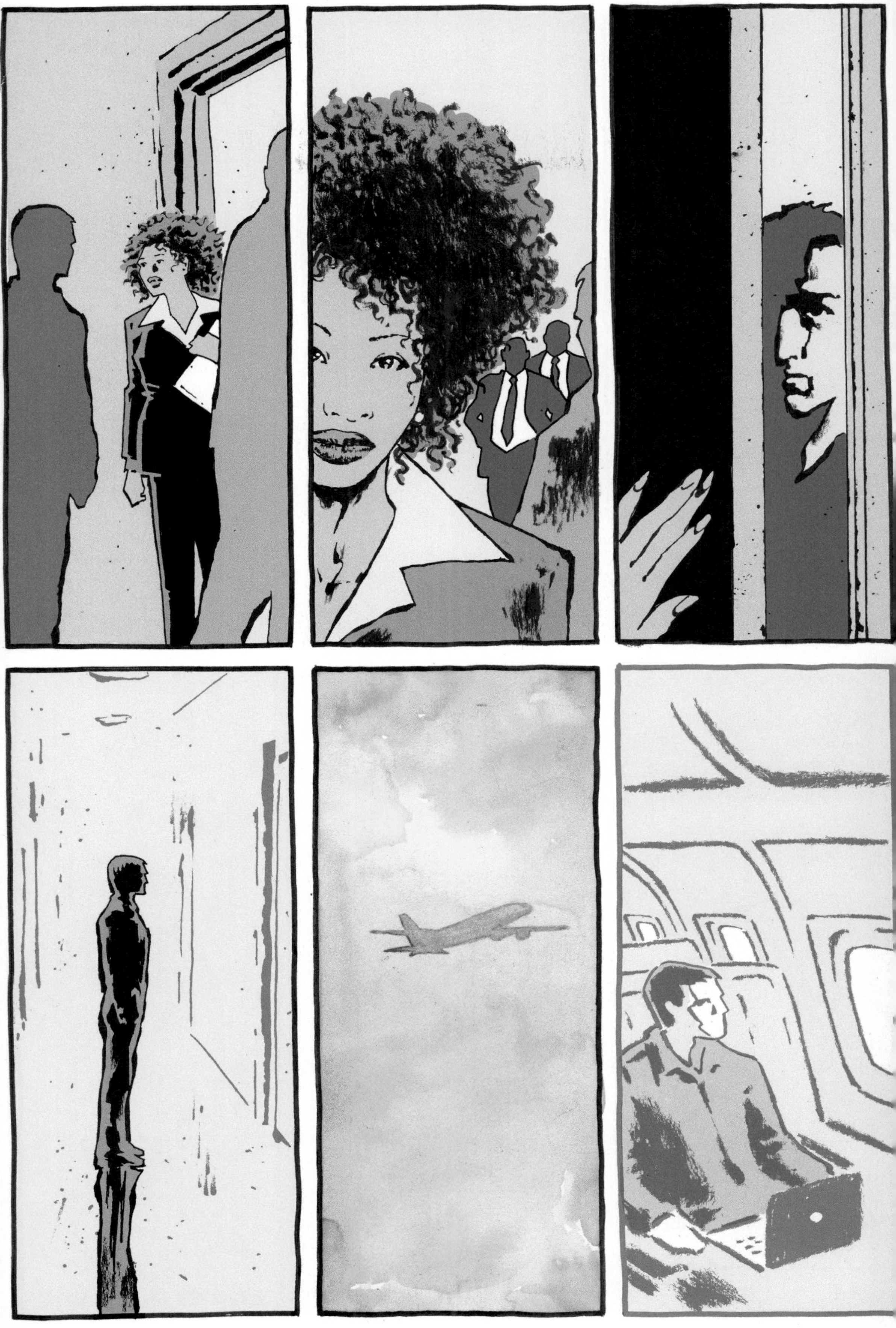

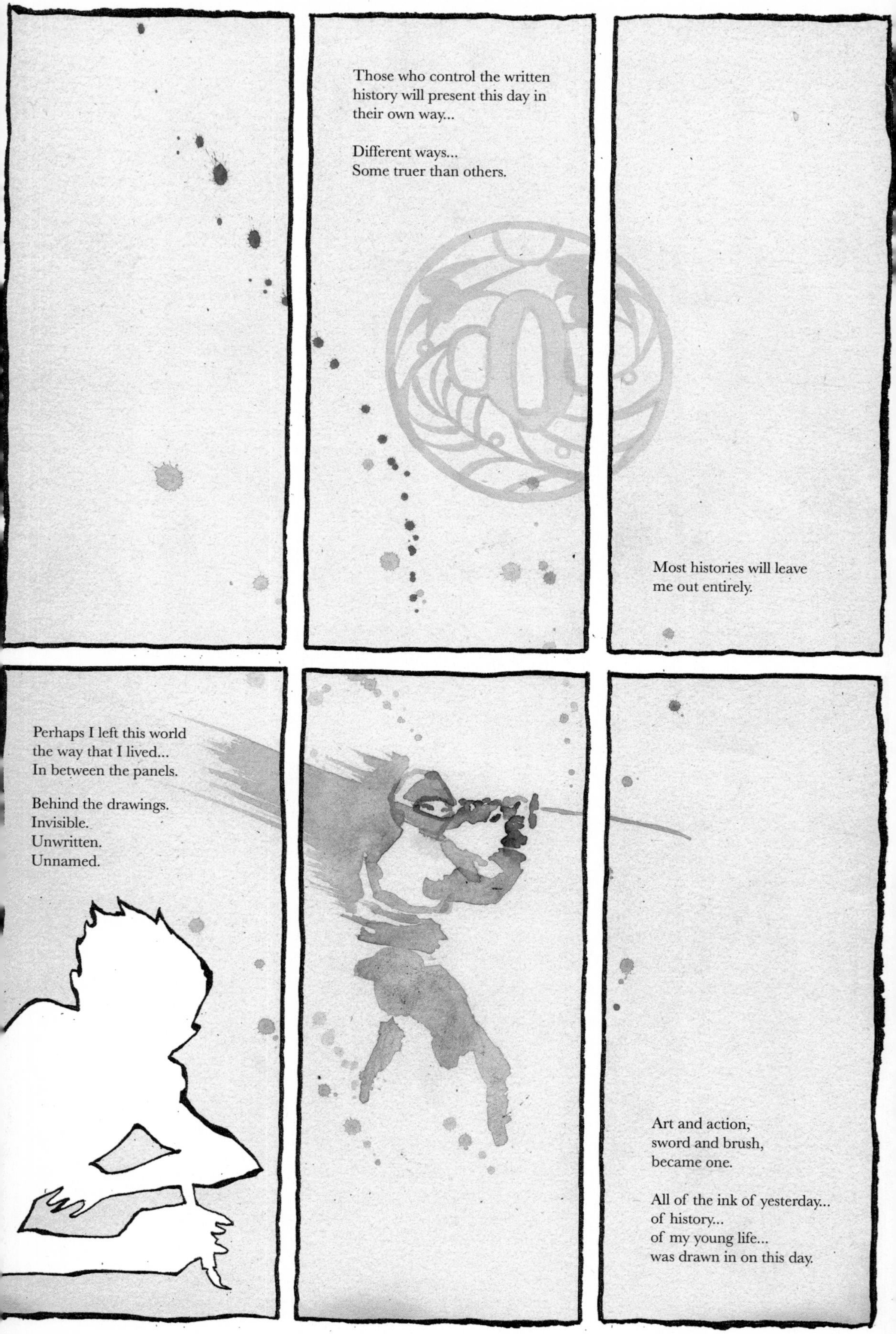
Those who control the written history will present this day in their own way...
Different ways... Some truer than others.
Most histories will leave me out entirely.
Perhaps I left this world the way that I lived... In between the panels.
Behind the drawings. Invisible. Unwritten. Unnamed.
Art and action, sword and brush, became one.
All of the ink of yesterday... of history... of my young life... was drawn in on this day.

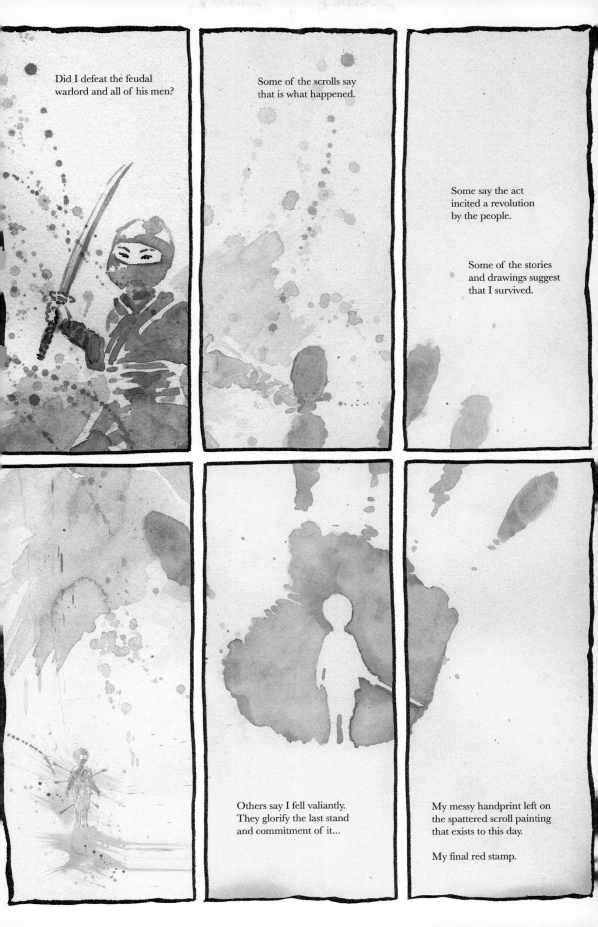

Did I defeat the feudal warlord and all of his men?

Some of the scrolls say that is what happened.

Some say the act incited a revolution by the people.

Some of the stories and drawings suggest that I survived.

Others say I fell valiantly. They glorify the last stand and commitment of it...

My messy handprint left on the spattered scroll painting that exists to this day.

My final red stamp.

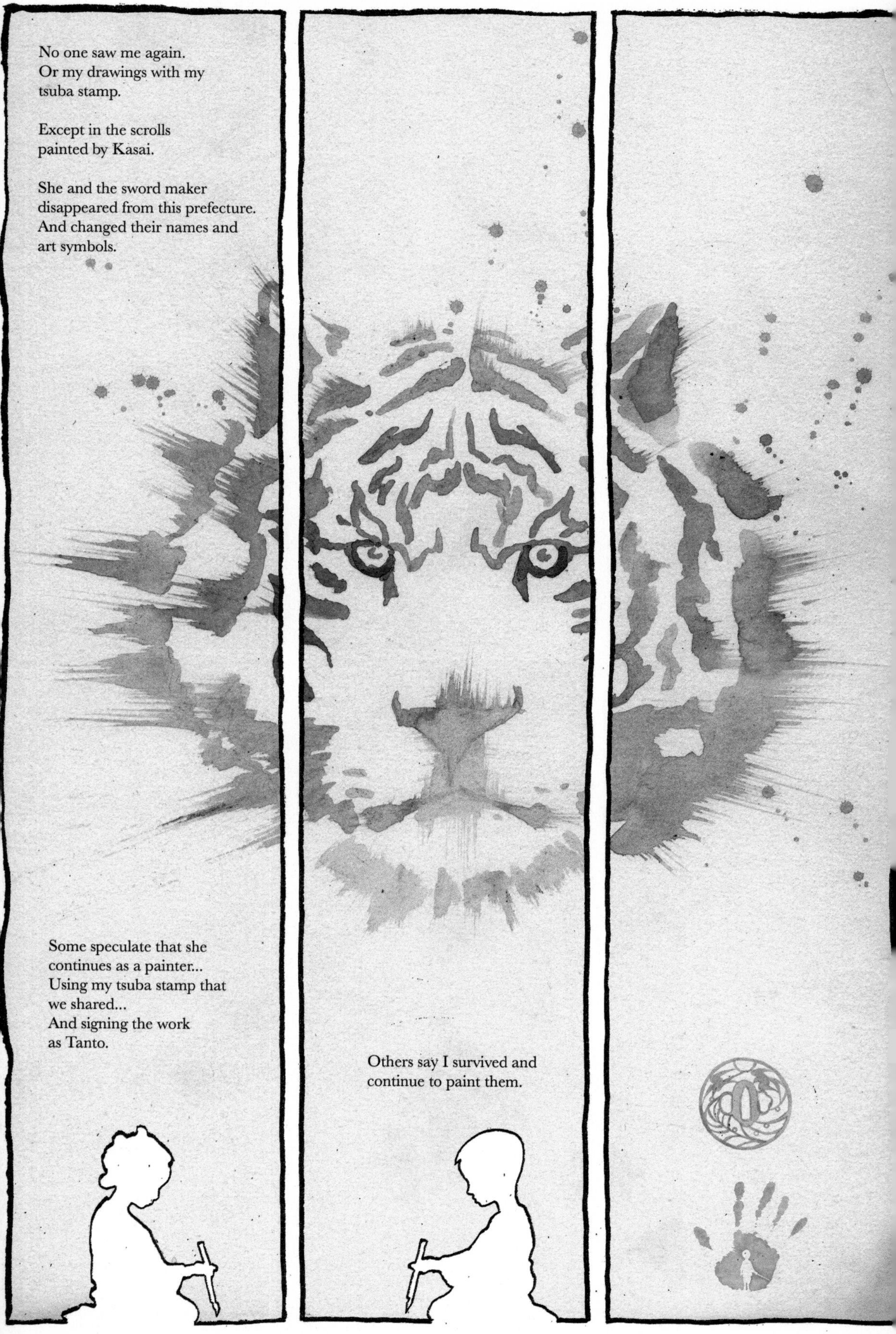
No one saw me again.
Or my drawings with my tsuba stamp.
Except in the scrolls painted by Kasai.
She and the sword maker disappeared from this prefecture. And changed their names and art symbols.
Some speculate that she continues as a painter... Using my tsuba stamp that we shared... And signing the work as Tanto.
Others say I survived and continue to paint them.

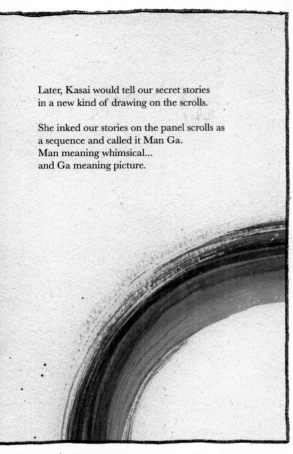

Later, Kasai would tell our secret stories
in a new kind of drawing on the scrolls.

She inked our stories on the panel scrolls as
a sequence and called it Man Ga.
Man meaning whimsical...
and Ga meaning picture.

It is said that she passed this
art down to her children,
and it blossomed to an art form
on the branches of her family tree.

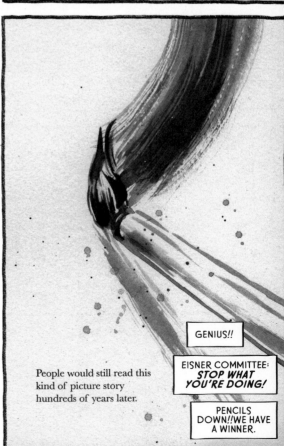

People would still read this
kind of picture story
hundreds of years later.

GENIUS!!

EISNER COMMITTEE:
**STOP WHAT
YOU'RE DOING!**

PENCILS
DOWN!! WE HAVE
A WINNER.

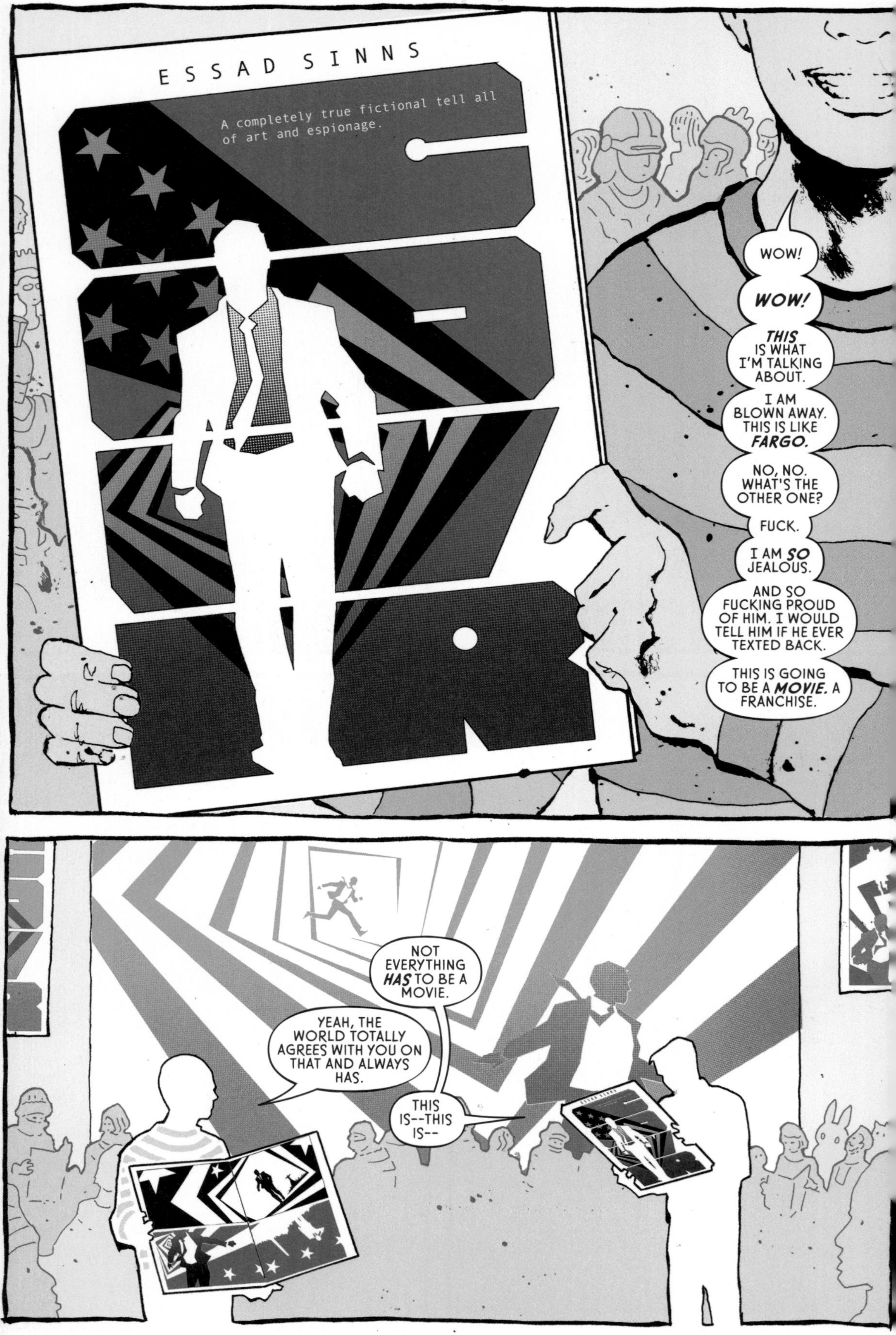
ESSAD SINNS
A completely true fictional tell all of art and espionage.
WOW!
WOW!
THIS IS WHAT I'M TALKING ABOUT.
I AM BLOWN AWAY. THIS IS LIKE FARGO.
NO, NO. WHAT'S THE OTHER ONE?
FUCK.
I AM SO JEALOUS.
AND SO FUCKING PROUD OF HIM. I WOULD TELL HIM IF HE EVER TEXTED BACK.
THIS IS GOING TO BE A MOVIE. A FRANCHISE.
NOT EVERYTHING HAS TO BE A MOVIE.
YEAH, THE WORLD TOTALLY AGREES WITH YOU ON THAT AND ALWAYS HAS.
THIS IS--THIS IS--

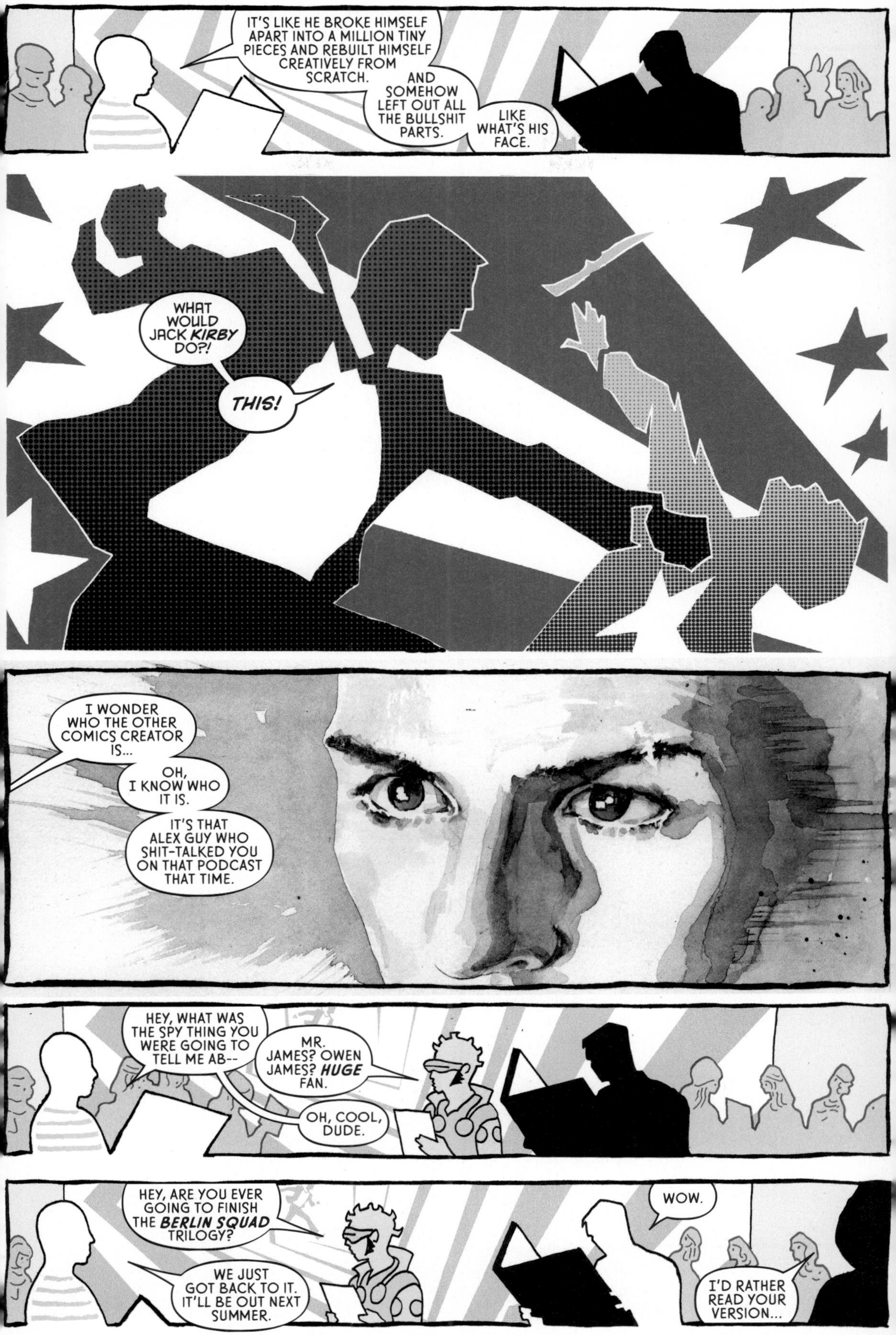
IT'S LIKE HE BROKE HIMSELF APART INTO A MILLION TINY PIECES AND REBUILT HIMSELF CREATIVELY FROM SCRATCH.
AND SOMEHOW LEFT OUT ALL THE BULLSHIT PARTS.
LIKE WHAT'S HIS FACE.
WHAT WOULD JACK *KIRBY* DO?!
THIS!
I WONDER WHO THE OTHER COMICS CREATOR IS...
OH, I KNOW WHO IT IS.
IT'S THAT ALEX GUY WHO SHIT-TALKED YOU ON THAT PODCAST THAT TIME.
HEY, WHAT WAS THE SPY THING YOU WERE GOING TO TELL ME AB--
MR. JAMES? OWEN JAMES? *HUGE* FAN.
OH, COOL, DUDE.
HEY, ARE YOU EVER GOING TO FINISH THE *BERLIN SQUAD* TRILOGY?
WE JUST GOT BACK TO IT. IT'LL BE OUT NEXT SUMMER.
WOW.
I'D RATHER READ YOUR VERSION...

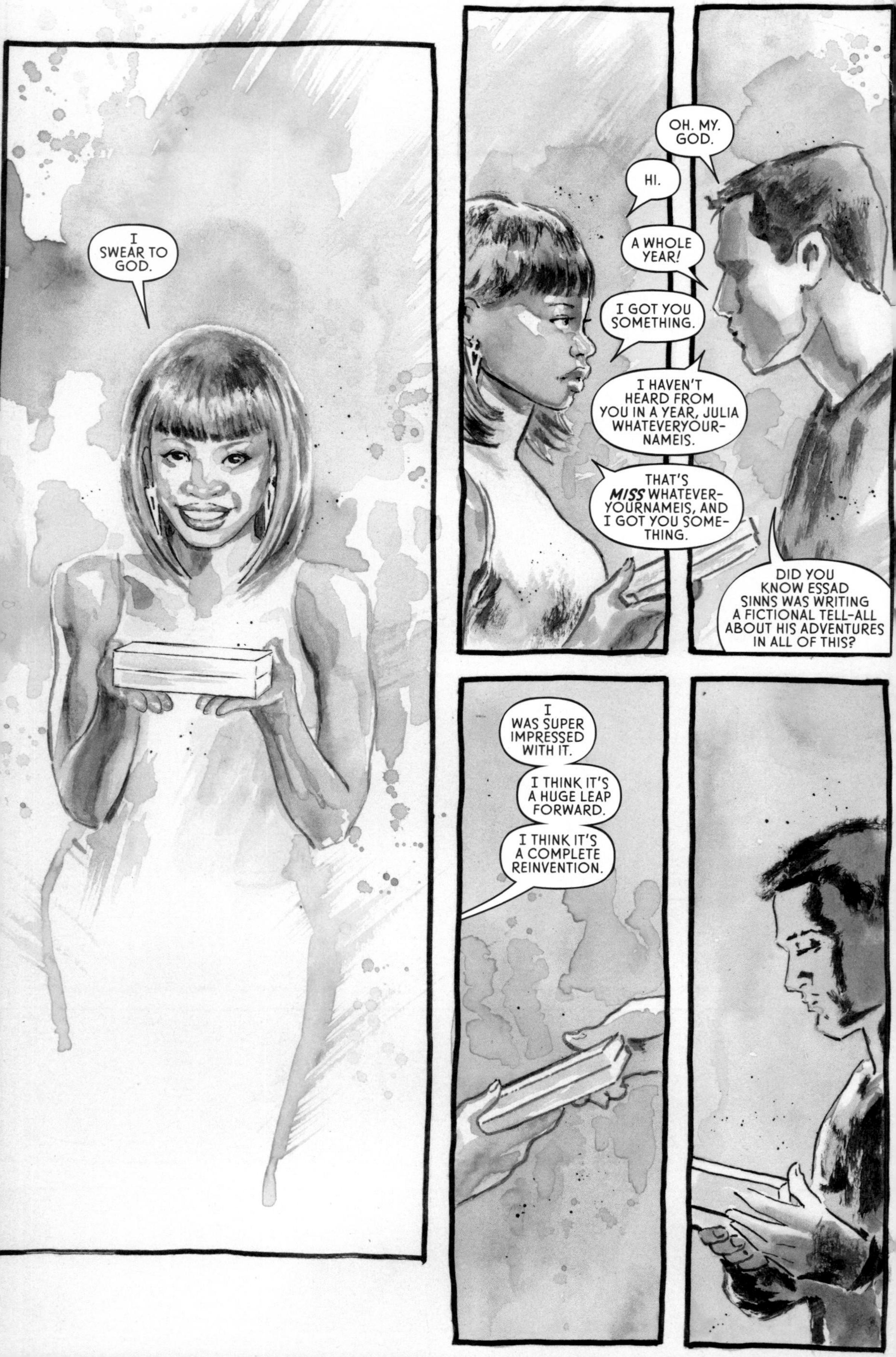
I SWEAR TO GOD.
HI.
OH. MY. GOD.
A WHOLE YEAR!
I GOT YOU SOMETHING.
I HAVEN'T HEARD FROM YOU IN A YEAR, JULIA WHATEVERYOURNAMEIS.
THAT'S *MISS* WHATEVER-YOURNAMEIS, AND I GOT YOU SOMETHING.
DID YOU KNOW ESSAD SINNS WAS WRITING A FICTIONAL TELL-ALL ABOUT HIS ADVENTURES IN ALL OF THIS?
I WAS SUPER IMPRESSED WITH IT.
I THINK IT'S A HUGE LEAP FORWARD.
I THINK IT'S A COMPLETE REINVENTION.

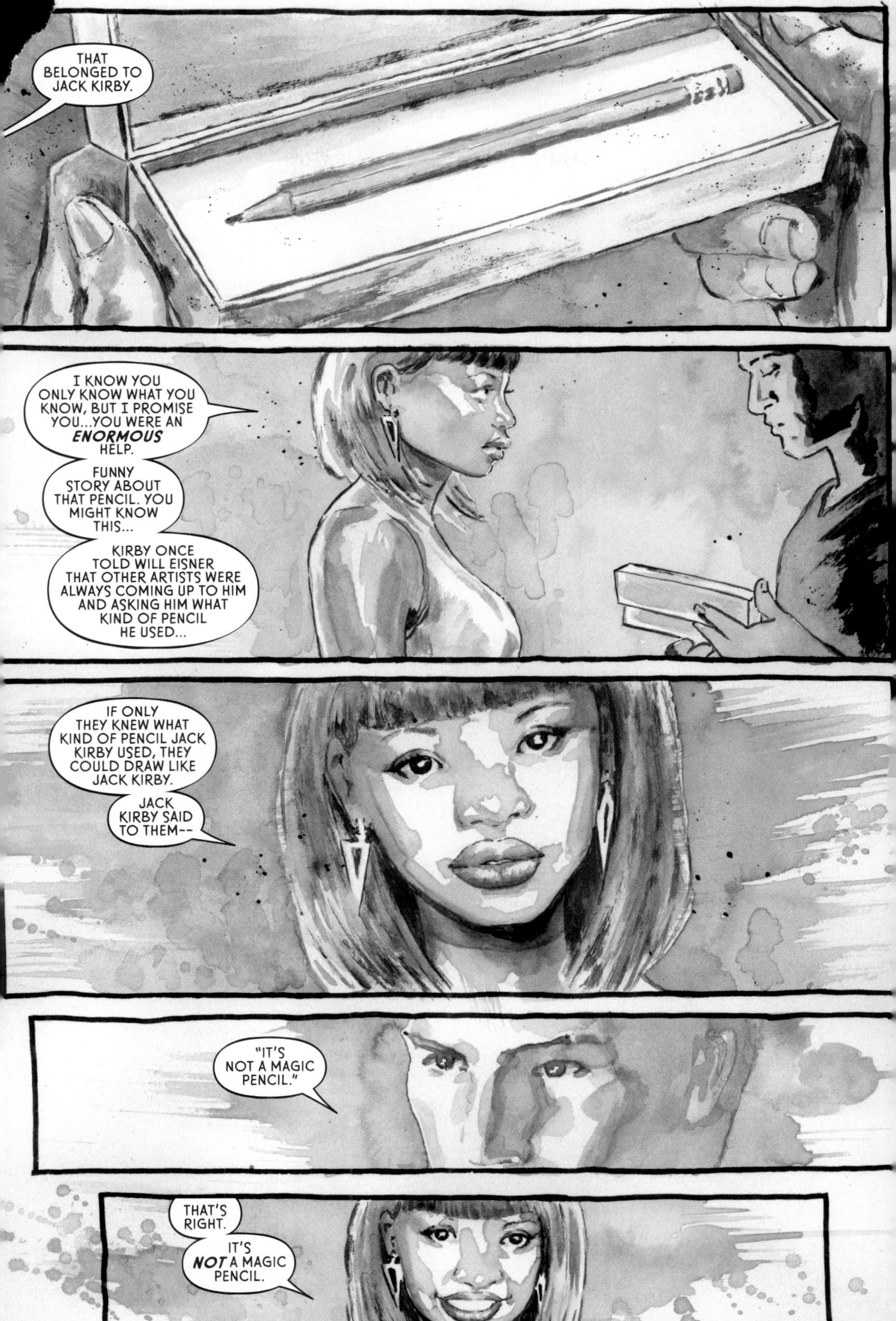
THAT BELONGED TO JACK KIRBY.
I KNOW YOU ONLY KNOW WHAT YOU KNOW, BUT I PROMISE YOU...YOU WERE AN ENORMOUS HELP.
FUNNY STORY ABOUT THAT PENCIL. YOU MIGHT KNOW THIS...
KIRBY ONCE TOLD WILL EISNER THAT OTHER ARTISTS WERE ALWAYS COMING UP TO HIM AND ASKING HIM WHAT KIND OF PENCIL HE USED...
IF ONLY THEY KNEW WHAT KIND OF PENCIL JACK KIRBY USED, THEY COULD DRAW LIKE JACK KIRBY.
JACK KIRBY SAID TO THEM--
"IT'S NOT A MAGIC PENCIL."
THAT'S RIGHT.
IT'S NOT A MAGIC PENCIL.

I **WILL** SEE YOU AGAIN, MAX.

I REMAIN, EVEN MORE SO NOW, YOUR BIGGEST FAN.

SHUT UP.

I REALLY HOPE THAT'S THE ONLY REASON YOU EVER SEE ME AGAIN.

BUT IF I COME TO YOU AND IT'S THE OTHER THING...

...WE'LL NEED SOME MAGIC SOMETHING.

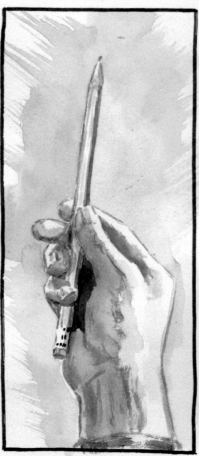

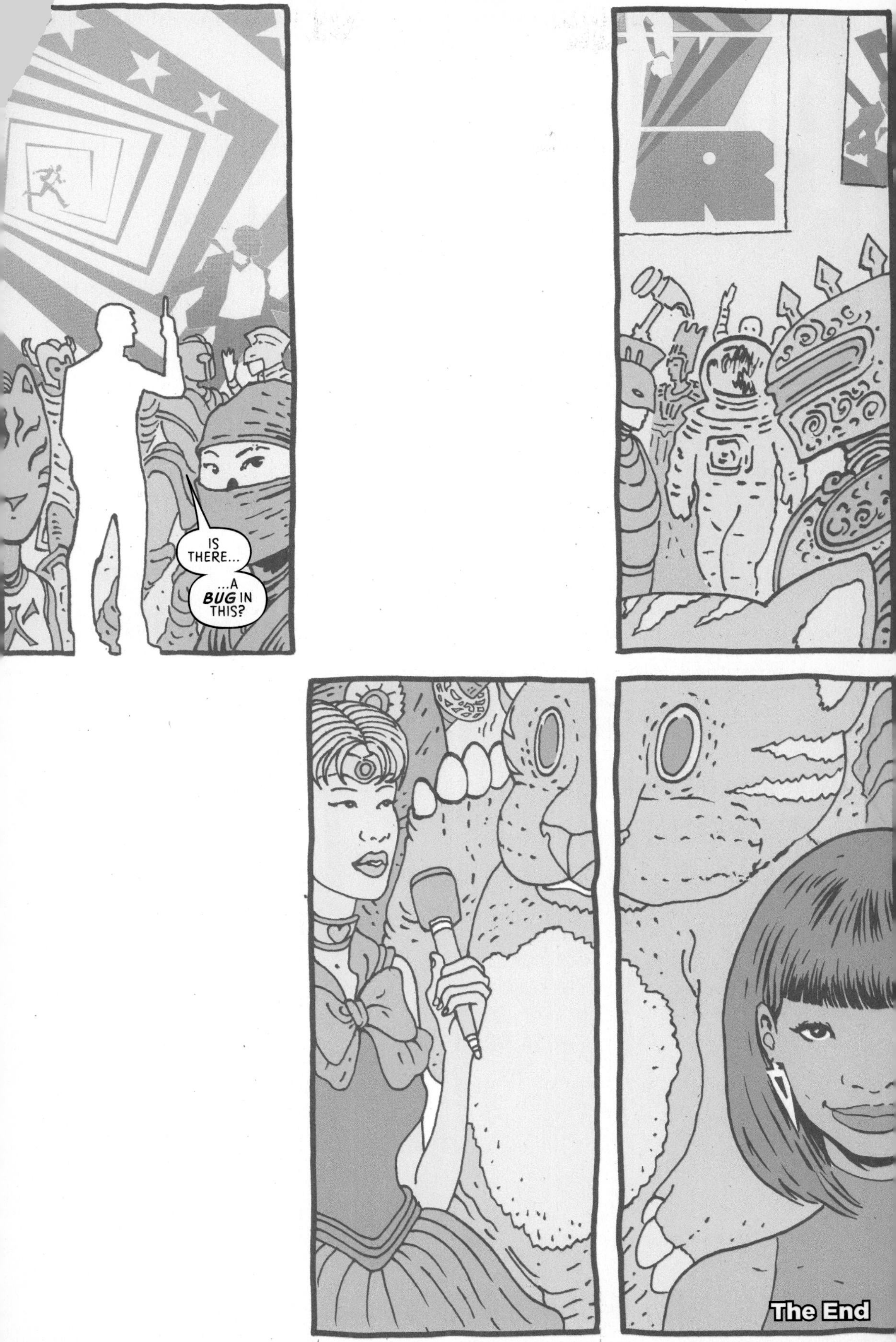
IS THERE...
...A BUG IN THIS?
The End

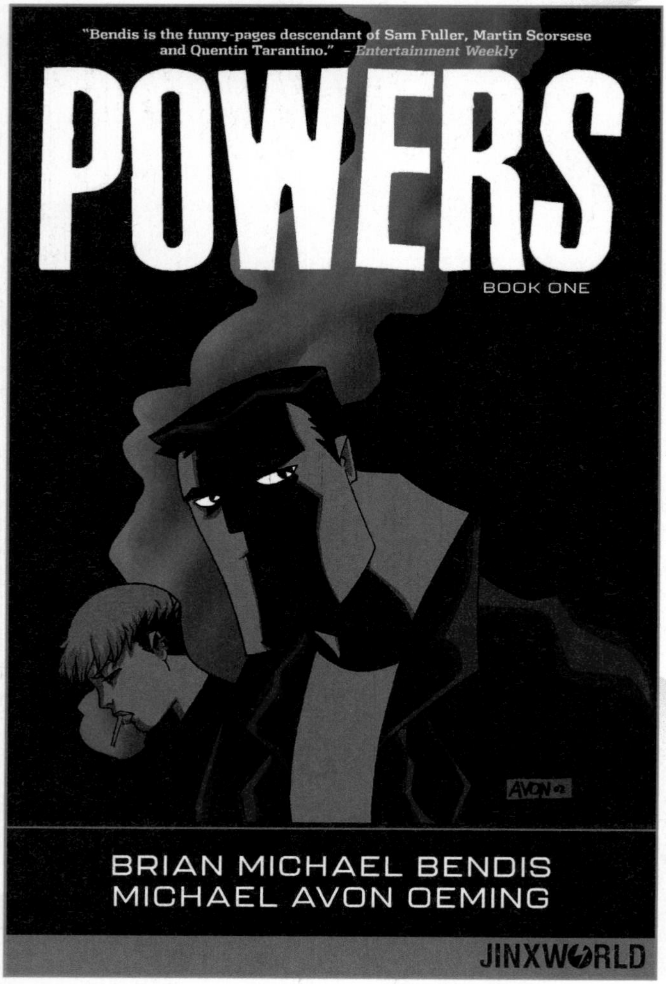
"Bendis is the funny-pages descendant of Sam Fuller, Martin Scorsese and Quentin Tarantino." – Entertainment Weekly
POWERS
BOOK ONE
BRIAN MICHAEL BENDIS
MICHAEL AVON OEMING
JINXWORLD

"One of the coolest comics on the planet."
–IGN

"Boundary-pushing."
–WIRED

"Filled with plot twists, this series both exalts superheroes and places them in a real-world context."
–LIBRARY JOURNAL

POWERS

BOOK ONE

BRIAN MICHAEL BENDIS
MICHAEL AVON OEMING

ALSO BY BENDIS AND OEMING:

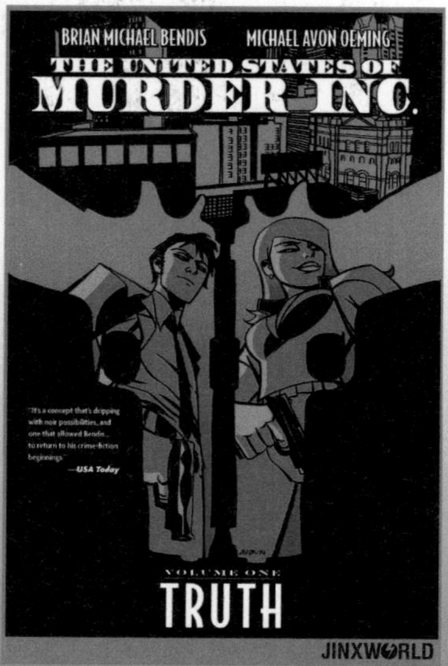
BRIAN MICHAEL BENDIS
MICHAEL AVON OEMING
THE UNITED STATES OF
MURDER INC.
VOLUME ONE
TRUTH
JINXWORLD

THE UNITED STATES OF MURDER INC. VOL. 1: TRUTH

"It's a concept that's dripping with noir possiblities."
–USA TODAY

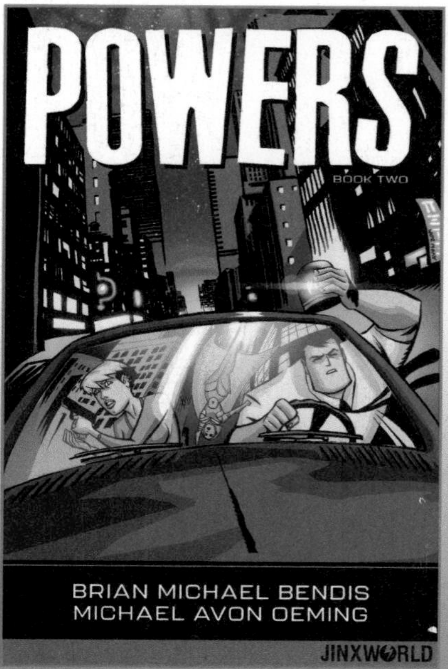
POWERS
BOOK TWO
BRIAN MICHAEL BENDIS
MICHAEL AVON OEMING
JINXWORLD

POWERS BOOK TWO

Get more Jinxworld graphic novels wherever comics and books are sold! JINXWORLD